UNDERSTANDING INVERTEBRATES

UNDERSTANDING INVERTEBRATES

By

Dr. Amita Sarkar

Dept. of Zoology

Agra College

Agra (U.P.)

(India)

DPH

DISCOVERY PUBLISHING HOUSE PVT. LTD.

NEW DELHI-110 002

Published by:

Namit Wasan

DISCOVERY PUBLISHING HOUSE PVT. LTD.

4383/4B, Ansari Road, Darya Ganj
New Delhi-110 002 (India)
Phone : +91-11-23279245; 23253475; 43596065
E-mail : discoverybooksindia@gmail.com
discoverypublishinghouse@gmail.com
namitwasan9@gmail.com
web : www.discoverypublishinggroup.com

***First Edition:* 2010**

ISBN: 978-81-8356-544-8

Understanding Invertebrates

Preface

The present title "Understanding Invertebrates" has been written for those students interested in careers in diverse fields of biological sciences. It provides a structured approach to learning by covering all the important topics in a uniform, systematic format. The book has been comprehensively designed incorporating recent advances in this fast moving field. It also provides accessible information on molecular biology in compact form for undergraduate students in biology and related life sciences. It is intelligible to the educated layman, though it deals with some complex ideas. It is an adequate text for all the requirements of students in this area. In addition, busy lecturers who require a quick reference compendium will find it useful, particularly for tutional planning. Simple, yet hopefully clear figures and tables are provided throughout the book.

The over-riding goal of this book, and indeed of the whole *Understanding series,* is to present the essential information concering molecular biology in a compact, readily accessible form which leads itself to student learning and revision. The convergence of various approaches has generated a rich panorama of detail, the significance of which we are still attempting to unraval. The present text has been written as an introduction to this rapidly growing field.

To make the work more comprehensive and informative, the author has consulted many authoritative books, research journals, abstracts, monographs etc., so there can be no claim to originality except in the manner of treatment.

The author expresses his thanks to his friends and colleagues whose continue inspirations have initiated him to bring out this book.

The author expresses his gratitude to Mr. Wasan and staff of M/s Discovery Publishing House Pvt. Ltd. for their whole hearted cooperation in the publication of this book.

In the mean time, the author will remain sincerely responsible for any shortcomings of the book and be grateful to the readers for their suggestions and constructive criticism for the continuous betterment of the book. He takes this opportunity to appeal to the readers to send their suggestions straightaway to his Publisher.

Author

Contents

1

INTRODUCTION

Let us understand, first, that all phyla of animals are invertebrates. Even the Chordata, in which we ourselves are situated, are invertebrate in origin; and primitive members of the chordate phylum survive as invertebrates. It is only that the conspicuous branches of the Chordata have developed a distinctive skeletal support that sets this phylum apart.

Though it is very interesting that most of the chordates possess an internal, segmented bony device—the vertebral column—this is only one of innumerable wonders of nature. Were we not anthropomorphically inclined, this characteristic would probably not be enough to warrant the predominant position which vertebrates occupy in our minds. As Aristotle has written, "We therefore must not recoil with childish aversion from the examination of the humbler animals. Every realm of nature is marvellous . . ."

Perhaps the most marvelous of all of the properties of living organisms, and one that all of them possess in common, is their capacity for building up their own substance. In this respect the living world, as a whole, is dependent for its existence upon the nonliving. There is no chemical. element within protoplasm that is not also found in the inanimate environment.

But, with the notable exception of water, which is the chief molecular component of the organism, the compounds most characteristic of protoplasm—such as carbohydrates, fats and proteins-are absent in inanimate nature. From this simple fact it becomes evident that living forms have the capacity for synthesis of their own constituent materials, while the nonliving world supplies the reservoir of matter and energy upon which life draws to increase its substance. How do living things obtain the materials required for growth? The answer to this question lays down the prime distinction between the plant and animal kingdoms, and we shall find that it leads to a hypothesis which can be very helpful toward developing an understanding of animal groups.

WHAT IS AN ANIMAL?

The difference between the plant and animal kingdoms is most basically a chemical one. With exceptions that can at present be ignored plants contain, and animals lack, chlorophyll. In the typical plant the relationship of the organism to the inanimate environment is therefore quite direct. Through the means of photosynthesis, and interrelated processes, a mass of living plant material is built up.

It should be clearly realized that in the presence of chlorophyll a living organism can carry on its nutritive functions in situs, since carbon dioxide, water, and sunlight are of general distribution. There is no need to seek them out and, consequently, there is no need for locomotion.

Therefore, except for some of the most primitive members, there are no locomotory structures in the plant kingdom. In the absence of chlorophyll an organism must be able to find access to preformed organic reservoirs of energy; in other words the bodies of other living things, either dead or alive. The significant point to be noted is that such foods must be sought out and, if animate as they usually are, it is likely that they must be pursued and captured.

Pursuit and capture become the main theme of animal life and, as a consequence, locomotion is a predominant characteristic of the animal kingdom. Of course, as with all general statements, there are exceptions to the rule that animals move about. For example, barnacles are sedentary in a phylum, the Arthropoda, which is otherwise composed of highly active animals. Again, the animals of the sponge phylum, when adult, lack the ability to move from place to place.

Parasitic animals form a category of exception which is imaginary rather than real. Parasites need to move about from place to place for their food, but here the place is a host in which the parasite abides briefly or even for a number of generations before it moves on to a new location, another host. In spite of exceptions, real or imaginary, it may be said that movement from place to place is of the very essence of animal nature.

And, while movement is primarily essential in relation to nutrition, there are also other needs for locomotion which include such aspects as escape from enemies, migrations, and mating. It is clear that animals need to move about. Various special organs and devices have been evolved to meet the need. The nature of these may be used to serve the purpose of integrating the many invertebrate groups, which would otherwise stand apart on the basis of their specialized characteristics.

This will be our hypothesis: that animal life can be best understood from the viewpoint of locomotory adaptations, for such are basic to the animal mode of life. At the beginning—perhaps a billion and a half years ago, by some estimates-life consisted of primordial forms dispersing slowly, as they became more numerous and more varied in their adaptations, over the great bulk of inanimate matter that composes the earth. Animals were comparatively simple in their patterns of structure then.

They had no need for the quick movements required of most of the highly competitive forms of today. They could probably get along very well with a simpler symmetry, perhaps of the radial type, correlated with the more placid existence then possible. As time went on and animal numbers steadily increased, competitive clash for available food became the primary factor in survival.

More animals turned from direct nutrition as herbivores, upon plant materials, to the pursuit of other animals. These, the predators, developed highly specialized mechanisms for pursuit. Others, the prey, became adept at evasion; often by means of locomotory devices more effective than those of the predators. Of course some animals and even entire groups of animals, like barnacles and sponges, did not take part in the mode of life centered around the property of speed.

Those which settled down to sift food out of their immediate environment are the sedentary forms. Many animals from various groups, and sometimes groups as a whole like the tapeworms, invaded the bodies of involuntary host animals and became parasites there.

In some cases the parasitic relationship was gradually altered to the more harmonious one of mutualism, in which both participating forms benefit, and in rare instances the two types of animal life became indispensable to each other and could exist only as a single complex; such, for example, as the termite and its intestinal flagellates.

WHAT KINDS OF ANIMALS ARE THERE?

A tremendous variety of animal forms arose. The clarification of the relationships between them has taken, and continues to take, arduous investigation. Moreover, taxonomists are always at work seeking out living forms which have not as yet been described, and always there is the need for cleaning house to avoid the duplicate use of the same scientific name for different animals. Also to settle, by laws of priority, upon a single name for a single species where it has been the subject of multiple discovery.

We should not look down upon taxonomy, nor regard it as a burdensome chore. Taxonomy is as essential to the effective pursuit of other branches of biological endeavor as is classification of books for use in a library. Biology without taxonomy could be compared to a library in which books are simply piled in random heaps.

Granting the need and the usefulness, we must realize at the same time that taxonomy is subject to a substantial amount of disagreement among the experts, and is subject to continual changes. This is so because taxonomy is intended to be based on the natural relationships between organisms, i.e., the relationships traceable to direct biological derivations. Natural relationships so defined cannot in many cases be established with any degree of certainty.

One should be fully conscious that all science is subject to change and that the current state of knowledge possesses no greater virtue in ultimate truth than earlier stages that have now become historical curiosities. When this is understood we then know that we need to be very clear as to the definition of that which is called a "fact."

Was it a fact in Aristotle's time that rats were generated out of the mud of the river Nile? Was it a fact in the eighteenth century that an embryo was fully preformed in all of its parts within the egg, or within the sperm? It appears that a fact is a currently accepted concept, agreed to in the light of prevailing belief.

Its value may be only temporary, but it is as essential to continued progress as each step of a stairway. We cannot accept any step as final if we are to transcend it. A mastery of current "facts" alone, without an understanding of their transient value, is a dead end in scientific knowledge; but a mastery of the facts, full of misconceptions and errors though they may be, is essential in order to have a basis from which to proceed to the next, more perfect, stage.

Since the publication of the "Origin of Species" in 1859, biological studies have been deeply coloured by the search for evolutionary relationships. The first concepts of evolutionary change assumed the form of a "ladder," and groups of greater complexity were thought to arise from those of lesser complexity in successive order.

Soon this view was found to be untenable and the "tree" plan took its place, in recognition of the evidence that no definable present group arose from any other coexisting group.

The "tree" plan assumed that living organisms represent end branches along various evolutionary lines, and that the end branches are related to each other only in common branches which have become extinct. It should not be overlooked that the chief source of evidence for deriving evolutionary relationships is paleontological. This evidence is strongest in the more recent sedimentary rock formations and is of the greatest value with regard to the origin of vertebrate classes.

On the other hand the earliest fossiliferous rocks, those of the lower Cambrian, already contain the most evolved invertebrate phyla. This shows that the main invertebrate stems were laid down in Precambrian times. For fossil studies the rocks of that era have deteriorated beyond systematic value.

Thus the firmest pillar of evolutionary evidence—paleontological—is not available for determining basic invertebrate relationships. This, together with the fact that many invertebrate groups are without substantial, solid bodily parts to facilitate fossil formation, accounts for the greater uncertainty in invertebrate taxonomy than in that of the vertebrates.

Subkingdoms

The animal world may be divided into three subkingdoms:

The Protozoa

The protozoan subkingdom includes those animals whose bodily features are derived from the substance of a single cell. There are therefore no tissues and organs as such. In genera where colonies are formed the constituent cells show little, if any, division of labor among them. In no case do the cells of a colony arrange themselves into outer and inner layers, in the manner of the other two subkingdoms.

The Parazoa

This is the subkingdom of the sponges. While usually included with the Enterozoa as a single subkingdom called the Metazoa, sponges have developed morphological and physiological features peculiarly their own. Although multicellular like the Enterozoa, unlike the Enterozoa they lack a digestive tract, and they differ from both Protozoa and Enterozoa in the absence of locomotory structures.

The Enterozoa

We might say that this is the subkingdom of animals with "guts." Although in exceptional cases it may be lacking, Enterozoa generally are characterized by the possession of a digestive cavity. The digestive cavity is a feature of sufficient importance to justify separation of Parazoa and Enterozoa into two categories each of subkingdom rank.

The three subkingdoms are very unequal in coverage. About 30,000 species are included in the protozoan subkingdom, contained in the single phylum Protozoa (although it has been suggested that each of the classes of protozoans might be elevated to phylum rank). Likewise, the subkingdom Parazoa is composed of the single phylum Porifera, with some 5000 known species.

With the exception of Protozoa and Porifera, all other phyla of the animal kingdom are found in the subkingdom Enterozoa, in which hundreds of thousands of species have been described. It should be of interest to us to know that in the time of Aristotle less than 500 species of animals were recognized. Twentyone hundred years later (1758), Linnaeus listed about 4000 species.

In the table herewith are some current estimates of the number of living species within various phyla. The first column is from Pratt's *Manual of the Common Invertebrate Animals* (1935), and the second is derived from Storer's *General Zoology*. From discrepancies between the two compilations it can be inferred-correctly-that the basic project of discovery of animal kinds is still incomplete. New species are being described constantly. Sometimes a species is discarded, as in the case of the "sponge" Oscarella malabonensis, which is now said to be a spongy mass of other, minute animals (reference listed with the sponges).

Older phyla of animals are being reviewed and divided into smaller groupings-for example, the modern separation of the Onychophora from the arthropod phylum. Genus, species and even phylum names are being changed, sometimes with distressing frequency. As studies become more intensified in one group or another, the number of known species in that group spurts ahead.

Within the Nemathelminthes, which are receiving increasing attention, it has been estimated that about 80,000 species may now be known, with a predicted ultimate total of 500,000, to make it the second largest phylum. It is evident, then, that the world of living animals includes perhaps a million living species already described by man, with more to come.

Efforts to arrange animals in related groups are very old, and criteria have changed with the times. In the days of Aristotle the basic plan was very simple. Two major categories were recognized. The lower animals, the invertebrates, were "animals without blood." The vertebrates were "animals with blood." Only 500 species were involved. Life for the taxonomist, and for the general student too, was less trying then.

Even the classification of the middle nineteenth century appears very strange today. The animal kingdom was at that time said to consist of four "Departments"

1. Department of Vertebrates
2. Department of Articulates
3. Department of Mollusks
4. Department of Radiates.

Most fascinating to us will be the composition of the "Department of Radiates." Here we find the sponges, the coelenterates, the ctenophores, the echinoderms, and the enteropneustan protochordates (Balanoglossus), strange bedfellows for today's taxonomy.

To arrange living organisms in a natural classification means to place them into groups according to evolutionary origin. This is a difficult task as we have already pointed out, particularly with invertebrates. No one can contend that animals as they appear today necessarily closely resemble the primitive ancestral stocks from which they arose. That would be a denial of evolutionary process and effect.

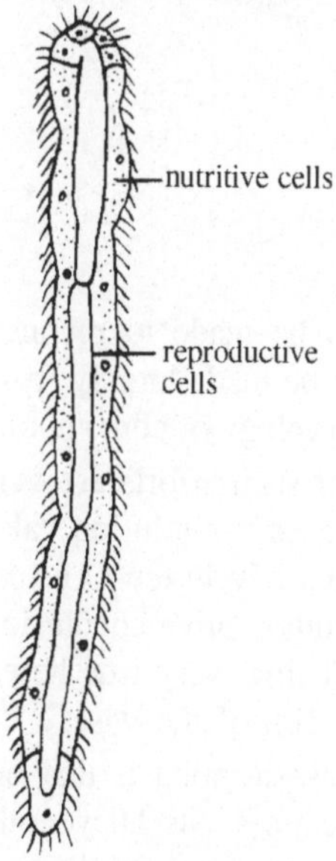

Figure 1.1: Dicyema, a mesozoan.

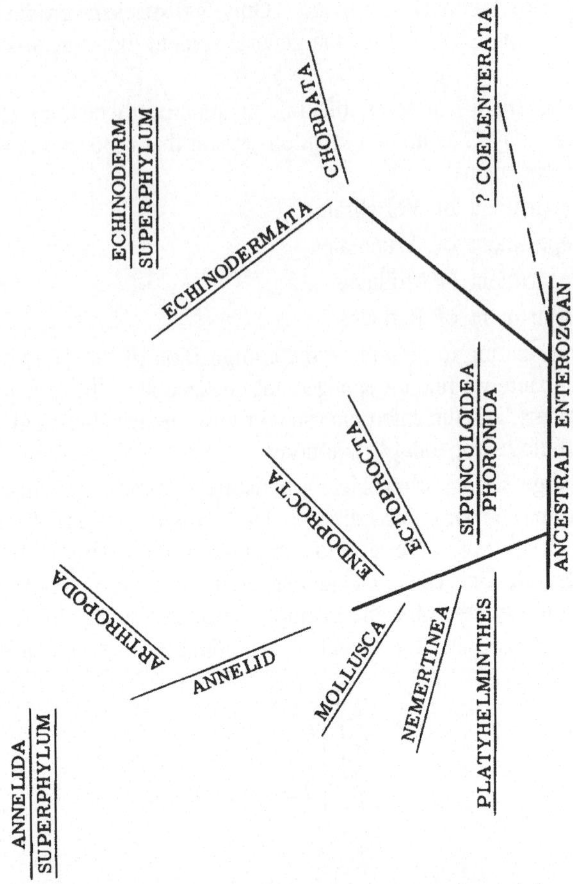

Figure 1.2: Major pathways of evolution within the Enterozoa.

Yet attempts need to be made to reconstruct the origin of ancestral forms, and they must be made largely from a study of the comparative morphology and embryology of contemporary groups.

The limitations of such efforts are very severe, and should not be disregarded. No one saw evolution take place. Fossil remains of invertebrates are comparatively few. The case is built on "circumstantial evidence." Equally authoritative conclusions are, therefore, sometimes diametrically opposed. It is very true here, as elsewhere, that "modest doubt is . . . the beacon of the wise."

An interesting case in point is that of the group Mesozoa (which is composed of two classes, the Dicyemida and the Orthonectida). All of the Mesozoa are parasites, the Dicyemida within the kidneys of cephalopod mollusks and the Orthonectida in mollusks, echinoderms,

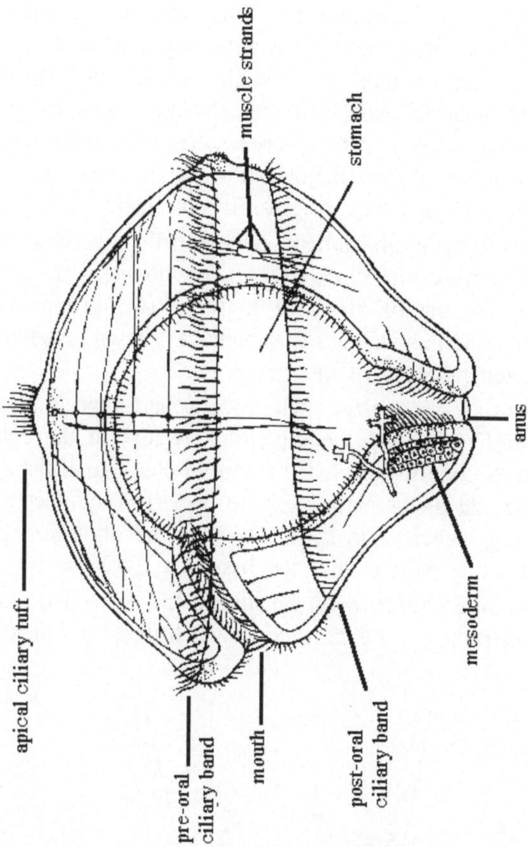

Figure 1.3: A trochophore larva.

annelids and flatworms. The body of the Mesozoan consists of an outer layer of ciliated cells which also performs nutritive functions by means of intracellular digestion. The interior of the animal is composed of reproductive tissue. (In the Dicyemida it has been shown that sexual maturity of the parasite does not occur prior to sexual maturity of the host, a point of interest to endocrinologists.)

One view as to the relationship of the Mesozoa to other animals is that they are a group of flatworms, atrophied in structure through parasitism, and to be included with the phylum Platyhelminthes. If this is so then they are entitled to no special prominence.

The other view taken of the Mesozoa is that they are the most primitive of the Enterozoa. In this case they would immediately take on outstanding significance with regard to the origin of the Enterozoa. They would show that Enterozoa did not arise in the form of a gastrula with an interior cavity surrounded by nutritive cells, as in the Cnidaria (Coelenterata), but that the first evolutionary step in setting up the succession of multicellular animals that led to such forms as the arthropods, the mollusks, and the chordates had to do with the reproductive rather than the nutritive system. There appears to be general agreement as to the existence of two major pathways of evolution within the Enterozoa, even though their origins are not clear.

One leads to the establishment of the annelid superphylum and the other to the echinoderm superphylum, as shown in the chart. The evidence for the origin of phyla in these two groups is chiefly embryological, and this includes four points as shown in the table. First there is the general form of the larva.

Two types are recognized. The trochosphere type is found in the annelid superphylum, and the dipleurula occurs in the echinoderm superphylum. Secondly there is the nature of cleavage of the zygote. In radial cleavage all of the early axes are in perfect symmetry with the axis of the egg, whereas in spiral cleavage the blastomeres are laid down in a rotating pattern after the first two divisions.

The third difference between the annelid and echinoderm superphyla lies in the determination of the time at which the part which each cell

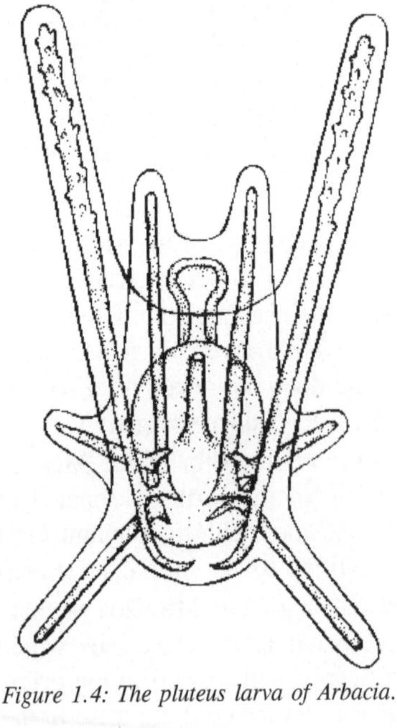

Figure 1.4: The pluteus larva of Arbacia.

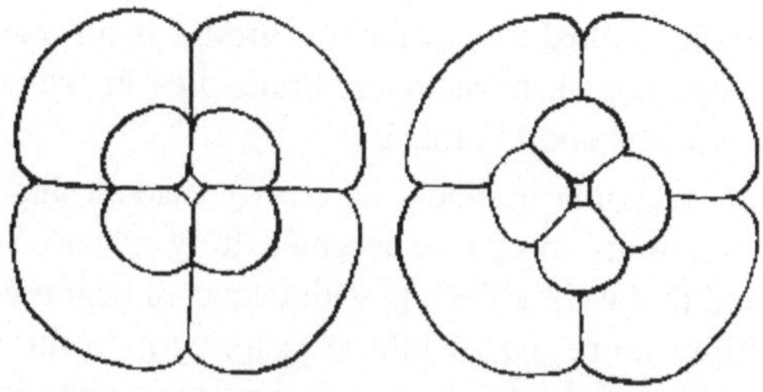

Figure 1.5: Radial cleavage at left and spiral at right.

will play in the body of the adult becomes fixed. In mosaic development the fate of each cell of the embryo is determined from the beginning, while in the equipotential manner of development the capacity to form any part of the organism, or all of it, is retained by all of the early blastomeres.

Only in that type of development is identical twinning possible. Finally, the two pathways of evolution differ in the method of coelome formation. In the schizocoelic animals the coelome is formed by means of a separation in an initially solid mass of mesoderm, unlike the enterocoelic method where a layer of cells forms a pocket to enclose a coelome within.

The uncertainty involved in establishing evolutionary origins is again demonstrated by the fact that Rotifera, Nematoda, and Chaetognatha are omitted by Carter who believes that "we cannot at present reach any worthwhile conclusions about their relationships." Hyman evidently does not concur since she does attempt to place them.

	Annelid Superphylum PROTOSTOMIA	***Echinoderm Superphylum DEUTEROSTOMIA***
Appearance of larva	trochosphere	dipleurula
Nature of cleavage	spiral	radial
Type of development	mosaic	equipotential
Origin of coelome	schizocoelic	enterocoelic

In figure elsewhere in this chapter the category "Protostomia" corresponds to the "annelid superphylum" of Carter, while the "Deuterostomia" are the equivalent of the "echinoderm superphylum," as noted in the table. It is of additional interest that in the Protostomia the embryonic blastopore, which leads into the primitive digestive cavity in the gastrula stage, becomes the functional mouth of the adult, whereas in the Deuterostomia this opening closes over, and an anus develops here.

Thus the longitudinal axis of the two groups is reversed. That which is the mouth opening in most invertebrates lies in the position of the anus of echinoderms and chordates.

From the foregoing it should be clearly evident that no scheme of phylogenetic relationship can be accepted fully as fact. It must always be remembered that we are dealing with events of origin which occurred in all probability more than a billion years ago. In the absence of an adequate fossil record we must rely on the uncertain evidence of comparative structure and embryology of present-day forms, the latter being very far removed from those we are attempting to visualize.

Under such circumstances no one can say with absolute certainty what the true relationships of the invertebrate groups really are.

Since taxonomy is an expression of relationships, classification is subject to the same limitations that apply to evolutionary origins. Accordingly, taxonomic arrangements differ from text to text according to the evolutionary views of the authors. Any undue concern over this situation can result only from the failure to understand the fundamental conditions outlined above.

As we proceed through the pages of this book, the following outline should be consulted frequently for purposes of orientation.

I. Subkingdom Protozoa—consists of animals which may be said to be acellular, or unicellular.

1. Phylum Protozoa

II. Subkingdom Parazoa-consists of multicellular animals without locomotory organs or digestive tracts.

2. Phylum Porifera

III. Subkingdom Enterozoa-consists of multicellular animals typically with locomotory organs and digestive tracts.

A. Acoelomate phyla-in *which there is no body cavity between the digestive tract and the body wall.*

1. With mesenchyme cells derived from the ectoderm.

3. *Phylum Cnidaria,* or *Coelenterata*

4. *Phylum Ctenophora*

2. With mesenchyme cells derived from the entoderm.

5. *Phylum Platyhelminthes*

6. *Phylum Rhynchocoela,* or *Nemertinea*, or *Nemertea*

B. *Pseudocoelomate Phyla—*in which there is a body cavity between *digestive tract and body wall, derived from the* *blastocoel of the embryo, and separating the mesoderm from the endoderm.*

7. *Phylum Endoprocta*
8. *Phylum Trochelminthes*, or *Rotifera*
9. *Phylum Gastrotricha*
10. *Phylum Kinorhyncha*, or *Echinodera*
11. *Phylum Acanthocephala*
12. *Phylum Nematomorpha*
13. *Phylum Nemathelminthes*

Aschelminthes
worms with a pseudocoel
(ascus=bladder,
helminth=worm)

C. *Coelomate phyla-in which* there is a body *cavity between* the digestive tract and the body wall, a cavity which is situated within *the* mesoderm, and *with* mesoderm derived from embryonic endoderm.

1. *Enterocoelic phyla*—in which the coelome arises as pouches from the embryonic enteron, and the embryonic blastopore closes. These are the Deuterostomia.

14. *Phylum Chaetognatha*
15. *Phylum Echinodermata*
16. *Phylum Chordata*

Echinoderm Superphylum

2. *Schizocoelic phyla*—in which the coelome arises as a split within the mesoderm, and the embryonic blastopore becomes the mouth of the adult. These are the Protostomia.

17. *Phylum Annelida*
18. *Phylum Sipunculoidea*
19. *Phylum Echiuroidea*
20. *Phylum Onychophora*
21. *Phylum Arthropoda*
22. *Phylum Bryozoa*, or *Ectoprocta*
23. *Phylum Phoronida*
24. *Phylum Brachiopoda*
25. *Phylum Mollusca*

Coelhelminthes
worms with a true coelome

Annelid Superphylum

THE SIZE OF INVERTEBRATES

Correlated with the *presence* or *absence* of *chlorophyll* in living organisms there is the *presence* or *absence* of cell walls. Unlike plants, in which the cells are enclosed in rather stiff cellulose walls, the cells and tissues of animals are necessarily soft. This is so in order to allow for the contractility which is essential for locomotion in the animal kingdom.

Soft bodies, however, generally lack the mechanical strength to attain large size, particularly on land where the buoyant effect of water is not present to offset weight. So we may regard the structural adaptation of animal cells for movement as a factor limiting the size of the organism. Shells or skeletons of invertebrates, when they appear, are located near or on the surface and seem to be designed primarily for protection of the soft body.

With skeletons located on the outside of the body, thickness and weight rapidly become limiting factors, and, unless the animal becomes sedentary in habit, preclude a large body. It is only among the vertebrates, whose skeletons are internal and are thoroughly integrated into the mechanism for movement, that comparatively large bodies are the rule.

Among invertebrates bodies are generally small. There appears to be considerable survival value in small size. The set-up of nature is such that the individual plays its role not in self-maintenance but in reproduction. In nature there is no value in building up a large body when a small body will do as well for passing life from one generation to the next. It is the succession and not the individual which counts. However, with increasing competition for food, the larger and more powerful animal possesses the obvious advantage, other things being equal, of being able more easily to overpower its prey. But the ability to seize food against smaller contenders is more or less offset by the greater amount of food required to reach a mature, reproductive stage.

It is evident that the size of an animal is not a simple consideration. Among invertebrates, as a group, smaller amounts of food are sufficient, the body can be built up more quickly, and reproduction occurs sooner and in greater numbers. These are important factors in evolutionary survival. Composed as they are of animals that are usually small, large species of invertebrates stand out. These are, accordingly, of exceptional interest.

The largest known invertebrate is a giant squid, *Architeuthis princeps,* which inhabits arctic waters. Architeuthis is a "sea monster," and may exceed fifty feet in length. In northern waters, too, is the jellyfish, *Cyanea capillata,* weighing about one ton; with a disc up to seven feet in diameter and tentacles trailing more than a hundred feet.

These two, from the least evolved and most evolved enterozoan phyla, are probably the largest of the invertebrates. In the same phylum with Cyanea, but among the polyps, is the hydroid *Branchiocerianthus imperator* of the northern Pacific, which stands over two feet in height. Its magnitude can be best appreciated in comparison with a common *Hydra*.

KNOWN OBJECTS ACCORDING TO WEIGHT

	Weight in grams
The Earth	$10^{27} \times 6$
largest whale	10^{9}
basking shark	10^{8}
giant squid	10^{7}
largest jellyfish	10^{6}
largest clam (*Tridacna*)	10^{5}
Japanese spider crab	10^{5}
average human	10^{5}
largest polyp (*Branchiocerianthus*)	10^{4}
largest worm	10^{4}
rat	10^{3}
mouse	10^{2}
Goliath beetle	10^{2}
South American bird-eating spider	10^{2}
largest protozoan (*Nummulites*, a *foraminiferan*)	10^{1}
common earthworm	10^{1}
humming bird	10^{1}
honey bee	10^{0}
largest ant	10^{0}
Amphioxus	10^{0}
smallest vertebrate (*Phyllobates*, a frog)	10^{-1}
house fly	10^{-1}
Hydra	10^{-2}
flea	10^{-3}
smallest mollusk (*Acme stussineri*)	10^{-4}
smallest polychaet (*Syllides opisthodonta*)	10^{-5}
smallest beetle	10^{-5}
human ovum	10^{-5}
largest Paramecium	10^{-6}
Vorticella	10^{-7}

Entamoeba histolytica	10^{-8}
Trypanosoma gambiense	10^{-9}
human erythrocyte	10^{-10}
malarial protozoan (maximum size)	10^{-10}
haemoglobin molecule	10^{-18}
water molecule	10^{-22}
electron	10^{-27}

Among crustaceans, where sizeable bodies are fairly frequent, the Japanese spider crab *Macrochira kaemp feri* is notable, with a leg span of up to twelve feet. There is also the marine isopod, *Bathynomus giganteus* of the Gulf of Mexico, which measures a foot in length and several inches in width.

Worms, too, sometimes attain considerable dimensions. *Megascolides gippslandicus,* a Tasmanian earthworm, reaches a length of six feet or more and *Eunice rousseaui,* a polychaet, may be over three feet in length. We would probably find most impressive, however, the sixty-foot length of *Diphyllobothrium latum,* a tapeworm which lives in the human intestine, or even the six-foot length of *Dracunculus medinensis,* a roundworm found under the skin in man.

In Haldane and Huxley, *Animal Biology*, there is a listing of known objects according to weight. From this compilation it may be ascertained that the range in size of invertebrate animals is quite extensive. The giant squid, on the one hand, weighs some 10 million grams. The malarial organism, when full grown within the red blood cell, weighs one ten billionth of a gram.

Twelve invertebrates in this listing are larger than the smallest vertebrate, and four of them are larger than man. It should be understood, however, that size is no criterion of "importance," as importance is measured by human standards.

The malarial organism, despite its extremely minute size, is the cause of one of the most devastating of human diseases. Insects are, economically, the most outstanding of invertebrate groups, yet the very largest is smaller than a mouse.

The giant squid, despite its size, is little more than a fascinating curiosity. Every invertebrate, regardless of size, demonstrates by its existence that it is able to perform all of the functions of life. Each, under the conditions of its own habitat, is able to obtain food, grow, and reproduce. Therefore, each is a "success."

2

The Subkingdom Protozoa

Protozoans are usually thought of as one-celled animals. This idea is reasonably correct, but it would be much better to consider the protozoan as a non-cellular animal. In this *subkingdom*, within the confines of a single cell, we find all the structures and capacities for carrying on a full life.

The protozoan is a very remarkable animal. Whereas in Enterozoa we find elaborate musculature and impressive organs of various kinds for moving about, the protozoan moves by means of specialized parts (*organelles*) of its single-celled body. In higher organisms there are intricate appendages for grasping food, organs for digesting food, and still others for expelling undigested residues, while the *protozoan* does all this with parts of its single cell.

And similarly with *secretion*, sensation, coordination, reproduction, and every function associated with the animal organism. Where the higher organism requires *organ-systems* with innumerable cells, the protozoan gets along fully as well with its one cell. Nor is there any function in a multicellular animal which the protozoan cannot also carry on, sufficient for its needs. Present-day protozoans represent the original animal world, when animal life first came into being.

All other phyla evolved later and are therefore younger than the protozoan. This means that protozoans have had a longer period in which to "try out" various forms than any other animal group. It should be expected, accordingly, that a stock of such *ancient* lineage be composed of *complicated* organisms, and it would be surprising if they were not.

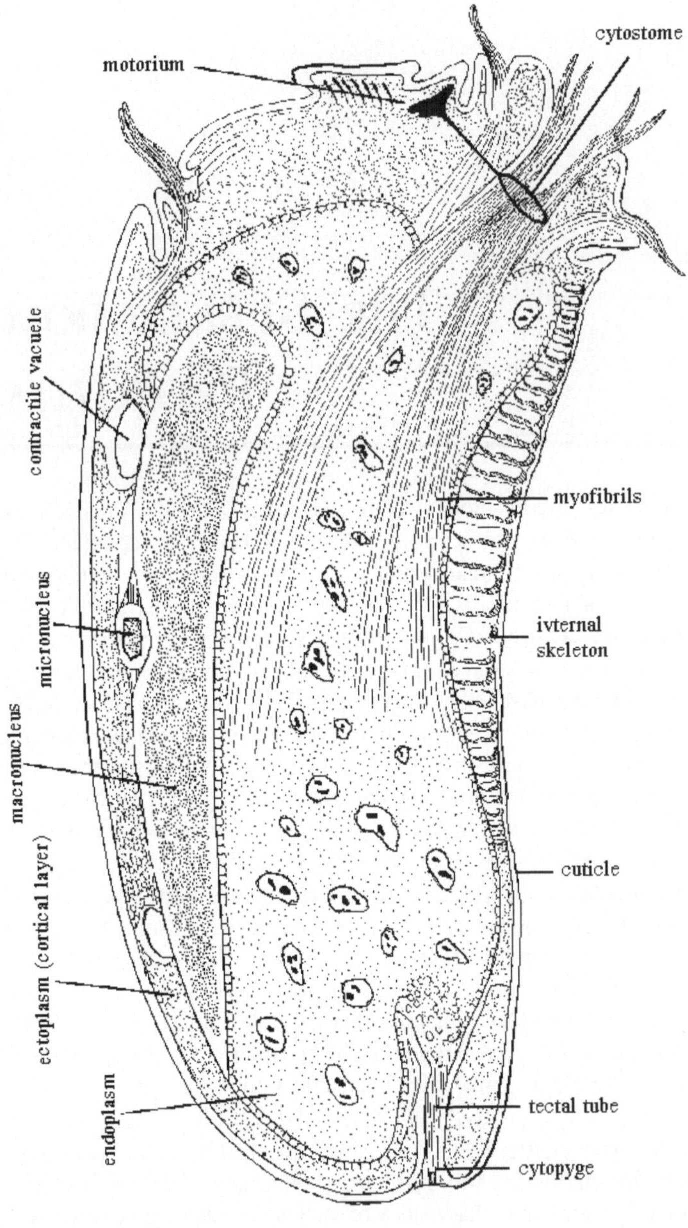

Figure 2.1: The complexity of a protozoan, as illustrated in Diplodinium.

As a matter of fact, protozoans are by no means simple. Some, as Amoeba, which appear to be simple, may very well be atrophied in some aspects of their structure. Others, like Diplodinium, show remarkable complexity.

In the higher animal the pattern of organization extends over many cells. More or less separate functions are allocated to different groups of cells. As a consequence individual cells may be comparatively simple in structure since a high level of versatility is not required of them. Among protozoans, which carry on all of the functions of life without cellular compartmentation of the body, the converse is true.

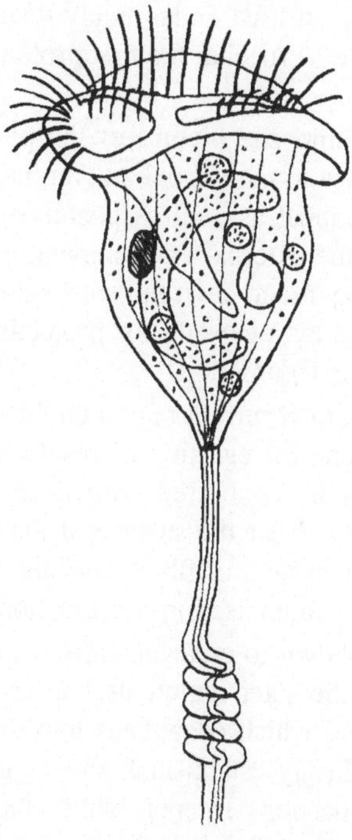

Figure 2.2: Vorticella.

Nowhere in the animal kingdom is so much functional and structural complexity compressed into so minute a body, so that a completely functional animal can exist within a single cell. It is not difficult to understand why Ehrenberg, in 1838, was led to believe that protozoans were complete animals in the same sense as the larger forms. He described the contractile vacuole as a beating heart. The radiating canals were, in his opinion, blood vessels. The food vacuole was regarded as a stomach; and the nucleus as a sex organ.

It is only in the perspective of time that these views have become quaint and we should not, therefore, be too dogmatic about our present-day views, for time has yet to pass judgment on them. Leeuwenhoek, in 1675, opened the door to the world of protozoans. As with many great discoveries, this one awaited the tool; the microscope was needed to detect the protozoan. Leeuwen hoek, the deviser of the former, was, fittingly, the discoverer of the latter.

And so it happens that the oldest of animal phyla is the most recently known to man. As the astronomer gazes into the far reaches of the heavens, so the protozoologist has continued to peer into the world of microscopic animal life. Today many thousands of organisms stand in our records where Vorticella, the first protozoan to be described, once stood alone.

Let us examine a composite picture of the protozoan as we now know it. There is a surface to the animal and an interior; the difference between the two is functional as well as positional. The surface is in immediate contact with the external environment, and its structure and properties equip it for response to environmental stimulation. The surface may be partially enclosed by a capsule for protection, and it is usually provided with devices for locomotion.

There is a permanent or recurrent region on the surface for ingestion of food and, similarly, one for egestion of residues. These, the mouth and anal openings, may be connected with ducts of pharyngeal and rectal nature, respectively. Near the surface of the organism it may be possible to demonstrate a system of fibrils serving in the manner of the nervous system of higher animals, for coordination of responses.

The fibrils can be shown to emanate from a motorium, somewhat analogous to a brain. In the outer region also, there may be found small capsules of ejectable fluid which coagulates into threads. The function of these remains to be firmly established; the suggestion that they are protective is open to question. Deeper within the organism there is frequently a skeletal system of calcareous, silicious or proteinaceous nature.

Skeletal adaptations in such small animals are perhaps somewhat surprising, but they are by no means uncommon. Sometimes, as we shall see later, they are characteristic of entire orders. Circulating in the cytoplasm are droplets of more or less clear fluid surrounded by protoplasmic membrane. These are the so-called "vacuoles," but they are not, as the name would imply, empty. The contractile vacuoles contain liquid which is periodically discharged to the environment.

The presence of contractile vacuoles is correlated with fresh-water habitat; they are believed to be of hydrostatic function, bailing out the water which, in this environment, constantly enters the organism under osmotic drive. Others, the food vacuoles, hold the particles that the protozoan ingests to meet its nutritive needs.

Of many types of more or less solid bodies, like crystals and granules, nuclei are especially significant. But more elusive than any of these visible structures is the innate organization of the protoplasm itself, which gives to each kind of protozoan its specific form and behaviour.

The Functions of an Animal

Whether they be simple or complex in visible structure, all forms of animal life are characterized by functions that they possess in common. These functions center around locomotion and nutrition. We shall now briefly explain some of them, for they apply to protozoans and others alike.

Sensation

Sensation is the capacity to receive stimuli. It is a crucial property of the animal organism since only by means of adequate sensitivity to a changing environment is the animal enabled to avoid unfavourable influences and to take advantage of factors that are favourable. All animals, including protozoans, are more or less sensitive to light, to touch or contact, to gravity, to sound and to vibrations, to heat, to electrical stimulation, and to chemical materials of various sorts.

When an organism is highly sensitive to a stimulus of a certain kind, we say it possesses a low threshold of sensitivity to that stimulus. Conversely, when the organism is relatively insensitive to certain stimuli, its threshold for those stimuli is high. In general, the development of low thresholds involves the evolution of specialized sensory organs.

For example, sound vibrations if very intense may affect an animal without ears, while vibrations of much smaller magnitude will be received by an animal which possesses ears. Ears, in this example, are organs of low threshold to sound stimuli. Among the protozoans Amoeba, without any specialized structural adaptations for the purpose, is sensitive to light, while other protozoans with eyespots are much more sensitive.

Coordination

Coordination is the function of transmission of stimuli within the body in such a way that an integrated response occurs. The most obvious type of coordination is that which is performed by a nervous system or, in protozoans, by a neuromotor system. Coordination also occurs without nervous systems. For example, the digestive secretion of the pancreas is coordinated with that of the intestine by means of a chemical substance, the hormone secretin.

This is a true form of coordination, for integrated behaviour results, yet no nerve action is involved. Similarly, in the locomotion of Amoeba there is coordination of pseudopodial outflow in the absence of a neuromotor system, while among ciliates a neuromotor system is involved.

Locomotion

Locomotion is the function of movement from place to place. Evidently all movement is not of the locomotory type. The circulation of blood, the passage of food through an alimentary tract, or of a food vacuole through a protozoan-these, too, are movements, but they are not locomotion.

Locomotion involves the transport of the organism as a whole. Therefore it has special significance-in the search for food and "society," and the avoidance of enemies, as already pointed out.

Alimentation

Alimentation will be used to include all of the functions which contribute directly to the nourishment of the animal. In the order of their occurrence *ingestion* is the first process of alimentation. Ingestion involves the transfer of food from the environment to the interior of the animal.

This transfer occurs through an opening called the mouth and into a space within which physical and chemical work can be done to convert the food into soluble constituents. This work is called *digestion*. Digestion is essentially the conversion of food from crude bulk form into particles of molecular dimension which can be absorbed into the living protoplasm itself.

Digestion usually involves a preliminary mechanical phase called *mastication*, or chewing, which might take place in the mouth or even after the food penetrates more deeply into the alimentary system, i.e. within the stomach. The tearing of food into smaller fragments before entry into the mouth is also related to mastication.

Mastication alone cannot reduce food to particles of molecular size, but by making smaller fragments it does increase the surface on which digestive enzymes can act and thereby speeds the process of digestion. The final phase of digestion, by enzymes, is a chemical one.

There are always some materials that enter an alimentary system but cannot be digested. The discharge of such wastes is called *egestion*, or defecation. Egestion usually occurs through a separate opening, the anus, but in some of the less evolved animals it takes place through the mouth and, under unusual circumstances, it may take place through the mouth even when an anus is present.

Circulation

Circulation may be broadly defined as the distribution of any substance within the body, although the term usually refers to the movement of body fluids within a specialized system of vessels. In some phyla food may be transported within a digestive system, in which case the circulation system is referred to as a "*gastrovascular*" system. Gases may be distributed through tubules of a special system, the tracheal system.

Within single cells circulation usually takes the form of simple chemical diffusion. But by whatever method it occurs, the system of distribution must be adequate to bring together materials from various sources so that the chemical reactions necessary to build and maintain the organism can be carried on; perhaps equally important, it must be adequate to carry waste substances to organs of discharge.

Excretion

Excretion must not be confused with egestion. Materials which cannot penetrate the linings of the alimentary system are egested. Excretion, on the other hand, deals with the elimination of substances produced within and by the living protoplasm itself. Carbon dioxide is such a substance.

It is disposed of by respiratory process. Nitrogenous wastes, are usually eliminated by means of special excretory organs of the kidney type; and this, the disposal of nitrogenous wastes, is the common meaning of excretion.

Respiration

Respiration is a cellular function, but the oxygen required is obtained from the atmosphere and the carbon dioxide is returned to the atmosphere, the place of exchange being the surface of the animal. Most animals can live actively only in the presence of free oxygen, which they consume to support the metabolic activities that go on in all of their organ systems.

As a result of oxidations, carbon dioxide is formed. At permeable areas of the surface, ventilation is required so that diffusion gradients, to shift oxygen inwardly and carbon dioxide outwardly, can be maintained.

Ciliary action, undulations of the body, gills, lungs, tracheae, all of these are aids to ventilation on the outer surface of the respiratory membrane.

Circulation of the body fluids facilitates ventilation of the inner surface. Some animals have become more or less independent of oxygen. The lack of oxygen is not an insurmountable barrier to respiration. If we recall that oxygen in its chemical activity acts as a receiver of electrons it can be understood that other chemical systems might be and sometimes are adapted to the same function.

It is fortunate for animals living in such low oxygen environments as muds or the intestines of other animals that receivers of electrons other than oxygen are available.

Reproduction

Reproduction is, simply, the production of more of the same kind. Let there be no confusion about its meaning; sex and reproduction are not the same. Reproduction is most efficiently accomplished when only one individual is involved. Fission is its simplest expression. Sex is something added. Sex does not aid in the production of new individuals, but promotes variability among the offspring.

The almost universal presence of sex shows that variability is worth adding even at the cost of complications, for as the number of individuals involved in a function becomes greater, behavioural problems increase.

How simple is the life of an amoeba, which pauses on occasion and divides into two, contrasted with that of Paramecium in which nuclear specificity, maturation phenomena, mating types and lethal factors are all associated with sex-as we will see in more detail below.

It should be clear by now that there is no essential difference in the functioning of a protozoan as compared with a multicellular animal. In the evolution of the latter no new functions are added. It is only that there is evolved more elaborate structural machinery, i.e., systems of organs composed of many cells.

Life processes are basically functions of protoplasm. Specific structural specializations are adaptations, which may or may not be present. This is as true in the protozoan subkingdom as elsewhere.

SPECIALIZATION IN THE PROTOZOANS

Let us now consider these animal life functions with more specific attention to the protozoan subkingdom.

Sensation

With regard to sensation, protoplasm is generally sensitive to stimulation. Visible structures may be absent, as in Amoeba; indeed, in most protozoans there are no visible sensory organelles. Euglena with its specialized light-sensitive area and light-filtering pigment spot is an exception, as are also the dinoflagellates Proterythropsis and Erythropsis, in which the light-receptors are even provided with lens-like devices.

Coordination

As for sensation, there is in most protozoans no visible mechanism for coordination, which is in these instances a function of the apparently undifferentiated cytoplasm. In other genera the structural complexity of the mechanism for coordination may be very great. This has been demonstrated chiefly among the ciliates where there is a neuromotor system composed of a network of coordinating fibrils, within an outer layer known as the ectoplasm.

The fibrils run both longitudinally and transversely and connect with an organelle named the motorium, which is situated near the mouth. It has been shown that the destruction of the motorium results in the disorganization of the entire ciliary beat and that severance of a single neurofibril interferes with the beat of those cilia located posteriorly to the cut.

In the neuromotor system of protozoans a parallelism with the nervous system of the multicellular animals is evident. However, it should not be forgotten that the neuromotor system of the protozoans, intricate as it is, is developed entirely from and within part of a single cell, and is therefore not structurally comparable (homologous) with the nervous system in other phyla.

The most marked type of coordinated behaviour in a protozoan is of an inhibitory nature. We might say that a protozoan "knows" when to go away, and that there is great merit in knowing when to go away, here as in higher animals. It is the essence of discretion. In more technical terms, protozoans show avoiding reactions, or phobotaxis. When a paramecium enters a region of unfavourable stimulation it backs out, changes direction, and then proceeds once more.

This response may be repeated as many times as is necessary, until the course ahead offers favourable stimuli. In psychology such procedure would probably be included in the "trial and error" pattern of behaviour, which constitutes a basic method of learning. There is little evidence that protozoans profit from their learning experience through a subseq-uently improved capacity for response, though there is some evidence.

In lacking capacity to learn they would be far from unique, however, and should not be set apart on account of it from animals even of the most advanced groups.

Sometimes a protozoan shows a directive, or topotactic, type of behaviour. This appears to be a positive response of movement toward the source of stimulation, as shown by Amoeba, for example, in its pursuit of food.

It cannot be said with certainty that phobotaxis and topotaxis are basically different. Perhaps Amoeba, in pursuing a course directly toward the source of food stimuli, is actually showing the phobotactic pattern by avoiding those regions of its environment which contain no food stimuli. The behaviour of a protozoan is, evidently, subject to varied interpretation and the field of animal behaviour is not more lucid for protozoans than it is for higher animals.

Locomotion

We have taken it as a working hypothesis that movement from place to place is of the essence of animal nature and that, accordingly, emphasis on the structures evolved for locomotion will promote an integrated view of the animal kingdom. Here in the protozoan subkingdom is our first opportunity to test the hypothesis. We find at once that the

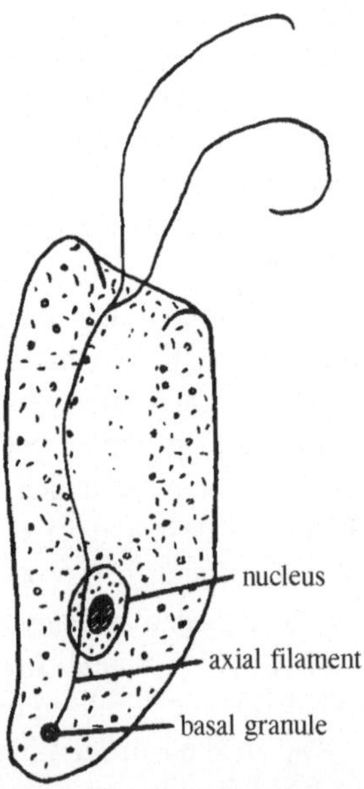

Figure 2.3: Chilomonas, showing deep anchorage of axial filament.

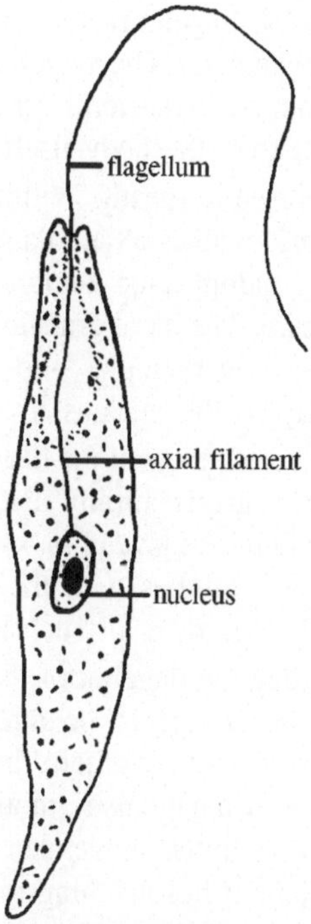

Figure 2.4: Euglena, showing axial filament.

classification of protozoans, which here as in other groups indicates scientific conclusions as to natural relationships, is based to a considerable extent upon the nature of their locomotory organelles.

There are three types of such organelles-the flagellum, the pseudopodium, and the cilium; and three classes-respectively the Mastigophora, the Sarcodina, and the Infusoria—are based on them. In some of the Sporozoa there also occasionally appear flagella-like or pseudopod—like structures. These are regarded as parallel developments. If identity with their counterparts in the other classes could definitely be shown, then such sporozoans would need to be removed from their class and placed with the class indicated.

They could no longer be regarded as sporozoans. It is only because of their minute size that the differences between protozoan locomotory systems are not as evident as are the differences between the locomotory organs of other phyla. In the description which follows it would be helpful to imagine them as of much larger dimension.

The Flagellum

The flagellum is a lashing thread capable of an undulating, whip like motion. In the simpler flagellates the flagellum extends forward and acts as a towing mechanism. The flagellum is believed to consist of an exceedingly fine tubular extension of the outer part of the body, often considerably longer than the body itself.

This part is the ectoplasmic sheath. Within, the sheath is traversed by one or more fine fibrils called axial filaments. The axial filament extends deeply into the endoplasmic region of the animal where it terminates in a basal granule. The basal granule may in turn be connected by means of another fibril-the rhizoplast—to the nucleus, or the axial filament may run directly to the nucleus itself.

The deep endoplasmic anchorage of the flagellum should be especially noted, for in this respect it is structurally distinguished from a cilium. The description of a flagellum here given has been obtained by observation with the light microscope. (Studies with the electron microscope are leading to revisions with regard to all such microscopic organelles).

The function of bending the flagellum is believed by some to reside in the filament, and straightening to be due to the elasticity of the sheath. A converse view is held by others, but whichever is the case, we have here an instance of antagonistic motion just as in muscle-one mechanism brings about an initial movement and another restores the part to its original position. It is something to think about, that all this can exist in a locomotory organelle produced from a very small part of a minute, one-celled animal.

The Pseudopodium

Pseudopodia are more diversified in structure than are flagella. One type is long and slender with an internal axial portion somewhat like a flagellum; but the central portion is fairly rigid, not vibratile as in a flagellum. This type is known as the axopodium and apparently has no direct locomotory function.

It has been suggested that the axopodium might have been derived by degeneration from the flagellum type of organelle. Some pseudopodia resemble axopodia but lack a differentiated central core and these are the filopodia. If short and thick, filopodia are known as "lobopodia." An important characteristic of the pseudopodium is its surface properties.

If the surface readily sends out branches and adhesions can form between the branches, this fact is recognized by the designation of a fourth type, rhizopodia. This is the type found in the common Amoeba, and all orders of Sarcodina with rhizopodia are placed in the subclass Rhizopoda. The theory has been proposed that the flowing, branching, and anastomosing type of pseudopodium shown by Amoeba has evolved from a flagellum through the loss of vibrating power followed by enlargement of the axial filament into a flowing mass. If so this is an evolutionary phenomenon no less remarkable than, for example, the transition from fin to wing among the vertebrates.

The Cilium

At first sight the cilium closely resembles a flagellum, with an ectoplasmic sheath and an axial filament. (The electron microscope reveals a composition of nine to eleven filaments, the central ones being sturdier and longer.) The fact remains that the cilium is restricted entirely to material from the ectoplasmic, or cortical layer, as it is known in this class.

Less basic for the distinction between ciliates and flagellates is the fact that there are usually many cilia and generally only a few flagella; but this is not always the case. In mode of action, the beat of a cilium is pendular, back and forth somewhat like an oar, with an effective stroke in which the cilium is held rather stiffly, and a recovery stroke in which it rolls back on itself.

While flagella generally tow the protozoan behind, cilia may be thought of as rowing the organism upon its way. The mechanical action of these organelles has been carefully studied by means of motion pictures which are then projected in slow time. Their rate of beat is not difficult to determine stroboscopically. When they appear to be motionless under intermittent lighting of known frequency, that is their rate of beat.

Such techniques provide interesting examples of the usefulness of selected tools in the study of specific biological problems. The most intensive studies of the physiology of protozoan locomotory organelles have been made upon pseudopodia. Ever since the genus Amoeba was discovered in 1755 by Rosel von Rosenhof, the flow of pseudopodia has fascinated the scientifically curious.

Generation after generation of students have peered at it in the classroom even as you do today, and generation after generation of biologists have devoted years to its study. It is illustrative of the difficulty of solving apparently simple problems of protoplasmic activity that no generally acceptable explanation of ameboid movement has ever been put forward. Such difficulties are not restricted to the protozoan subkingdom, however, for, in 1956, Heilbrunn said with regard to motion among the enterozoa that "at present no complete theory of muscular contraction is possible."

Physiologically the animal world is one world and the scientific problems of life are the same wherever one searches for them. Perhaps the most widely held view of ameboid movement-and this does not guarantee it against error-is that of Pantin who proposed a mechanism of viscosity changes.

On the basis of studies made with *Amoeba limax*, which moves by means of a single pseudopodium, Pantin suggested that the fluid endoplasm flows forward into the anterior ectoplasm, which is also fluid. The anterior ectoplasm is thereupon rolled laterally out of the line of motion and becomes modified from a sol to a gel.

At the posterior end of the animal the ectoplasm liquefies again and flows forward into the endoplasm. In this way a fluid interior core of the animal moves forward through a more solid exterior sheath. Even if this theory were fully accepted, how much does it really tell us? It is little more than can be seen under the microscope and only skirts the fringes of the biochemical explanation toward which we are striving.

Even though ameboid movement is an amazing feat of acrobatics, considered physically, it is nevertheless rather ineffective as a means of locomotion; for the common species of Amoeba plow along at a rate of not more than four or five microns per second (you might convert this to miles per hour) while ciliates and flagellates breeze by at several hundred microns per second.

We should not be too quick to accept any theory of ameboid movement, since explanations which appear to have merit for one species are difficult to apply to others. In Entamoeba, for example, pseudopodia consist only of ectoplasm. Since no endoplasm is involved, Pantin's theory does not seem applicable. It is always well to keep an open mind.'

ALIMENTATION

The nutrition of some protozoans is plantlike and consequently no alimentation is then involved. This is true of the Phytomastigina which may be regarded as the most primitive of the protozoans (although botanists usually include Phytomastigina with the algae). It is very difficult to draw a taxonomic line between algae and the earliest protozoans, and it would profit us little to attempt to do so.

Let it suffice to say that when animals and plants first appeared, the characteristics of the plant kingdom were gradually lost in the animal stem, and somewhere along the line it becomes possible to state that here, at last, is an organism which is fully animal. The Phytomastigina are motile and possess flexible bodies but they are nourished entirely or in part by means of photosynthesis, which they are enabled to carry on because of the presence of chlorophyll-bearing chromatophores. In very rare instances the Sarcodina may also have such chromatophores, perhaps of their own, as in the genus Paulinella, a testacean.

Sarcodina also may be in symbiotic relationship with plant organisms, a phenomenon which is especially notable among the radiolarians as in the genus Thallassicolla. Even among ciliates, e.g., *Paramecium bursaria*, chlorophyll-green has not entirely disappeared. Obviously the presence of chlorophyll cannot be accepted by itself as an indication of flora

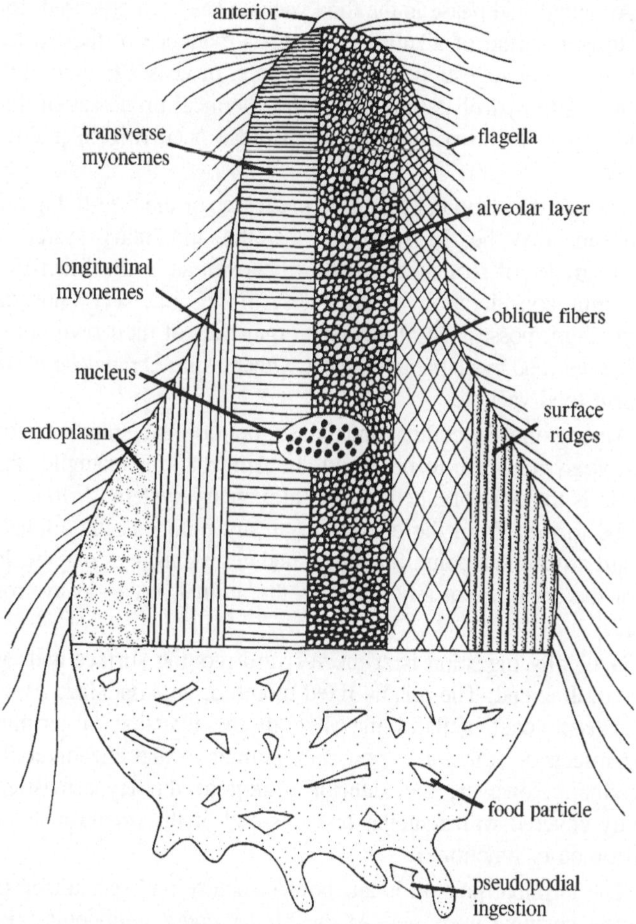

Figure 2.5: Trichonympha. At the posterior end nutritive processes are indicated. Anteriorly the intricate body structure is brought out. The surface ridges support the flagella and, successively, toward the left are shown differentiated regions deeper within the body. The longitudinal myonemes and the nucleus lie within the endoplasm.

versus fauna, since the question inevitably arises as to whether it is due to mutualism with algae.

The line between the earliest plants and the very earliest animals is a vague and tenuous one, as indeed it should be by evolutionary considerations. The prevailing method of nutrition in protozoans involves the ingestion of organic particles-sometimes dead, more often alive, like bacteria and other protozoa-within a droplet of water. In this way a food vacuole is formed, and here digestion takes place.

An initial acid phase in the food vacuole has been observed, followed by a longer period of alkalinity. There is evidence of the existence of amylases for the digestion of carbohydrates, proteases to digest proteins, and lipases to hydrolyze fats. Thus the chemical processes of digestion would appear to be no different than those occurring in multicellular animals.

Though the chemical digestive processes of the free-living holozoic protozoans may be the same for all, the alimentary system shows various grades of structural complexity, even as in the Enterozoa. We shall omit consideration of parasites. Some, like Trypanosoma and Plasmodium, possess no alimentary organelles of their own but take in predigested food available in the host. Others, like *Entamoeba histolytica*, do form food vacuoles.

Among the Sarcodina and Mastigophora the simplest structural digestive systems are to be found. In Amoeba, for example, the food vacuole is the only organelle of the alimentary system. A food vacuole may be formed from the ectoplasm at any point, as the animal flows forward around that point. Similarly, undigested residues may be dropped out of the organism at any point, as the animal moves away from that point.

Generally ingestion is at the forward-moving surface and egestion at the trailing end. There is no fixed mouth or anal opening. Among the Hypermastigidaeflagellates that live in the intestine of termites and other insectsthe situation is generally similar to that encountered in the Sarcodina. However, the anterior region of the Hypermastigidae is heavily covered with flagella, and this end of the organism is devoted to locomotory function.

The terminal portion is ameboid in nature and specialized thereby to serve nutritive purposes. At the hinder end pseudopodia are thrust out, food vacuoles are formed, and undigestible wastes are discharged. An interesting parallel may be drawn between the food vacuole and the tubular digestive system of higher organisms.

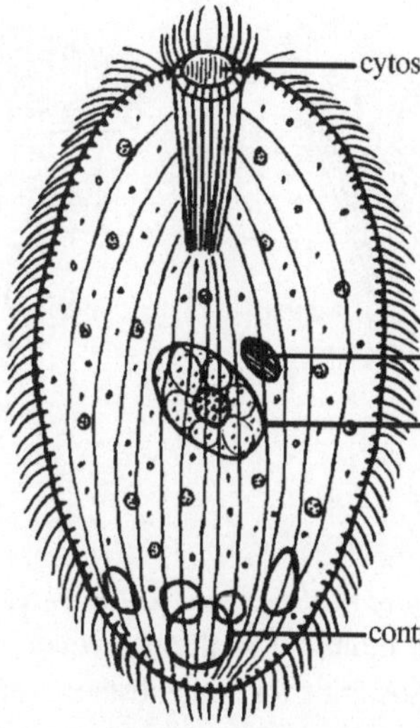

Figure 2.6: Prorodon.

As the vacuole begins to form, and to sink into the interior, its opening to the water of the environment may be thought of as a mouth and the tubular connection between the "mouth" and the partially engulfed vacuole may be thought of as an esophagus.

As the vacuole is completed it becomes the "stomach" and as it circulates around and around the interior of the animal it may be likened to the coiling of an intestine. In both the circulation of the food vacuole and the coiling of an intestine more time is provided for the action of digestive enzymes than would be the case if transit through the body were in a direct line from mouth to anus.

Finally, as the vacuole makes contact once again with the ectoplasm and breaks through it becomes, in effect, a rectum and its opening is the anus. Thus, without the differentiation of a variety of structural parts the food vacuole serves all of the purposes of such parts.

Infusorian Digestive Organelles

Among the Infusoria the situation is different. Although all are not equally equipped in this respect, many are quite intricate in their organelles for alimentation. The Protociliata, are all endozoic, e.g., Opalina in frog intestines, and in them there is a total absence of digestive structures. But this is exceptional. Ciliates generally have a mouth, or cytostome, in a fixed position.

The cytostome may be terminal at the very anterior end as in Prorodon, one of the Holotrichida. This is believed to be the primitive

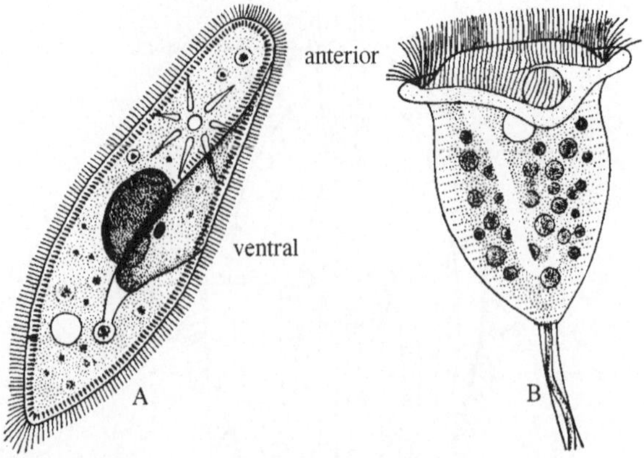

Figure 2.7: The symmetry of a ciliate. Paramecium, in relation to the mouth.

location of an infusorian mouth. Usually, however, the mouth is found to be shifted toward the posterior for some distance, and a food-funnelling depression of the surface, the oral groove or peristome, leads to it. When located in this way the mouth is taken to mark the ventral side of the animal, and the identification of right and left sides of the organism follows.

We thus encounter bilateral symmetry among the protozoans, a phenomenon that is made much of when it appears in higher phyla. Running from anterior to posterior, and on either the right side or the left side of the peristome, there may be found a series of brushlike bands of cilia. Together they form the so-called adoral zone. The adoral zone, in its progression posteriorly, may curve toward the right side, in a clockwise direction, or counter-clockwise, toward the left.

This difference has no functional significance, but is utilized in the classification of various orders of ciliates. The mouth itself may lie in the bottom of a pit-like depression, the cytopharynx. After formation at the mouth the food vacuole circulates for some time within the endoplasm and provides time for chemical phases of digestion and for absorption. Finally the indigestible residues in the food vacuole are discharged. In some ciliates this occurs at a random point but usually there is a fixed anal spot, the cytopyge.

There may even be a differentiated rectal tube leading to the anal spot, as in Diplodinium. A pause for reflection will show that Mastigophora, Sarcodina, and Infusoria are the same in their basic organelle for alimentation, the food vacuole, but that among Infusoria, accessory organelles are derived from the ectoplasm and serve the functions of ingestion and egestion. The parallelism between the advanced alimentary system of the ciliates and that of multicellular animals is quite intriguing.

It is remarkable that such could have been achieved among protozoans, considering that there was only one cell to work with on the one hand, while tissues and organs were "available" on the other. But it should be clearly kept in mind that regardless of the relative simplicity or complexity of the system, the function of alimentation is equal to the needs of the animal in all cases, or the organism would not survive.

RESPIRATION

The exchange of respiratory gases is accomplished in the protozoan, as in the higher animal, by diffusion across surface membranes. Rate of diffusion is controlled by the concentration gradients that exist between the organism and its environment. Since carbon dioxide is produced within the cell, the concentration of carbon dioxide in a favourable environmental medium is higher in the animal and this gas diffuses out (of course in dissolved form) through the surface.

The oxygen gradient runs in the opposite direction. Being consumed within the organism its concentration is greater outside, and oxygen diffuses inward. The total quantity of gas which travels into or out of the animal per unit time depends not only upon the concentration gradient but also upon the surface area available for diffusion. Both are subject to a certain amount of control.

Other things being equal, a smaller protozoan body respires more easily since the relative ratio of surface to volume is larger when the animal is small; and so fission becomes a dynamic factor in respiration. Such structures as the tentacles of Suctoria and the pseudopodia of Sarcodina also increase available surface and, with a constant diffusion gradient, allow more gas exchange than if these adaptations were not present. A different relationship of locomotory organelles to respiratory function is encountered in rapidly moving forms like ciliates and flagellates.

Here speed of movement acts to ventilate the surface. Carbon dioxide is quickly swept away and the motion of the animal carries it into areas where the oxygen supply may not have been depleted. Relationships of locomotory structures to respiration should be kept in mind, for it will not be difficult to find parallel adaptations appearing from time to time among multicellular animals.

EXCRETION

We have defined excretion, above, as the elimination of the waste products of protoplasmic activity. Indigestible wastes from the alimentary system are excluded from this process. Carbon dioxide, although derived from the activity of protoplasm, is not

ordinarily included in a consideration of excretion because it also falls within the scope of respiration. Besides carbon dioxide, water is an end-product of the oxidation of carbohydrate and might properly be regarded as part of the true excreta; but, as conventionally defined, excretion deals only with the elimination of nitrogenous wastes such as ammonia, formed in the breakdown of proteins.

Excretion occurs by diffusion through the surface in all protozoans. No specialized organelles, corresponding to the nephridium or kidney of the enterozoans, have been demonstrated. As defined in this way, there appears to be no essential relation of the contractile vacuole to excretion.'

The Contractile Vacuole

What, then, is the function of this vacuole? We need now to remember that any living cell acts as an osmotic system. Water is usually taken in from the environment, in accordance with the relative concentrations which prevail within and outside of the animal. In a hypertonic medium water would be lost.

For protozoans which live in sea water, osmotic balance can apparently be maintained without special devices, inasmuch as the osmotic concentration of sea water is close to that of protoplasm. For an animal living in fresh water the situation is different. Here more water is constantly being taken in than is given out through the surface. If there were no mechanism to do the work of disposal of excess water the organism would, at the least, swell out of normal shape and size and, in an extreme condition, it would rupture and disintegrate.

The presence of the contractile vacuole in freshwater protozoans and the fact that it is usually absent in marine and in parasitic forms therefore becomes significant. It has been shown experimentally that alteration of the salt content of the medium in which the animal lives affects the rate of pulsation of the vacuole.

When salts are added the rate slows, and when the medium is diluted the vacuole pulses more rapidly. The contractile vacuole appears to be, by present evidence, an organelle for controlling water content, and nothing more. The elimination of nitrogenous wastes remains, in protozoa, a function unassociated with specialized organelles.

REPRODUCTION

Now we come to the question of reproduction in the protozoans,

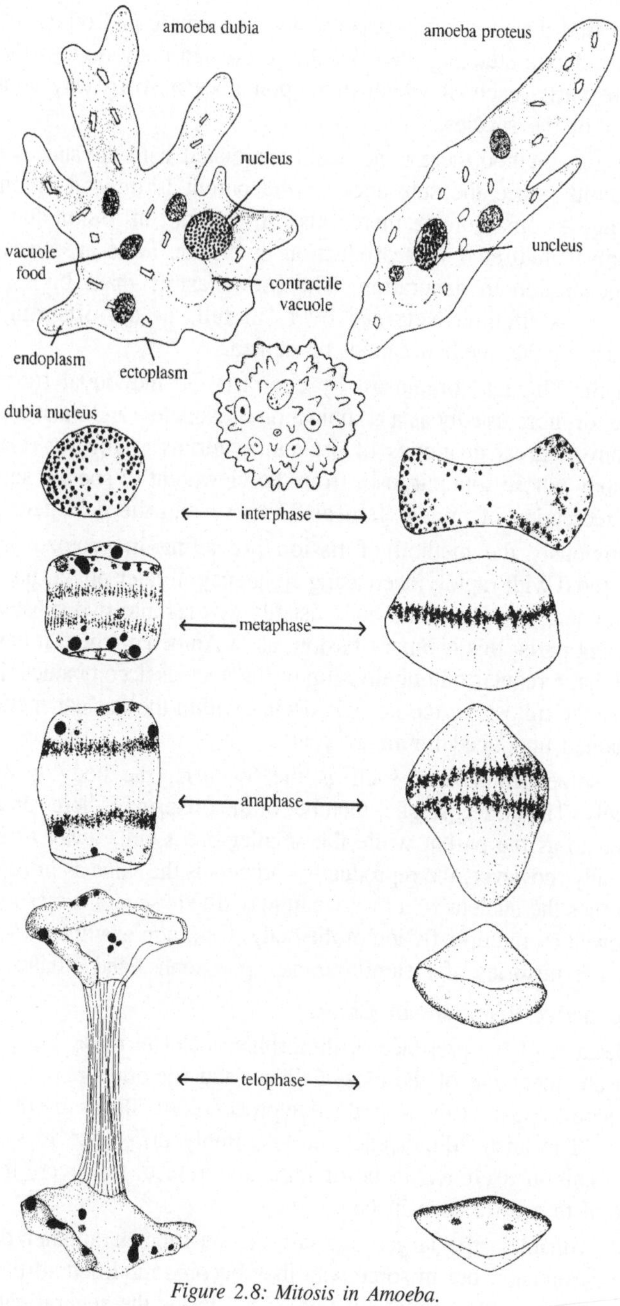

Figure 2.8: Mitosis in Amoeba.

and we find that it contains aspects that are simple and others that are complex. Upon attaining maturity the protozoan body divides into two or more parts, each of which thereupon goes its own way as a new member of the species.

By this method there is no death associated with the succession of generations, since the substance of the parent is divided among the offspring. At one moment there exists a "parent" in fission and at the next only "children." In reproduction by fission there are no corpses from generation to generation. The protoplasmic mass built by the parent in its lifetime is turned over, in full, to the offspring. The efficiency of this method cannot be denied.

In the "higher" organism, by contrast, the individual starts as a gamete, or more usually as a combination of gametes, and must consume and convert great quantities of organic materials to form a relatively huge body whose sole purpose, from the viewpoint of species survival, is the recreation of minute gametes to carry into the next generation.

Obviously the method of fission prevailing in protozoans, and encountered with rapidly decreasing frequency in later phyla, has much in its favour. The protozoan body usually divides into two substantially equivalent parts; this is binary fission, as in Amoeba, where it has been shown that a regular mitotic division of the nucleus accompanies fission. Because the mitosis of the nucleus occurs within the nuclear membrane it remained unnoticed for many years.

In some protozoans, such as the Suctoria, the body is divided unequally. The larger, sessile, member of the offspring is here sometimes referred to as the parent while the smaller one swims away as a bud. Essentially, however, the reproductive process is the same as in Amoeba. Sometimes the nucleus of a protozoan may divide several times and this is followed by multiple fission of the body. Common examples are found in the life histories of foraminiferans, sporozoans, and ciliates.

Reproductive Processes in Ciliates

Because of the presence of dimorphic nuclei in most, but perhaps not in all, members of the class Ciliata—and for other reasons which will become apparent-the reproductive processes of ciliates are of special interest. The term "dimorphic" means simply difference in size and shape. This in itself would be of little importance, however, if it did not point to a difference in behaviour.

Macronuclei—the larger ones-are at one time or another derived from micronuclei, but in some way they become modified so that they are capable only of amitotic division. Considering the general nature of

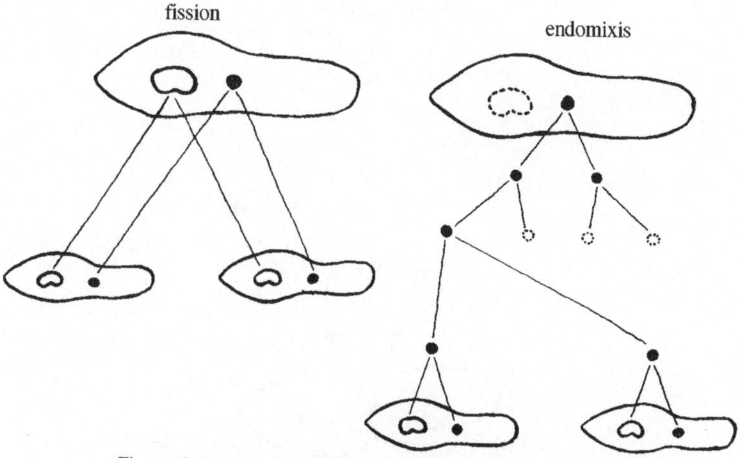

Figure 2.9: Fission (at left) and endomixis in Paramecium.

nuclei and their chromosomal derivatives, this is a very drastic modification. Micronuclei are diploid in nature and divide mitotically, in which case they retain their diploid condition; or they may become haploid by meiosis. Only the micronuclei of the ciliates are therefore comparable with nuclei in the higher animals.

In Paramecium more than in any other ciliate, reproduction has been the subject of considerable study. In most generations the fission of Paramecium is preceded by division of both nuclei, a division which is amitotic in the macronucleus and mitotic in the micronucleus. Meiotic division of micronuclei occurs in relation to conjugation of two individuals, and also in a peculiar uniparental "conjugation" which involves only one individual and is known as "autogamy," and possibly also in the process known as "endomixis."

While any one of these meiotic reproductive processes is going on the macronucleus is resorbed into the cytoplasm and plays no part. In endomixis each micronucleus divides twice and three of the daughter nuclei are then resorbed. The remaining micronucleus divides again and fission of the Paramecium ensues.

In the daughter cells the macronuclei are reconstituted from the micronuclei by division and enlargement of some of the latter. It is as if the macronuclei in time become senescent and die and must be reborn from micronuclei. If this is so it may be the first appearance of the phenomenon of senescence which in later phyla occurs in the body as a whole and removes it from the living, generation after generation.

A rejuvenating phase is apparently included in endomixis for after

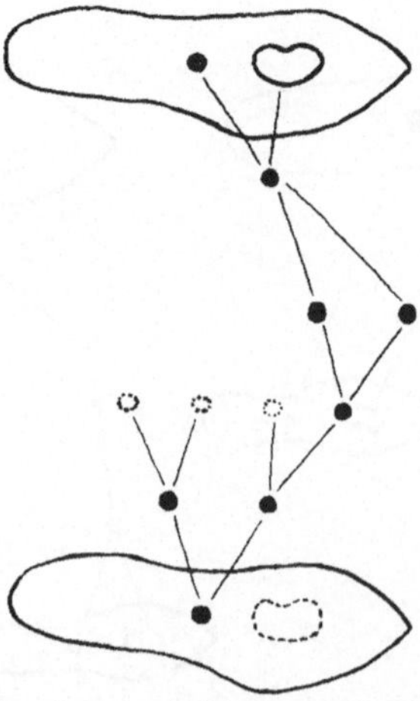

Figure 2.10: Aufogamy in Paramecium.

the phenomenon is completed the protozoan enters a period of rapid multiplication. However, the process of endomixis is still under dispute and its full significance is not clear. The fact that the macronucleus disappears suggests that the micronucleus is more basic and exerts a predominant influence upon the life of the organism.

In autogamy as in endomixis only a single parental organism is involved. The macronucleus is resorbed. The micronucleus divides twice. Three of the resultant micronuclei are also resorbed while the remaining one divides again. The two now present act as in gametes and fuse with each other. Division of this nucleus and fission of the organism then follow as in endomixis.

This peculiar process of uniparental sexuality is further complicated by the fact that it appears to be linked with "mating types." It has been observed only in species of Paramecium where there are two mating types (*P. aurelia* and *P. caudatum*) and not when there are more than two (e.g., *P. bursaria* and *P. multimicronucleatum*).

What is a mating type? Briefly, it is a hereditary line of the species in which there is a block of some sort which interferes with the tendency toward mating. Individuals within this line show little or no inclination to mate with each other, although reproduction by fission goes on as usual; and individuals of this mating type show varying degrees of attraction toward individuals of other hereditary lines within the species.

In some strains evidence has been found that toxic substances transmitted through the cytoplasm are involved in the mating block since the effect is less marked when the period of conjugation is cut short by experimental means, thus decreasing the time of cytoplasmic contact.' Perhaps there is something in the cytoplasm of Paramecia which is analogous to the factors controlling blood types in higher forms.

There is also evidence of an environmental effect on mating, because conjugation has been shown to be stimulated by such factors as starvation. Since this stimulation occurs more easily soon after endomixis and becomes lessened as the time after endomixis is greater, there is evidence of inter-relationship between environmental and hereditary factors. All of these aspects of protozoan life are still being studied and it is clear that much remains to be learned of the "life and love" of the "simplest" organisms.

Obviously, while the organelles for reproduction may be simple, the complexity of sexual physiology is very great. In conjugation a pair of Paramecia come together side by side and a protoplasmic bridge is set up between them. As in endomixis and in autogamy, macronuclei are absorbed into the cytoplasm and play no visible part. Micronuclei, on the other hand, become exceedingly active.

The micronucleus of each of the conjugants divides twice, forming four nuclei. Three of these dissolve and fade away, and the micronucleus that remains is of haploid nature. This procedure has been compared with gametogenesis in higher organisms. The single micronucleus now found in each of the conjugants then divides once again, so that each protozoan possesses two of them.

Up to this point the visible phenomena are the same as in autogamy. But now there is a mutual exchange of one of the micronuclei, each Paramecium with the other, and then the conjugants separate. Each exconjugant now carries two micronuclei as before, but only one is its own and the other has originated with its conjugating partner.

Now, again as in autogamy, the micronuclei in each Paramecium fuse into a single nucleus which divides several times. Some of these enlarge into macronuclei and the body cleaves by fission into a number of individuals sufficient to distribute the nuclei in accordance with the number characteristic of the species.

Since, besides the macronucleus, Paramecium may possess a single micronucleus as in the species caudatum, two micronuclei as in *P. aurelia*, four as in *P. multimicronucleata*, and eight as in *P. polycaryum*, the arithmetic of conjugation may, in itself, be quite taxing.

Endomixis, autogamy, and conjugation in the ciliates notwithstanding,

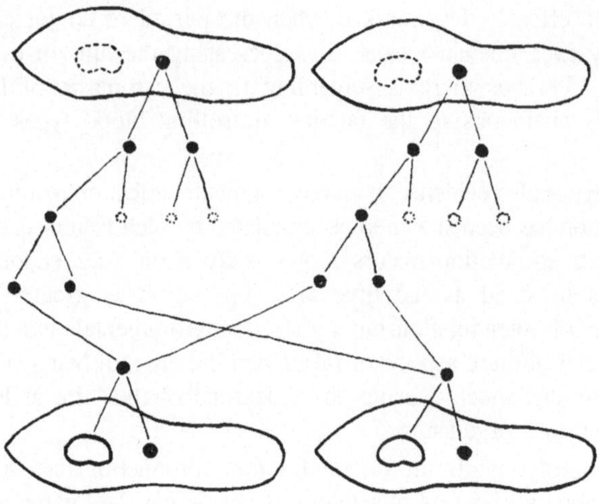

Figure 2.11: Nuclear behaviour in conjugation, Paramecium.

it should be clear that fission is the only method of reproduction found among protozoans, for only by fission is there an increase in the number of organisms.

Whether fission is direct, involving only nuclear mitoses, as in Amoeba, or when it is complicated by nuclear behaviour as in Paramecium, in either case fission is adequate to meet the reproductive needs of a protozoan; and there need be no death from generation to generation.

In as much as protozoans represent the first in origin of all animal phyla and their substance is carried forward from one generation to the next we observe here the longest possible line of continuity in living body-protoplasm.

TAXONOMIC AND OTHER CONSIDERATIONS

In preceding discussions we have had occasion to mention some of the groups, below phylum level, into which protozoans are classified. Let us now devote ourselves a bit more to the taxonomy of the protozoa, and note at the same time some of the interesting members and phenomena encountered. Some of you might have preferred that taxonomy be taken first.

Then we would have placed in orderly arrangement things we knew nothing about. By deferring taxonomy until now, it was necessary to use terms which only now will fall into proper relationship. In colloquial language it is "six of one or a half-dozen of the other" as to which method would have been better, since we eventually arrive at the same objective of greater knowledge and understanding of this distinctive branch of animal life included in the subkingdom Protozoa. Perhaps we have learned that a text is not like a suspense story. There is advantage in looking back and forth through its pages to compare and relate its various parts.

THE CLASS MASTIGOPHORA

The Mastigophora are considered to be the most basic, in origin, of all protozoan classes. They are distinguished by the possession of locomotory organelles named flagella (meaning a whip), already defined as hairlike structures with axial filaments deeply anchored within the endoplasm. But in addition to flagella, pseudopodia may also be present, as in the flagellate Mastigamoeba, which has both.

Or the flagellate may have pseudopodial means of ingestion, as in Trichonympha. Obviously, it is not always easy to recognize a flagellate. It is therefore helpful to know in addition that when a mastigophoran divides, it does so along the long axis of the body, i.e., by longitudinal fission. If this is observed in a living specimen, it is safe to assume that a flagellate is at hand. (Why should a flagellate divide on the long axis when other protozoans with elongated bodies divide transversely? Perhaps it is. the basal granule of the axial filament which determines the plane of the nuclear spindle.)

Further, if there is opportunity to study fixed and stained preparations, the absence of dimorphic nuclei would be an additional confirmation of flagellate affinity, although such absence might not eliminate all of the Infusoria. There is more to taxonomy than learning names. Sometimes a study of the entire life of an organism is necessary for proper classification.

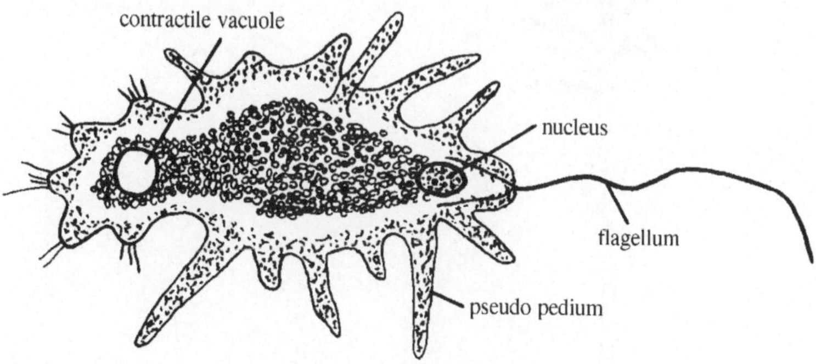

Figure 2.12: Mastigamoeba.

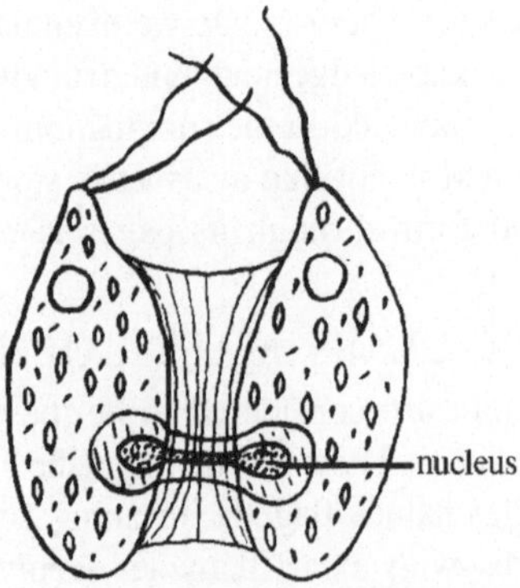

Figure 2.13: Longitudinal fission in a flagellate, Chilomonas.

Two subclasses of Mastigophora are now fairly widely accepted, One, the Phytomastigina, develops green chromatophores; but this group also includes closely allied species without such chromatophores. Because chromatophores are usually present, and because of the consequent capacity for holophytic nutrition by means of photosynthesis, the Phytomastigina are known as the plant-flagellates.

Also, the organisms in this subclass are able to store carbohydrate

Figure 2.14: Hydrurus, palmella phase.

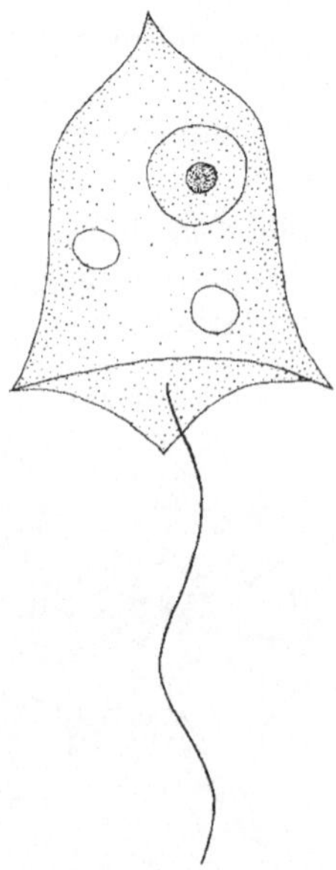

Figure 2.14A: Hydrurus, flagellate phase.

in the form of starch, as most plants do, whereas glycogen is the usual form of animal carbohydrate. Furthermore, some of the Phytomastigina show plantlike patterns of growth, as in the so-called palmella phase of Hydrurus, which alternates with the flagellate phase. It is understandable, then, why some zoologists ignore the Phytomastigina and why botanists include them with the algae.

But, in a group which evidently lies so close to the stem of origin of both the plant and the animal kingdoms the decision as to whether Phytomastigina are plants or animals is necessarily an arbitrary one. It is better for both zoologists and botanists to claim them than for both to ignore them. When we proceed from the subclass Phytomastigina to the subclass Zoomastigina we stand on firm zoological territory.

The members of this group do not possess chromatophores, do not have the capacity for photosynthesis, and do not store carbohydrate in the form of starch. Also, while the Phytomastigina do not usually possess more than one or two flagella, species with numerous flagella are common among the Zoomastigina. It is curious that conjugation, which is common among the Phytomastigina, is rare in Zoomastigina.

Nutrition in the Mastigophora

Very noteworthy among the Mastigophora is the variety of nutritive methods, which range from plant-typical synthesis and storage of starch as in Euglena, to typical animal-holozoic-digestion as in Peranema. There also occurs the unusual ability to hydrolyze wood cellulose in the Hypermastigida, which are found

in the alimentary tracts of termites and roaches. No other single group of organisms shows such versatility in nutritive chemistry as do the Mastigophora. This is understandable when it is remembered that Mastigophora lie at the physiological as well as the morphological foundation of the plant and animal kingdoms.

ORDERS OF THE SUBCLASS PHYTOMASTIGINA

The Phytomastigina are separable into a number of orders on the basis of the presence or absence of a gullet, and the nature of their food reserves. Together with the order we note a number of genera. The Cryptomonadida (Chilomonas), Euglenoidida (Euglena, Peranema), and the Chloromonadida (Vacuolaria, Thaumatomatyx) possess a gullet, or more technically a cytopharynx.

In addition the Cryptomonadida contain starch, the Chloromonadida have oily inclusions, and the Euglenoidida show paramylum, which is

Figure 2.15: Synura.

a form of starch that does not take the iodine stain. The members of the orders Chrysomonadida (Hydrurus, Synura), Phytomonadida (Volvox, Carteria), and Dinoflagellida (Noctiluca, Gonyaulax, Polykrikos, Proterythropsis) do not have a gullet. Of this group the Phytomonadida are starch-storing, the Chrysomonadida have oily inclusions, and the Dinoflagellida may have either one or the other.

A number of genera of Phytomastigina are outstanding because of

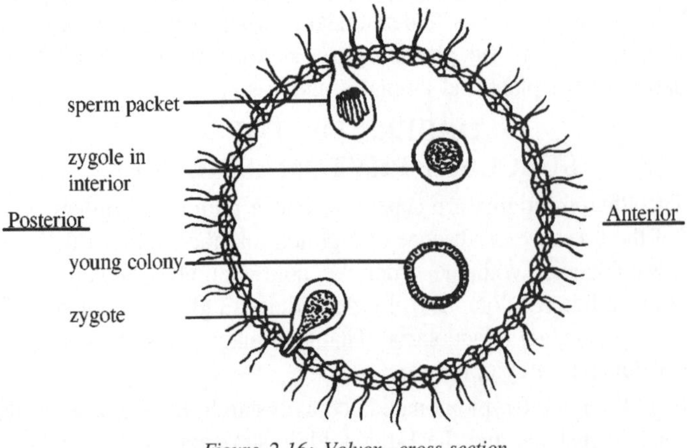

Figure 2.16: Volvox, cross-section.

points of special interest associated with them. Vacuolaria, like Hydrurus, furnishes an example of plantlike growth-the "palmella stage" already mentioned. The more usual forms—Synura, Volvox, and Polykrikos—further illustrate the marked tendency among the plant flagellates to form colonies of cells, a property which is much more outstanding here than among the animal flagellates.

Synura produces one of the structurally simpler colonies, which consists of a cluster of up to fifty biflagellate individuals. Synura is one of the Chrysomonadida, an order which is well known to sanitary engineers because of the production of aromatic oils.

When found in sufficient numbers in potable waters, various members of the order release oils which impart odors or flavors ranging from that of violets to those of putrefaction. Fishy odors are most common. The biologically rather obscure order Chrysomonadida is not, as we can see, without an impact of economic significance.

Volvox is expecially well known for the colonies it produces. Here all of the cells, which are biflagellate as in Synura, are arranged on the surface of a sphere. Each cell is responsive to light, and the flagellary beat is such that the same end of the colony is always directed forward in locomotion. The colony moves into zones of moderate illumination, and away from high intensity.

Extremes are avoided. It is also interesting that the colony is

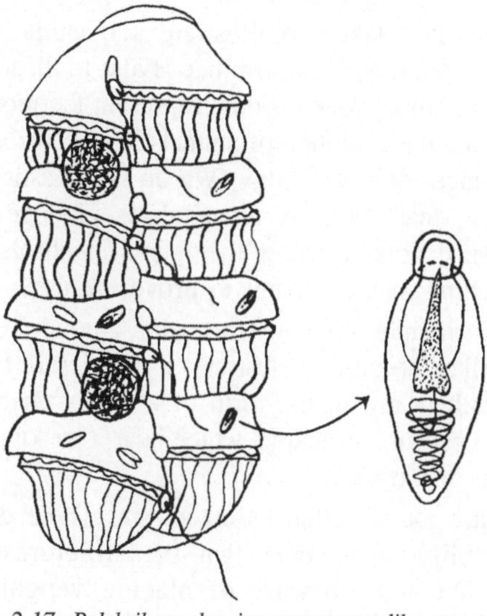

Figure 2.17: Polykrikos, showing nematocyst-like structures.

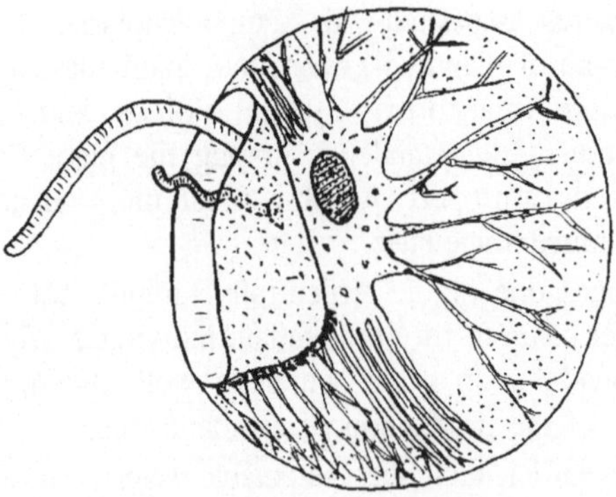

Figure 2.18: Noctiluca.

specialized along its axis in such a way that gametes arise from cells near the posterior or trailing region. Upon fertilization the zygotes sink into the interior, where they develop into young colonies. If this were a higher animal we would call it a state of pregnancy.

Why not in protozoans? A pregnant protozoan! Parturition, then, involves the rupture and destruction of the mother, as the young within grow beyond her capacity to contain them. We encounter for the first time the death of one generation and its succession by another. In some species of Volvox the colonies are monoecious; in others the sexes are separate. In the latter the male colonies escape such consequences of "childbirth."

Volvox is often taken to illustrate a blastula stage in animal evolution, and is followed by a form like Hydra to illustrate the gastrula. A cluster of cells, like Synura, would represent the morula. The theory behind this is that the evolution of animals has occurred in sequence as shown in the stages of embryology. We do not question the validity of this proposition, that ontogeny recapitulates phylogeny. However to utilize as evidence Volvox, one of the "plant flagellates," would appear to be overreaching in the attempt to prove the case.

As a final example of colony formation among the Phytomastigina we cite Polykrikos because it illustrates a rather rare type of colony in which the members are in the form of a linear chain. Polykrikos is interesting also because structures which bear a striking resemblance to the nematocyst of the phylum

Cnidaria are found within its cytoplasm. There does not seem to be any possibility whatsoever that the structures are related to nematocysts. We must beware of placing weight on superficial resemblances.

Noctiluca and Gonyaulax have in common the property of bioluminescence, or life light. (Let us avoid the use of the term "phosphorescence," since phosphorus as such is not involved. Adenosine triphosphate does figure in bioluminescence, but since it also plays a part in many life-energy reactions, is not specific in the production of light.)

Both of these genera contribute to the night-time luminescence of sea water, which is so fascinating to all who have had an opportunity to observe it. But not all of the properties of Gonyaulax are aesthetic. As Chilomonas, in fresh water, is one of the staple foods of amoebae, so is Gonyaulax a staple food of bivalve shellfish.

And, as the Chrysomonadida are noted for the production of oils which are aromatic to human senses, so is Gonyaulax known for its poisonous effect on man. When shellfish which have fed upon Gonyaulax are used for human consumption, the effect is frequently disastrous.

If certain Dinoflagellates are noted for their ability to produce light it is, in a sense, fitting that others should be noted for special organelles to receive light stimuli. So it is with Proterythropsis which achieves a protozoan peak in the possession of an eye spot complete with a refractive lens.

Before leaving the order Dinoflagellida let us mention that its members can be recognized by the presence of a surface groove in which there lies one of their two flagella. And before leaving this very interesting subclass, the Phytomastigina, we should point out that many of them may be found living in a relationship of mutualism within the bodies of other organisms-in other protozoans such as certain foraminifera, and even in higher animals. The association of Carteria, one of the phytomonads, with Convoluta, a flatworm, will be referred to in connection with the latter.

Zoomastigina

Before entering the subclass Zoomastigina which possess no chromatophores, let us cite Chilomonas, Peranema and Thaumatomatyx. These are exceptional Phytomastigina from various orders, in that they, too, possess no chromatophores. In this respect they are like Zoomastigina.

ORDERS OF THE SUBCLASS ZOOMASTIGINA

The subclass Zoomastigina is divided into orders chiefly on the basis of the number of flagella which these protozoans possess. The presence or absence of a mouth and of pseudopodia are additional criteria. We might point out here, as already noted in connection with Mastigamoeba and Trichonympha, that the presence of both flagella and pseudopodia is of frequent occurrence among the Zoomastigina.

In the order Pantastomatida the general surface of the flagellate is ameboid, and it becomes evident that the line between Mastigophora and Sarcodina is not as clearly cut as those who feel mentally comfortable only with definite taxonomic boundaries would like it to be. There are in the Pantastomatida, however, at least one and in some species many flagella which bear witness to Mastigophoran affiliation.

Among Protomonadida there is much less ameboid property, and sometimes none, i.e., pseudopodia are usually absent. In this order there are never more than one or two flagella. There is no mouth opening in the Protomonadida. Food is ingested by pseudopodia when such are present or, in the case of endozoic forms, by diffusion through the surface.

The order Polymastigida is identified by the presence of three to eight flagella and also a mouth opening. Many flagella concentrated around the anterior region are a feature of the Hypermastigida. In the absence of a mouth, food is taken in by pseudopodial action, usually on the posterior surface. In comparison with higher animals, specialization of the body for locomotion at the anterior and ingestion at the posterior is a rather unusual arrangement.

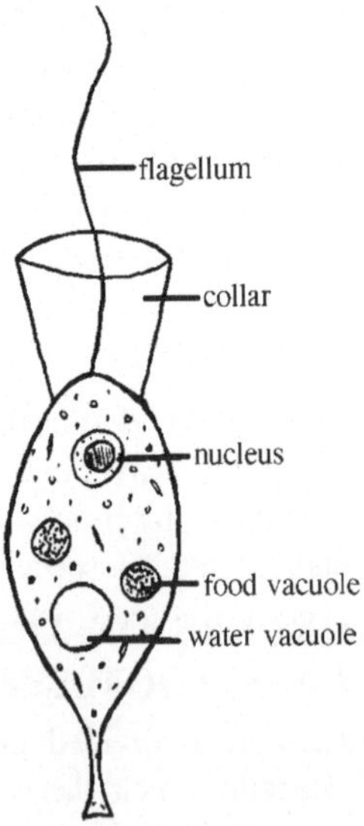

Figure 2.19: Monosiga.

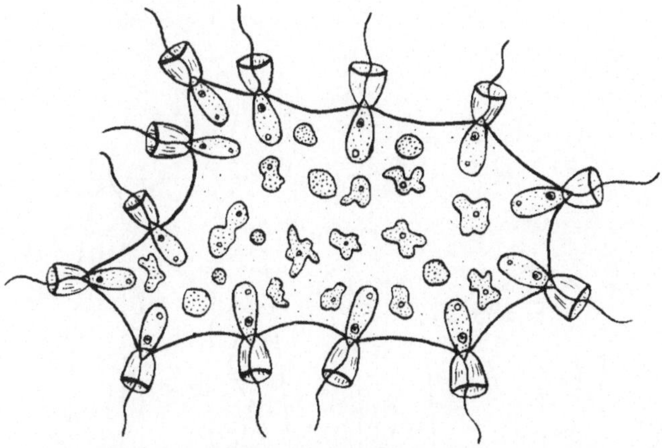

Figure 2.20: Proferospongia.

It is, however, an adaptation which appears to suit the Hypermastigida very well, as they tow themselves slowly through the intestinal contents of their hosts while their posteriors browse upon the small particles of cellulose in which they are immersed.

Panfastomatida

Mastigamoeba and Multicilia are examples of the Pantastomatida. Mastigamoeba is provided with a single flagellum and Multicilia with as many as fifty. (We see that we need to be careful about jumping to conclusions about the names that organisms have been given.

According to the name it carries, Multicilia should be a member of the class Infusoria). Mastigamoeba is often cited as a connecting link between Mastigophora and Sarcodina, but it is also true of other members of the Zoomastigina that they can form pseudopodia.

Protomonadida

The Protomonadida are especially interesting because of the collar-bearing forms to be found in this order. Similar structure is seen again only in the subkingdom Parazoa, and its presence here is taken as an indication of the origin of sponges. Monosiga represents a genus of solitary habit, while Proterospongia forms colonies, the outer portion of the colony consisting of collar-bearing cells while the inner cells are ameboid.

It is strange to find in the same order with these species such important parasites as the trypanosomes. In the illustration a number of Protomonads-Leishmania, Leptomonas, Crithidia, and Trypanosoma-are arranged in a structural series that indicates a possible origin of the

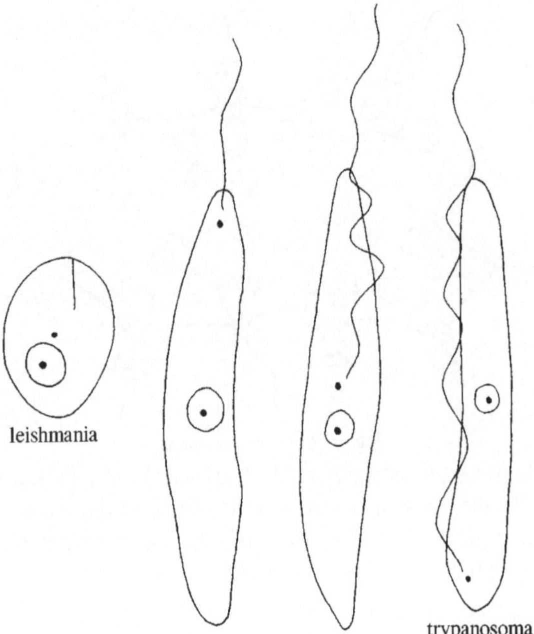

Figure 2.21: Stages in the life history of a rat trypanosome.

undulating membrane of the trypanosome. Evidently this undulating membrane is different in structure, and it differs also in function from that of ciliates.

Trypanosoma gambiense will be taken to represent the large group of protomonads which are endozoic, since it is a very important human parasite. *T. gambiense* lives in the human body fluids, particularly in those of the central nervous system. As the protozoans become numerous they cause fever, and accumulated toxic products of their metabolism bring on a narcosis of the nervous system which often results in the death of the host.

The parasites gain entry into the human host with the saliva of the bite of Glossina, the tsetse fly. Flies become infected when they feed upon the blood of infected humans or of cattle-related animals in which the protozoans can also exist. In the fly the trypanosome inhabits the alimentary tract, whence it migrates to the salivary glands, a favourable location for transmission to the human.

The variety of habitats of the trypanosome-the intestine of the fly, its salivary glands, human and cattle blood, cerebrospinal fluid-demonstrates an unusually wide tolerance to environmental conditions, a tolerance which is not to be expected and which does not occur in free-living protozoans. Besides this functional versatility, a trypanosome may go through a series of structural changes in its life history; a range of metamorphosis which, in its way, is comparable to the most drastic which are to be found among multicellular animals. In the rat trypanosome, for example, leishmanial, monadic, and crithidial phases are present. For the human parasite, however, such extensive changes are not known.

Polymastigida

Giardia will serve as an example of the order Polymastigida. Giardia possesses the maximum number of flagella for the order-eight-and these are in a bisymmetrical arrangement of four on each side. With its ventral sucking disc, this protozoan resembles a miniature trematode worm and, like some of the common trematodes, it lives in the intestines of various vertebrates, including man.

Hypermastigida

Also living within intestines, but in this case those of termites and roaches, are of course the members of the already mentioned order Hypermastigida. Because of their flagellate mutualists, termites have acquired an economic significance of the first rank, since it is on

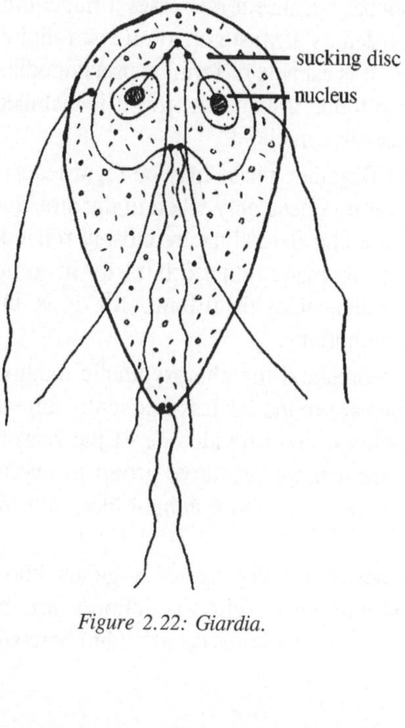

Figure 2.22: Giardia.

account of the digestive power of the flagellates that termites are enabled to feed on wood.

The termites themselves can do no more than masticate their food and swallow the pulp. If not for the role of the Hypermastigida the mass would lie chewed but undigested, clogging the alimentary tract and yielding no nutritive benefit. Such potential misfortune to the host is avoided because of the rare power possessed by these flagellates to hydrolyze cellulose.

The carbohydrate products formed are indirectly shared with the host, and both species thrive. If, by means of heat, high oxygen tension, and in other ways, the host is deprived of its digestive partners, then though it might for some time continue to chew, the insect nevertheless succumbs to the effects of inanition in the midst of abundance.

THE CLASS SARCODINA

Sarcodina are defined as those protozoans which possess pseudopodial organelles for locomotion. By now we should be fully aware that such definitions need to be applied with judgment and discretion. As we have seen, many flagellates have pseudopodia and, conversely, some Sarcodina have flagella. It is sometimes difficult to decide whether a given species should be placed within one class or the other.

Mastigamoeba, because it possesses a flagellum that is permanently present, is regarded as a Mastigophoran even though, along with many other flagellates, it is capable of forming pseudopodia. Naegleria, although this genus is also found in flagellate form, is included with the Sarcodina because it is usually ameboid.

Indeed, the flagellate phase may be regarded as immature or larval, since Naegleria reproduces only when in the ameboid form. It is evident that Mastigophora and Sarcodina are closely related and that taxonomic decisions need to be made rather arbitrarily in some cases. This should be reassuring rather than disturbing, for it is in accord with basic evolutionary assumptions.

Chromatophores-and the photosynthetic method of nutrition linked with these bodies-are found far less frequently among the Sarcodina than in the Mastigophora, and provide one of the reasons for assuming that Mastigophora are a more primitive group in evolutionary origin. The Sarcodina, as a class, are more animal-like, and the Mastigophora are more plantlike.

With the possible exception of a genus known as Paulinella in which chlorophyll-bearing chromatophores are believed to be self-produced, when chromatophores occur within Sarcodina they seem always

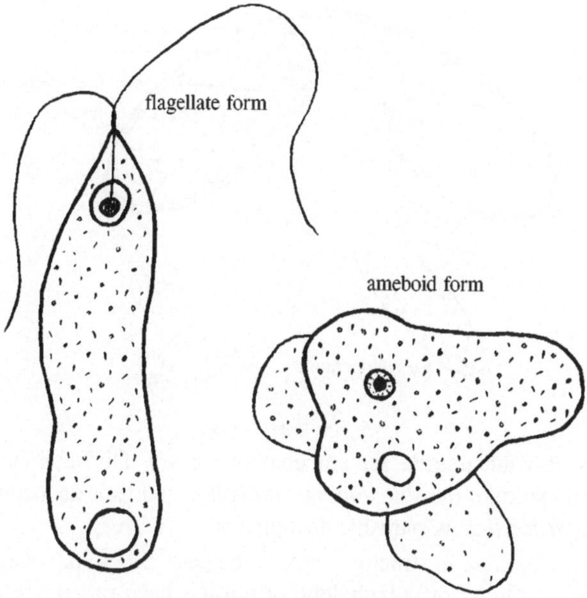

Figure 2.23: Naegleria.

to represent cases of mutualism with chlorophyll-bearing organisms. Among the Radiolaria particularly, as exemplified in the genus Thalassicolla, Phytomastigina are not uncommon as sym-

bionts. On the whole however, photosynthetic pigments are conspicuous among the Sarcodina only by their relative absence. Thus the class falls more definitely into the animal pattern of holozoic nutrition. At the same time we might note that the parasitic habit is not so frequently encountered and the curious capacity for digestion of cellulose is unknown.

ORDERS OF THE SARCODINA

With regard to habitat Sarcodina show a wide range of radiative adaptation. The orders Foraminifera and Radiolaria are marine, while Heliozoa and Testacea are found in fresh water. The order Mycetozoa (also known as Myxomycetes to the botanists) is terrestrial and sometimes parasitic, as in the case of the genus Plasmodiophora, which lives in the roots of the cabbage plant.

The common freshwater amoeba belongs in an order, the Amoebina, which is not restricted either to fresh water or to salt; and this order also contains endozoic forms. *Amoeba limax*, *Flabellula mira*, and some

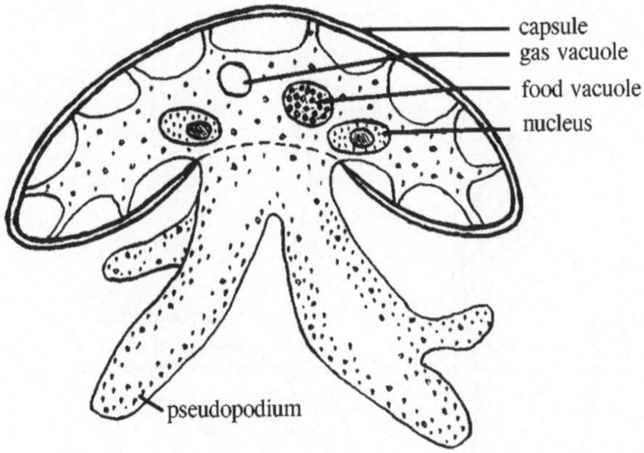

Figure 2.24: Arcella.

species of Vahlkampfia, are amoebas of the sea. Difflugia can survive in the moisture of the soil. *Entamoeba coli* is endozoic as a commensal, and *E. histolytica* is parasitic in humans.

So diversified in structure, too, is the class of Sarcodina as a whole that the possibility of polyphyletic origin has been raised, i.e., that the members arise from different evolutionary sources. If this could ever be shown to be the case, then reclassification would of course be necessary.

Order Amoebina

Amoeba, in this order, is often taken as a representative form of the class Sarcodina. Since amoeba itself is an animal of few visible structures, it is easy to be deceived into thinking of it as a simple animal, and this may erroneously colour one's view of the class as a whole. But living protoplasm, of whatever shape and form the organism may be, is never simple.

As evidence we may consider the fact that the same strain of protoplasm which is found in Amoeba has also produced genera of much greater structural complexity. This is evident especially in shells and skeleton.

Order Testacea

Arcella, forms a chitinous capsule or test, hence it is in the order Testacea. There is a single opening through which pseudopodia are extended. Upon the somewhat similar capsule of Difflugia, particles collected from the environment are cemented in a regular and specific pattern which differs in different species, thus indicating the presence of complex behaviour patterns in animals that are still rather simple from a structural viewpoint.

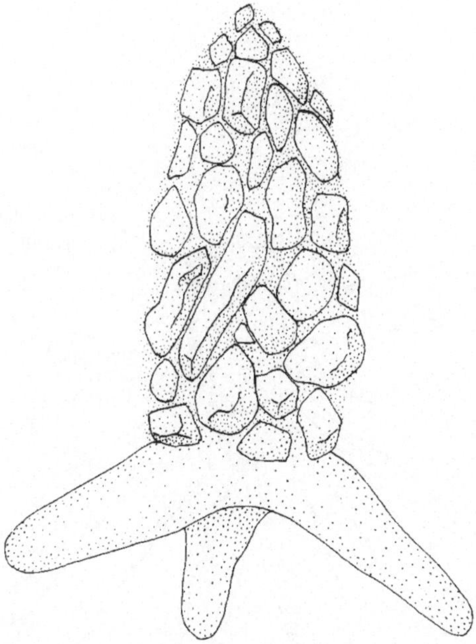

Figure 2.25: Difflugia.

Order Foraminifera

The Testacea are sometimes included with the Amoebina, and sometimes they are considered to be Foraminifera, but we shall take the simplest of the Foraminifera, e.g. Allogromia, as differing from the Testacea in the fact that the protoplasm which protrudes from the central opening of the shell forms a thin layer covering the entire shell.

Thus the shell comes to lie internally in the Foraminifera and may be regarded as an internal skeleton. In Arcella and Difflugia this is not so. The shell of the Testacea forms a cap outside of the protoplasm. In the more complex Foraminifera, skeletal chambers are formed to keep pace with the growth of the animal. In some, e.g., Nodosaria, the chambers are arranged in linear order. In others they are concentric as in Frondicularia.

Or they may be spiral in pattern as in Polystomella. It is the presence of many small pores in the shell, by means of which the pseudopodial layer is continuous with the protoplasm within, that gives the Foraminifera ("to pierce") their name. Foraminifera are an abundant and widespread group. Their shells, which are abandoned during reproduction, are very plentiful in the oozes which lie on ocean floors all over the world.

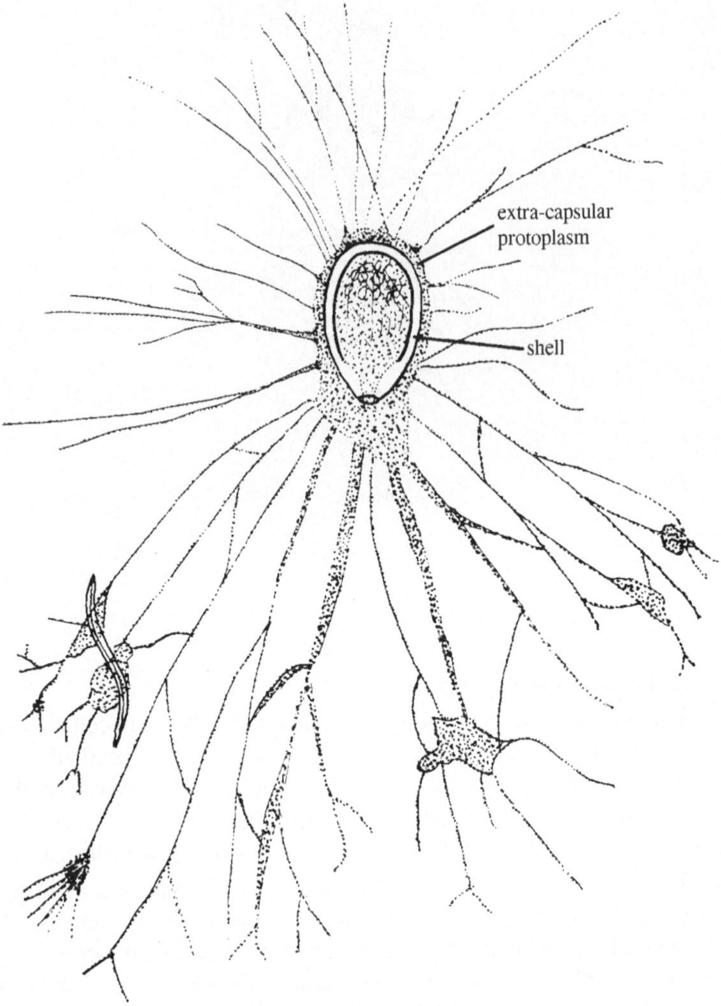

Figure 2.26: Allogromia.

In the Atlantic, Globigerina ooze is particularly prevalent. As time has gone on these oozes have become compressed into chalky layers in some regions. Where diastrophic upheavals of the ocean floor have occurred rocky islands can be seen, composed of the shells of countless generations of foraminiferans whose life and work went on below the surface of the sea. Such are the Dover Cliffs of England, which have played their part in human history. Also, the Egyptian pyramids are made of foraminiferan stone.

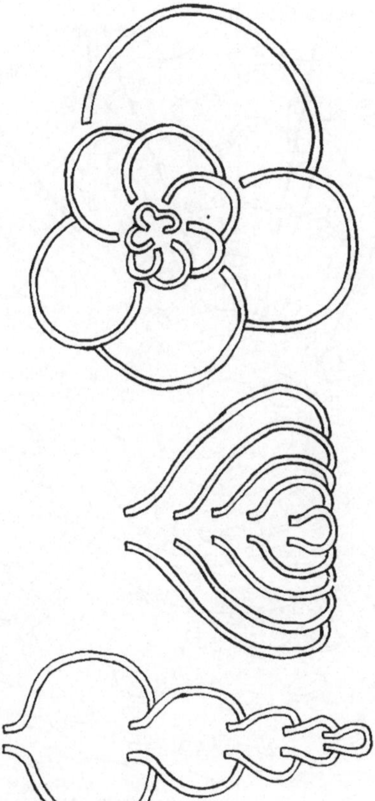

Figures 2.27, 2.28, 2.29: Chamber patterns of foraminiferan shells, as exemplified by Nodosaria. Frondicularia and Polystomella.

Order Radiolaria

Intricacy of skeletal structure reaches its protozoan peak among the Radiolaria. Actinomma is an excellent example.

The skeleton is silicious, a chemical structure characteristic of Radiolaria. The spicules are interwoven in the form of a porous sphere within the cytoplasm. Several such spheres are built up concentrically and supported, one upon the other, by radial struts.

A most amazing anatomical feature is that the innermost sphere lies within the nucleus. Nowhere else do we find a nucleus with a skeleton, and we cannot at present begin to imagine why a radiolarian nucleus should be provided with skeleton. All of this in the same strain of protoplasm which has produced the structurally "simple" Amoeba.

Polystomella

As a general representative of the class Sarcodina we shall take the

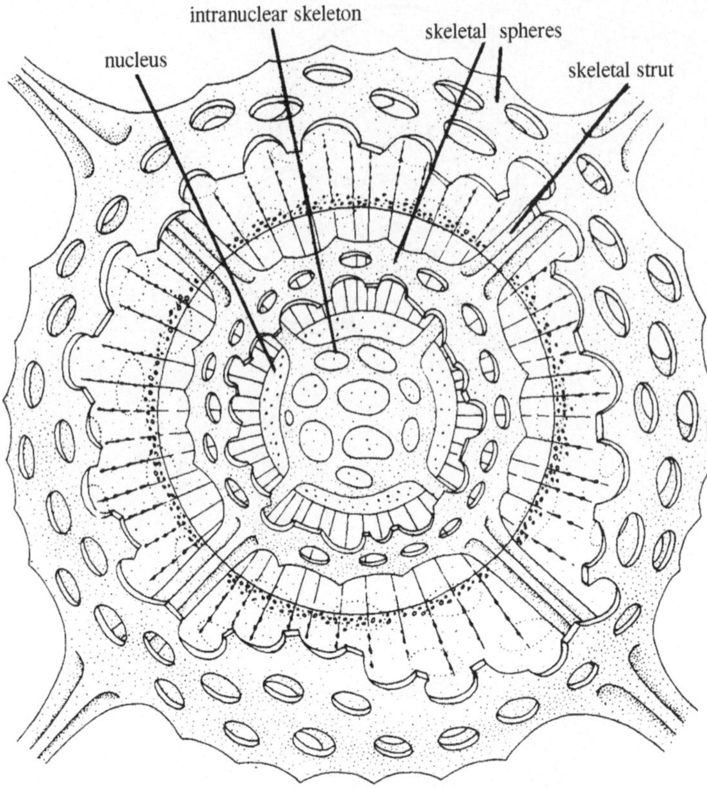

Figure 2.30: Concentric spheres of skeleton, Actinomma.

foraminiferan Polystomella. Polystomella is common along the shores of the sea, from the arctic to the tropics, and has also been found in water samples taken as deep as 300 fathoms (1800 feet). Pseudopodia capture small particles of food, such as diatoms, and the food is digested in a vacuole formed by the common protoplasm of several pseudopodia fused together.

In this interesting way the problem of carrying a larger body through smaller skeletal openings into the central protoplasm is circumvented. It is digested food which diffuses through the foramens. As the organism grows, additional chambers of shell are added to accommodate the enlarging protoplasmic mass and the shell is wrapped, by growth around itself, into a coil of chambers of increasing size.

In appearance therefore Polystomella resembles a miniature snail (and it was so regarded by the early taxonomists, when protozoology had not yet come of age). A perforated plate is laid down across the mouth

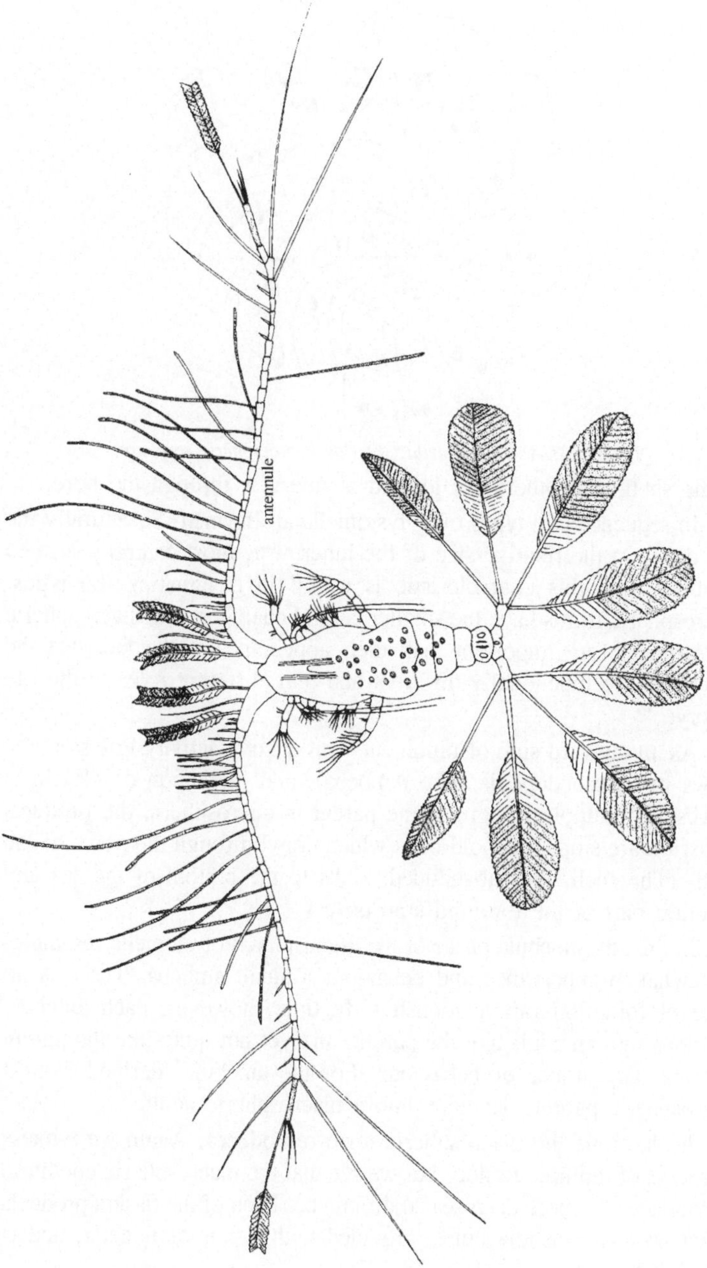

Figure 2.31: Polystomella, mature form.

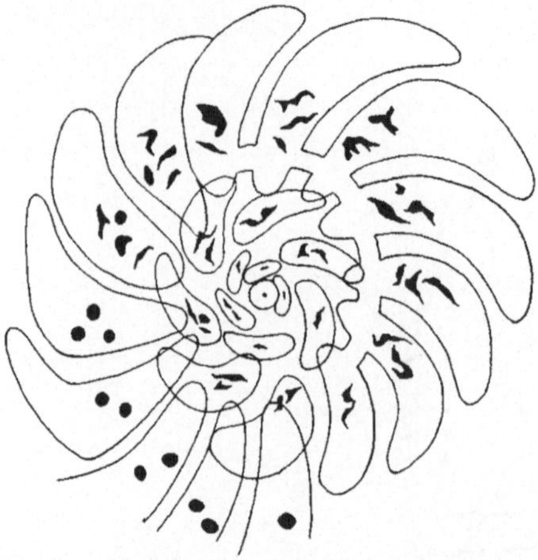

Figure 2.32A: Polystomella, showing micro spheric structure.

of the shell, and others are located at intervals through the bore.

In sequence two types of Polystomella are formed. Structurally the two differ in the relative size of the innermost, most centrally located chamber; and this characteristic is useful in designating the types. Microspheric forms have the smaller central chamber, and macrospheric the larger. More important than their appearance is the fact that the two types are functionally different and play different roles in the life history.

As an outward sign of imminent reproductive activity Polystomella draws in its pseudopodia (like Amoeba), and thereupon divides by a process of multiple fission. If the parent is microspheric the products of fission are small ameboid cells which crawl through the pores of the shell. (The shell, thus abandoned, sinks to the bottom of the sea and becomes part of the foraminiferan ooze.)

In this, the amebula phase of the life history, Polystomella resembles somewhat in appearance and behaviour a small amoeba. There is no trace of foraminiferan relationship. In time, however, each amebula develops into an adult like the parent; and yet not quite like the parent in either appearance or behaviour. For the amebula, derived from a microspheric parent, develops into a macrospheric adult.

In due time the macrospheric form reproduces. Again we witness a process of multiple fission, but we see that the macrospheric condition is evidence of a more deep-seated difference. Each of the fission products is not now an amebula but is provided with a pair of flagella, and is called a flagellula.

Figure 2.32B: Amebulae of polystomella.

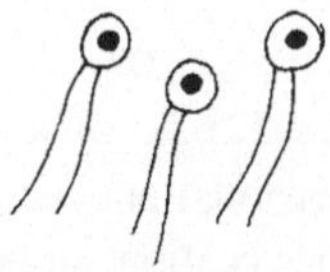

Fig. 2.32C. Flagellulae of Polystomella.

The flagellulae swarm out of the pores of the shell which again settles to the bottom of the sea. In the flagellula stage Polystomella resembles a mastigophoran, but the resemblance is of short duration. The flagellulae are evidently incapable of living alone and, when two meet, they fuse together and assume an ameboid form from which the microspheric generation is again produced.

Thus the life history of Polystomella includes two types of individuals, the microspheric and the macrospheric. Since these differ in appearance they illustrate the phenomenon of dimorphism. Functionally the microspheric form is the asexual generation, and the macrospheric is sexual. They follow each other in alternating sequence of generations, or metagenesis.

Metagenesis incorporates the superior efficiency of uniparental fission as a reproductive method for increasing numbers in one generation and, in another, includes the invaluable benefits of variability which are associated with sex. It is not surprising that metagenesis appears from time to time in the various classes of the protozoan subkingdom, as well as in certain phyla of multicellular animals.

Review of the Class

Among the Sarcodina a life history such as that of Polystomella is not unique. Trichosphaerium, a testacean, shows a similar history. Trichosphaerium is not typical of the Testacea, however, because it is of marine habitat and possesses a perforated shell, but the shell is not covered by protoplasm as in Foraminifera.

The life history of Amoebina is simple in contrast. There is only

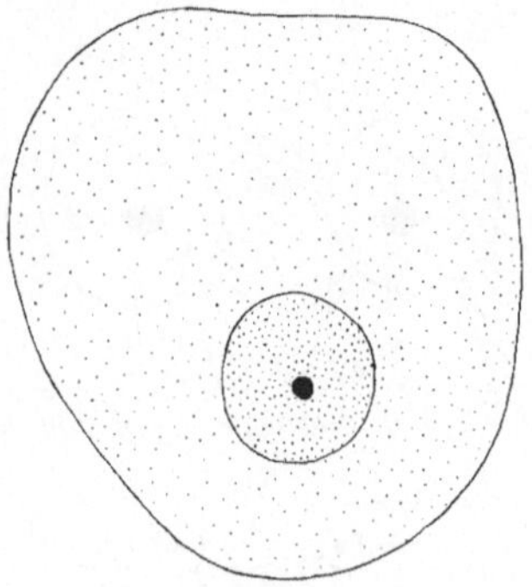

Figure 2.33: E. histolytica.

growth and fission, with occasional encystment to tide over a period of adverse conditions, such as desiccation. In habitat Amoebina show more diversification than any other order of Sarcodina.

We are accustomed to think of them as freshwater forms because the best known representatives live in fresh water, like *Amoeba proteus* and *Amoeba dubia*. But the large, multinucleate Pelomyxa is an inhabitant of stagnant water and *Amoeba limax* is one of several forms (given above) which live in the sea. Others of the Amoebina are entozoic. *Entamoeba gingivalis* feeds, without apparent harm to the host, upon bacteria in the mouth of humans.

E. coli behaves similarly in the large intestine of man. But with the most outstanding of the entamoebae it is quite a different story. *E. histolytica* ("histolytica" means "tissue-destroyer") is a highly virulent form which preys on tissue cells and on blood cells, causing the sometimes fatal disease known as amoebic dysentery. Compare the characteristic Entamoeba nucleus with those shown previously to illustrate fission.

Some of the genera mentioned in our discussion of the Sarcodina are shown in the following frame of taxonomic reference which, in wisdom, should not be accepted as final. Classification has changed in the past, and will change in the future.

Aside from the specialist, who seeks the ultimate but unattainable truth in taxonomy for its own sake, the merit of classification lies in the degree of its helpfulness toward understanding the forms we deal with. We believe that the following, though simplified and perhaps not fully "up to date," will be helpful.

Class Sarcodina

subclass Actinopoda—radiating, unbranched pseudopodia of the axbpodium type.

of free-living forms, as are also the majority of the Mastigophora and Sarcodina, we shall accordingly take them next. The Sporozoa are all parasites and we shall take them last.

While the decision to consider the Sporozoa with Mastigophora and Sarcodina on taxonomic grounds as Plasmodroma is (we believe) debatable, the decision to separate them by themselves on ecological grounds is clear cut. Let us then proceed with the Infusoria. We shall grant that there is little evidence of close evolutionary relationship between them and the two preceding classes.

In contrast to the Mastigophora, with which they might be confused, Infusoria generally possess large numbers of locomotory hairs, while Mastigophora usually have few. But, again, this is not always the case. In the flagellates Multicilia and Trichonympha, for example, large numbers of flagella are found. In ciliates such as Vorticella, on the other hand, ciliation is greatly reduced and in the Suctoria cilia occur only in the larval stage, being lost during metamorphosis.

The structural distinction between cilia and flagella, and the difference in their mode of action, have already been pointed out and need not be repeated. Ciliates have other diagnostic characteristics besides the cilium. The complex cortical layer, containing besides cilia such inclusions as the neuromotor apparatus and the trichocysts, is especially noteworthy. Trichocysts (as those of Prorodon) sometimes closely resemble the nematocysts of Cnidaria. Perhaps partly for this reason they have been assigned a similar function, but the function of trichocysts is still very uncertain.

The presence of dimorphic nuclei, although perhaps not found in all, is an extremely important characteristic of the class. Conjugation, for the purpose of exchanging nuclear material, is also an outstanding property. And finally transverse fission-at right angles to the long axis of the body-may be cited.

The class of cilia-bearing protozoans is divided into those which possess cilia at all times, and those which have them only -in the larval stage. These two groups are sometimes separated as the classes Ciliata and Suctoria, respectively, but we shall retain them as subclasses of the class Infusoria; for which there are both grounds and precedent.

ORDERS OF THE SUBCLASS CILIATA

While ciliates are recognized as such because of the presence of cilia, the several orders are distinguished on the basis of the distribution of the cilia over the body. Uniform distribution of separate cilia over

order Radiolaria—central chitinous capsule. *Examples:* Thall
Actinomma.

order Heliozoa—no central capsule.

subclass Rhizopoda—branched or anastamosing pseudopodi
filopodium or lobopodium types.

order Mycetozoa—no shell, skeleton, or central capsule, a
cellulose-covered spores or cysts. This order is also
botanically under the name Myxomycetes, the "slime mol

order Amoebina—no shell, skeleton, central capsule, or ce
Examples: Amoeba, Entamoeba, Pelomyxa.

order Testacea (also known as "Foraminifera Monothalamia")
calcareous shell of single compartment and single opening
not covered by protoplasm.

Examples: Arcella, Difflugia, Trichosphaerium.

order Foraminifera (also known as "Foraminifera Polythalamia
calcareous shell usually of several chambers and with many
enclosed by protoplasm.

Examples: Allogromia, Polystomella.

THE CLASS INFUSORIA

As we have seen from the evidence of mutual possession of fla
and pseudopodia, the Mastigophora and the Sarcodina are closely rel
The question which then had to be decided was which class shoul
taken first in evolutionary order. From the widespread presenc
chloroplasts among the Mastigophora it was logical to consider the
closer in origin to the plant kingdom, and to have them precede
Sarcodina.

When we view the remaining two classes of protozoans, there
no such simple solution open to us. In recent years there has bee
tendency to include the Sporozoa with the Mastigophora and the Sarcodi
as the subphylum Plasmodroma; and to separate the cilia-bearing for
in a second subphylum, the Ciliophora. But we venture to suggest t
the relationships implied between the Sporozoa and the other classes
the proposed subphylum are not capable of sufficient proof.

The class Sporozoa includes only parasitic forms and the evolutiona
effects of the parasitic habit upon structure are often very profound
Basic homologies may not only be diminished and lost, but new adaptation
may appear which are misleading with regard to taxonomic relationship

We therefore prefer to proceed with the remaining two classes on
the basis of ecological considerations. Since the Infusoria are a class

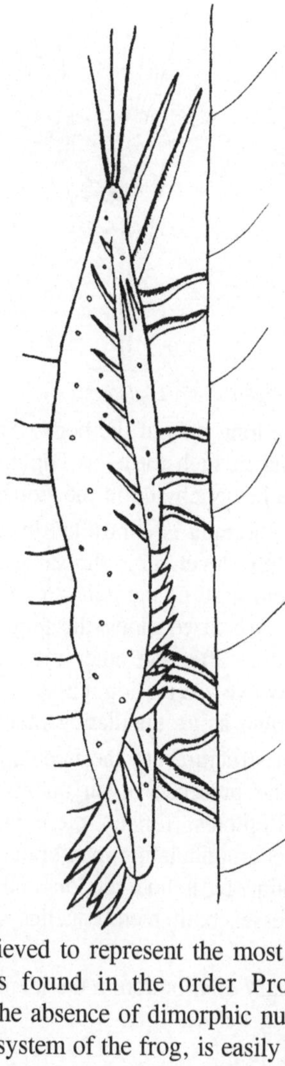

Figure 2.34: Stylonichia.

the surface is believed to represent the most primitive condition. This simple pattern is found in the order Protociliata, which is also distinguished by the absence of dimorphic nuclei. Opalina, which lives in the alimentary system of the frog, is easily obtainable as an example.

Most ciliates possess locomotory organelles which are composed of cilia fused together in one or more of the following ways: Sometimes a small tuft of cilia from a localized area is fused into a single, larger and more powerful unit, called a cirrus.

Cirri are used like little legs, for crawling, as in Stylonichia. Fusions of cilia may also be found as adaptations for swimming. Paddle-like organelles are created when the cilia are fused side by side in

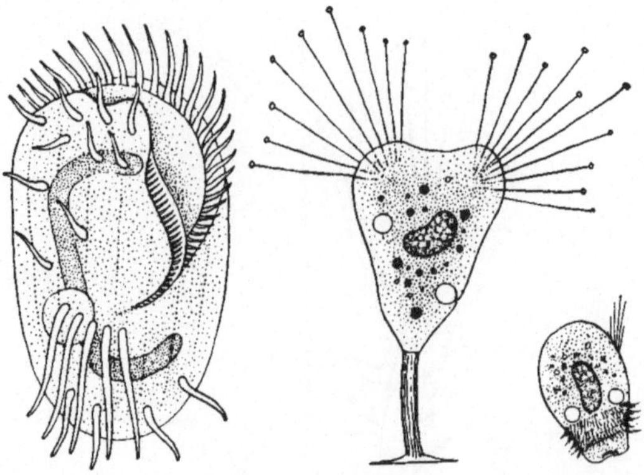

Figure 2.35: Euplotes.

plates at right angles to the long axis of the body. These are known as membranulae and are found in such forms as Diplodinium where they aid in plowing through the heavy chyme in the stomachs of ruminants.

The action of the membranula is controlled by the fact that all of its constituent cilia are at one level, i.e., the same distance from one end of the body, and therefore all of the cilia are stimulated to beat at the same time. Often cilia are fused along the long axis of the body. In sequence, then, one cilium after the other receives the stimulus to contract and a rhythmic wave of motion passes over the organelle which, in this case, is known as an undulating membrane.

Note how different in structure are the undulating membranes of ciliates and flagellates. The presence of an undulating membrane is illustrated in the ciliate Euplotes. Finally there is the membranelle which, in action, resembles an undulating membrane but is structurally composed of cilia fused obliquely, in both the longitudinal and transverse planes. Blepharisma possesses both membranelles and an undulating membrane.

The helpfulness of ciliary distribution in the identification of orders is brought out in the listing below:

Order Protociliata

In this order the protozoans are uniformly covered with unfused cilia. There are no dimorphic nuclei, and there is no conjugation process. In the sexual life heterogametes are produced. Fission is longitudinal. This is, obviously, an atypical order, and it is regarded as a primitive one.

Order Holotrichida

Members of this order, such as Prorodon, Paramecium, and Didin-

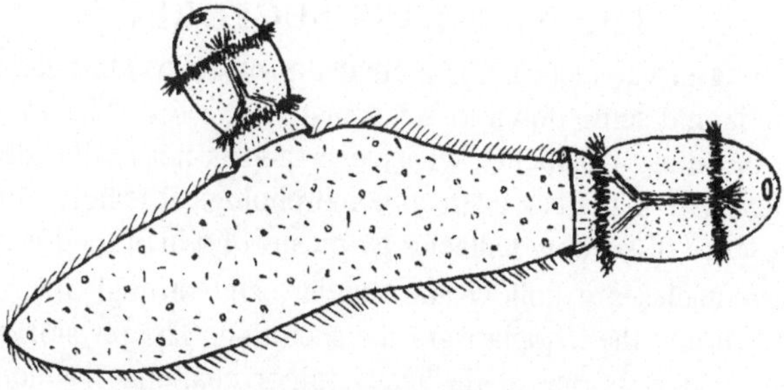

Figure 2.36: Didinia attacking paramecium.

ium, also possess a relatively simple covering of cilia, and they are in accord with all following orders in that the nuclei are dimorphic and that conjugation does occur. Two of the examples given, Didinium and Paramecium, provide a very striking example of the predator-prey relationship. Paramecium will not long survive in the same culture with Didinium.

Order Heterotrichida is distinguishable by membranelles in addition to dispersed ciliation over the body. The membranelles are situated in a groove which curves toward the left around the mouth; the mouth being taken to mark the ventral aspect of the animal and right and left sides designated accordingly.

Blepharisma is an interesting example of this order because, being lavender in hue, it illustrates colouration in protozoans. With reference to nutrition, Blepharisma serves as an example of cannibalism among protozoans. If a small Blepharisma is observed within a larger one it has entered by way of a food vacuole and is not, as students sometimes report, a young one about to be born.

Nyctotherus, frequently found in the intestinal contents of the frog in company with the protociliate Opalina, is another member of the present order. *Order Hypotrichida* is most markedly characterized by the presence of locomotory organelles in the form of cirri, adapted for crawling, as in Stylonichia. In correlation with the crawling habit the body of Stylonichia is much flattened dorsoventrally.

Also a hypotrich is Kerona, the "Hydra-louse," which evidently steps lightly in a chemical sense as well as a mechanical, for it is able to crawl on the body of Hydra without causing the discharge of nematocysts.

Order Peritrichida has cilia only about the mouth, in a band curving toward the right. Within this order is the famous Vorticella, the first protozoan known to man.

THE SUBCLASS SUCTORIA

A young-larval-suctorian is a ciliated protozoan. Only later does it lose its cilia and settle down to a sedentary adult life. The adult shows no trace of ciliary organelles whatsoever and is not easily identifiable as an Infusorian. The most distinctive morphological feature of the adult is the presence of sucking tentacles by means of which food is ingested.

The tentacles are hollow and tubular, and through them food is drawn down into the cytoplasm of the suctorian. The physiology of the suctorian tentacle is one of the many minor challenges which always confront those who seek explanations as to how things work.

Besides suctorial tentacles there are also some with sticky surfaces which hold the prey (this too is a physiological problem; what is the chemistry and physics of the formation of a "sticky" surface membrane?) while the others draw the food in. While there are questions as to the closeness of the taxonomic relationship between Suctoria and Ciliata, there is none about the nutritive relationship, for the Suctoria are predators and the Ciliata are often their prey.

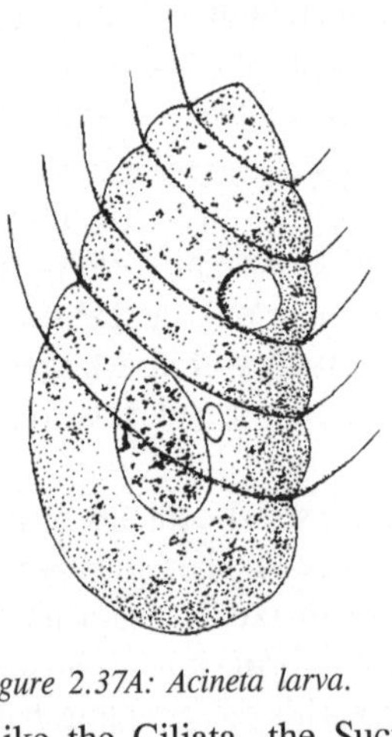

Figure 2.37A: Acineta larva.

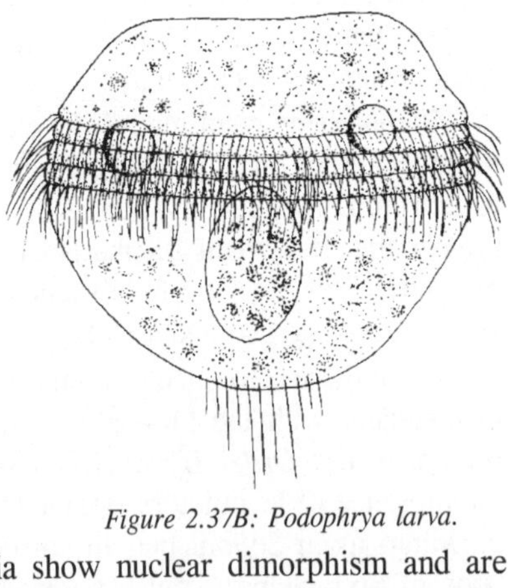

Figure 2.37B: Podophrya larva.

Like the Ciliata, the Suctoria show nuclear dimorphism and are similar also in the conjugation process. Fission is, however, never equal. One of the daughter cells becomes a ciliated bud which only later comes to resemble the other in size and in the presence of tentacles. The loss of cilia in the adult condition and their reappearance in the young (larvae) may be regarded as a recapitulation phenomenon on a par, for example, with the appearance of gills in the young amphibian.

The form of adult Suctoria may be relatively simple as in Podophrya; it may be much branched, as Dendrosoma; and sometimes quite bizarre,

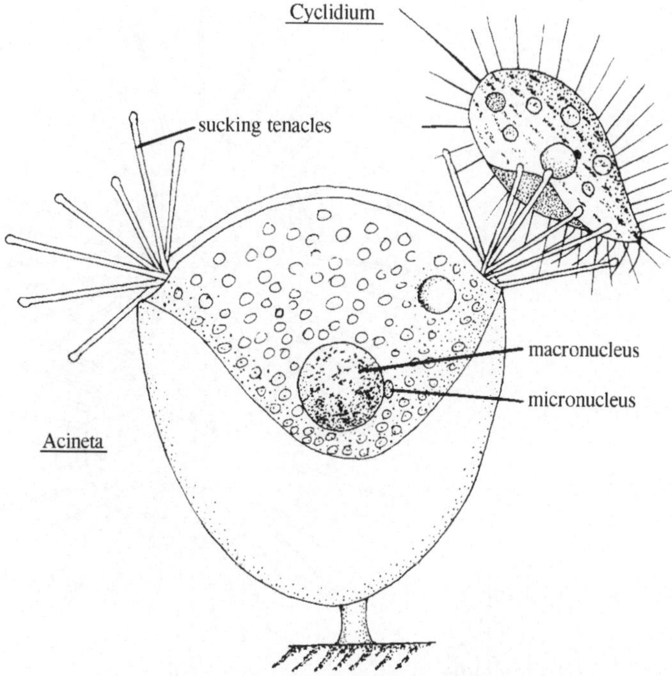

Figure 2.38: Acineta feeding on Cyclidium.

as Dendrocometes. Choanophrya, attached to the crustacean Cyclops, is noted for exceptionally long tentacles. The habitat of Dendrocometes is upon the gills of the crustacean Gammarus, and we can understand that this is a fortunate location for a sedentary protozoan.

Not itself being able to move through the environment, the environment is brought to the protozoan in the form of a stream of water created by the host, which carries food, oxygen, and other necessities. Some of the Suctoria are endozoic; even so within members of their own class. Sphaerophrya, for example, is found within Paramecium and Stentor. Other Suctoria aspire to higher endozoic affiliations-Allantosomas lives in the alimentary tract of the horse.

THE CLASS SPOROZOA

Of all of the minute animals in existence, among the sporozoans we find some of the most minute. Here are forms which can find sufficient nourishment, grow, and reproduce a multitude of young, all within the confines of a host cell which is itself exceedingly small, e.g., an erythrocyte (red corpuscle). It is something to conjure with, this capacity for maintaining a specific structure and a definite way of life with so

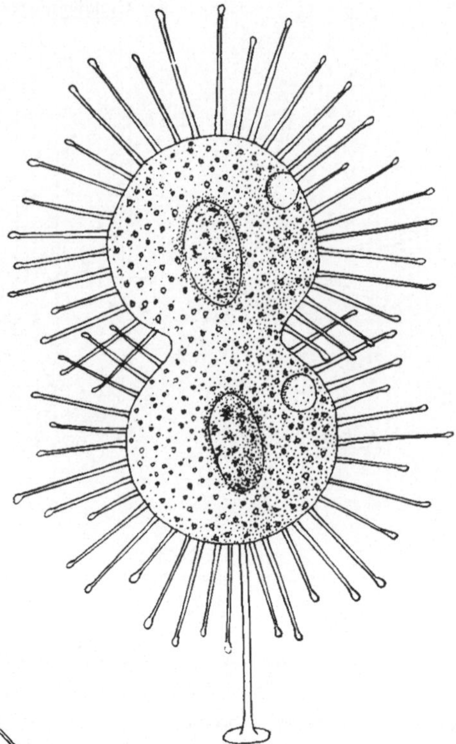

Figure 2.39A: Early budding in Podophrya fixa.

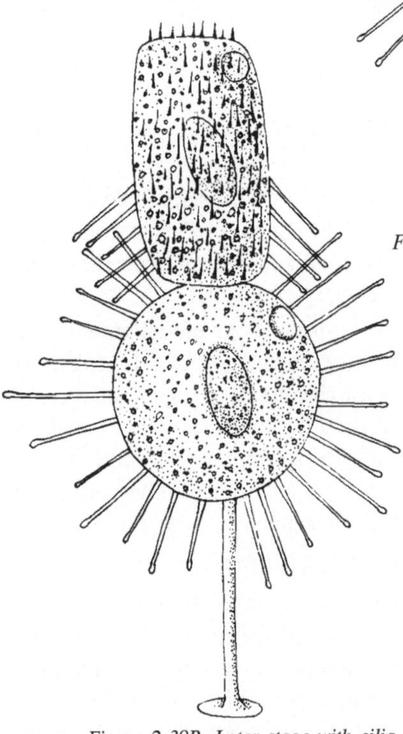

Figure 2.39B: Later stage with cilia replacing ten tacles of bud.

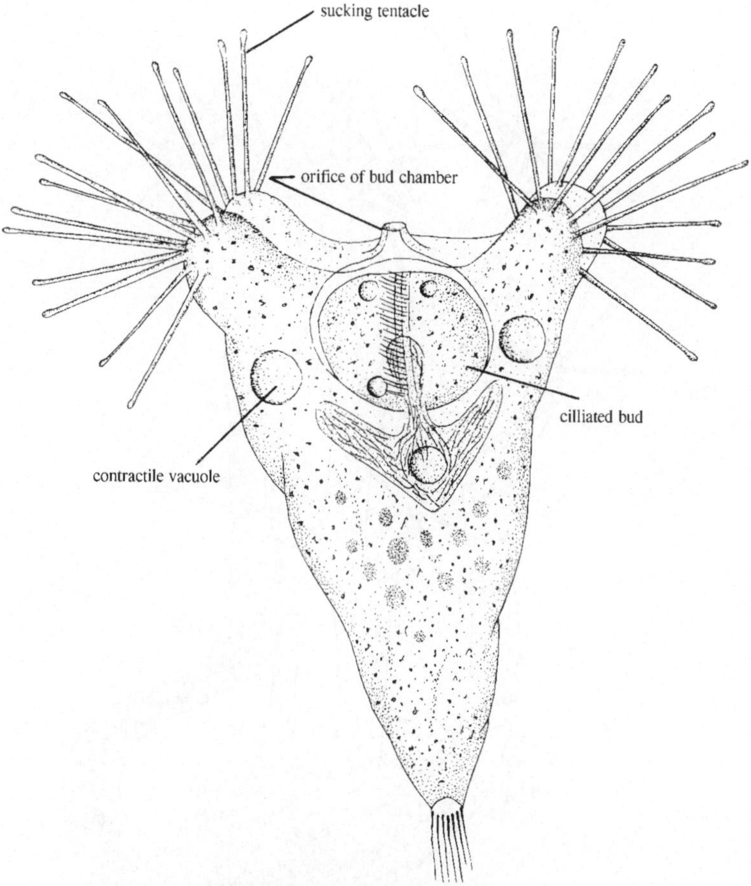

Figure 2.40: Podophrya quadripartita, with ciliated bud in bud chamber.

little substance. All of the Sporozoa are parasites, but so are some of the members of each of the other classes. It follows therefore that when a protozoan addicted to the parasitic habit can be recognized as a member of the Mastigophora, the Sarcodina, or of the Infusoria, it is there included.

Only when such affiliation cannot be established, is the organism placed with the Sporozoa. While parasitism alone does not identify a sporozoan, concomitant absence of the characteristics of the other classes does so identify it.

The free-living mode of existence must have preceded the parasitic

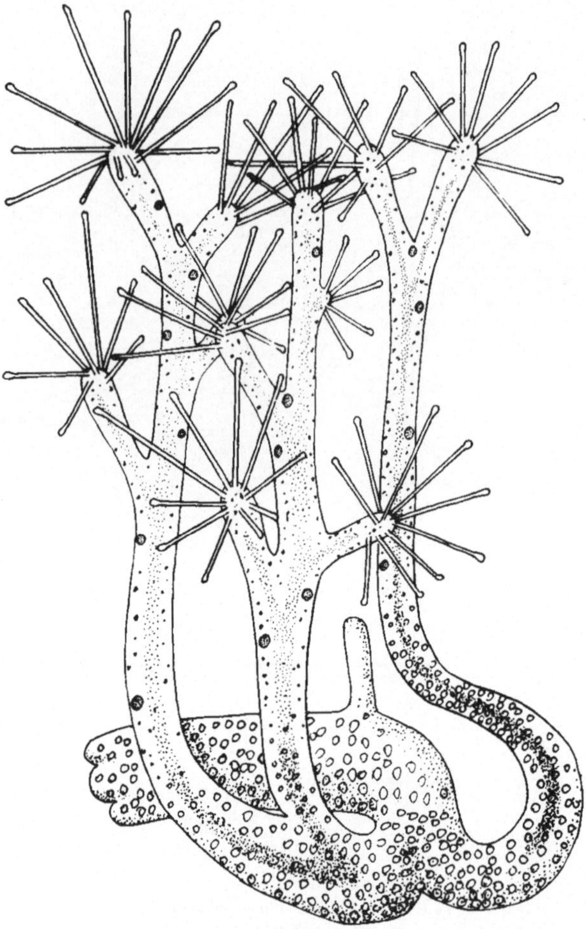

Figure 2.41: Dendrosoma.

way of life, for hosts had to be available before parasites could come into being, and it may be that the Sporozoa are "polyphyletic"; i.e., they were evolved from all three of the other classes. Parasitism has stripped from the sporozoans all of the distinctive structural characteristics of their free-living ancestors, and it has at the same time impressed upon them all a similar life history.

The nature of the life history becomes a positive factor for grouping them together and it accordingly takes on a special significance. We shall first take the life history of *Piroplasma* (Bibesia) *bigermlina* and show by comparison its similarity to that of Plasmodium, which will follow.

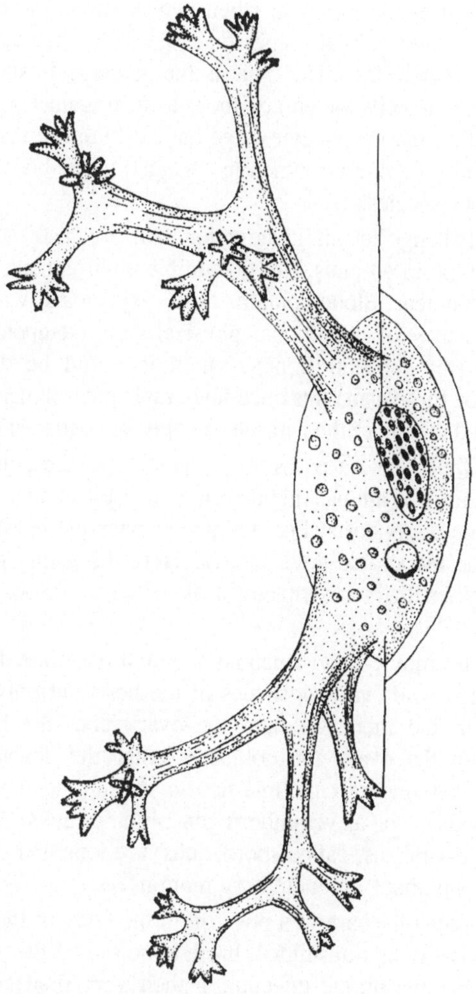

Figure 2.42: Dendrocometes, attached to gill of Gammarus.

The Life History of Piroplasma

Piroplasma is a sporozoan which is adapted for life in two different kinds of hosts. One is an invertebrate-the tick *Margaropus* (or Boophilus) *annulatus*. The other is a mammal of the bovine type. When cattle are infected the disease is of great economic importance. In symptoms it is considerably like the malaria of humans, and is commonly known as Texas fever of cattle. Doubtless, the tick is also sick, when infected, but no one has troubled to work out the symptoms and effects in the invertebrate host.

The tick acquires the infection when it feeds upon the blood of a diseased mammal, and only at a specific stage in its mammaldwelling period is the sporozoan infective. This is the gametocyte stage, and it consists of sporozoan cells which are about to form gametes. Although developed in cattle, the gametocyte stage has no future in that host. Its life can go on only if the environment is changed to the body of a tick, and of the proper species.

This is a challenge to our imagination. An organism is produced and lives for a time in an unusually favourable environment, for blood is such an environment. Blood contains food, oxygen and water, and it provides a constancy of conditions, physical (e.g., temperature) and chemical (e.g. salt concentrations), which it would be difficult to duplicate. Yet for Piroplasma this once-favourable environment becomes unfavourable, and the life of the parasite can only be continued elsewhere.

This is as well, since a parasite that could live through all of its generations within one animal might well find itself extinct at the end of one generation of its hosts! For the gametocytes the intestine of the tick becomes the favourable environment. Here the gametocytes form gametes and, by fertilization (syngamy), the zygotes, or ookinetes, are produced.

Ookinetes are motile in an ameboid way and penetrate through the intestinal wall to invade various tissues of the host; but only for those ookinetes which find their way into the ovary does the life history continue. Within the ovary the ookinetes enter the developing tick embryos. Here they undergo multiple fission and in time come to infest the salivary glands of the as yet unborn generation of ticks. At this time the Piroplasma organisms, called sporozoites, are long and slender and capable of moving about by undulatory motions.

Since the sporozoites are in a position in the body of the tick from which they can easily be transmitted through the saliva, the young ticks are capable of passing on the infection at their very first feeding after birth. This is one of the interesting adaptations in the life history of Piroplasma, that the young ticks become infected while still in the body of the mother. In this way, for each adult tick which contracts the infection, many of the next generation transmit it. Thus the weakest link in the life history of a parasite-the transfer from host to host-is strengthened.

In its cattle host, Piroplasma lives a life entirely different from the one it led in the tick. It invades the erythrocytes, where it feeds, grows, and reproduces. The young escape into the blood plasma and infect other erythrocytes, and the cycle is repeated over and over again. Symptoms of the disease of Texas fever appear when sufficiently large numbers of erythrocytes are affected. Then, occasionally, the life history takes a different turn in some erythrocytes.

Gametocytes-with which we began this account-are formed. For them, if they remain in the mammal, it is the end of the road. They can survive there (floating in the blood stream) for some time, but a change in environment is required for the development of the succeeding stage in the cycle.

It should be recalled how small the erythrocyte is—7.5 microns in diameter-to appreciate how much smaller is the parasite which can live, grow, and reproduce in this miniature cosmos. How intriguing that an animal so small can contain the hereditary factors to control its intricate behaviour!

The Life History of Plasmodium

In its essential aspects the life history of Plasmodium, the human-malaria-causing sporozoan, is similar to that of Piroplasma. But the hosts, of course, are different. The invertebrate host of Plasmodium is the Anopheles mosquito. Man himself is the mammalian host. Here, as in the Piroplasma life cycle, there is a combination of the first animal phylum, the protozoan, with the one most recently evolved.

In the human host, malarial infection presently reaches the stage of gametocytes. A mosquito feeding at this time draws the gametocytes into its stomach, where gametes are formed. By the fusion of male and female gametes a motile zygote is created. At this stage Plasmodium

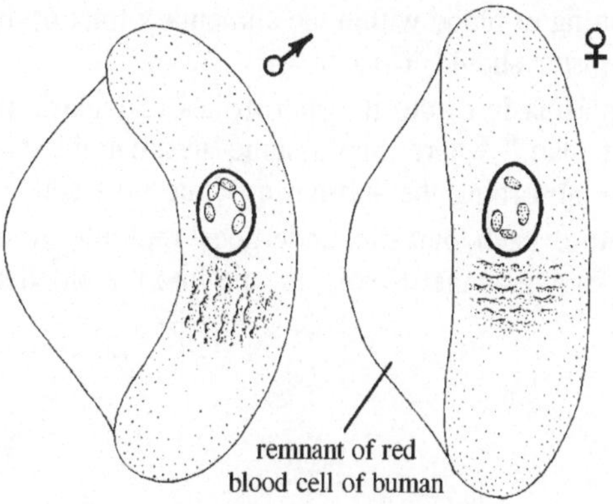

Figure 2.43: Gametocytes of malaria, as they are drawn into the mosquito.

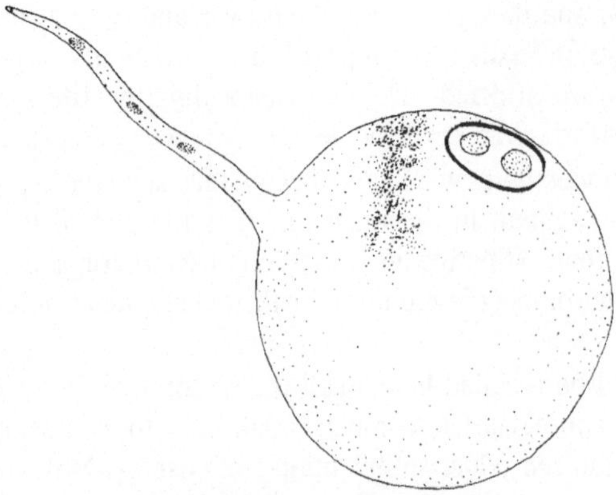

Figure 2.44: Fusion of male and female malaria gametes.

is ameboid in form and, acting like an entamoeba, it penetrates the intestinal wall of the mosquito. On the side facing the haemocoelic cavity encystment takes place. Within the cyst many sporozoites, which are flagellate in shape and form, are produced by multiple fission. Upon rupture of the cyst the sporozoites escape into the haemocoel and find their way to the salivary glands whence, on opportunity, they are injected into the blood stream of the human.

To understand the mechanism of transfer from the mosquito to the human host it is necessary to know something of the physiology of a mosquito's bite. In its first phase the bite involves the inoculation-the spitting-of a bit of saliva. This is not for the purpose of adding insult to injury but, by means of an anticoagulant carried in the saliva, to prevent the clotting of blood within the alimentary tract of the mosquito, obviously a disaster should it occur.

Like Piroplasma in cattle, the sporozoites of malaria penetrate the erythrocytes of man," where they assume an ameboid shape and take nourishment by absorbing the substance of the host cells.

When mature each parasite undergoes multiple fission and the progeny, now known as merozoites, escape into the blood stream when

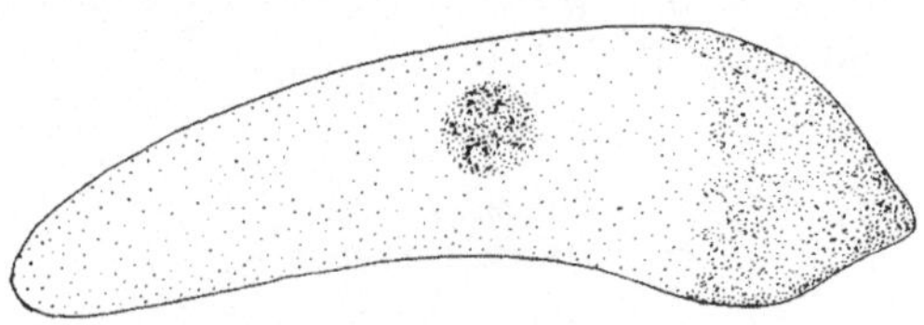

Figure 2.45: Motile zygote of malaria.

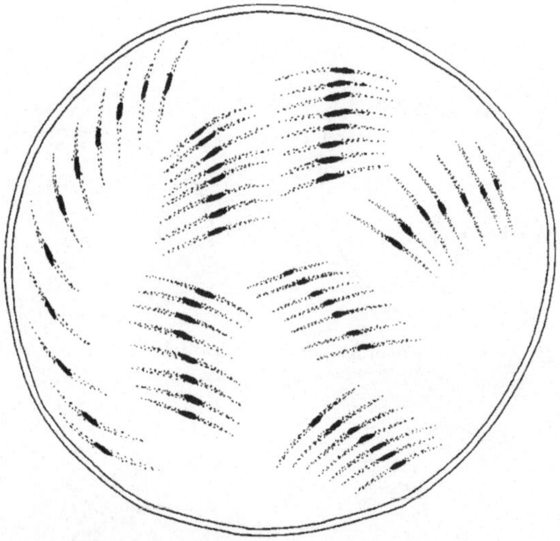

Figure 2.46: Sporozoite cyst of malaria.

the shell of the wornout erythrocyte ruptures. Merozoites enter fresh erythrocytes and this phase of the life cycle is repeated for countless generations. Because of the genetic uniformity of the parasites and of the environmental conditions, it is not difficult to understand why the procedure remains in similar phase from corpuscle to corpuscle, and as increasingly large numbers of corpuscles are simultaneously destroyed, the symptoms of malaria begin to appear.

The cyclical chills and fever of malaria are apparently not due to the loss of blood cells but are attributable to the shock which comes upon release of toxic malarian metabolites into the blood plasma when many corpuscles are ruptured at the same time.

In a small percentage of human erythrocytes the parasites develop into gametocytes and remain as such, in arrested development, unless ingested by an Anopheles mosquito. No other environment will do, for they will not develop within the common Culex mosquito, for example, nor in any of the other blood-sucking insects that feed upon human blood.

This is an interesting example of the specificity of adaptation, for Culex mosquitoes do serve as a host for bird-malaria parasites. While the life history of a sporozoan in all cases includes an alternation of sexual and asexual generations, it does not always involve an alternation of hosts. The entire life history of the sporozoan *Eimeria schubergi*, for example, is carried through within a single host, the centipede Lithobius.

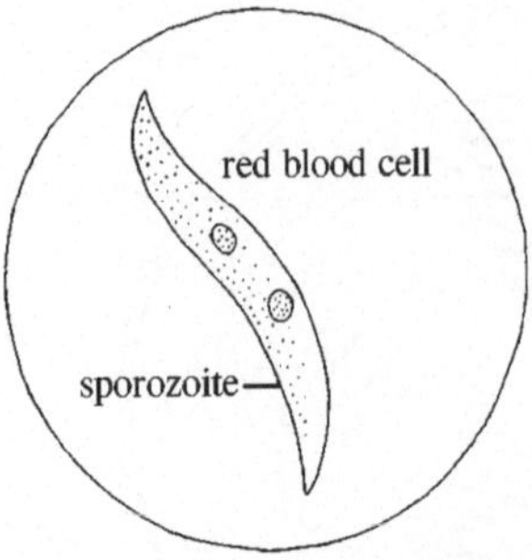

Figure 2.47: Sporozoite within human erythrocyte.

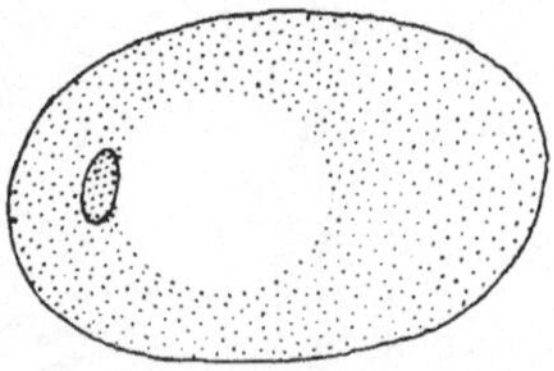

Figure 2.48: Ameboid growth phase of malaria.

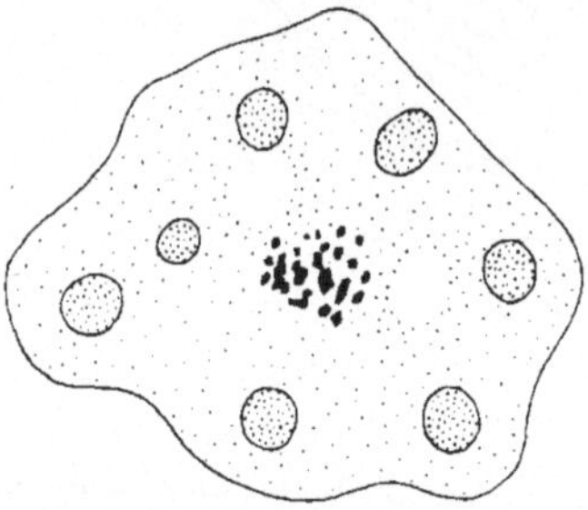

Figure 2.49: Multiple fission within erythrocyte.

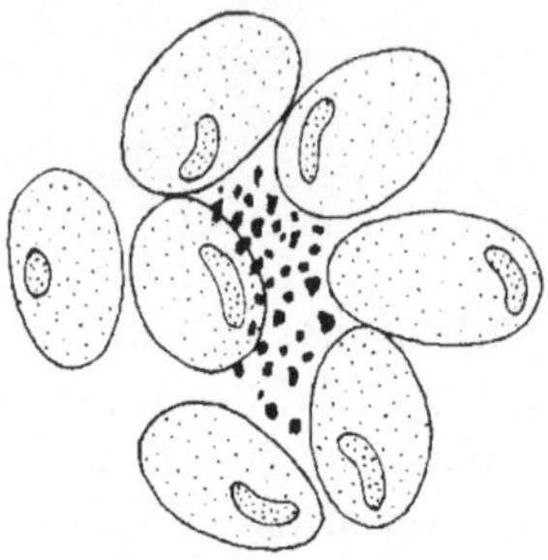

Figure 2.50: Dispersion of daughter merozoites.

From one host to another the parasites are transferred in contaminated food. They penetrate the epithelial cells of the intestine, and reproduce there asexually. Without change of hosts asexual generations are then followed by gametocytes, gametes, and zygotes.

The zygote develops into a sporocyst in which, by multiple fission, sporozoites are produced. Cysts are eliminated with the feces and enter other centipedes by way of the mouth.

Telosporidia and Neosporidia

In the sporozoans so far considered all of the substance of the parental organism is consumed in the fission processes. This is true of the subclass Telosporidia, which includes the commonly known sporozoa. Another subclass, the Neosporidia, is identified by the fact that offspring are formed and released continuously from within a parental form which retains the bulk of its substance and its identity throughout the process of fission.

Included with the Neosporidia is an order known as the Cnidosporidia, which is mentioned because of a point of special interest. One of the

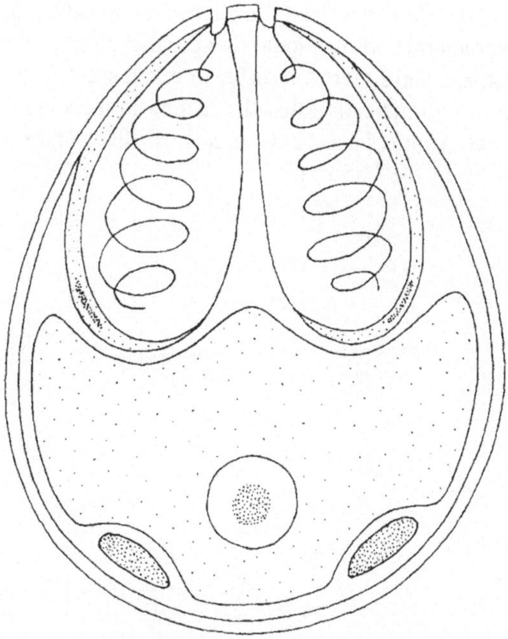

Figure 2.51: Cnidosporidian, showing two thread capsules.

structural features of the group is a capsule containing an inverted coiled thread.

When the Cnidosporidian is ingested by the host the thread is everted and serves to anchor the parasite to the tissues of the intestine. In appearance, and somewhat in action, the polar capsule resembles a nematocyst, which will be found to be an outstanding characteristic of the phylum Cnidaria. This is another interesting case of parallelism in evolution, for there appears to be no possibility of relationship between the two.

As we close our consideration of the subkingdom Protozoa let us remember that no other phylum of animals has developed a completely functional body within the limits of a single cell; a body which, in its complexity of structure and the intricacy of its behaviour, goes far beyond what might at first thought be regarded as the limits of possibility for a single cell.

Protozoans are small animals, but they are not simple animals. They have been in existence longer than any other group and it would be too much to expect them to have retained the primitive simplicity which may have characterized them on origin.

In their evolution they have developed a considerable number of adaptations-structural and functional-that parallel those of the Enterozoa. That the Protozoa and Enterozoa differ in this respect from the Parazoa may be taken as an indication that the factors influencing the evolution of the first two groups have been somewhat alike, and different from those operating in the Parazoa.

3

The Subkingdom Parazoa

Things were different in the time of Gerard, if the use of natural sponges was then well known. In that respect we have retrogressed. Sponges are now rare in everyday life, at least those "wrought of the foame and frothe of the sea." In our generation the objects generally known as sponges are manufactured products "wrought" with the aid of modern chemistry.

Cellulose and rubber sponges, entirely divorced from the sponge phylum, have largely replaced the original product, and most of us who have seen a natural sponge have encountered only the dried remains of one. It may be true even among biologists that few have observed the spongeanimal in the living state. It is necessary, therefore, that we disregard the voice out of the past and that, by all means, we do speak of sponges.

WHY "PARAZOA"?

With the sponges we enter the second great subkingdom of the animal world, the subkingdom Parazoa. "Para" means beside or alongside; "zoa," of course, is the plural of "zoon," which means "animal." Why "alongside animals"? There must be something very unusual about sponges, as indeed there is. Let us find out.

First, sponges differ from other animals in that they do not move about from place to place. Locomotion is found only in the larval stage. As adults, sponges are invariably fixed in one location for life. In other animals locomotion is a primary function essential to survival, and it becomes a key to the understanding of their nature and evolution. When locomotion is lacking in multicellular animals other than sponges it is a matter of secondary adaptation to very special conditions.

Secondly, sponges do not possess an alimentary tract in any shape or form. There is no common space provided for the discharge of extracellular enzymes and for communal digestion. Sponges can never have a full stomach, nor an empty one, for they have no stomach at all.

Further, sponges stand apart from other multicellular animals in that they lack all trace of a nervous system. Such apparatus, so vital to the harmony of integrated function in other animals, is completely unknown in sponges.'

No organs of locomotion, no digestive tract, no nervous system - it is enough to show why sponges are thought of as "alongside animals." They are clearly off the beaten track. They have evolved along lines peculiar to themselves and are entitled to a separate subkingdom, the Parazoa.

HOW "SUCCESSFUL" ARE SPONGES?

Let us not be too hasty in our judgment of the Parazoa. In spite of the unusual omissions in their anatomy, they are a highly successful group. How shall we measure their success? We find that though they are among the earliest multicellular animals to have arrived upon the evolutionary scene, no genus of sponge is known to have become extinct. Sponges have come, and they have survived. But, on the other hand, no other type of animal life is known to have arisen from the sponges.

Once a sponge, always a sponge, has apparently been true for hundreds of millions of years. It is not incorrect to state that sponges are a blind alley in evolution, but it is misleading. We can also take the view that the Parazoa are a group in which evolutionary maturity was early attained. Within a single phylum there evidently arose so excellent an adaptation to natural conditions that no changes outside of the pattern of the phylum were necessary for survival; none such has occurred, at any rate.

By contrast, the Enterozoa have been characterized by a continuing evolutionary restlessness. One phylum after another has come into being, but none has achieved the equilibrium characteristic of the sponges—the "dead-end group." Whether we regard them as dead-end animals or as animals with near-perfect adaptation is of little moment to the sponges; they are likely to continue their placid existence upon the sea-bottoms of the world while more "advanced" phyla succumb to the intensities of rapid life and, on occasion, become extinct. Thus, among multicellular animals, two pathways of evolution have been followed.

These center around the presence or absence of locomotion. In the Enterozoa-beginning with the Cnidaria and terminating with the Chordata-life, in most cases, depends upon effective pursuit of food. A premium is therefore placed upon rapid movement, and stresses of competition are set up which, from phylum to phylum, bring forth ever greater complexity of structure.

The expenditure of energy involved in movement makes necessary the development of a specialized alimentary system for processing food. And the intense level of activity required for the pursuit of food, or'for the evasion of capture, is not possible without devices for quick bodily coordination. Hence the nervous system, and the specialized sensory organs associated with it.

There being no corresponding need for them, locomotory, digestive, and nervous systems are unknown in sponges. (We cannot here go into philosophical considerations with regard to the relationship between evolutionary "need" for an adaptation and the mechanism of origin. It will suffice for us to note the presence of certain functions and structures in one subkingdom and their absence in the other.)

In contrast with Enterozoa, it is clear that sponges are unusual; so unusual in fact that they were not at first thought of as animals at all. As a result of the work of Robert Grant in 1836, however, they have since occupied a firm position in the animal kingdom, different though they are from other animals.

Grant named them the Porifera and it is fitting that the sponge genus Grantia should be named for him; and rather sad that this genus name is being replaced, first by Sycon, now by Scypha. However, Scypha is regarded as taxonomically correct for the American genus widely known as Grantia, the latter name having erroneously been carried over from a European sponge.

The Larval Form of Sponges

Sponges generally are marine animals. A few inconspicuous genera-e.g., Spongilla, Ephydatia, Tubella-live in fresh water, but the typical sponge lives in the sea. It is now known, of course, that young sponges arise from other sponges, and not from the "foame or frothe" of the sea. They arise by sexual activity, as a result of the fertilization of gametes, or asexually by parental budding.

Whether the young sponge begins its life as a zygote or as a bud, a swimming larva is almost always developed. To a sedentary animal

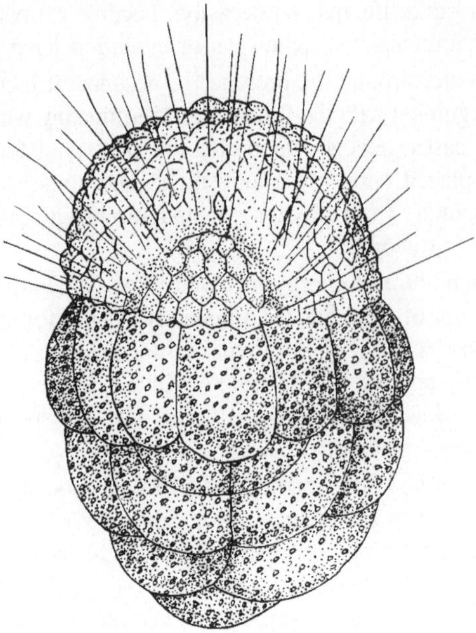

Figure 3.1: Amphiblastula larva.

like the sponge, a motile larval stage is of especial significance. There is thus afforded the opportunity of moving away and settling in a region of lesser competition for food than would be the case in the immediate vicinity of the parents.

And dispersal of the species means also that there is less danger of extinction through catastrophic change in one locality. While animals with highly developed locomotory powers often have motile larvae, the benefits to them would be mainly of a different kind such, for example, as enabling the young to remain afloat until they are able to cope with conditions on the bottom.

The larvae of most sponges are distinctive in appearance. One half of the typical larva is composed of flagellated cells, while the other half is not, whereby it is called an "amphiblastula"; this larva is best illustrated in the class Calcispongiae, where it is present in all but a few of the most primitive members.

Little is known of the development of the Hyalospongiae, which inhabit deep water, but sponges of the class Demospongiae also go through an amphiblastula stage. In the family Spongillidae, which lives in fresh water, there is again a swimming larva, but it is completely covered with flagella.

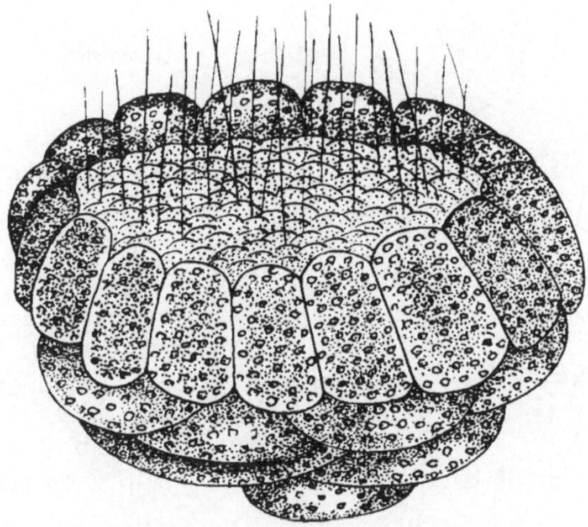

Figure 3.2: Flagellated layer of larva turned inward.

During metamorphosis the flagellated cells of the amphiblastula larva are turned inward and become a layer of collar cells, or choanocytes, similar in structure to those found among the choanoflagellate protozoans. With the translocation of the flagellated cells, structures for locomotion are lost from the surface, and they are not replaced.

The organism ceases to move through the environment and becomes attached. With the arrival of flagellated cells in the interior, the environment begins to move through the animal, and the life of the adult sponge begins. It is interesting that it is the same mechanism which provided locomotory power to the young animal which later becomes the means of moving the environment through the adult.

The Sponge as a Pump

The body of a sponge functions as a pump. Not being able to wander about in its environment, the sponge draws the environment to itself. Its sides are perforated ("Porifera") by many small openings, the ostia, through which the water is drawn. These small streams traverse the interior and combine to form a jet which is forced out of the main body opening, the osculum.

The power to maintain a flow of water is derived from the beat of the flagellated cells, the choanocytes. All of the needs of the animal-nutritive, respiratory, excretory, and reproductive-are served by the water stream. No other phylum of animals is built to function in exactly this way.

It has been estimated that, while passing the choanocytes, the water

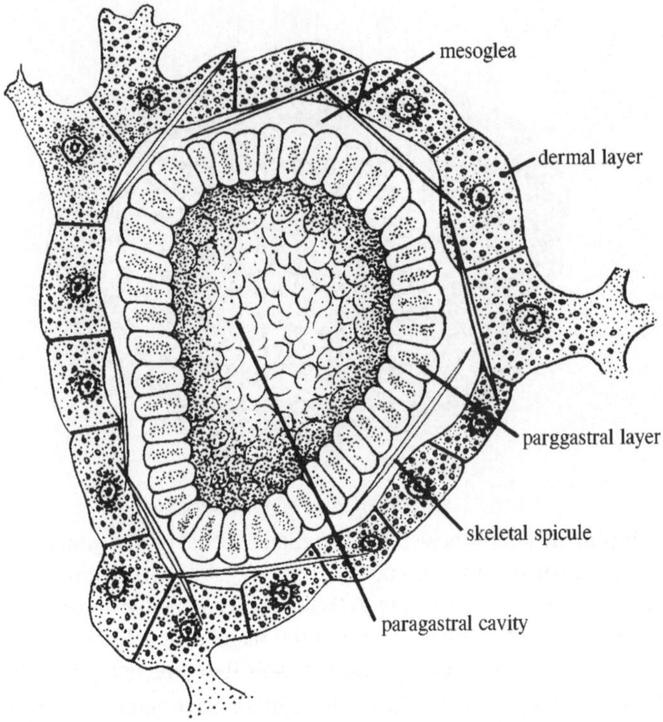

Figure 3.3: Section through young sponge, flagella and pores not shown.

current of a sponge (Leucandra, or Leuconia) runs at a velocity of about fifty microns per second. This rate of flow is well within the speed range of a ciliated or flagellated protozoan moving freely through the water.

By the time the ostial streams have been combined into the oscular jet, the speed of the current may be 25,000 microns per second, or even more. The volume of water discharged each minute is about equal to the volume of the sponge body itself. (For skeletal material alone, a tremendous water turnover is required, since for each ounce of skeleton about a ton of sea water must be processed.)

Under unfavourable conditions it is believed that water intake may be reduced through contraction of the porocytes. These are the cells that form the ostia. The most significant mechanism for the control of rate of water flow is, however, at the output rather than at the intake.

With the amount of water intake at the ostia remaining constant, constriction of the osculum, the exhalent opening, results in an increase of velocity there. This is an effective way of casting out discharges such as metabolic wastes, and sperm, beyond the zone of the suction that might carry them back again through the ostia.

Structure

The body of the sponge is not only made up of many cells, but it is made up of cells of many types. Moreover, the cells are arranged

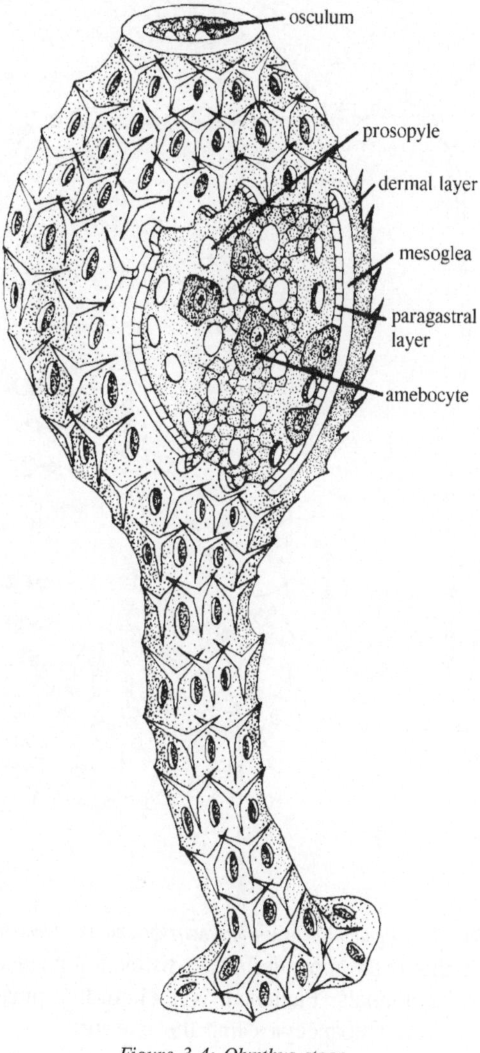

Figure 3.4: Olynthus stage.

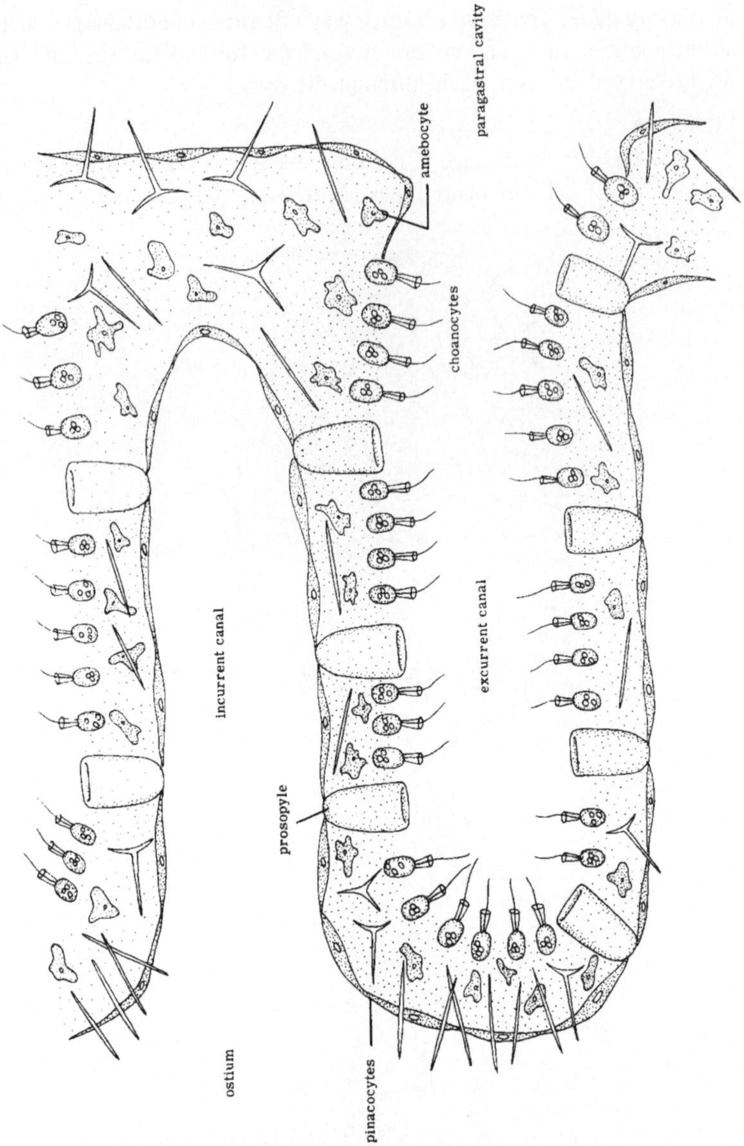

Figure 3.5: Relation between an incurrent and excurrent canal.

in layers, and this is the most definitive distinction between protozoans and multicellular animals. Flattened, epithelium-like pinacocytes make up the outer cover. Choanocytes line the interior.

The outer layer of cells is usually known as the dermal layer, and the inner one is the paragastral. Again we encounter the prefix "para," which here indicates that this is not a true digestive layer but something "alongside" it, something which only stands in its place. Between the dermal and the paragastral layers is a matrix known as the "mesoglea" which contains numerous wandering cells, the amebocytes.

The ameboid type of cell is nowhere more versatile, nowhere more fascinating, than it is in sponges. The mesoglea and the cells within it are collectively known as the mesenchyme of the sponge. The dermal layer, the mesenchyme, and the paragastral layer together make up a tripartite body wall which would be impervious if it were not for the microscopic canals, the prosopyles, which abundantly run through it. Prosopyles are canals that are either found within the porocytes, which are apparently single cells, or made up from several cells.

The central region of the sponge, surrounded by the body wall, is known as the paragastral cavity or spongiocoel. The content of the spongiocoel is environmental water, somewhat modified in composition by the activities of the animal. The working description given above is helpful toward a basic understanding of the structure of a sponge.

Actually, the simplicity outlined exists only in an early stage of development of the calcareous sponges-the Olynthus stage—and in the adult condition of a very few primitive genera like Leucosolenia. In all other sponges the choanocytes do not line the paragastral cavity directly, but are folded into adjoining canals or pockets. When choanocytes are found within canals, they occur only within the excurrent canals.

The opening of the excurrent type of canal is into the paragastral cavity; and the peripheral end of the canal is closed. Incurrent canals lead from the sea water into the body wall, and are closed at the inner

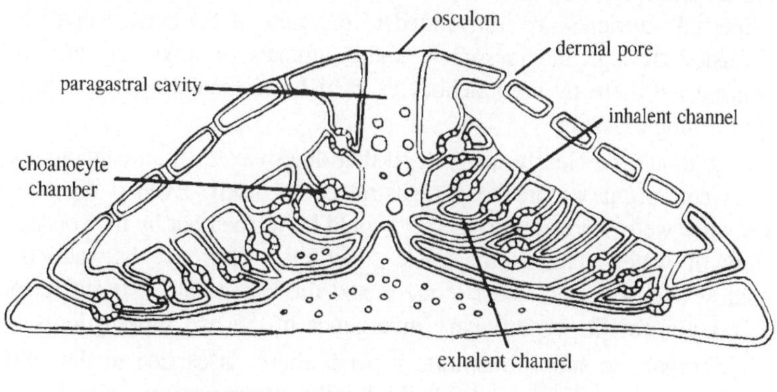

Figure 3.6: A complex canal system, Spongilla.

end. The incurrent canals contain no choanocytes. Water is sucked into the incurrent canals through the ostia and then into the excurrent canals through the prosopyles.

From the excurrent canals the water is forced into the paragastral cavity and, finally, outward through the osculum. The genus Grantia (Scypha) illustrates this level of structure and function. In the most complex canal systems the choanocytes are restricted to small chambers that are supplied with water from the sea through inhalent channels.

Discharge to the central paragastral cavity is through exhalent channels. A water system of this type is found in Euspongia, the common bath sponge, and the innumerable little chambers account for its highly porous nature.

A water system with the choanocytes in the central paragastral space is known as the Ascon type; when choanocytes are in the excurrent canals it is the Sycon type, and when located in special chambers we have the Rhagon type. From the simplest to the most complex, all sponges fall into one of these three types.

Function

Everything the sponge requires for growth and maintenanceand sperm involved in reproduction-enters with the water stream. Food wastes, metabolic excreta, and reproductive products-the larvae-depart in the water stream. As water flows through the body, food particles are engulfed chiefly by the choanocytes by means of pseudopodial processes located near the base of the collar.

Much of the food is digested within vacuoles in the choanocytes, in the protozoan manner, and indigestible residues are passed into the water stream to be swept out of the body through the osculum. Dissolved (digested) nutrients are transmitted to the cells of the dermal layer by diffusion through the mesoglea, and fragments of food may also be transported there by the amebocytes, which are themselves capable of performing digestion.

It should be clearly understood that digestive function cannot, and does not, occur within the paragastral cavity itself. Even if digestive enzymes were secreted into it, they would be washed out by the constant flow of water. This is the basic functional difference between the central body cavities of the Parazoa and the Enterozoa. It is sufficient to account for the evolutionary divergence of the two subkingdoms.

Oxygen, to supply respiratory needs there, is carried to the cells in the inner recesses of the body by the water stream, which also removes carbon dioxide and the nitrogenous wastes of metabolism.

Respiratory and excretory requirements of the dermal layer are served directly by the surrounding sea water.

Even though there is no nervous system to coordinate the activities of the cells of a sponge, a remarkable level of cellular cooperation nevertheless prevails. This is especially evident in the behaviour of amebocytes.

The Amebocytes

Besides their role in nutrition, amebocytes are active in many other ways. In reproduction, they give rise to the gametes of the sponge. Also, when sperm arrive in the incurrent water, amebocytes engulf the sperm cells and conduct them to the ova, where they are released to perform their assigned function. So we find amebocytes serving the purpose of genital tubules.

In a method of asexual reproduction amebocytes cluster together to form buds, more specifically known as gemmules. A gemmule is surrounded by a double-walled protective coat containing radially arranged spicules. This is constructed by assisting amebocytes which do not take a more direct part in reproduction, for when the gemmule is released the assisting amebocytes remain behind in the parent sponge.

Although they do not originate from zygotes the gemmules of marine

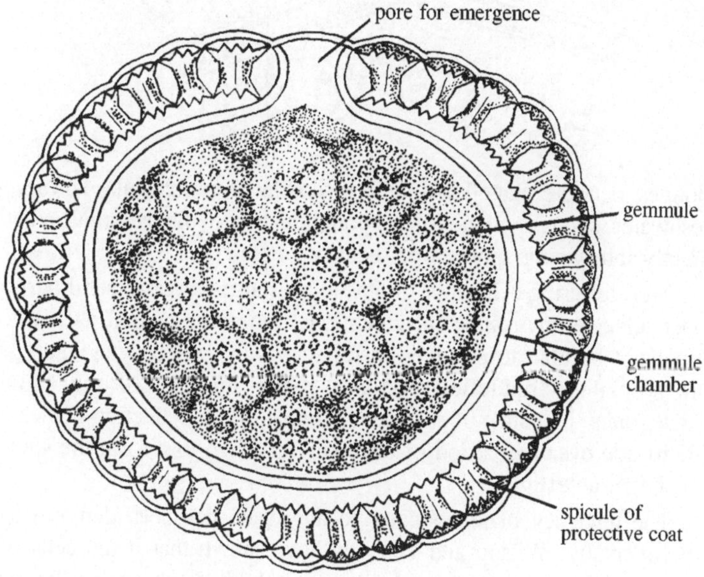

Figure 3.7: Sponge gemmule, Spongilla.

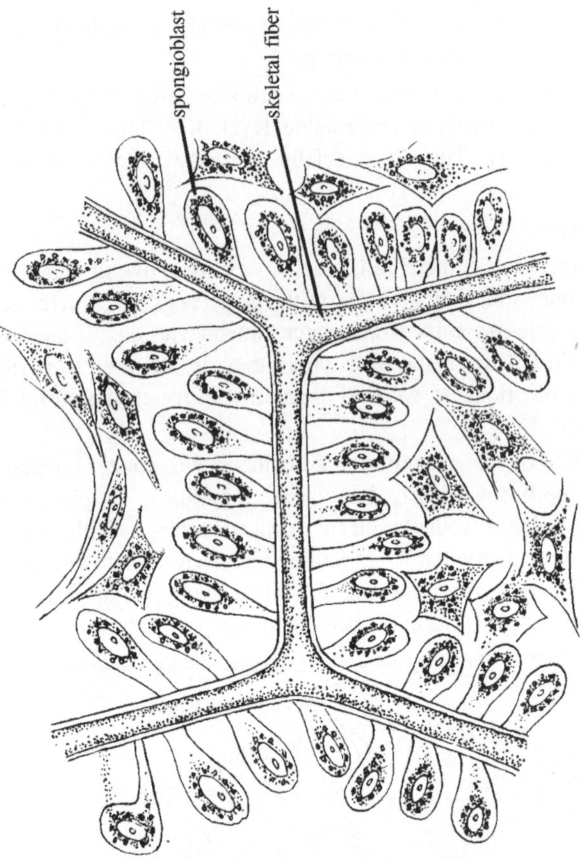

Figure 3.8: Spongioblasfs fabricating keratin fiber.

sponges become flagellated and resemble amphiblastula larvae. In freshwater sponges alone (the Spongillidae) do the gemmules hatch directly into young sponges of sedentary habit.

The clustering behaviour of amebocytes also serves a useful purpose under adverse environmental conditions, when the animal as a whole would not be able to survive. In this event the amebocytes aggregate into so-called "reduction bodies," while the rest of the sponge disintegrates. In a state of suspended animation the reduction bodies are able to tide over the period of adversity and then to reform the sponge at a favourable time.

The tendency of amebocytes to aggregate has been demonstrated experimentally. Wilson and Peabody have shown that if the cells of a sponge are forcibly separated by pressing the body through a fine silk mesh, the amebocytes thereupon move together again and rebuild the

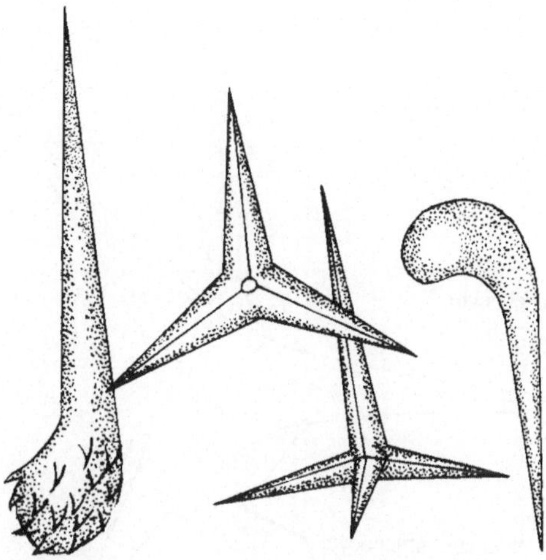

Figure 3.9: Lime spicules of various sponges.

body, dragging non-motile cells with them. As they are in reconstruction amebocytes are also active in construction, particularly of the skeleton. Some amebocytes, thereby known as spongioblasts, secrete skeletal material of a chitinous, or proteinaceous, nature.

If the secreting amebocytes are predominantly or entirely of the spongioblast variety, then the skeleton is fibrous like that of the bath sponge. But amebocytes may also secrete a mineral product, and they are then known as "seleroblasts" (Greek *skleros*, "hard"). One variety of scleroblasts forms spicules of lime, another of hydrated silicon dioxide, glasslike in composition.

It is well to note that all of these types of amebocytes are found in sponges that live in the same environment, where the same raw materials are available to them. It follows that the nature of the skeleton is due to the specific chemical behaviour of the amebocytes. But amebocytes of sponges are not the first living cells to show such selective powers.

Among the Sarcodina we saw that the Foraminifera take calcium carbonate out of the sea for their skeletons while the Radiolaria, in the same medium, use silicon. The method of procedure in the fabrication of skeleton provides one of the most intriguing examples of coordination to be encountered among sponges. A calcareous spicule, for example, is first laid down as an intracellular structure within the cytoplasm of a "founder" amebocyte.

When the spicule grows too long to be contained within a single

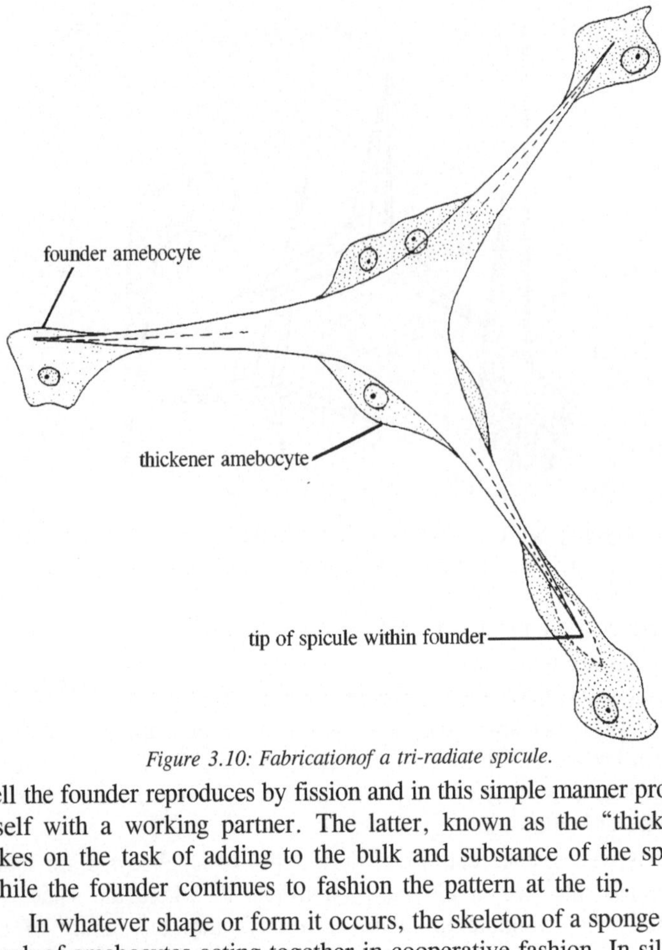

Figure 3.10: Fabricationof a tri-radiate spicule.

cell the founder reproduces by fission and in this simple manner provides itself with a working partner. The latter, known as the "thickener" takes on the task of adding to the bulk and substance of the spicule, while the founder continues to fashion the pattern at the tip.

In whatever shape or form it occurs, the skeleton of a sponge is the work of amebocytes acting together in cooperative fashion. In silicious skeletons a single scleroblast forms a simple spicule.

Many-rayed spicules are the product of a group of scleroblasts. Long spongin fibers are the fused secretions of many spongioblasts. Essentially, a cell works alone when the spicule to be made is small and of simple design. If it is large or complex, the original cell may produce whatever assistants are needed, by fission. Or, assisting cells may be called up from the mesenchyme.

This is a manifestation of coordinated behaviour beyond anything the protozoan subkingdom has to offer, and it is an evidence of the physiological complexity which underlies structural organization even of superficial simplicity.

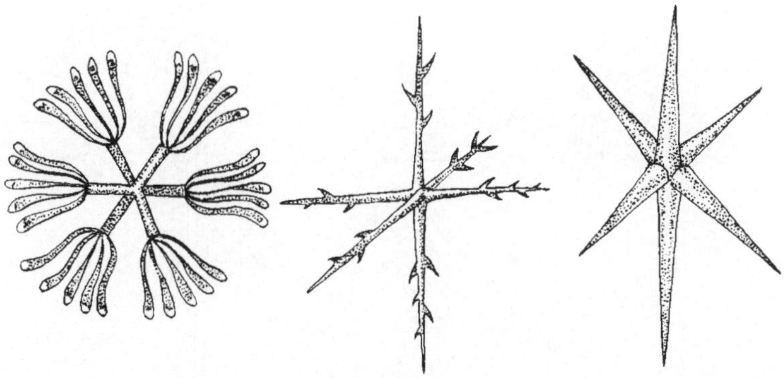

Figure 3.11: Some six-rayed silicious spicules.

Sponge Taxonomy and Distribution

From classes down to individual species the taxonomy of sponges depends greatly upon the chemical nature and structural pattern of the skeleton. Therefore it may be said that classification of Porifera is based upon the labors of amebocytes. In the class Calcispongiae are found those amebocytes which secrete spicules of calcium carbonate. Two orders are recognized according to the gross shape given the paragastral chamber.

In the order Homocoela we find a simple saclike paragastral cavity, as in the sponge Leucosolenia of the Ascon type. A spongiocoel with radiating canals is characteristic of the order Heterocoela in which Grantia and Leuconia are found. In the two remaining classes, the Hyalospongiae and the Demospongiae, there are silicon-secreting amebocytes, besides others.

The Hyalospongiae have six-rayed spicules and include such forms as Hyalonema, the glass-rope sponge, and Euplectella, the Venus flower basket. These are among the most beautiful and most intricate sponge skeletons. The class Demospongiae is the most diversified with regard to skeleton. Silicious spicules are present, but they are not of the six-rayed type as in the Hyalospongiae. Besides, some of the Demospongiae have proteinaceous skeletons and some even no skeleton at all.

In the order Tetractinellida there are silicious spicules of a four-rayed pattern, which distinguishes them from those of the Hyalospongiae; and, unlike the Hyalospongiae, all of the Tetractinellida are found in shallow waters as, for example, the sponge Chondrilla. Related to Chondrilla is the interesting sponge Chondriosa in which support for the body is derived from a stiffened mesoglea, there being no spicules at all.

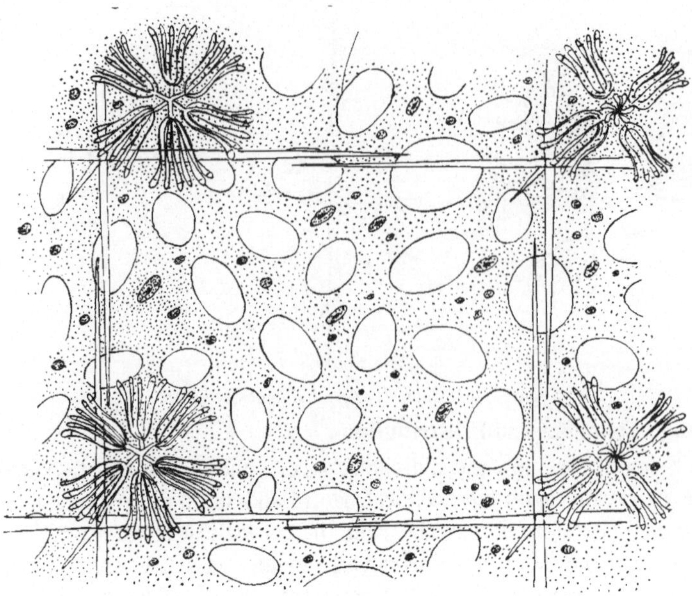

Figure 3.12: Lattice work of one of the Hyalospongiae.

Most of the Demospongiae are in the order Monaxonida. Their spicules are of silicious composition as in the class Hyalospongiae and in the order Tetractinellida but, as the name implies, those of the Monaxonida are built on a single axis. Besides the large spicules we have just referred to, known as "megascleres," there are also smaller less distinctive ones, the "microscleres."

Microscleres are of variable shape and do not have the taxonomic significance of megascleres. In addition to silicious spicules the Monaxonida possess spongin- or keratin-forming amebocytes which produce a proteinaceous substance to bind the glassy spicules together in the framework of the skeleton. In some forms spongin may predominate and the animal consequently resembles the bath sponges in texture. Suberites is such a Monaxonid sponge and it shows the added extraordinary feature of being able to move about from place to place.

However, this is a false motility as it is due to a crab of the genus Dromia which is associated with the sponge in the same manner as hermit crabs are associated with snail shells; for protection. The rule that no adult sponge possesses the power of locomotion remains inviolate. The Monaxonida show a very large range in bulk of skeleton.

Among the Spongillidae, a monaxonid family of freshwater habitat, the skeleton is very light and fragile and the members of the family are

Figure 3.13: Four-rayed spicules of Tetractinellida.

found as encrusting growths upon the stems of aquatic plants and other solid objects. In the sea, on the other hand, the monaxonid skeleton is often very massive as in the genus Poterion, the "Neptune's Goblet, which grows in a large cuplike form and has a heavy stemlike base buried in the sea bottom. Chalina the "Dead Man's Fingers," is a common, rather flexible sponge which may be taken to represent an average Monaxonid.

Also among the Monaxonida are the bright red Microciona and the boring sponge Cliona; the latter often found sunken into coral formations and mollusk shells.

Both the Monaxonida and the Tetractinellida are generally inhabitants of shallow waters, but the Monaxonid genus Cladorhiza may be cited as an exception since it has been dredged from down to 3000 fathoms, a depth usually associated with Hyalospongiae.

The order Keratosa of the class Demospongiae is usually found in warm and shallow waters. This group, in which there are no calcareous or silicious spicules to act as deterrents to their "proper use," contains the sponges of commerce of which Gerarde was aware. The skeleton is in the form of a tight mesh of fine proteinaceous fibers; capillary action in the fine spaces between the fibers accounts for absorbent properties.

The Keratosa skeleton lends itself to many household, medical, and industrial uses for which synthetic sponges are only poor substitutes. The finest bath sponges grow in the Mediterranean Sea, although the Gulf of Mexico and other areas around the world are also known for commercial sponge fishery. It is not an unprofitable mode of livelihood,

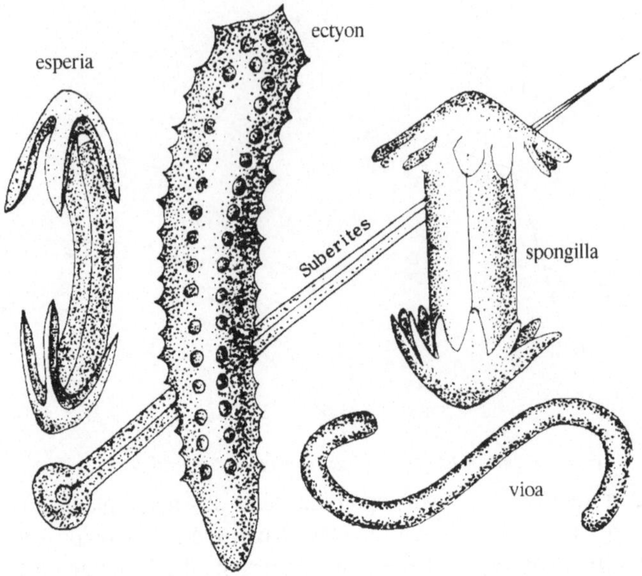

Figure 3.14: Monaxonid spicules of various sponges as shown.

and the Keratosa impart to the subkingdom Parazoa a considerable economic importance. Spongia, the most common bath sponge, and Hippospongia, the "horse-sponge," are examples of the group.

In view of the wide variation in the skeletons of Demospongiae, it is not surprising to find one order that forms no skeleton at all. This is the order Myxospongida, of which the genera Oscarella and Malisarca are examples. It is also true of the genus Chondriosa in the order Tetractinellida of Demospongia, as cited above.

In concluding let us list some of the rather formidable taxonomic terms we have employed:

Class Calcispongiae, also known as Calcarea, is made up of the orders Homocoela and Heterocoela, the latter containing the genus Grantia or Scypha, the sponge which is best known to students.

Class Hyalospongiae, also known as Hexactinellida, forms sixrayed silicious skeletons of the most beautiful and intricate design.

Class Demospongiae is made up of the orders Tetractinellida, Monaxonida, Keratosa, and Myxospongida. This is the most variable of the classes, and includes the commercial sponges.

The lack of locomotory organs, digestive system, and nervous structure makes of the Parazoa a most unusual animal group. But let us be aware that the state of being unusual is merely comparative. If

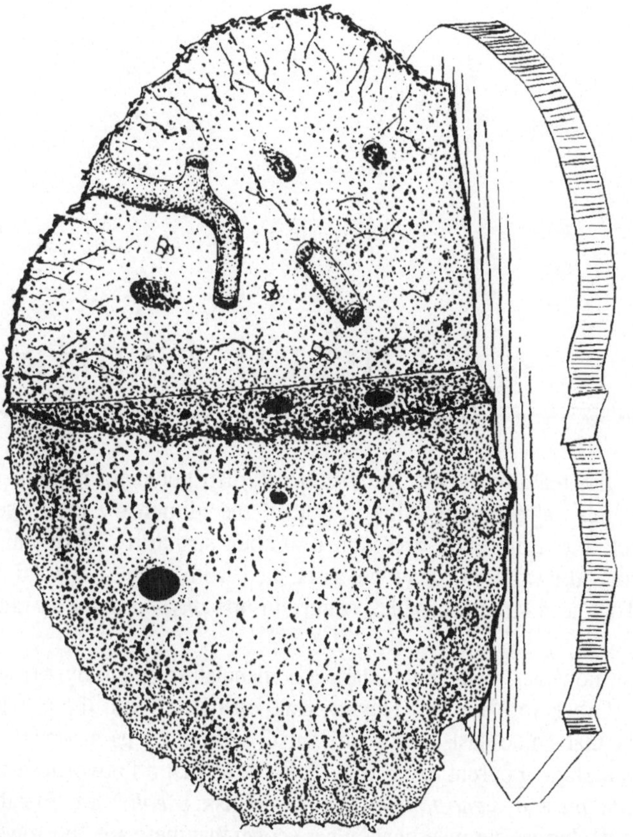

Figure 3.15: Spongia.

sponges were more conspicuous and better known, and other multicellular animals less so, then the latter would be unusual. At any rate in nature there is no lack of merit necessarily associated with the unusual. The Parazoa are certainly different from the Enterozoa.

In the latter there is a gut to be filled. In order to fill it a predatory way of life becomes common. Prey speeds up to escape predator, and predator speeds up to capture prey. It is a life of rapid movement, tense nervous systems, and often empty bellies. Which is the "better" way of life, that of the Parazoan or that of the Enterozoan? In nature the test is that of survival. Up to the present both of these ways of life have survived.

4

Phylum Cnidaria

Some of the features of the *Enterozoa* are distributed throughout the phyla of this subkingdom. This is true of the alimentary tract itself, for which the Enterozoa are named. Other structures, like paired locomotory *appendages*, may be associated with only a few of the phyla. To find a structure which occurs in one *phylum* alone is rather rare.

Such, however, is the cnidoblast, a nomenclature begun by Aristotle from the Greek for "nettle." Having gone on record with the absolute statement that cnidoblasts occur only in *Cnidaria*, let us at once now entertain certain apparent exceptions. It happens that a flatworm or two (*Microstomum* and *Stenostomum*) and a mollusk (*Aeolis*) are found to possess cnidoblasts, but investigation has shown that these are "borrowed" in a very *remarkable* way from cnidarians ingested as food.

Why are the cnidoblasts not digested? We do not know. Also, by what means are they moved to the surface of the "host" animal without being discharged, and there to function as if they were still part of the cnidarian which produced them? These are attractive questions, which are as yet not answered.

Structures which resemble cnidarian stinging cells might also be adduced, such as the polar capsules of the cnidosporidian protozoans and similar objects in the *flagellate Polykrikos*. They are not enidoblasts, but then how can we account for the *resemblance*? Here we have a case of the occasional parallelisms which appear from time to time in groups not related to each other.

On close inspection, the polar capsule and the *cnidoblast* bear only a *superficial* resemblance. It should be noted that the polar capsule is

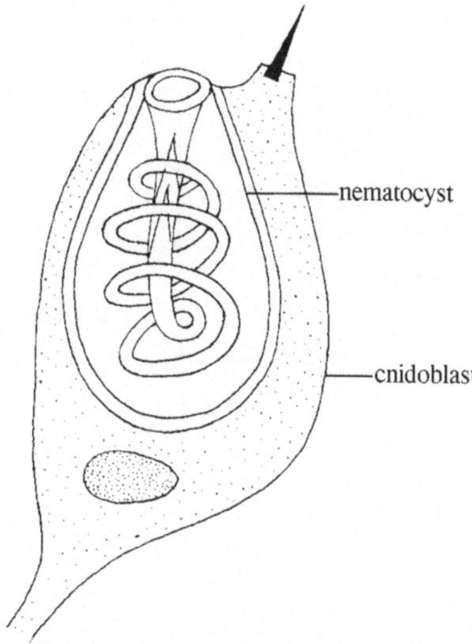

Figure 4.1: A cnidoblast.

a *protozoan* organelle composed of only a very small part of a cell while the cnidoblast is an entire cell in itself. Then it will be realized that there can be no basic relationship between the two.

It is fully accurate to state, therefore, that no animals besides cnidarians are capable of producing the cnidoblast cell type, and that practically no animals except enidarians possess cnidoblasts. This furnishes good and sufficient reason for naming the phylum "*Cnidaria*," a name that was first used by *Aristotle* and revived more recently by the zoologist Hatschek.

Let us make it clear that the cnidoblast itself possesses no stinging power, but it does have the unique capacity for forming the cyst—like capsules within its cytoplasm which are known as nematocysts. It is the *nematocyst* that stings. Each nematocyst contains an inverted, hollow thread, coiled to accommodate its length.

On appropriate stimulation the thread is forcefully everted by means of the contraction of the cytoplasm of the cnidoblast, and the fluid contained in the capsule is inoculated through its tip. This fluid contains *hypnotoxin*, a substance of undetermined *chemical* composition but of well-known effect. The effect can easily be observed in the relationship between Hydra and Daphnia, and human contact with jellyfish in the sea attests to the nature of the sensation.

The nematocysts of the "*Portuguese Manof-War*," while not as widely experienced by humans, are among the most potent, and enable

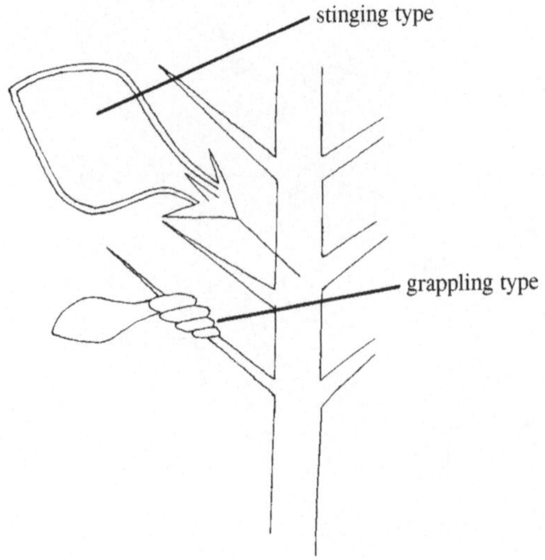

Figure 4.2: Two types of nematocysts.

these members of the first Enterozoan phylum to prey upon some members of the most advanced Enterozoan phylum. *Physalia* easily subdue fish and are dangerous to humans. (It is interesting that a little fish, of the genus Nomeus, is not harmed.)

To complete the picture on nematocysts, we should note that not all of them are of the stinging type. Another kind, for example, ejects *grappling threads*, which hold fast to the *prey*.

Additional Cell Types Found in Cnidaria

Besides cnidoblasts the body of a cnidarian is composed of cells of several other types. Cells of a *muscular* type, the myocytes, are present in large numbers. They account for the contractility of the body and also provide a mechanism for movement from place to place. The *myocyte* of the cnidarians is not a highly *specialized* cell.

Neither in structure nor in origin is it like the muscle cell that appears later in the *Enterozoan* series. A true muscle cell is derived from embryonic mesoderm, and the whole cell is *contractile*. Among the Cnidaria, mesoderm is not found in all of the classes of the phylum and when found is present only in *rudimentary* form. Besides, cnidarian myocytes are not drawn out like true muscle cells but are, instead, provided with basal *elongations* in which the contractions occur.

The direction of orientation of the basal processes determines the nature of the effect upon the body. *Myocytes* are found chiefly in the epidermis and in lesser numbers in the *gastrodermis*.

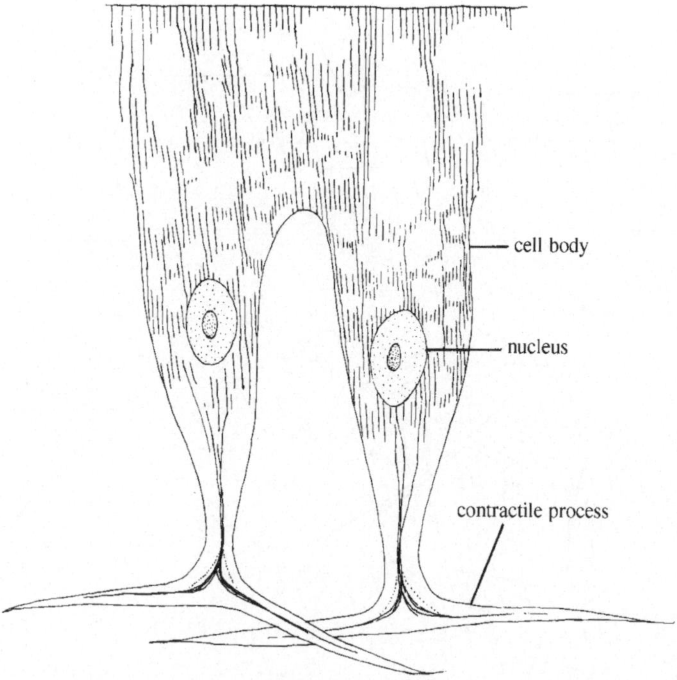

Figure 4.3: Myocytes of Hydra.

Glandular cells, for secreting digestive enzymes into the gastrovascular space, are associated with the gastrodermis. Like myocytes, these cells are especially significant of the Enterozoa. They make possible extracellular digestion: the existence of proteolytic enzymes in the Cnidarian digestive cavity has been demonstrated. Such a *phenomenon* is, of course, unknown in the *Parazoa*.

Also highly noteworthy in *cnidarians* is the neurocyte, or nerve cell, specialized for the conduction of stimuli in the form of nerve impulses. The neurocyte is built somewhat on the same structural pattern as the myocyte. From a central cell body fibrillar processes radiate outward and run between the *dermal* and *gastral* layers. The *fibrils* are longer than those of a *myocyte* and, of course, they are not of contractile nature.

By their property of length they facilitate the passage of stimulation. It is known from studies of nerve transmission in more advanced nervous systems that the limiting factor upon the speed of transmission is the number of cell contacts, or *synapses*, which the impulse must cross. *Elongated* cell processes reduce this number for a given distance, and

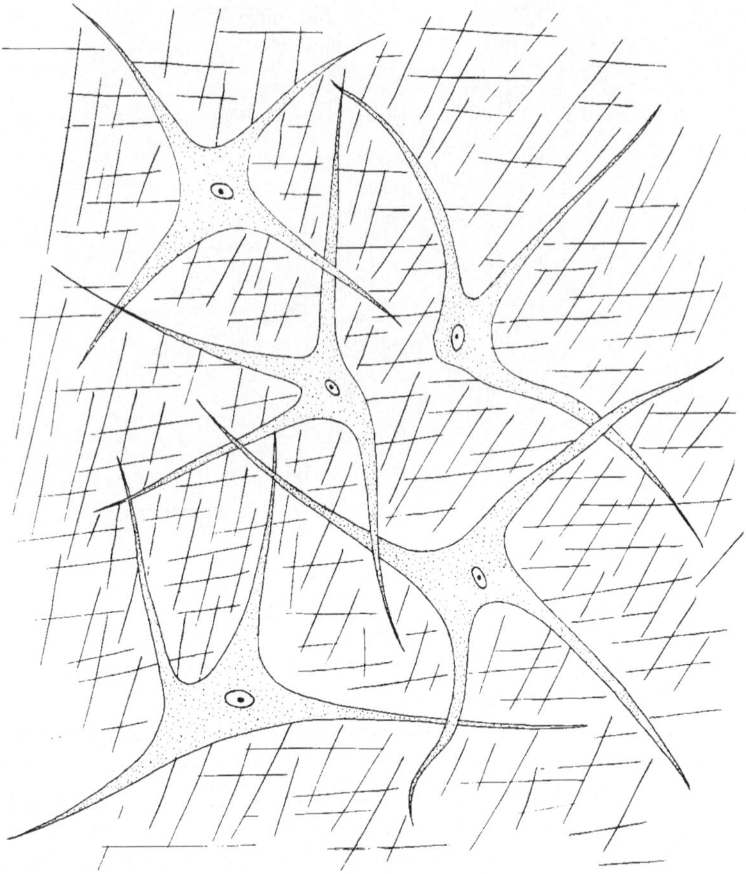

Figure 4.4: Neurocytes of an anemone.

thereby speed the passage. As compared to those later evolved, however, the cnidarian neurocyte is only a *rudimentary* cell. More specialized nerve cells have the property of polarization.

One end is then provided with *receiving* processes, the dendrites, and transmission is unidirectional via a long *fiber* known as the *axon*. The fibrils of a cnidarian neurocyte are physiologically equivalent. They receive and *transmit* in any direction. The fact that neurocytes and myocytes appear simultaneously and for the first time in this phylum should not be overlooked. A *natural* inference is apparent, that a nervous system is primarily correlated with *movement*.

Together with the *digestive*-glandular cell, these are the three cell types that are most intimately tied in with the different *pathway* of evolution taken by the *Enterozoa*, from that taken by the Parazoa. In the noncellular mesoglea, which lies between epidermis and gastrodermis, amebocytes wander in greater or lesser number. *Interstitial* cells, of an embryonic character, lie tucked between the bases of the dermal (epidermal) cells.

Interstitial cells become active in regenerating a wounded body, by giving rise to cells of other types as needed. In some cases the origin of germinal cells, the gametes, is also attributed to the interstitial cells. In the bases of polyps (the *cylindrical cnidarians* typified by the Hydra), *mucus-secreting* cells are significant.

Gas-forming cells are found in the floats of the Siphonophora (see below), such as the Portuguese Man-of-War. The hard parts of hydrocorallines and of corals demonstrate the presence of skeleton-secreting cells. *Sensory* cells are widely distributed in dermal layers, and flagellated cells in gastral layers.

Within the mesogleae of the *Scyphozoa* and the *Anthozoa* there is found a small amount of fixed contractile tissue that is regarded as the first appearance of true mesodermso far as we can tell from surviving species, of course.

It is apparent that the general *resemblance*, at first sight, between a simple cnidarian like Hydra and the Ascon sponges is purely superficial. The types of cells present are quite different. These differences are carried forward into behaviour, and the motility and nutrition of the cnidarian stand in sharp contrast to the fixed shape and protozoan-like digestion of the sponge.

Cell Layers, Mesoglea, and Body Form

In the discussion of cell types we noted their arrangement in layers. The body is composed of an outer covering of cells, the dermal epithelium or epidermis, and an inner gastral epithelium or gastrodermis.' Between the two there is more or less of the *jelly*-like mesoglea. The gastral epithelium surrounds and forms the enteron, which is usually known as a gastrovascular system because of the accessory function of food distribution which it performs.

In the area around the mouth there are a number of mobile, fingerlike *prolongations* of the body, which are tentacles. This completes the basic pattern of body structure. By *virtue* of the relative amount of jelly-like substance which is included between the two cellular layers, and without any other essential deviation from the general plan, a *cnidarian* may exist in one of two *seemingly* different forms.

With little jelly the polyp or *hydranth* type results, as in the very

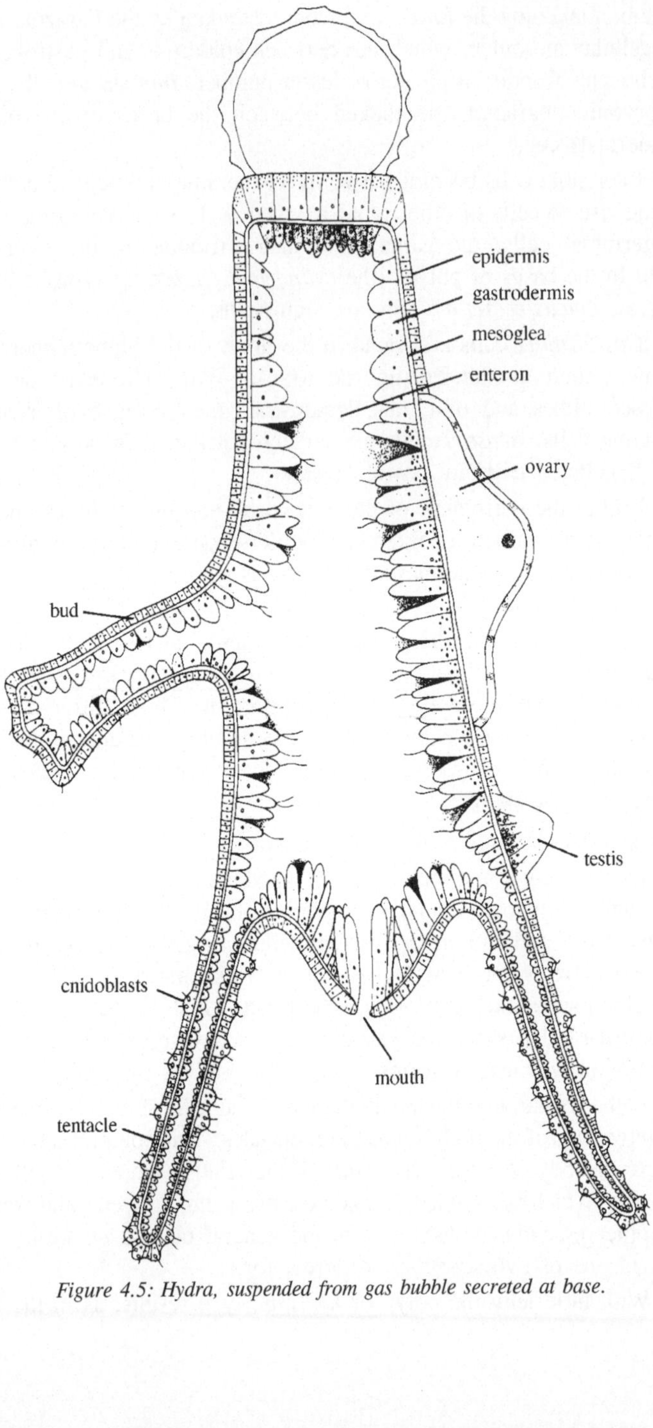

Figure 4.5: Hydra, suspended from gas bubble secreted at base.

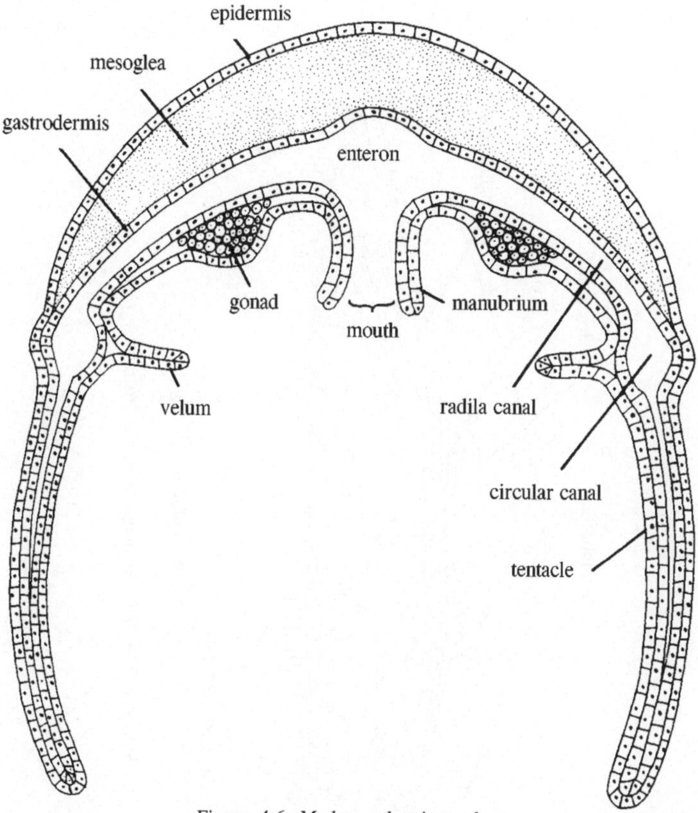

Figure 4.6: Medusa, showing velum.

familiar genus Hydra. *Locomotory* powers are slight in polyps, or the animals may even be completely sessile. In such cases contractility serves nutritive purposes.

With an increase in jelly there results a *drastically* different animal. This is the *medusa* or *jellyfish*. As a *jellyfish* the cnidarian is adapted for the *swimming* habit; even though its powers in this direction are usually not very pronounced. We really cannot expect them to be.

The animal is enlarged and bulky with jelly, while the *contractile* tissue is limited to the thin covering layers. This does not provide a sound *mechanical* basis for locomotion. While the polyp and the *medusa* neither look alike nor do they act alike, anatomically they are only deviations of the same plan of structure.

Additional proof is found in the fact, brought out below, that the medusa type may be directly produced by *budding* from the polyp.

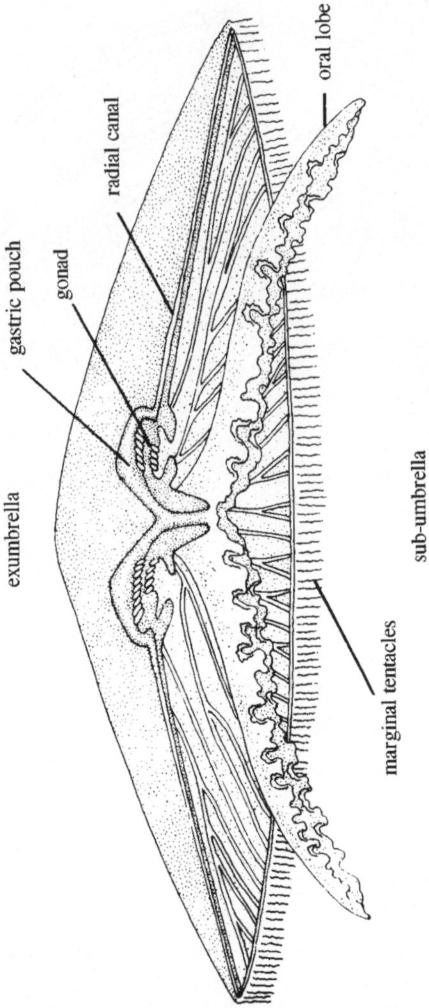

Figure 4.7: Aurelia meduasa, side view in hemisection.

In some *genera* of *cnidarians*, as *Hydra*, only the polyp phase exists. In others, e.g., Liriope, only the medusa is known. But in large measure cnidarians show both polyp and medusa in the same life history. *Aurelia* belongs in the last category, and it will be taken as a reference type for the phylum.

Aurelia

As a jellyfish Aurelia is found floating and *pulsating* gently in the surface waters of all oceans. The body can be described as being in the shape of a *flattened saucer*, up to one foot in *diameter*. The opening into

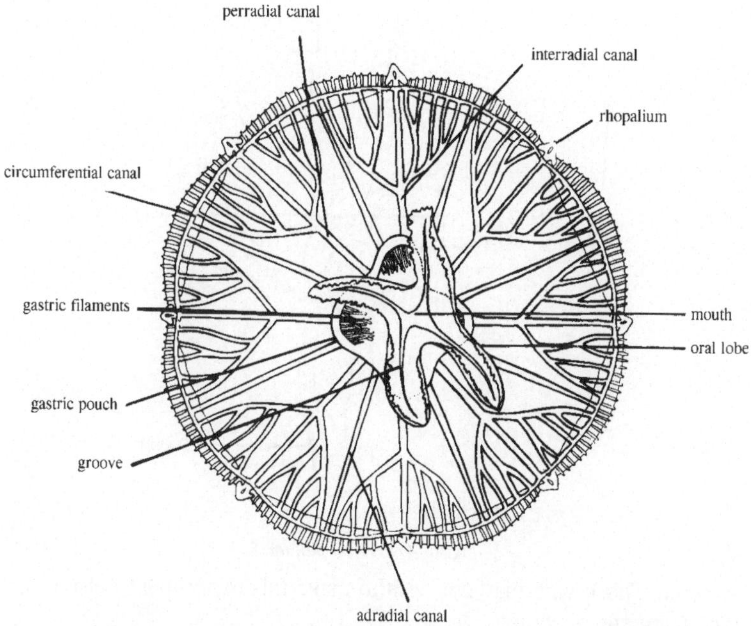

Figure 4.8: Subumbrella view of young Aurelia, about 2 cm. in size.

the *gastrovascular* system runs through a short stalk known as the manubrium, which hangs from the center of the *concave* side of the saucer. This is the oral, or subumbrella, side of the animal.

Its apposite, the aboral or *exumbrella* side, is unbroken by any projecting structure. Although Aurelia is usually oriented with the exumbrella side upward and the *subumbrella* side downward, it would be in error to designate them as *dorsal* and *ventral* since such terms are applicable only to animals of bilateral symmetry.

The mouth of Aurelia is not round, but four-cornered. From each corner a conspicuous oral arm is suspended. On the inner side of each arm, along its length, there is a *flagellated* (perhaps *ciliated*) *groove*. For subduing small organisms to be taken in as food, the arms are provided with *numerous* small *tentacles prolifically* studded with cnidoblasts.

There are longer tentacles around the outer margin of the umbrella which are also provided with cnidoblasts, for defense against larger animals. The nematocysts of *Aurelia* are not powerful enough to *penetrate* human skin, at least of the tougher varieties.

Direct personal knowledge as to the effect of *nematocysts* can readily be gained by contact with Cyanea, a form closely related to

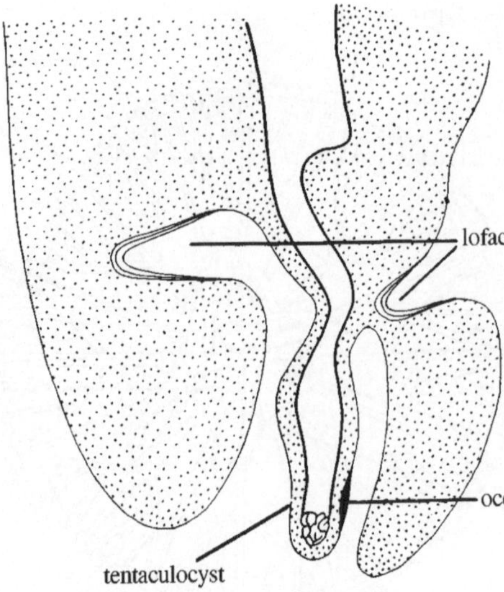

Figure 4.9: A rhopalium.

Aurelia. Those who may not wish to make this experiment must accept the statement on faith.

Tucked into notches of the umbrella margin are eight sensory organs (why are they not "*organelles*"?) called "tentaculocysts" or "rhopalia". The most noticeable feature of the rhopalium is a short tentacle which is weighted at its free end to form a *balancing* organ, for sensitivity to *gravitational stimulation*. Most specifically this is the "*tentaculocyst*."

There are also patches of optically and chemically sensitive cells incorporated into the structure of the *rhopalium*. Through their contact with a network of nerve cells the rhopalia control the rate and magnitude of the swimming pulsations of the umbrella. A more vigorous or more frequent contraction on one side swings that side of the body forward in the direction of movement.

While the effect of each rhopalium is somewhat localized in its own vicinity, it has been demonstrated experimentally that the influence of each is also felt completely around the animal. This is shown by the fact that swimming movements continue even when all but one of the rhopalia are removed. When the last is excised all swimming reactions cease.

The effective contraction of the umbrella is produced by a zone of contractile cells concentrated about the lower *margin* at the outer edge of the body. The entire edge of the umbrella acts as a continuous swimming fin, and the animal moves ahead with the aboral side in the lead. The *recovery* phase appears to be due only to the *elasticity* of the body.

While the swimming behaviour of Aurelia is neither rapid nor very purposeful in direction, such *qualities* of motion are not essential since swimming is not utilized in the pursuit of prey. Cnidarians are not capable of *capturing* food by running it down. In *compensation* they are equipped with *nematocysts* for immobilizing any food organism with which chance contact is made.

THE GASTROVASCULAR SYSTEM

By way of a short gullet the mouth leads into a centrally located stomach, which is extended into four side-chambers called gastric pouches. The presence of *gastric* pouches and particularly the fact that these are well supplied with gastric filaments bearing *cnidoblasts*-apparently for dealing with food organisms not yet fully subdued-is a characteristic of medusae of the class Scyphozoa.

The stomach and its pouches, because of their relative spaciousness, are adapted for *extracellular digestion*. But the movement of food into the animal does not stop here. From each gastric pouch two *unbranched* radial canals, specifically known as the adradials, lead to the circumferential canal at the outer margin of the body.

Thus the *stomach* contents, partially digested, enter the circumferential canal at eight points. Many small canals arise from the circumferential and carry material back toward the stomach. We might, for reference purposes, call these the afferent canals. Afferent canals are organized into definite groups.

Four such groups, geometrically arranged, comprise the perradial system. These four groups combine into four perradial canals, which lead directly to the stomach. The *perradials* pass between, and not into, the gastric pouches. The remaining afferent canals which drain the *circumferential* combine to form four so-called *interradials*. The latter feed into the gastric pouches.

It will be noticed that the gastric pouches receive two flows of material. One emanates from the stomach and travels outward. The other comes in from the interradial canals. Why do not these currents oppose and *neutralize* each other? There is structural *provision* against this *contingency*.

Extending from the floor of each gastric pouch and running parallel to its outer curvature are two *gastric ridges* (*gastric ridges* are another characteristic of medusae of the *scyphozoan* class). Material coming into the pouch from the interradial canals is guided around the outer wall of the pouch by the ridges, whence it is conducted back into the *stomach* via two exhalent channels. In this way interference with material coming into the center of the pouch from the stomach is minimized.

The circulation of gastric contents is completed by the emission of four streams, one through each corner of the mouth. The grooves of the oral arms are continuations of the exhalent system. It is apparent that this elaborate system is adapted not only for digestion but also for the distribution of food within the animal; hence *gastrovascular*.

The complete passage around the system takes about twenty minutes, and the extracellular digestion which was begun in the stomach is supplemented by intracellular, since the canal system is lined with cells capable of *pseudopodial ingestion* and of digestion within food *vacuoles*.

In our study of the gastric pouches there is an unavoidable impression of a structurally and *physiologically crowded* condition. Water currents move in and water currents move out. Canals and channels lead in and out. Ridges aid in "*traffic control*." There is no doubt that conditions are crowded; moreover, this is not all that goes on in the *gastric pouch*.

Reproduction

Lying in the floor of each pouch, following its outer curvature, is a somewhat horseshoe-shaped organ, the gonad. This is indeed a curious location for reproductive organs, within the digestive system. *Alimentary* and genital associations are rare; urinary and genital much more common. But here, in *Aurelia*, digestive and genital systems operate in *harmony*, and show that the state of being *peculiar* is only a relative one.

It is a situation that is strange only because in higher forms things are so different. It is interesting that cnidarians could survive in competition with more evolved forms when the *gastrodermis* is so burdened with *nutritive*, *circulatory*, and *reproductive* functions.

Perhaps their survival can be attributed to the exclusive possession of the cnidoblast. The sexes of Aurelia are separate. An individual contains either four testes or four ovaries, one in each gastric pouch. Since the gonads arise from the gastrodermis they are embryologically of endodermal origin.

Eggs or sperm are discharged into the solution of *gastric juices* found in the pouch and, apparently none the worse, continue on their destined course. *Sperm* are *swept* out at once, through the *corners* of the

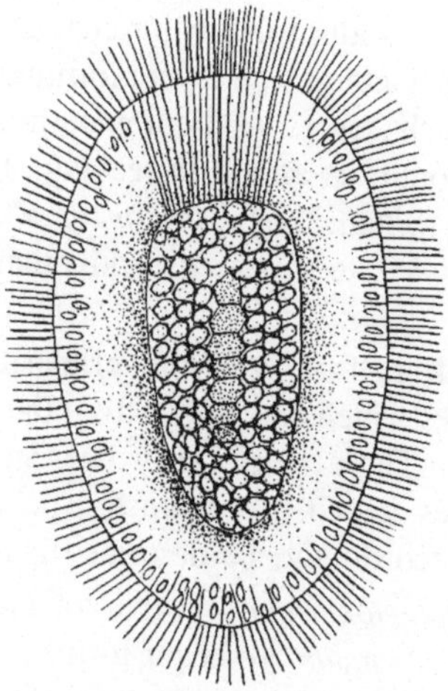

Figure 4.10: Aurelia planula larva.

mouth. Since Aurelia generally swim in groups, or schools, the school soon moves through a diluted suspension of sperm. There is nothing to prevent the sperm from being carried into the mouths of other animals, and nothing does.

Sperm enter through the center of the mouth, with the inhalent current. Impregnation is by way of the mouth. Perhaps it is the presence of sperm in the gastric system of the females which stimulates them, or *irritates* them, to discharge their eggs, and then *fertilization* occurs in the stomach. When compared withh later *phyla*, the *sex* life of these first *enterozoans* is very strange, but here it is normal behaviour.

After fertilization the *zygotes* emerge from the corners of the mouth of the females, as sperm did in the case of the males, and the young cleaving *embryos* become entangled in the folds of the oral arms which, as we have seen, are *continuations* of the *exhalent system*.

It is interesting that the arms of the females are provided with extra folds which are adaptations for holding the young. This may be regarded as a secondary *sexual characteristic* giving these animals a kind of "*motherly*" quality, which appears again in later phyla. In the arms of the "*mother*" *Aurelia* swimming planula larvae are developed. In due time the planulae free themselves, and leave.

The free-swimming life of the planula phase is brief. Soon it settles and becomes attached. The *planula* now undergoes a metamorphosis into a *polyp* form. As contrasted with the bulk of the *jellyfish* phase of Aurelia, the *polyp* is very small.

Nevertheless it shows all of the major characteristics of a cnidarian polyp. There are dermal and gastral layers forming a tubular body, with a single opening which serves as both mouth and anus. There are tentacles about the mouth, as an aid in feeding. This polyp of Aurelia is known as the "*scyphula,*" or "*scyphistoma*", a little *Hydra*-like animal. Its life, attached to *seaweeds* and other solid objects, is a sedentary one.

Structurally it differs from a Hydra primarily in the presence of four longitudinal ridges which extend out from the gastrodermis into the gastrovascular cavity. These *ridges* may be regarded as rudimentary mesenteries, structures which are characteristic of the polyps of the *Anthozoa* and will, accordingly, be described later.

Although the *scyphistoma* may survive for many years, it does not attain sexual maturity. *Gonads* are never formed. Sometimes, although this is very rare, the scyphistoma does not reproduce at all. In this event *metamorphosis* may take place directly into a *miniature medusa*, which eventually becomes adult. This transformation is direct evidence

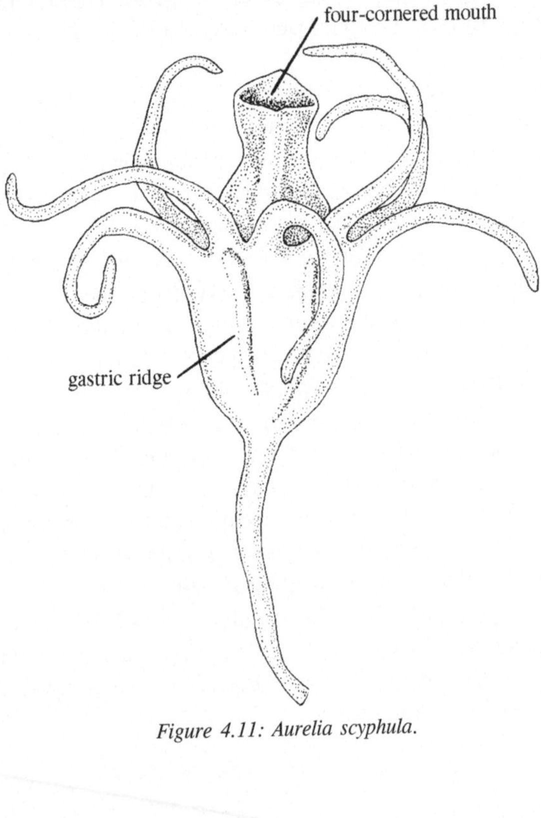

Figure 4.11: Aurelia scyphula.

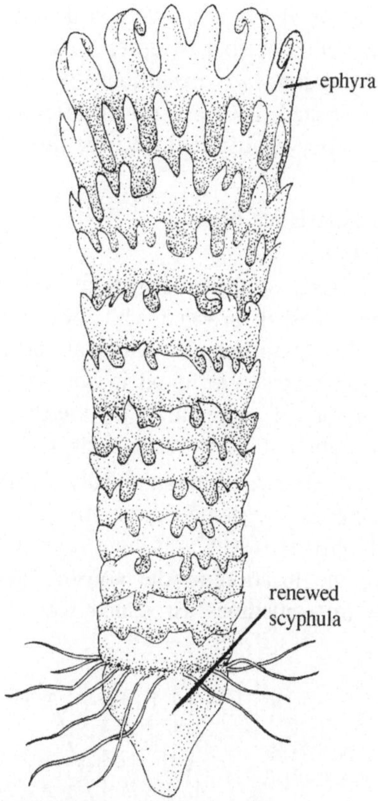

Figure 4.12: Aurelia strobila.

of the essential sameness of the polyp and medusa plans of structure. Commonly *scyphistomae* do *reproduce*, but only by asexual means. Additional scyphistoma stages may be budded from lateral outgrowths of the base of the original individual, so that a colony of *Aurelia* polyps comes to owe its origin to a single *fertilized* egg.

Eventually, however, the scyphistoma changes the nature of its budding behaviour. *Constrictions* arise at the oral end, in a transverse *orientation*. Each of these is a bud which completes its separation and swims away. Often additional buds begin to be formed before the first is released, and several may then be attached to the single *scyphistoma* base.

Such a complex is known as a "*strobila*" and the process is one of strobilization. Reproduction by means of *strobilization* usually occurs during the colder months of the year. The transverse buds formed by the scyphistoma are named *ephyra*. They are minute members of the *medusa* phase, but are *scrawny* and *incomplete* in structure. The margin of the umbrella is not yet filled out but is represented, somewhat like spokes on a wheel hub, by *rudimentary* extensions upon the ends of which the tentaculocysts are situated. By a process of differential growth the gaps between the *tentaculocysts* are filled, and the little *ephyra* becomes the adult *jellyfish*.

Taxonomic Characteristics of Polyps and Medusae

Now, on the basis of the information attained by the study of Aurelia as a type, we shall proceed with further consideration of the phylum Cnidaria. Structural features which are useful in differentiating between the various classes are found in both the polyp and medusa. Each possesses points of recognition by means of which it can be identified as a member of its respective class.

The presence or absence of longitudinally oriented gastric *partitions* known as "*mesenteries*"—although these are sometimes found only as rudiments called "*gastric ridges*"—is significant in the identification of the *polyp*. Also, the location of the gonads varies in the different classes. *Gonads* are sometimes associated with the gastral layer and

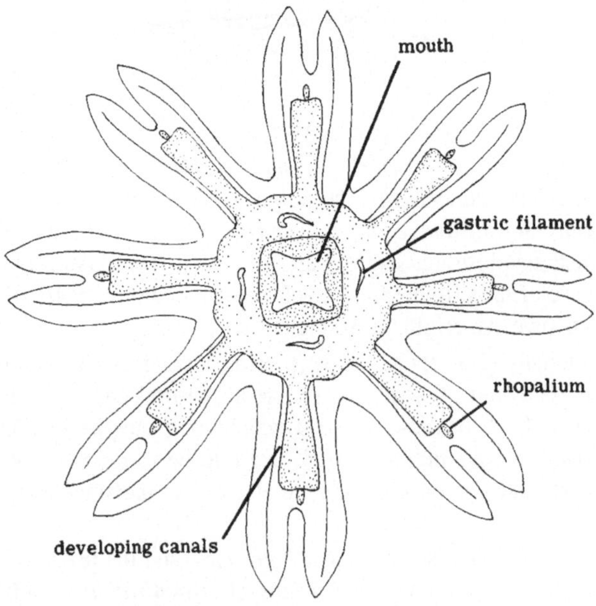

Figure 4.13: Aurelia ephyra, oral view.

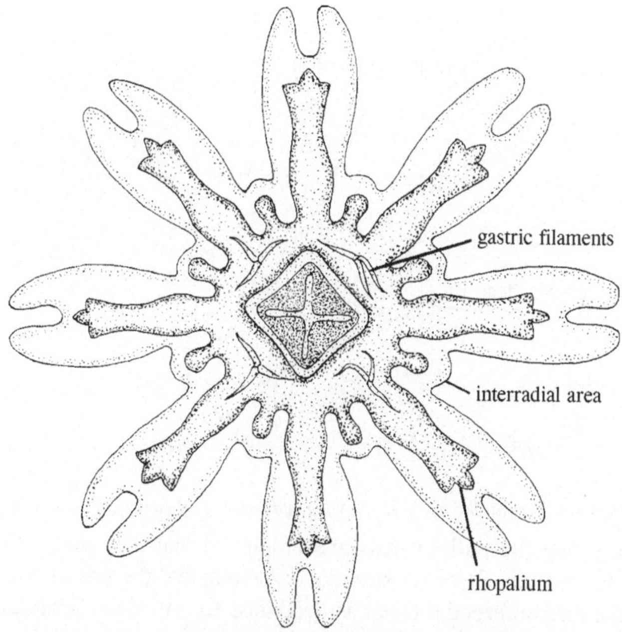

Figure 4.14: Aurelia ephyra, about 2 mm, in size.

sometimes with the dermal. Another differentiating feature is the nature of the lining of the mouth. In more primitive forms *gastrodermis* and epidermis meet at the mouth, whereas in the *embryology* of more evolved polyps the ectoderm is turned inward and comes to line the beginning of the alimentary tract.

Since in this event the *endoderm* does not extend as far as the mouth, the gastrodermis here is accordingly composed of tissue partly ectodermal and partly endodermal in origin. A portion immediately behind the mouth is derived from ectoderm. A gullet lined in this way with tissue of ectodermal origin is a "*true*" gullet, and is known as a "*stomodaeum.*" The taxonomic association of a polyp is, then, determined by its mesenteries, its gonads, and its gullet.

The term "true," as used above in a biological sense, is in need of a word of definition. There is no implication of veracity, or the lack of it. "True" simply means that the structure so designated is like that of animals later evolved; that it runs true to advanced form. This usage will be encountered again, as in "*true appendage*," or "*true coelome.*"

Of the criteria that are useful in the classification of the medusa phase-in the *cnidarian* classes in which such phases *occurperhaps* the most outstanding is the nature of the system of *gastrovascular canals*.

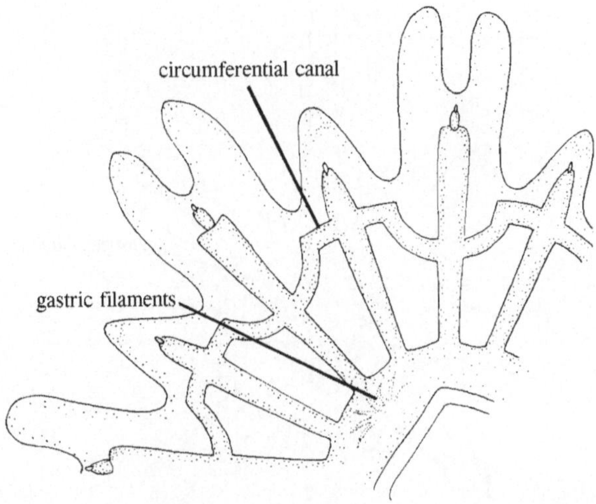

Figure 4.15: Aurelia ephyra, showing appearance of circumferential canal.

In one group the radial canals are simple, in that they do not branch; while in the other there is extensive branching and the branches connect with the circumferential canal as described for Aurelia. *Structurally*, it seems that the type of canal system is correlated with the size of the animal, because the *branching* type is a general feature of large medusae, while the *non-branched* is a *characteristic* of the small.

From a physiological basis it appears safe to conclude that the greater amount of digestive surface provided in a branching system is necessary for the *nutrition* of the larger animals, and conversely for the smaller. Another feature for the distinction of *medusae* is the presence or absence of a velum. The *velum* is a circular shelf extending inward from the margin of the *umbrella*, on the *subumbrella* side.

There is a central opening in the velum through which water can be drawn into the subumbrella region, and by contraction of the body water is discharged through this opening. The constricted velum opening serves to increase the *velocity* of the *emerging* water stream and the presence of such mechanism serves the purpose of converting a paddle-like *swimming* stroke of the umbrella into *jet* action.

Structurally, a true velum is characterized by the fact that there are no *endodermal* derivatives-such as elements of the gastrovascular system-within it. Also, a velum contains a special ring of nerve tissue, which is otherwise absent in the umbrella. As was also the case in the polyp, the *location* of the *gonads* has taxonomic significance for *medusae*.

Gonads are found associated with the *epidermal* layer, with the advantage of direct discharge of gametes into the environment, or they are found in the gastrodermis in which case perhaps the *gastrovascular* circulation is of assistance in bringing the *gametes* together. Finally, in one type of medusa there are thread-like *gastral* filaments within the stomach, as in *Aurelia*. In other types these are absent.

Classes of the Cnidaria

On the basis of such criteria *Cnidaria* are divided into three classes:

Class Hydrozoa

Polyps lack mesenteries, have their gonads in the epidermal layer, and are without a stornodaeum. Medusae of the same class lack gastric filaments, gonads are located in the epidermal layer, radial canals are unbranched, and a velum is usually present.

Class Scyphozoa

Polyps possess rudimentary gastric mesenteries but no stomodaeum. Nor, since these never become sexually mature, are there gonads. Like the polyp, the medusa also has outgrowths from the *gastrodermis* in the form of gastric filaments; and *gonads* are located in the *gastral* layer.

Most distinctive of these medusae is the complexity of their gastrovascular system, as *manifested* in the extensive branching of the radial canals. Finally, scyphozoan medusae lack that important aid to locomotion, the velum. Some possess a so-called *velarium*, a thinned-out portion of the umbrella margin which, unlike a true velum, contains branches of the *digestive* system but no nerve ring.

Class Anthozoa

Unique in that no medusa phase is formed, and therefore the distinctive features of the class are all in the polyp phase. The polyps have a large and well-defined stomodaeum and a gastrodermis of very complicated structure due chiefly to a system of mesenteries. These two features alone separate them *sharply* from *Hydrozoan* polyps and, besides, the gonads are in the *gastrodermis*.

It will be noticed that in *Anthozoa* there is no medusa phase. In the Scyphozoa, on the other hand, there is a much de-emphasized polyp phase and, in some of the deep water forms, no polyp is known at all. Among *Hydrozoans*, while both phases are often well developed, one or the other may also be reduced.

In all cnidarians sexual maturity is attained in the medusa phase, if there is one. For this reason the polyp has sometimes been regarded as a larva and the *medusa* as the adult. A view more generally held is that both polyp and *medusa* are individuals, in which the more primitive ancestral form-the *medusa -reproduces* sexually, while the polyp is asexual in its reproductive habit. The life history of a typical cnidarian thus involves an alternation of asexual and sexual generations, a *phenomenon* known as *metagenesis*, which we have also *encountered* among *protozoans*.

Since there exists considerable variability within the classes of Cnidaria, let us conclude our *consideration* of the phylum with a brief discussion of each class.

HYDROZOA

Hydrozoans are widely distributed in the sea and only a few genera are found in fresh water; the much studied Hydra being atypical in this

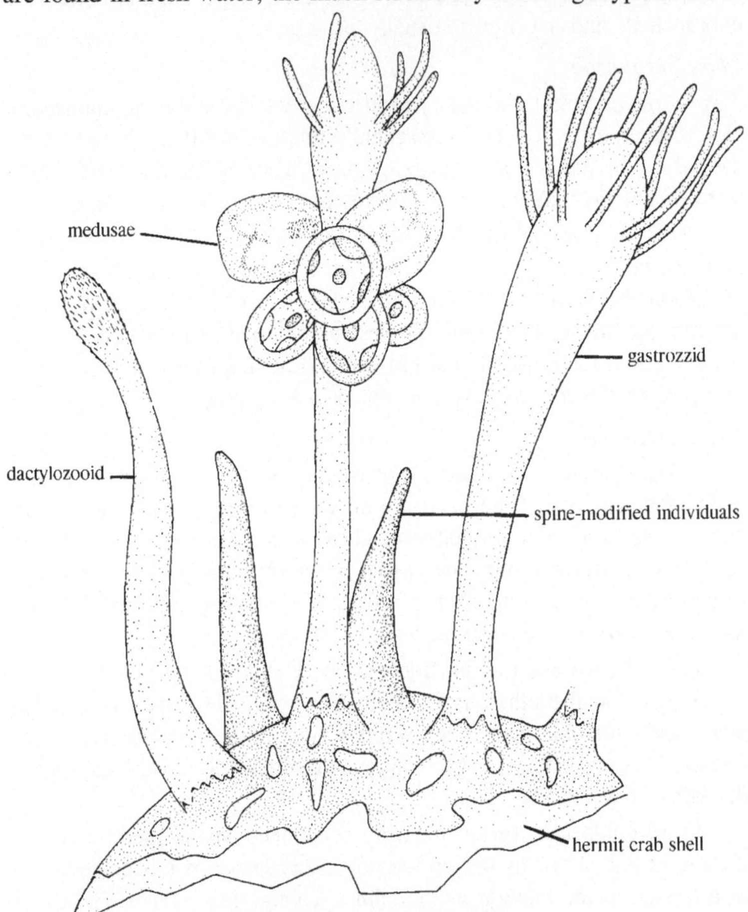

Figure 4.16 A: Hydractinia colony.

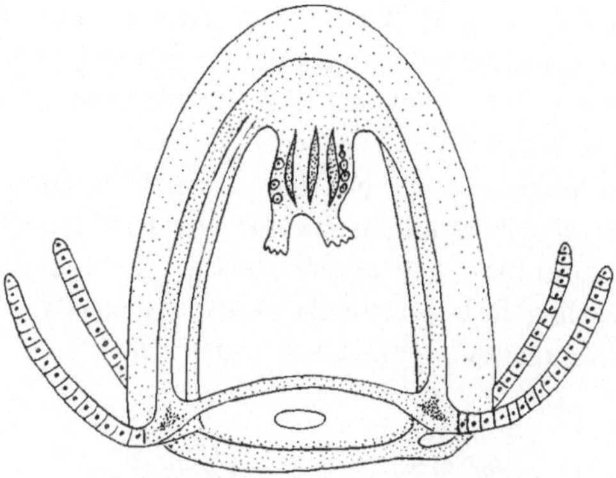

Figure 4.16 B: Hydracfinia medusa.

respect. Nor is *Hydra typical* with regard to life history, since there is no medusa phase. Craspedacusta is also found in fresh water. Here the medusa is relatively large, up to two centimeters in diameter, while the polyp-once thought to be a separate genus, "*Microhydra*"—is only one tenth as long as the medusa is wide.

Of colonial forms *Cordylophora* is perhaps the only one which is not marine, although it may be found in brackish water as well as in fresh. These examples show that, while *Hydrozoans* are basically marine, there has been some evolutionary penetration into waters of lower salinity.

Marine hydrozoan polyps range in size from the tiny Protohydra, about 3 mm. long, to the gigantic Branchiocerianthus of Pacific deeps (down to 3000 fathoms), which may stand six feet tall. *Medusae* are mostly microscopic like that of Obelia, though some, e.g., Tima, a "*giant*" of the class, attain a diameter of two or three inches. It is interesting to note historically that into the nineteenth century, *polyps* were referred to as the males and medusae as the females of the same species.

Colonial hydrozoans form inconspicuous *aggregates* of a few small individuals, as in Craspedecusta, and range to the large Siphonophoran group which includes such as Physalia, the "*Portuguese Man-of-War.*" The latter, from float to the ends of the trailing individuals, may cover a span of fifty feet, or more. Hydrozoan polyps generally reproduce asexually, by budding, and the buds may separate from the parent as in Hydra.

More usually buds remain attached, and in this manner *colonies* are built up. *Budding* may result in upright colonies, as in *Obelia* and

Bougainvillea, both common forms, or individual buds may spread laterally from stolons, producing an aggregation like that of Hydractinia, which lives in a relation of mutualism with hermit crabs, according self-evident benefits to both.

When hydrozoan polyps bud they generally produce polyps like themselves. But they may also, as in *Corymorpha* and *Branchiocerianthus*, form medusae. In these two genera budding never produces a polyp. This is a puzzling fact, for fragments experimentally removed from these polyps do *reconstitute* themselves as such.

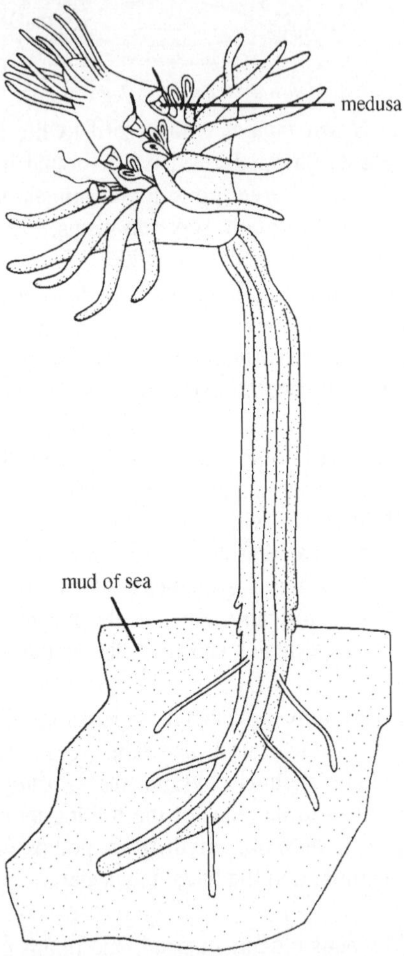

Figure 4.17A: Corymorpha, forming medusae.

In many forms polyps branch out by budding into a modified phase, the gonozoid; and this phase gives rise to medusae, also by means of buds. Sexual reproduction among the *Hydrozoa* is confined to the medusa phase, except in a genus like Hydra, where no medusa is formed.

While gamete formation is a property of the medusa and budding is not, as in all natural phenomena an exception can be found, since medusae of the genus *Rathkea* are known to form buds.

Life History of the Hydrozoa

Genera which exist in only one phase have, of course, no metagenesis. But this is very rare. Hydra, as everyone knows, is found only in polyp form. Craspedacusta was once thought to exist only in the medusa phase, until its relationship to the polyp "*Microhydra*" was discovered, and a life history between the two established.

So also with the medusa Gonionemus until eventually it was demonstrated that the polyp "*Haleremita*" developed from *Gonionemus* eggs. It still appears, however, that there are some medusae-evidently few and far between-which do not form a polyp phase. No polyp, for example, is known to be associated with the *medusa Liriope*. In their respective phases, then, *Hydra* and *Liriope* stand very much alone.

Obelia

It is typical of hydrozoans to show a life history which includes both polyps and medusae. Each is adapted to make a *contribution* to the welfare of the *species*. The polyp appears better able to serve the purposes of *nutrition*, especially in *colonial* form where a larger water expanse can be covered.

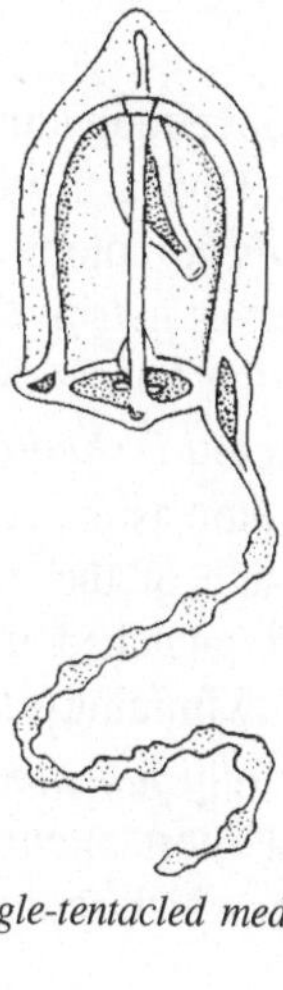

Figure 4.17 B: Single-tentacled medusa of Corymorpha.

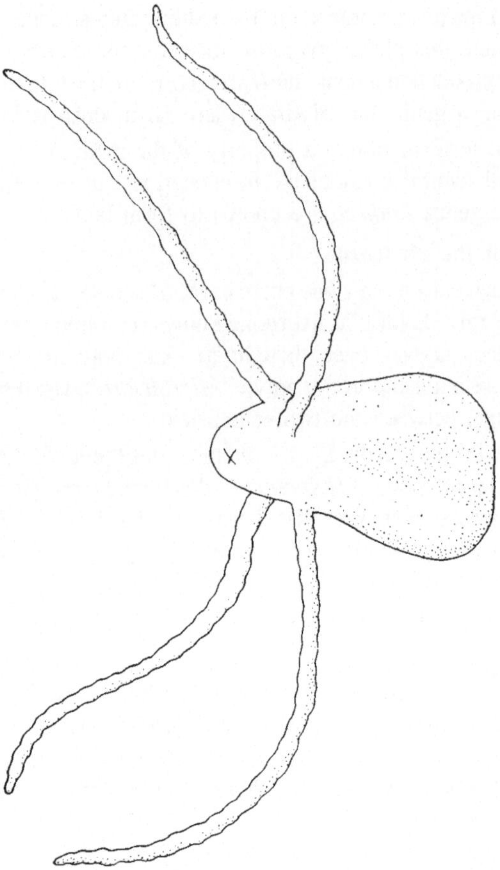

Figure 4.18: Teh polyp of Gonionemus.

The *medusae*, as reproductive individuals, can usually herd together for the mingling of gametes. Obelia is often taken as an example of hydrozoan life history. The *Obelia* colony is composed of two types of polyps. One, the *hydranth*, serves nutritive purposes, and the other, the *gonozooid*, is specialized for the formation of *medusae*.

Within a protective *skeletal sheath* medusae are budded by constriction from a central protoplasmic stalk of the *gonozooid*, known as the blastostyle. The oral side of the medusa is differentiated first, while the aboral end remains attached until the time comes for the release of the bud as a free-swimming *planktonic* animal.

The Obelia medusa is a fully *functional* animal. There is a mouth located at the distal end of a short *manubrium*; the mouth leads to a centrally located stomach from which four *unbranched radial canals* run

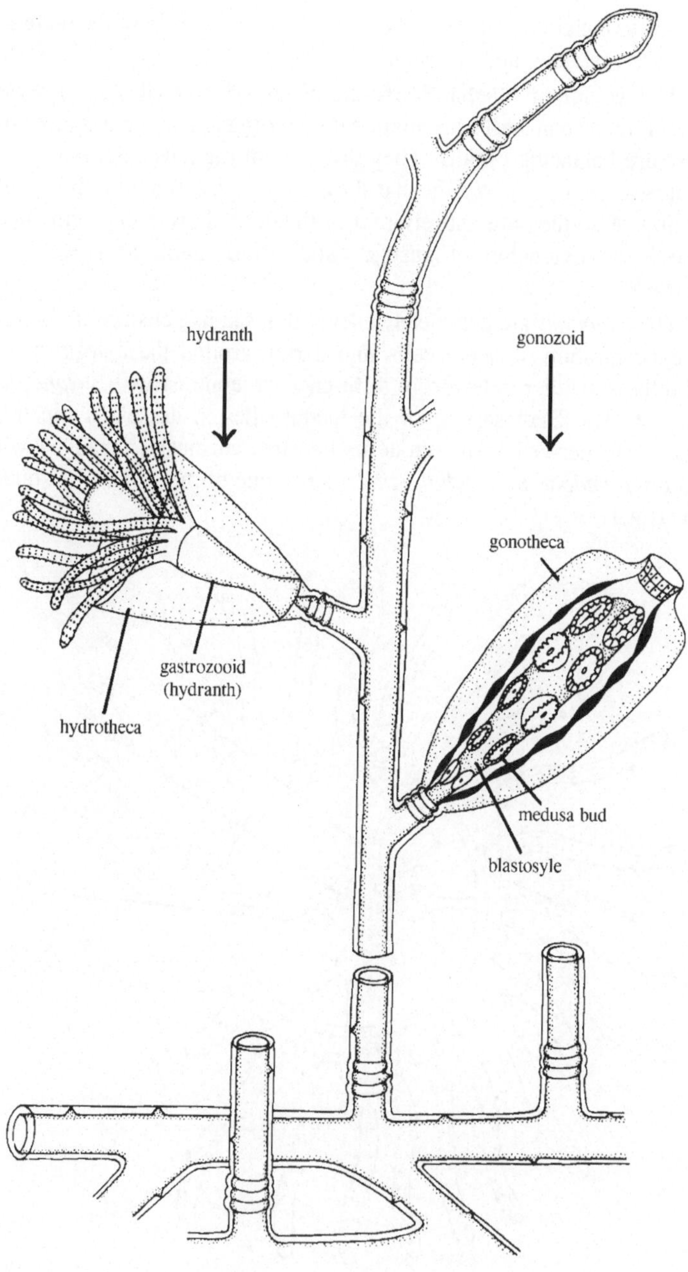

Figure 5.19: Individuals of the Obelia colony (schematic).

outward to the circumferential canal. At the outer margin of the umbrella there are *tentacles* and a *velum*.

The velum of Obelia, however, is of very small size. Located between tentacular bases are eight sensory organs known as statocysts. These are balancing organs. They differ from the tentaculocysts of the Scyphozoa (e.g., *Aurelia*) in that they are adapted for only this single function. Also they are entirely part of the dermal layer in origin, since there is no extension of gastric canals into them, as there is in tentaculocysts.

The *statocysts* are completely enclosed in sac-like chambers. Finally, the concentration of nerve cells into a ring around the margin of the umbrella is another noteworthy difference, in contrast with *scyphozoan* medusae. The chief service of the medusa lies in its sexual function. Gonads are derived from ectoderm but are, curiously, arranged with relation to *endodermal radial canals*, since one of the *gonads* lies under each canal.

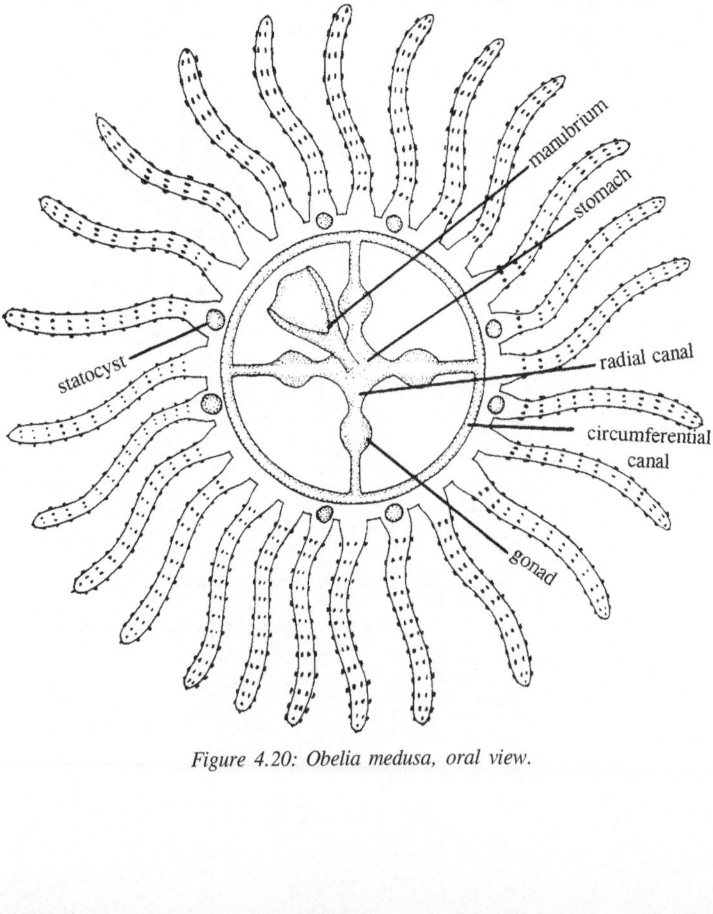

Figure 4.20: Obelia medusa, oral view.

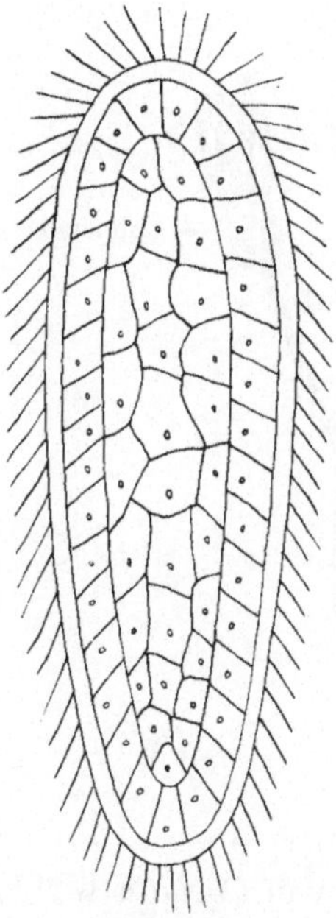

Figure 4.21: Obelia planula larva.

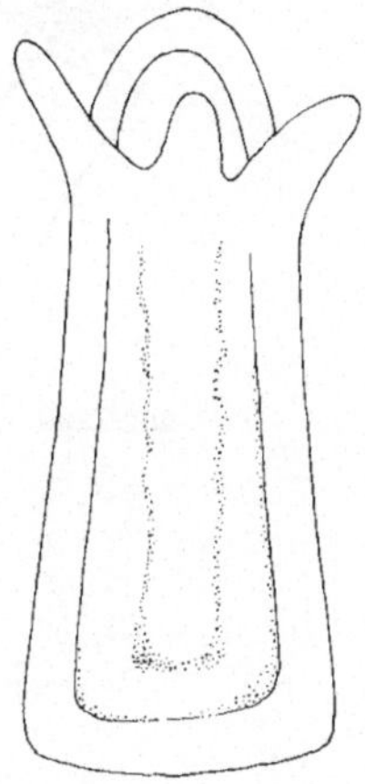

Figure 4.22: Protopolyp of Obelia.

The sexes are separate, and when individuals become mature, gametes are shed into the water, where fertilization takes place. A free-swimming larva, *uniformly* covered with *flagella*, is a distinctive phase of the development. This, the planula, possesses most of the cell types found in the adult. *Cnidoblasts*, *neurocytes*, *myocytes*, *glandular cells*, and other types are present.

Though at first solidly composed of cells, the shift of endoderm cells toward the *periphery* leaves a cell-free interior that becomes the first rudiment of the gastrovascular cavity. It should be noted that the outer *flagellated* cells have no subsequent relation to the *central cavity*, since they do not shift *inward* as they do in the *sponges*.

The *planula larva* is characteristic of *Cnidarians*, just as the amphiblastula is of sponges. This is another way of saying that the group affiliation of animals may often be *determinable* early in their life. It is not necessary to wait until they develop the leatures of the adult. Upon attachment the *planula metamorphoses* into a *polyp* which, by growth and *budding*, builds up the colonial group of *Obelia*.

The colony of *polyps* is surrounded by a *chitinous* tubular *jacket* or *exoskeleton* (narrow around the stalks and wider to accommodate the gastrozoids and *gonozoids*) which gives it a measure of *support* and

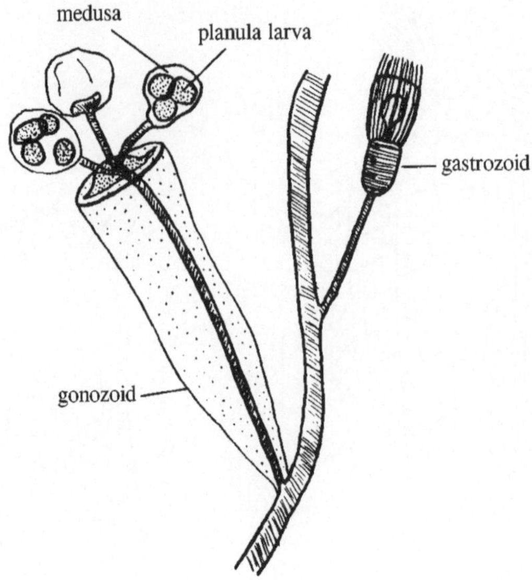

Figure 4.23: Gonothyrea.

protection. It is evident that the life history of *Obelia* is well balanced in that both phases, the *hydranth* and the *medusa*, are free-living and functional.

Other colonial *Hydrozoans* may lack such balance due to partial suppression or lack of full development of one of the phases. In Gonothyrea, for example, the medusae are never released but remain attached to the blastostyle by an aboral stalk of *tissue*. The advantage of swimming medusae to bring the *sexes* together is therefore lost in *Gonothyrea*.

This condition is hard to understand, and may be evidence that the medusa phase is a more recent evolution from the *polyp*, but this is the converse of the view *currently* held. More likely it indicates suppression of the medusa phase in the *Gonothyrea* life history.

Polymorphism among the Hydrozoans

Hydrozoans that exist in only a single shape or form are rare. Almost always there is at least a *dimorphic* condition, with polyp and medusa. In Corymorpha, for example, a larger polyp buds off small medusae directly from the region of the tentacles. *Corymorpha*, like *Tubularia* and *Branchiocerianthus*, is *dimorphic*.

Obelia is *trimorphic*, having added the gonozooid type of polyp especially for the production of medusae. In *Hydractinia* there are four types of *individuals*, adding to the other three the *dactylozooids*. These show a reduced *gastrovascular* system or even none at all, and a very high concentration of cnidoblasts. As a consequence dactylozooids are adapted for the *capture* of food and for the defense of the colony, but not for feeding.

The highest level of polymorphism to be found in the *Hydrozoan* class (or in the *Cnidarian phylum*, or even elsewhere in the animal kingdom) appears in the *Siphonophora*. *Medusa* and *polyp phases*, and various modifications of both, are here integrated into a single functional complex. *Stephalia* is such a complex.

Physalia is another. Its float, or pneumatophore, is believed to be a modified *medusa* in which the epidermis, by invagination, has come to lie inside. (It has been proposed that the aurophore of *Stephalia* is represented in the pore, or major opening, of the *Physalia* float.) In the floor of the *pneumatophore* there is a mass of gas-secreting cells responsible for the *maintenance* of *buoyancy*.

The pneumatophore rides on the surface of the sea. Suspended from it and extending many feet downward, in accordance with the size of the specimen, are the other members of the colony. It is believed that in stormy weather release of gas through the *pore* allows the colony to sink into a region of lesser turbulence, and secretion of a renewed supply causes *re-emergence*.

But, if so, this mechanism is not particularly responsive since, after an onshore wind, great numbers of Physalia may be found beached. In life Physalia is a very beautiful animal, with changing hues of rose and purple colouration. These are soon lost after preservation.

Although *Physalia* can be blown along by wind action upon the float, in the related genus Vellela the pneumatophore is actually modified into a sail-like structure which appears to be especially adapted to catch the wind. And so without motive powers of their own such animals are enabled by the wind to troll through the water and capture many a good-sized fish, of a phylum much more evolved than their own. Such prey is then digested down to the bare skeleton, through the combined action of the *gastrozooids*, applied like so many suction cups.

Classification of the Hydrozoa

It has now been brought out that there is considerable diversity in form and structure within the *Hydrozoa*. There is considerable ,diversity, too, in the various schemes of classification which have been proposed for the class. Perhaps, some day, all authors will agree. *Characteristics* of both *polyp* and *medusa*, when both are present in the life history, are utilized in arranging members of the *Hydrozoa* into related groups.

Hydroidea

This order is recognized as one in which the polyp stage is well developed, and the medusa is small or even completely absent. A *proteinaceous* (*chitinous*) skeleton is usually present in *Hydroidea*, although *Hydra* possesses none. The *skeleton* takes the form of a sheath which *envelops* the *organism*.

When the skeleton surrounds the gonozooid, with its blastostyle and developing medusa buds, the resulting group may be known taxonomically as the "Calyptoblastea" ("*calypto-*," *covered*). Or, if the medusa is the basis for classification, the group may be known as the *Leptomedusae* ("*lepto-*," small).

In those Hydroidea where the skeleton does not cover the blastostyle the term "*Gymnoblastea*" ("*Gymno-*," naked) is applicable. If named for its medusae, then "Anthomedusae" is the word ("*antho-*," flower), for these medusae are bell-shaped in contrast to *Leptomedusae*, which are flattened like a saucer.

Among the *Hydroidea* the student will be most familiar with these: *Hydra*, *Protohydra*, *Tubularia*, *Corymorpha*, *Branchiocerianthus*, *Hydractinia*, *Obelia*, *Gonothyrea*, and *Polyorchis*. The order *Hydroidea* contains some of the most familiar *hydrozoans*. Because it is an interesting point of contrast with the order that follows, it is pointed out that the statocysts of the Hydroidea are composed entirely of *epidermal* tissue.

Trachylina

In this order the polyp phase is reduced, or may be absent, and the medusa is relatively large and well-developed. Cells known as *lithocytes*, which secrete the balancing part of the statocyst, are of endodermal origin. *Gonionemus* and its diminutive *polyp-phase* "*Haleremita*," *Craspedacusta* and its tiny polyp "*Microhydra*," and *Liriope*, in which no polyp is known, are in this order.

Skeletons "come and go" among the orders of the Hydrozoa. The Hydroidea show a *proteinaceous* exoskeleton. In the *Trachylina* there is none.

Hydrocorallina

This order is marked by the heaviest skeleton to be found among hydrozoans. It is of calcareous composition and, in this respect, Hydrocorallina may be associated with *coralline algae*, *calcareous Polyzoa* (*Bryozoa*), and *Anthozoan corals*; all of which contribute to coral island and reef formation in warm seas. In the de-emphasis of the medusa phase, *Hydrocorallina* are somewhat like *Hydroidea*.

The medusa of the genus *Millepora*, for example, is much reduced. In Stylaster no *medusa* is known.

Siphonophora

In this order, again, there is no *skeleton*. As mentioned previously, it is most noted for *polymorphism*. No better example of structural and functional differentiation among individuals of the same genus and species can be found anywhere, not even among the insects in which such differentiation is often *spectacular*.

Individuals of the hydranth type are much more apparent in a *Siphonophoran* colony than are medusa types. It is interesting, therefore, that it is believed by some that the entire colony *originates* from a medusa phase.

THE SCYPHOZOA

Of the *scyphozoans* ("*scypho-*," cup), Aurelia has already been considered as a general type form for the phylum. Aurelia may be small or large. In the *polyp* phase, as a *scyphistoma*, it is only a millimeter or so in height. As a medusa it can reach a diameter of a foot or more. But Aurelia is neither the smallest nor the largest of the *Scyphozoa*.

Pelagia forms a fivecentimeter *umbrella*, and may be considered among the smallest of *scyphozoan medusae*. (*Compare*, of course, also with Hydrozoan medusae.) On the other extreme, among the Scyphozoa, there are great gobs of jelly, weighing several hundred pounds. Such is *Cyanea arctica* with an umbrella of seven feet or even more in diameter, and tentacles trailing for as much as one hundred feet below.

A few of the *Scyphozoans*, such as *Haliclystus* and *Lucernaria*, show the *astonishing feature*, among jellyfish, of a *sessile habit*, for which

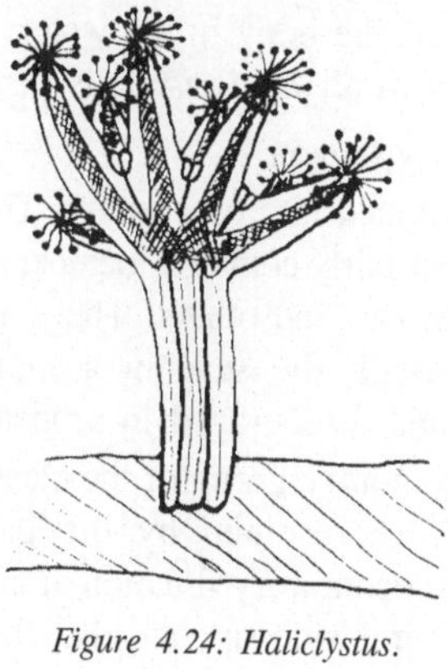

Figure 4.24: Haliclystus.

they are adapted by means of an aboral attaching stalk. Some, as *Chrysaora*, are *luminescent*, and *contribute* to the *widespread bioluminescence* of the seas.

All Scyphozoans are marine. None, apparently, has been able to penetrate the fresh-water realm. In the sea, most are found near the surface, but a few genera extend their range down to about 2000 *fathoms*. In our treatment of *Aurelia* we have already included the characteristics of the class.

Jelly

Now a little more with regard to "*jelly*" since it is, obviously, the jelly that makes the jellyfish. Covering the jelly, the epidermis is only a very thin layer, comparatively, except where it gives rise to other structures such as the tentacles and oral arms. Within the jelly the gastrovascular system consists only of slender tubules, except for the stomach and gastric pouches.

The jelly forms the bulk of the jellyfish. Although the jelly contains wandering ameboid cells-derived from the *endoderm*-and also some strands of solid tissue, for the most part it is a *noncellular mesoglea*. It is the action, by *contraction*, of the umbrella which imparts *locomotory* power to the animal.

Contractile cells are arranged, in the form of circular fibers, around the outer margin of the subumbrella. From the anatomy it is obvious that locomotory movements cannot be very *vigorous*. The jelly bulk of the animal to be moved is too large to be managed effectively by the *amount* of *contractile* tissue available to do the *job*.

And so the *scyphozoan* moves by gentle pulsations which are sufficient to change depth, to come together in schools for reproductive purposes, and for the orientation of the body in the water. But for the pursuit of food its locomotion, as in all *cnidarians*, is *insufficient*.

Classification of the Scyphozoa

Scyphozoans are divided into two orders. The order *Discomedusae* contains Aurelia and other fairly common members of the class *Scyphozoa*, such as *Cyanea*, *Chrysaora*, and others. These are the forms which go pulsing sluggishly through the seas in a manner which might be characterized as tired and discouraged in a normally vigorous animal.

And this is the locomotory group of the class *Scyphozoa* for, in the order *Stauromedusae*, represented by the genera *Haliclystus* and Lucernaria, there is no locomotory function at all. The members of the latter order are found oral side up, attached by means of an *aboral* stalk. In this position they simply lie and wait for things to come their way, thus foreshadowing the mode of life of the *Anthozoan* class.

THE ANTHOZOA

With the Anthozoa ("*antho-*," flower), which include the nonskeleton-forming group of sea-anemones and the skeleton-forming corals, the phylum Cnidaria will be completed. In some of the *anthozoans* there may be hundreds of tentacles arranged around the mouth, and colouration is often brilliant and varied. The class is, therefore, aptly named. Even luminescence is sometimes present, as in the genus *Pennatula*, so that optical awareness extends into the night; but such, of course, bears no relation to flower like qualities.

Among anthozoans there is no other way of life than a sedentary one. *Polyps* give rise to polyps, and there is no alternation of generations. There are no *medusae*. In this respect the Anthozoa are a unique class among cnidarians, for medusa phases are represented within both of the other classes.

Unlike the *scyphozoan*, the *anthozoan* polyp does attain sexual

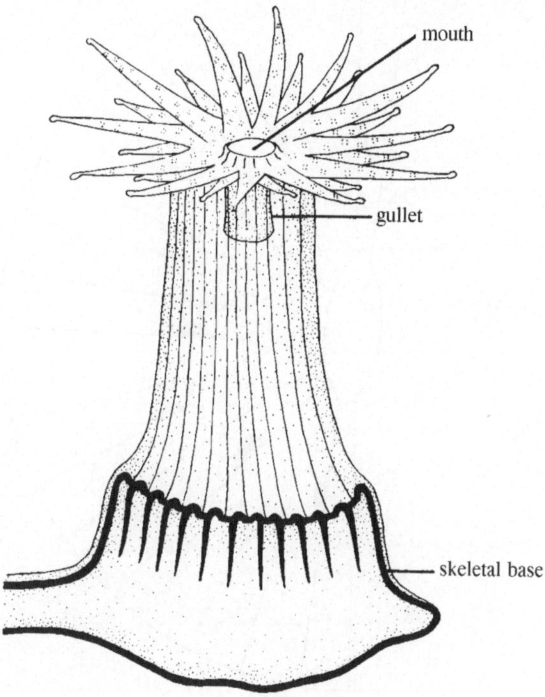

Figure 4.25: Haliclystus.

maturity-as also, but very rarely, does the polyp of the *hydrozoans*. Gonads of *anthozoans* are formed from endoderm and are found in the gastrodermis, like those of the *scyphozoan medusae*. It is interesting to speculate on the possibility of relationship between anthozoans and the sessile *scyphozoan* medusae in the order *Stauromedusae*.

Actinia

Though *Metridium* is often taken as representative of the class Anthozoa, the pattern of growth of Metridium is usually quite irregular. The genus Actinia, found along the eastern shores of the Atlantic-that is, on the European and African coasts-is much more constant in its characteristics, and is therefore preferable as a type.

The body wall of the anthozoan is folded inward at the oral end to form an *ectodermally* lined tube. This is a true gullet, and is one of the distinctions of anthozoan as contrasted with hydrozoan polyps. Since the oral end is flattened at right angles to the length, the *general* shape of the body is that of a squat *cylinder*.

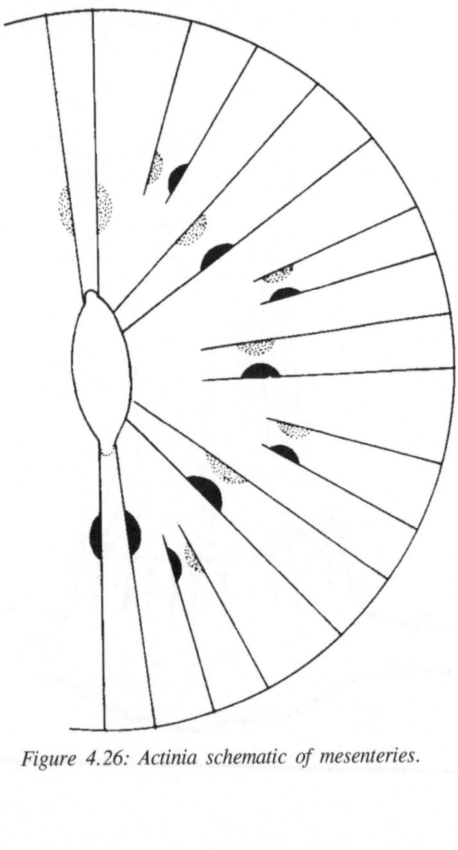

Figure 4.26: Actinia schematic of mesenteries.

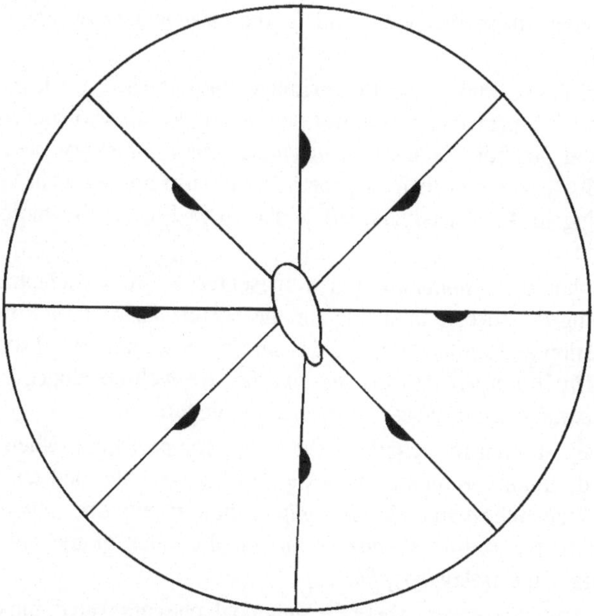

Figure 4.27: Alcyonium mesentery arrangement.

On the oral surface there are *numerous tentacles* which are arranged in *concentric circles*, with the largest number of tentacles contained in the outermost ring. Proceeding inward from the edge of the oral disc, there are in *Actinia circles* of 96, 48, 24, 12, 6, and again 6 immediately around the mouth; 192 tentacles in all.

Thus a large table-like area is adapted for food *capture*, and by consecutive action of the circles of tentacles the food is passed to the center of the oral disc where a slit-shaped mouth is situated. To *ingest* food the entire mouth is opened as required. Also, the corners of the mouth are somewhat *agape habitually*, to give entry into *flagellated* (or ciliated) grooves which extend *lengthwise* on the inner side of the *stomodaeum*.

These, the siphonoglyphes, help to maintain a current of water through the *gastrovascular system* and are of *significance* in *respiratory ventilation* of the interior of the body. Some of the features of the internal *anatomy* of the *anthozoan* are forecast in the *scyphozoan polyp*, for the gastric ridges of the *scyphistoma* may be taken to represent *rudimentary mesenteries*.

The anthozoan also possesses such narrow *mesenteries*, and in *addition* others of various widths. Some of the *mesenteries* extend the full distance from the body wall to the *stomodaeum* where they are attached.

These are known as the primary *mesenteries*. Besides gastric functions, the primary *mesenteries* help to support the stomodaeum, and hold it in position. Other *mesenteriessecondary*, *tertiary*, and so on-successively narrower than the *primaries*, are also *present*. (The condition prevailing in Actinia (*simplified*) is shown in Figure elsewhere in this chapter.)

It should be *understood* that mesenteries are an adaptation for increasing the surface available for the performance of such functions as digestion and *respiration*, besides serving other purposes brought out below. *Incorporated* into the *mesenteries* are well-developed bands of *longitudinal* muscle. These are *retractor* in function.

They shorten the length of the body, for protection when such is required, and act as an aid to egestion of undigestible food residues. In some of the anthozoans, like *Alcyonium*, there is only one *siphonoglyphe* and all of the *retractor muscles* are on the sides of the *mesenteries* which face the *siphonoglyphe*.

In *Actinia* however, where the siphonoglyphes are paired, the retractor muscles are also paired. One set faces one of the *siphonoglyphes*, as in Alcyonium, and the other set is oriented in the opposite direction, toward the *opposite* siphonoglyphe. With respect to these structures Actinia, with other anthozoans, shows bilateral *symmetry*.

Since an over-all radial symmetry is also in evidence, the animals are said to be *biradially symmetrical*. Due to the elaboration of special structural features at the edge of the mesentery, called mesenteric filaments, the free edges of the mesenteries are *trefoil* in shape. The mesenteric *filament* is a compound structure and it has compound functions.

Upon it there are flagellated cells to aid in the circulation of the contents of the gastrovascular cavity, concentrations of cnidoblasts to deliver a “coup de grace” to such food organisms as may still require it, glandular cells for secreting digestive enzymes into the enteron, and, near the base of the filament there are gonads which, it should again be noted, are of endodermal origin.

The upper part (at the oral end of the body) of the primary and secondary mesenteries is perforated by ostia to allow the movement of fluid between adjoining *intermesenteric* pockets of the gastrovascular cavity. The upper part of these mesenteries also contains transverse muscle bands which, on contraction, cause the mouth to gape open for the entry of food. Through the action of a *peripheral sphincter* muscle the entire oral disc of tentacles can be constricted and covered over.

Contractility is, of course, a *prominent* feature of the body wall of the anemone, as well as of the mesenteries. There are longitudinal and transverse strands of contractile cells in both the column of the body and in the tentacles. By means of these the body may be expanded with tentacles extended, like a "*flower*"; or the entire organism may be contracted into a wartlike *protuberance adhering* closely to the substrate on which it is attached.

A slow, creeping *locomotion* is also possible, and the location of the animal in its environment gradually changed thereby. Movements are coordinated by an undifferentiated network of nerve cells, much as in the *hydrozoan* polyp. The sex life of *Actinia* is very similar to that of Aurelia. Again we find an association of the genital with the gastric. Sperm are drawn in by way of the mouth. *Fertilization* and development occur in the "*stomach*," that is, in the coelenteron near the base of the stomodaeum. While in most anthozoans larvae are released in the characteristic planula stage of cnidarians, thus providing a free-swimming dispersal phase, in Actinia *embryos* are retained until the young *anemones* are formed.

By a quick birth contraction of the body the young are then delivered through the mouth into the water outside. Reproduction by budding from the fringes of the pedal disc is common in other anemones, like Metridium. It is interesting to observe this process in a marine aquarium and to see miniature little animals separate from the parent and go their own way,

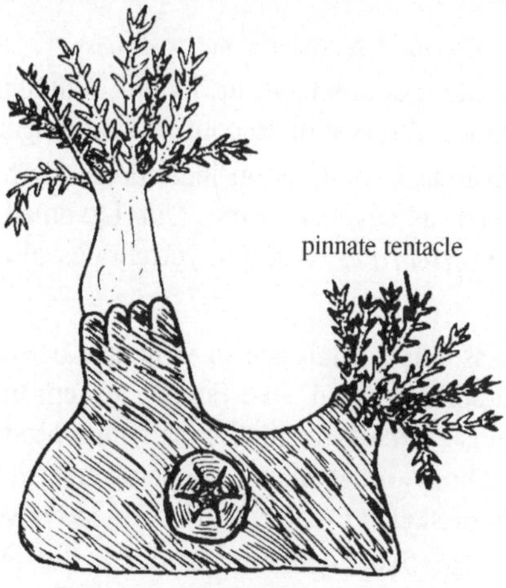

Figure 4.28: Renilla, the "sea-pansy."

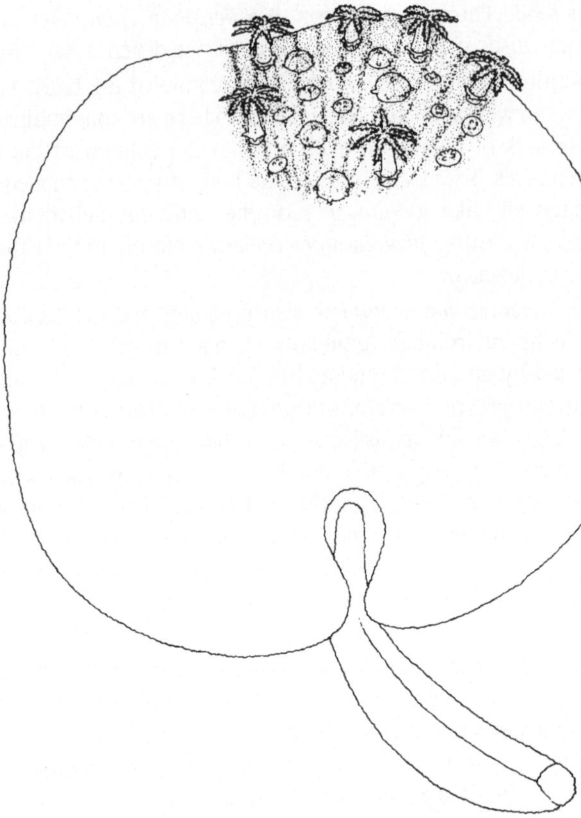

Figure 4.29: Renilla, the "sea-pansy."

but this *asexual* method is unknown in *Actinia*, although this *genus* has been under continuous observation in confinement longer than any other.

In the marine aquaria of London individuals of *Actinia* have been retained for as much as seventy years. This is something of a record for longevity in *invertebrates*, and for vertebrates also.

Corals

There is no essential difference in structure between an anemone like Actinia and a solitary coral, like Fungia, except that the pedal disc of the latter contains *skeleton*-forming cells which produce a calcareous base into which the body of the animal can be contracted to a considerable extent. The ridges of skeletal material are formed between *mesenteries*.

Most corals, e.g., *Astrangia*, are colonial, but the individuals of Astrangia are fairly distinct and each secretes a full calcareous cup which is clearly identifiable in the *aggregate* mass. Sometimes, though, when colonies are formed, fission of the individuals is not complete and this is reflected in the nature of the skeleton. In the brain coral, Meandrina, it is difficult to deduce from the skeleton where the living individuals which produced it were located. Not all colonial forms produce bulky skeletons like that of *Meandrina*.

Some, as Madrepora, build upright antler-like growths and others form skeletons of different shapes, each according to its own kind. A remarkable fact to remember is that these aggregate coral colonies, and their skeletons, are always derived from a single egg.

It would be interesting to know how many eggs are responsible for the great masses of *calcareous* stone which are *incorporated* into the reefs and *atolls* of *tropical* seas.

Orders of the Anthozoa

The corals and the anemones we have so far mentioned belong in the order *Zoantharia*. These animals have a calcareous skeleton, or they have none. They generally possess two *siphonoglyphes* and their mesenteric muscle bands are arranged in sets so that one set faces one of the *siphonoglyphes*, and the other set the opposite *siphonoglyphe*.

Perhaps the most useful of the recognition characteristics of the Zoantharia is that their tentacles are not branched, i.e., they are of the non-pinnate type. The rest of the *anthozoans* are placed in the order Alcyonaria, which have pinnate tentacles. This is not only a *morphological distinction*. It is a *feature* of growth.

When the body branches, buds are produced, when the bud branches, tentacles are formed, and when the tentacles branch a taxonomic feature appears. In the Alcyonaria the budding-gradient extends out into the tentacles. Not so in Zoantharia.

Alcyonaria are provided with only one siphonoglyphe and the mesenteric muscles are all on the side toward the *siphonoglyphe*. Furthermore, unlike Zoantharia in which the skeleton is *external*, Alcyonaria have an endoskeleton formed in the mesoglea and *derived* from *skeleton*-forming cells that have wandered in from the ectoderm.

The difference in location of skeleton is, therefore, a *dynamic* one due to cell migration. Among the *Alcyonaria* we have the genus Alcyonium, which has given the order its name, and also such attractive forms as Tubipora, the organ-pipe coral; Pennatula, the sea-feather; Gorgonia, the sea-fan; *Corallium*, the "*precious coral*"; Renilla, the sea pansy; and many others of equally intriguing shape and colour.

CONCLUSION

From time to time we shall pause in our presentation for the purpose of re-examining our guiding hypothesis in the light of gradually *accumulating* information. Do the *cnidarians*, from *Hydra* to *Renilla*, as we have seen them, make any contribution in support of the viewpoint that focus upon locomotory adaptations will promote an integrated understanding of the many *diversified phyla* of which the animal kingdom is composed?

Here, in the Cnidaria, there is a *phylum* in which the powers of *locomotion* are very *poorly* developed. Yet the predatory way of life has been successfully maintained. The reasons for the low level of locomotory technique have been presented, and are not difficult to understand. Contractile cells in this, their first appearance among *Enterozoa*, are not highly *specialized* for locomotion, nor are they present in number or mass *sufficient* to the task of moving the *comparatively* bulky body from place to place with any degree of ease.

Also the body plan of structure-basically radial and sometimes biradial-is not designed for rapid movement. Under such *conditions* success in predation would ordinarily not be expected. How can we account for it? How does it happen that the oldest phylum of the *Enterozoa* has *survived* without modification of their *predacious* method of *nutrition*?

It seems that this has been possible only because of the presence of nematocysts, an exclusive feature of *Cnidarians*, by means of which pursuit is eliminated as a factor in feeding. Instead of "*running down*" its prey, the *cnidarian* need make only casual contact, brought about largely by the movement of the prey *itself*.

This means that feeding is an accidental rather than a purposeful function; but not requiring the energy for rapid locomotion, nutritional needs are low and can be fulfilled by occasional feedings. In the *phyla* to come, let us observe the development of more efficient *structural* features for locomotion or, in the absence of them, *determine* whether adequate *compensations* are there also present.

5

PHYLUM PLATYHELMINTHES

There are more kinds of worms than one would ordinarily dream. There are flatworms, roundworms, ribbonworms, hairworms, segmented worms, arrow-worms, peanutworms, and even more. Biologically each of these is in a distinct category, but all must have something in common, or they would not be known as worms.

A study of the phylum Platyhelminthes will begin to show what manner of animal a worm is and, specifically, will bring out the nature of the first of the worms, the flatworms. Profound biological events have transpired to produce the wormlike plan of body structure, whose full significance will not be evident until it can be shown what evolved from the worm.

That will come a good deal further along. In order to appreciate a worm we must keep in mind for contrast the more or less radially symmetrical, jelly-bloated, and sluggish bodies of the first enterozoans. Then it becomes apparent that in the worm for the first time in evolutionary history the body of a multicellular animal has been drawn out along a single axis, on a bisymmetrical plan of structure.

This is deeply significant because locomotion can now be accomplished in a unidirectional manner. And with one end of the body habitually moving into new areas of the environment ahead of the rest of the animal, sensory organs can be concentrated at this end and they can be developed to higher levels of specialization.

The chief nervous coordinating centers are associated with the sensory organs at the anterior end and, in this way, a head begins to come into being. At the opposite end, lacking these structures, is the tail. It is interesting that in the first worms, the flatworms, oral and anal do not correspond with head and tail, for the alimentary system still retains the more or less radial pattern found in previous phyla, and is perhaps a little "slow" in catching up with the new design.

Just as the animal stabilizes its direction of movement, it also steadies its position while moving. One side stays down with relation to gravity and contact, the other up; and dorsal and ventral become distinguishable. With anterior head, posterior tail, ventral bottom and dorsal back, right and left follow.

For the pattern of an animal with these newly differentiated regions we have a new name-"bilateral symmetry." And it takes no stretch of the imagination to see that, with bilateral symmetry, new potentials of adaptation are opened up. One surface becomes adapted for contact and locomotion, the opposite for concealment and protection; one end becomes specialized for sensation and ingestion, the opposite for egestion.

These potentials are not realized all at once, but in time, as phylum follows phylum, they come. For the first worms, the Platyhelminthes, more has here been added to the body plan than the change in shape and related features already mentioned. The structure of the middle layer, between epidermis and gastrodermis, has been greatly revised.

This region is no longer essentially a jelly-like substance with wandering cells (and, sometimes, a few strands of fixed tissue) within it. It is now a solid area with some fluid spaces. There has been a reversal of "phase," we might say. And the significance of this change runs far deeper than the physical. There are profound physiological implications. But we will look into these after a description of anatomy.

The epithelia, or covering layers, of invertebrates-Chaetognatha excepted-are composed of only a single layer of cells. The layer that is spread out over the outer surface of the body is entirely derived from embryonic ectoderm and it is named the epidermis. Lining the interior of the enteron is the gastrodermis.

While the gastrodermis originates largely from the embryonic endoderm, often there is more or less invagination of ectodermal tissue at the external openings of the various systems, particularly the digestive system. Between the epidermis and the gastrodermis there may be a minimum of substance as in a Hydrozoan polyp, or a mass of material may be developed here which comes to compose the bulk of the body.

This mass is known as the mesenchyme. The mesenchyme of cnidarians and ctenophores is basically a jelly but it also contains a certain amount of cellular material, most of which has migrated in from the ectoderm.

In flatworms, however, some of the actively dividing cells of the embryonic *endoderm* slip into the space between ectoderm and endoderm. These cells become the embryonic mesoderm, and from them the differentiated cellular masses of the platyhelminth mesenchyme arise. Thus, in *Platyhelminthes*, "true" mesoderm is encountered in large mass for the first time. True mesoderm is provided for in embryological procedure and is derived from embryonic endoderm.

With each of these three regions definite functions are associated, and each of the regions is structurally differentiated accordingly. The epidermis is specifically concerned with such functions as sensation and *locomotion*, and the epidermis also contains the openings which lead into and out of the body.

The gastrodermis of flatworms retains digestive activity but loses the curious relationship to reproduction which was seen in previous phyla. The *mesenchyme* is now essentially a region of muscle; but nervous system originating from ectoderm sinks into it, and reproductive and excretory systems are newly derived from it.

It is probably in relation to the replacement of the noncellular with the cellular in the mesenchyme that we can account for the sharp falling off in bulk of the animal body which occurs in the Platyhelminthes, in contrast to jellyfish and ctenophores. Distribution systems-for oxygen, for food, and for the removal of nitrogenous wastes-are not yet highly developed, and for deep-lying cells this is an acute problem.

One solution to the matter of supply is to have no cell too far either from the outer surface or from the gastric epithelium. This the flatworm has achieved in the shape of the body. Another solution is found in the fact that the body is small. Small size in itself provides a relatively greater surface for the volume involved than if the size of the animal were large.

In spite of small size and flat shape, there is evidence that this first evolutionary "experiment" in replacing mesoglea with mesoderm was not an overwhelming success. There is so much more living substance to feed. Mesoglea required no appreciable nutrition. Mesoderm does. It would seem that the animal would be required to move about more to pick up sufficient food, and yet structures for effective locomotion are conspicuous only by their absence.

The musculature at this stage serves largely for orienting the body.

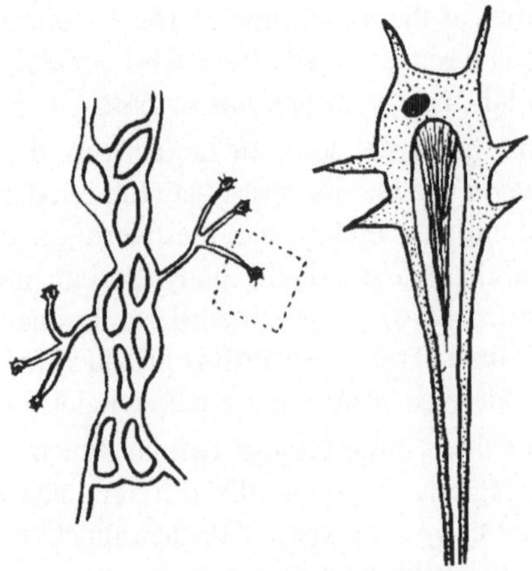

Figure 5.1: Excretory canals and flame cells of Euplararia, a single flame cell enlarged.

The animals can bend, wriggle and squirm; and only to a limited extent can they swim, by means of bodily undulations. On the whole, primitive ciliary locomotion is still much in evidence in flatworms. What is the animal to do? It has a large "family" of living cells to feed, and does not possess the locomotory means for hustling.

It should now be clear why two whole classes of the three in the platyhelminth phylum, and some of the members of the third, became adapted as parasites under the pressures of competition from later forms of life. In the parasitic mode of life the problems introduced by a body newly filled with cells are more easily overcome.

Parasites do not need rapid movement in search for food in amounts sufficient to supply the new cellular region. Food is plentiful all around. The fact that movement is at a low level itself keeps nutritive requirements down, since energy needs are correspondingly low. With a body not strained metabolically there is less need for oxygen and this, apparently, can be supplied by simple diffusion even into the innermost cells, since the body is flat and the distance of any cell from the surface is therefore not too great.

Also, because of the low metabolic level, there is a damped-down production of nitrogenous wastes and a special excretory system is perhaps not to be expected. Nevertheless, the animals of this phylum, for the first time, do (or may) possess an excretory system. Therefore it appears that excretion is the most limiting of the various factors we have been discussing in relation to mesoderm.

Classes of Platyhelminthes

Further understanding of the flatworms will come sooner if we consider the three classes that compose the phylum. These are the class Turbellaria, which is made up almost entirely of the freeliving forms, and the classes Trematoda and Cestoda which consist entirely of platyhelminths which have acquired the parasitic habit.

TURBELLARIA

Turbellaria are generally marine in habitat. Therefore Bdelloura, which is found in ocean waters, would be typical in this respect. However, Euplanaria-also known as Planaria and as Dugesia-is very widely used as a type form, and it lives in fresh water.

Euplanaria and Bdelloura both belong in the order Tricladida, in which crawling by ciliary means (and by means of minute muscular contractions) is 'a common method of locomotion; but Bdelloura can also swim by muscular undulations of the margins of the body.

On the basis of the structure of the gastrovascular system, the class Turbellaria is divided into the orders Acoela, Rhabdocoela, Tricladida, and Polycladida. While the Turbellaria stand out as the only class of free-living flatworms, even in this class the order Rhabdocoela contains members that have taken the way of parasitism-within the digestive tracts of echinoderms and mollusks.

In the Acoela the mouth leads into a loosely packed mass of digestive cells, not arranged in the form or shape of a digestive tract, but functioning as such. Food particles are engulfed by phagocytic cells and digested intracellularly.

It is interesting to note this unusual situation, in which a mouth serves a mass of cells that have not gone beyond the physiological level of protozoans in their nutritive behaviour; just as these animals, on the whole, have not gone beyond protozoans in their method of locomotion.

The genus Convoluta is particularly interesting, for it appears to have given up all new horizons in locomotion and digestion as a "bad job." We find this flatworm lying quietly in the sunlight upon the sand flats at low tide, subsisting upon the products of photosynthetic activity carried on by Phytomastigina with which it has set up a mutualistic relationship.

We might interpret this as evidence that in some of the first triploblastic animals the newly introduced mass of mesodermal cells is more of a burden than an advantage. It appears that the Acoela should be able to make good use of a helping hand from the plant kingdom, for they lack not only a differentiated digestive tract but also the excretory system with which other flatworms are provided. There is no reason to doubt that their plant partners aid in relieving the animals of their metabolic waste products, which would be useful to the plant.

Except for the Acoela, all other orders of the Turbellaria possess a morphologically differentiated digestive system. This may be only in the form of a simple, unbranched sac, as in the Rhabdocoela. In the Tricladida, which are most widely known, the system consists of three main branches, as in Euplanaria.

This is the order commonly referred to as "planarians." Leptoplana may be taken as a representative of the order Polycladida, in which there are a large number of branches to the gastrovascular system; which is here most reminiscent of the condition in scyphozoan medusae. Lacking a circumferential canal, however, the continuous circulation seen in the Scyphozoa cannot take place. We find instead an ebb and flow through the mouth.

The absence of an anus must be a distinct physiological handicap to the flatworms. But if there were to be one anus, there would have to be many-one at the end of each canal. Nature has accomplished many oddities, but hardly ever an animal of multiple ani. Nevertheless, in the flatworm Cycloporus we encounter even this.

Although turbellarians are a marine group, some have moved rather far from the typical realm. Freshwater forms, like Euplanaria, are the

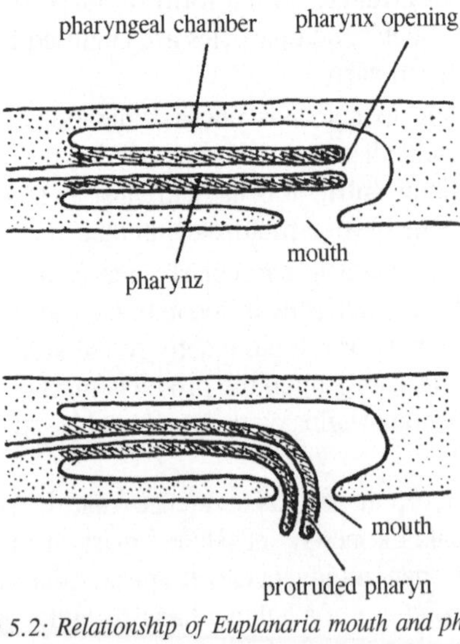

Figure 5.2: Relationship of Euplanaria mouth and pharynx.

most commonly seen; and others, as Mesostoma, occur in mountain waters up to an elevation of 15,000 feet.

It is a strange sensation for humans unaccustomed to high altitudes to penetrate to this height, and it imparts an odd feeling of comfort to find recognizable forms of life there even though they are only on the flatworm level. As it is with altitude, the temperature limits of tolerance are also wide in Turbellaria.

While Mesostoma can live in cold mountain waters, Microstomum may be found in hot springs of almost fifty degrees centigrade, which humans would find quite uncomfortable (heat a pan of water to the indicated temperature and try it; your Fahrenheit thermometer will read 122').

For the first time in multicellular animals, we find terrestrial forms among the flatworms. Bipalium-perhaps the largest of the turbellarians, since it attains a length of about sixteen inches -is found on land, in the tropics. Here is one of the infrequent examples of ciliary locomotion in the terrestrial environment, and it is made possible by the fact that Bipalium lays down a mucus track upon which it glides by means of especially well-developed ventral ciliation. Let us note at this time that a ciliated epidermis is a characteristic of the Turbellaria. Absence of cilia is therefore significant in the other classes of the phylum.

Euplanaria

Now, with Euplanaria as an example, we shall explore the anatomy of a turbellarian. It will be helpful to compare Euplanaria with a scyphozoan of the Aurelia type, and the comparison is facilitated if we assume that the umbrella of Aurelia is drawn out into elongated form.

In each case the body is covered with an epithelium derived from ectoderm, and the digestive system is lined by a gastrodermis entirely or mainly of endodermal origin. With the shape of Aurelia as assumed, the mouth of both animals lies in a midventral, or nearly midventral, location.

While in Aurelia the mouth marks the junction of tissues ectodermally and endodermally derived (respectively), Euplanaria possesses a true stomodaeum because of the embryological invagination of the ectodermal layer at the mouth.

Alimentary System

In Euplanaria the mouth does not itself serve for the ingestion of food, but this statement is not as extraordinary as it may sound. The mouth leads into a pharyngeal chamber in which there lies a protrusible pharynx. In the process of feeding the pharynx is thrust out through the mouth and ingestion is directly into the pharynx.

Although teeth are absent the strong pumping action of the muscular pharynx, aided by digestive enzymes, enables it to separate small particles of food and draw them into the gastrovascular system. Within the animal, through the phagocytic behaviour of the gastrodermal cells, digestion is in large part intracellular.

Sensory and Nervous Systems

Whereas the sensory organs of Aurelia consist of eight tentaculocysts which are evenly distributed around the margin of the umbrella, in Euplanaria organs for sensation occur in pairs. There are two eyes on

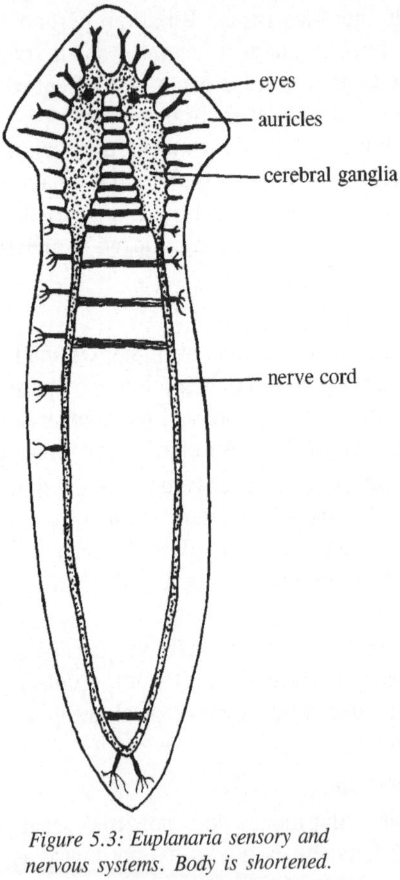

Figure 5.3: Euplanaria sensory and nervous systems. Body is shortened.

the dorsal surface of the "head," which is not yet fully a head-there is no mouth here, for example. A pair of lateral chemosensitive auricles, provided with ciliated grooves for more effectively sampling the nature of the medium, is also part of the head.

In some other flatworms the distribution of eyes is more comparable to Aurelia. Polycelis has multiple eyes, in two diffuse groups on the anterio-lateral margins of the body. Leptoplana has eyes in four groups, and Geoplana has its eyes scattered all around the margin of the body.

Under the elongated condition postulated for Aurelia, the nervous system would take the form of a rather diffuse oval ring of nerve cells. This is somewhat similar to the condition in Euplanaria. In the latter, however, the nerve cells are condensed into definite cords somewhat like the heavier concentrations of nerve cells in the vicinity of the tentaculocysts of Aurelia.

Euplanaria shows two major nerve centers-the pair of cerebral ganglia that lie appropriately near the eyes. In addition to the nerve ring, or nerve cords, there is in both animals a diffuse subepidermal nerve cell network.

Musculature

Between epidermis and gastrodermis the main bulk of the Aurelia body consists of a mesenchyme which is largely noncellular. The Euplanaria mesenchyme, on the other hand, is a spongy parenchyma filled with tissues and organs mainly of mesodermal origin; foremost among these being true muscle.

In the outer region of the body the muscle strands are oriented in a circular pattern around the short axis of the body and their contraction accordingly constricts and lengthens the body. The inner muscle strands run longitudinally. Contraction of the longitudinal muscle shortens and thickens the body. In the pharynx the above order of arrangement of muscles is reversed.

Reproductive System

The reproductive system, which in Aurelia was associated with the gastrodermis, now in Euplanaria is derived from the mesoderm and lies within the mesenchyme. Special ducts, for the transport of genital products, appear for the first time.

Many testes are spread along each side of the body. These are drained by a pair of sperm ducts which lead into a muscular penis found in the genital chamber. A genital pore allows the penis to be extended out of the chamber for copulation.

Like almost all Platyhelminthes, Euplanaria is hermaphroditic. There is much to be said in favour of this condition. First is the fact that only an arithmetic pair of two animals, and not the more selective biological pair of male and female, is required to carry on the reproductive process. Also, one mating produces two batches of young.

Obviously, hermaphroditism has the potential of being more productive of young forms and more economical of parental forms than does the dioecious condition. Euplanaria carries its ovaries in its head, just behind the eyes; a rather unusual location for gonads. Oviducts run the length of the animal to the genital chamber, and along the way receive the products of yolk glands which are dispersed throughout the body.

As a pocket extending out from the side of the genital chamber there is a pouch which serves a vaginal purpose. At copulation the penis of each worm, reciprocally, is introduced through the genital pore into the vaginal pouch of the other and sperms are mutually discharged. After copulation the sperm migrate along the oviduct and fertilize the eggs upon their release from the ovaries. As the zygotes then move down the oviducts they are joined by yolk cells.

Each zygote, together with a group of yolk cells, is encapsulated and laid through the genital pore. In the physiology of this system provision is made for nourishing the cleaving embryo. In about fourteen days, a minute worm hatches out of the capsule. Thus in the Platyhelminthes, the deeper location of the gonads necessitates ducts for genital discharge, found in this phylum for the first time in the animal kingdom.

Specialized portions of the genital ducts serve as organs of sexual contact, and fertilization is internal. It should be understood that discharge

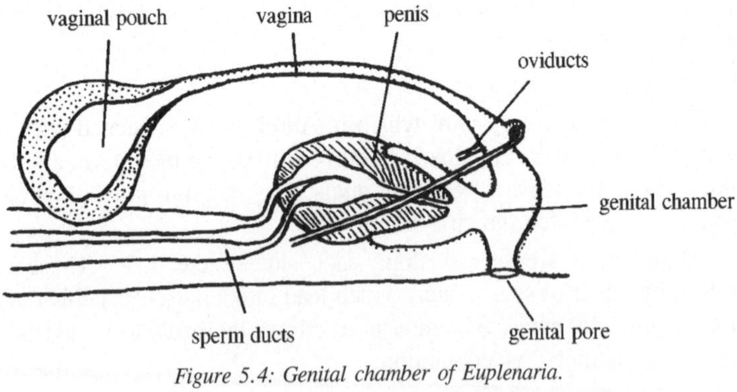

Figure 5.4: Genital chamber of Euplenaria.

of gametes into the water would not be as certain to insure the bringing together of gametes as is fertilization within the confines of the genital system. The provision of yolk for nourishment of the embryo so that it is enabled to hatch out in a feeding condition is an adaptation which likewise should not be overlooked.

In all cases we shall find that the reproductive system of flatworms is highly developed. The consequent production of greater numbers of offspring in a more advanced stage of embryology-and also the widespread parasitic habit in the phylum-are factors which tend to compensate for the difficulties of adjustment to the newly developed triploblastic plan of body structure.

EXCRETORY SYSTEM

The present cellular status of the mesenchyme relieves the epidermis of the need for contractile function, and relieves the gastrodermis of reproductive function. Each of these layers can now serve more primary uses. The epidermis, being an environmental contact layer, can now be more fully adapted in relation to environmental stimulation, and the gastrodermis can be devoted exclusively to gastronomic function.

But the development of the mesenchyme as a cellular region results in the formation of metabolic wastes that are secluded from contact with the fluids of either the environment or the gastrovascular system. Provision is required for ventilation, and such provision is found in a specialized excretory mechanism now appearing for the first time.

This first excretory adaptation of a multicellular animal is in the form of a diffuse system of scattered flame cells. Each of the cells contains an invaginated fluid area in which there is located a tuft of cilia. The beat of the cilia, in life, imparts to the tuft its characteristic flickering appearance-hence the name. (The flickering of the ciliary "flame" may be observed most easily in rotifers under high magnification, but detection requires care and patience.)

The action of the cilia presumably tends to move the fluid out of the pocket of the hollow cell into a connected excretory canal. There are two systems of canals in Euplanaria, one along each side of the body, and they are drained by a series of excretory pores on the dorsal side.

A distinction is often drawn between excretory function-that is the disposition of nitrogenous wastes-and the maintenance of water balance in the body. It is true that more or less water doubtless finds its way into the animal under the impetus of osmotic pressure, and that the excretory system plays a role in osmoregulation.

However, it should be noted that water is also inevitably produced in the body by oxidation of carbohydrate. This is a true excretory product, and it is excreted through the flame cell system. Even if the flame cells discharged water only, they would still be excretory organs.

But besides, at least part of the end-products of protein metabolism, i.e., nitrogenous wastes, must also find their way out through the flame cells; and so the flame cell serves both in true excretion and for water regulation, as do the excretory organs of higher animals.

The ramifying nature of the excretory and of the digestive systems at this level of evolution can be understood in relation to the absence of a separate system for circulation. Since there is no circulating body fluid, which would carry materials from the tissues to localized organs for processing, these "organs" must here extend to the tissues where such materials are formed or are needed.

Excretory Systems in the More Evolved Enterozoa

Having briefly considered the first appearance of specialized excretory structures among the simpler animals, we will interrupt the discussion of flatworms for a general consideration of excretion as a metabolic process, and the ways it is carried out by morphological adaptations.

A living cell is a consumer and also a producer. The cell consumes materials required to build up and maintain the complex organization of its protoplasm. These substances are the nutrients. In its activity the cell also produces substances that are disposed of outside of the cell boundaries. These are excreta, and the function which deals with them is known as excretion.

We have seen that, with the appearance of a mesodermal cell mass to replace the noncellular mesoglea, the need for excretion becomes critical to the organism as a whole. Then, in the Platyhelminthes, a special excretory system is first evolved.

Just as matter cannot enter the cell except when dispersed into particles of molecular size, which can be held in true solution, so also nothing can leave the cell that is not in the same conditionegestion in phagocytic cells is, of course, excepted.

If we confine ourselves to a single tissue cell there is no special problem involved in excretion. The process occurs by means of molecular diffusion in accordance with concentration gradients, as in protozoans. For example, one of the substances constantly being produced within the cell is carbon dioxide.

As a consequence the concentration of carbon dioxide molecules within the cell sooner or later exceeds the concentration level outside. By the process of diffusion these molecules tend to disperse from regions in which they are more highly concentrated and this leads them to move out of the cell.

Cells produce many kinds of diffusible substances, which may be wastes to the producing cells themselves, but not necessarily so to the organism as a whole. Carbon dioxide itself is such a substance. On the one hand it is a cellular waste of metabolism, but on the other it enhances the ability of the protoplasm to take up oxygen.

In this respect a cell waste acts as a hormone, catalyzing a vital protoplasmic function. Other substances, too, discharged as wastes by specific types of cells, exert hormonic effects on the growth and function of the organism.

With this understanding that cells produce many kinds of chemical materials as a result of their metabolism and that these materials are wastes in the sense that they are discharged from the cells, we shall confine our consideration of excretion to its usual meaning, i.e., the disposal of the common wastes of protein metabolism. Since proteins are distinctively nitrogenous substances, the wastes produced in protein metabolism are nitrogenous wastes.

At their simplest, protein derivatives are in the form of ammonia (NH_3). Ammonia is toxic to life and if allowed to accumulate in any appreciable concentration would harm the organism. Therefore it must be kept in diluted form. This requires much water, and indicates why water is so much a part of the excretion process. It also shows why ammonia is a suitable nitrogenous excretion only in aquatic animals, where water is plentiful and expendable.

When the conditions as stated are proper, the formation of ammonia provides a good mechanism for the disposal of nitrogenous wastes. Ammonia diffuses readily through cell membranes and is easily gotten rid of. By combination with carbon dioxide ammonia can be converted to urea, $CO(NH_2)_2$. In comparable concentrations urea is less toxic than ammonia. The organism can tolerate larger amounts of urea. But, like ammonia, urea is highly soluble and the problem of water attraction remains. Even though the toxicity factor is reduced, on physical (osmotic) grounds the tissues can-not tolerate much urea.

An accumulation of any soluble substance has the osmotic effect of holding an amount of water bound in the tissues until the substance is disposed of. If urea were produced in the organism faster than it could be discharged there would be the stresses of swelling to contend with. It is interesting that by the conversion of ammonia to urea the animal is also relieved of the end products of carbohydrate metabolism, since carbon dioxide and water are formed in the oxidation of carbohydrates.

Not only is the carbon dioxide utilized in the chemical change of ammonia to urea, but the water serves to transport the urea out of the animal. Inasmuch as water is so closely tied to the excretion of metabolic wastes, we might expect that this would express itself in the chemical adaptation of terrestrial animals to this function. For many terrestrial animals water is a very scarce commodity, and their survival might depend on the ability to conserve water within the body.

In this light we can understand the evolution of uric acid as an excretory product. Uric acid ($C_5H_4O_3N_4$) is only slightly water-soluble. Accumulated nitrogenous wastes are precipitated out of solution as uric acid, which can be stored in minimal amounts of water. Uric acid also has the virtue of low toxicity. But, being only slightly soluble, uric acid cannot be readily moved out of a living cell.

Therefore transport across the cell membranes must take place in simple form such as ammonia. Only within the tubules of the excretory system-where movement of the waste requires no further passage across living cell membranes—is it feasible for the conversion to uric acid to take place. The phylum Platyhelminthes is the first to show a tubular excretory system.

This is a system of the protonephridial type; in which the tubules are closed at their inner ends by flame bulbs. Later on we shall encounter more advanced excretory structures in which the tubules are open at both the inner and outer ends. (How will copious loss of the body fluids be prevented?) There are also invertebrate excretory systems composed of compact organs localized in one region of the body.

These require a circulating body fluid to carry the wastes to them for separation. While in most invertebrates excretion is performed by a system separate and distinct from other systems of the body, this is not always so. In insects, for example, there is an unusual uroalimentary association in which the excretory tubules discharge into the alimentary tract, and the excreta are subject to the dehydrating properties of the lower intestine where water is reclaimed from them.

The urogenital association, so well known among vertebrates, finds its counterpart among invertebrates like annelid worms, where the nephridia may serve to transport genital products during the reproductive season.

TREMATODA

Competitive stresses of life in the open are absent in the Trematoda since all the members of the class are parasites; with all of the advantages and special difficulties of that mode of life. Young flukes (note the dangers of popular terminology, since a "fluke" is both a fish and a worm), however, are free-living like Turbellarians, and like Turbellarians they are provided with a ciliated epidermis for swimming and with a pair of eyes for phototactic response.

But the young free-living fluke, known as a miracidium larva, has no alimentary system and no reproductive system. As a miracidium it lives a very limited life. It swims restlessly, but cannot feed. It is not attracted to other individuals of its own kind but, upon contacting the soft body of another animal, it is induced to whirl and bore against the surface.

If the host is suitable -usually a snail-the miracidium may succeed in puncturing the skin, with the aid of a digestive enzyme externally secreted by the apical snout. Thereupon, utilizing its muscular power, it squirms through into its host. Usually at this time, or very shortly thereafter, the miracidium sheds its epidermis, including eyes and cilia,

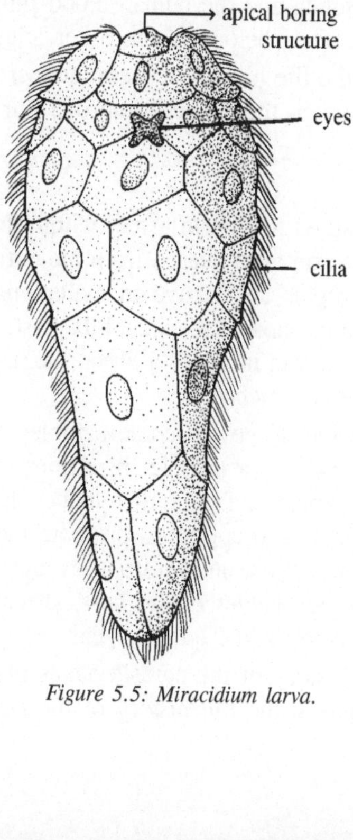

Figure 5.5: Miracidium larva.

so ending the phase of resemblance to members of the class Turbellaria. It is interesting that trematodes in the adult stage are diploblastic, but clearly this is not the primitive diploblasty of previous phyla like the Cnidaria.

It is secondarily acquired as an adaptation to parasitism, through the loss of the epidermis. The outermost part of the post-miracidium body consists of a protective cuticle, thought to be derived from the mesenchyme.

The lack of an epidermis, and its replacement *in position by the cuticle, is one of the important structural differences between adult trematodes and the turbellaria. A more obvious difference is the presence of muscular suckers ("trema," sucker). The appearance of a hypertrophied section of the oviduct, to form a uterus for the storage of eggs in large numbers, is also a noteworthy feature of the trematodes not found in turbellarians.

On the basis of their life history Trematoda are divided into two groups. Some, like the genus Polystoma of the frog, live in only a single host and are accordingly placed in the order Monogenea. More usually, two or more hosts are involved in the life of a trematode. Of such, the sheep liver fluke Fasciola and the human blood fluke Schistosoma are prominent examples. They belong in the order Digenea.

Let us examine the life history of these and certain other members of the Trematoda, and in the process improve our knowledge of the class.

Polystoma

Polystoma is adapted for life in urine, within the bladder of frogs. Eggs of the mature worm are released from the parent in the spring of the year-when the frog is also active in ovulationand are discharged with the urine through the cloacal opening of the host. After embryonating for about four weeks within its shell, a larva, the miracidium-with cilia and two pairs of eyes-is hatched.

The frog eggs have by now become tadpoles and the miracidium attaches itself to the gills of a tadpole, by means of a circle of hooks at the posterior end. Whatever factors then induce metamorphosis of the tadpole to an adult frog also appear to promote metamorphosis in the parasite, for when the tadpole metamorphoses and resorbs its gills the parasite migrates to the bladder of the host, sheds its epidermis, and the six attaching suckers of the adult appear.

The whole life history of the parasite takes place in a single host and is synchronized with the life history of the host.

Fasciola

The year 1883 was outstanding in parasitology, for then the first life history of a trematode was completely worked out.' This is a task only for the consecrated. Sometimes many years of discouraging search are needed to track a parasite through its various forms and hosts.

Many life histories are still open, despite devoted efforts. The first completed life history was that of the sheep liver fluke, *Fasciola hepatica*, now a classic example of the group.

Egg cells of the adult fluke, which resides in the liver, are discharged with the feces, via bile duct and intestine. Embryonation produces the miracidium with its significant apical structure for boring into the next host, in this case the snail Lymnaea. If unsuccessful in finding a host, the life span of the miracidium is limited to a few hours.

Within the snail the miracidium is converted into a sporocyst stage, wherein asexual reproduction by means of internal budding takes place. The buds, known as rediae, leave the confines of the sporocyst and infiltrate farther into the tissues of the host where they again reproduce by the same method as before.

Within a number of weeks after a miracidium enters a snail, parasites in the cercarial stage emerge from it. The cercaria is a free-

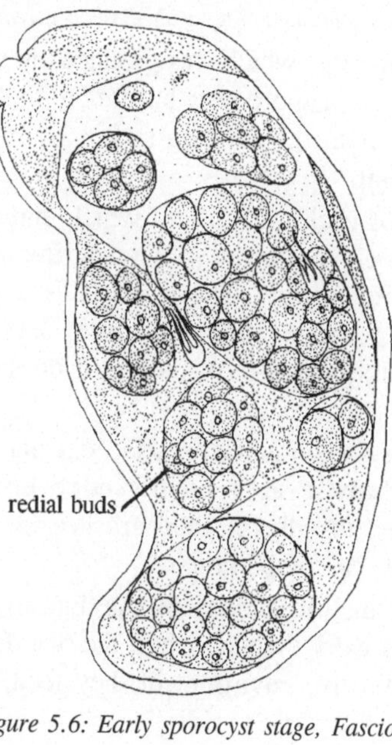

Figure 5.6: Early sporocyst stage, Fasciola.

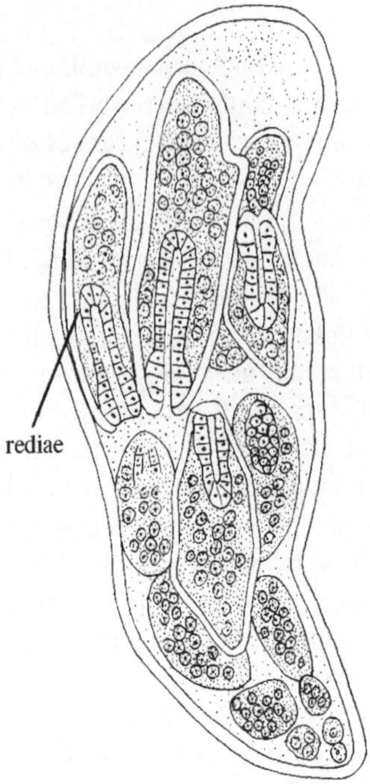

Figure 5.7: Later sporocyst stage with developed rediae. Fasciola.

swimming, free-living stage which was produced in the snail by budding from redial ancestors in a sporocyst; but unlike the miracidium, which moved by means of cilia, the cercaria swims by muscular undulations of the tadpole-like tail.

The fact that, for each miracidium which enters the snail, tens of thousands of cercariae swim away, obviously improves the chances of completion of the life history. The cercaria is a young fluke of the sexual generation. It possesses the rudiments of the organ systems of the adult. Although at first a free-living form, it does not long remain as such.

Soon it encysts, as a metacercaria, casting off its tail in the process. If sheep browse at a pond's edge upon grass to which metacercariae happen to adhere, the parasites are ingested and their life history continues to completion.

The cyst wall is dissolved away by the digestive juices of the host, and the young flukes work their way into the bile duct and arrive in the liver. In this rich nutritive environment they feed, grow, and become sexually mature.

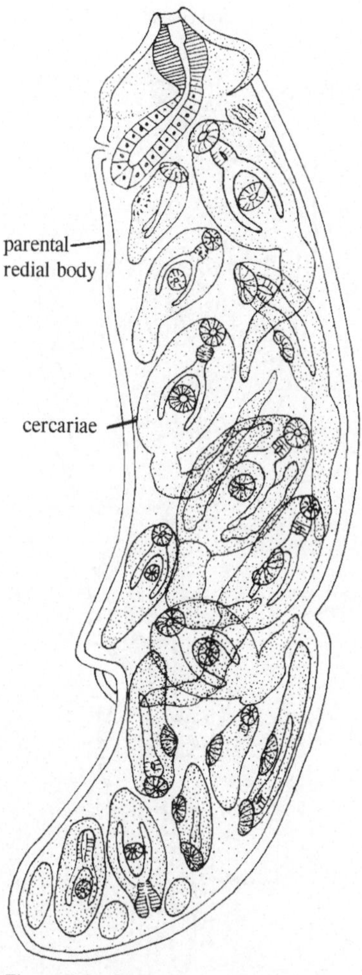

Figure 5.8: Cercarial sporocysf, Fasciola.

Body Structure of a Trematode

As we have seen, an adult fluke differs from a turbellarian in the lack of an epidermal layer with its derivatives, the cilia and the eyes. It is therefore significant that these parts are present in the young liver fluke, of miracidial stage, where they provide an instance of the biological phenomenon of recapitulation.

The miracidium is free-living and the adult is parasitic. Obviously the loss of structures is due to evolutionary atrophy, a process of negative selection in relation to the parasitic habit. For an animal situated

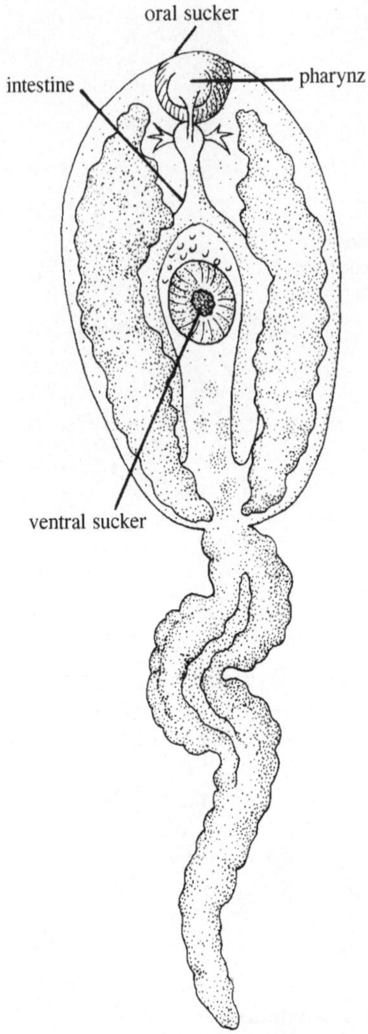

Figure 5.9: Cercaria, Fasciola.

as it is deep within the tissues of the liver, eyes would be a useless extravagance of structure; and the small translocations of the parasite within the liver are better effected by muscular movements than they would be by ciliary action. When these changes due to parasitism are excepted, then a trematode and a turbellarian have much in common.

In both, the digestive tract is of the vascular type. Euplanaria, with the mouth ventrally located, has three main branches to the gastrovascular system.

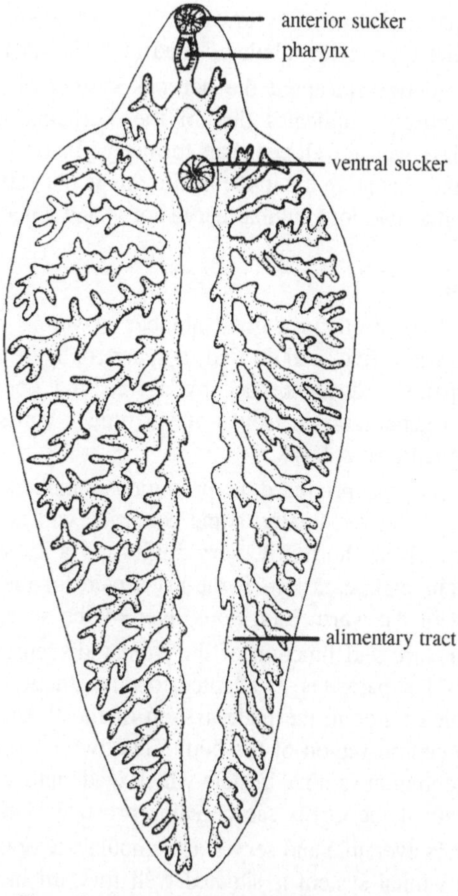

Figure 5.10: Fasciola gastrovascular system.

In Fasciola there are two main branches. But in the latter the mouth has moved forward in position, and now lies within an anterior sucker. It is as if the anterior branch of the triclad were moved completely out of the body as the mouth shifted forward. About one third of the distance from the an terior sucker there is another, but this is a holdfast structure and has nothing to do with ingestion.

The excretory system of Trematoda, like that of the Turbellaria, consists of flame cells, or flame bulbs as they are sometimes called, which drain into excretory tubules. Something new has been added in the trematode in the form of a urinary bladder, which collects wastes from the excretory canals and discharges them through a single terminal pore at the posterior end of the animal. In both of these classes of flatworms, and in the one to follow also, the excretory system is of the protonephridial type, with tubules closed at their inner ends.

Little need be said about the nervous system of the Trematoda, since it so closely duplicates that of the Turbellaria. The cerebral ganglia are less well developed than formerly. In view of the absence of eyes and the change in the mode of life this is not surprising. Besides cerebral ganglia, two longitudinal nerve cords and a nerve net complete the system.

Reproduction

Beca t of the need for a great number of young in the life cycle we might expect to find, and do find, a hypertrophy of the reproductive system. A parasite does not occupy a free and open range. From generation to generation or from time to time it can survive only by change to specific new hosts.

Young must be produced in prodigious numbers and cast forth widespread so that, eventually, some cercariae will arrive in the liver of additional sheep hosts. A very high mortality rate among the youngmiracidia and cercariae—is the price paid for the life of ease led by the adult in the warm, nutritious liver of the sheep.

The structure and function of the trematode reproductive system, like that of other parasites, is adapted to this situation. There are two much-branched testes in the male system of the fluke, one behind the other in the central region of the body. The two sperm ducts combine and form a common seminal vesicle which leads into a muscular cirrus sac. The wall of the cirrus sac contains prostate glands.

The sac is eversible and serves as a copulatory organ. The opening of the male genital system is situated well forward in the animal, just behind the fork of the two main intestinal canals. In the female system there is a single branched ovary which lies between the acetabulum (ventral sucker) and the testes.

A short oviduct conducts the eggs into a long coiled uterus which opens at the base of the cirrus sac, near the male gonopore. Apparently to facilitate fertilization, there is a separate duct, Laurer's canal, which extends inward from the copulatory opening on the dorsal side of the animal and meets with the oviduct. The latter is also joined by a common yolk duct which, through subsidiary ducts, drains the very extensive system of yolk glands.

The point where the oviduct and yolk duct join marks the beginning of the uterus. The uterus is a large and much coiled structure built to accommodate the eggs, enlarged with yolk, that descend from the ovary in a never ending stream. But the uterus is more than a storage organ. Its first run is surrounded by shell glands, or Mehlis' glands, and is referred to as the ootype. Here each egg, with its measure of yolk, is enclosed in a capsule. The main portion of the uterus, which follows, is utilized for egg storage. Aside from the general overdevelopment of the system, the appearance of a uterus is the chief distinction between trematode and turbellarian reproductive structures.

Comparative Life Histories of the Trematoda

We have seen that the new way of life in the Trematoda removes the need for open competition for food, and eliminates locomotion as a limiting factor in survival. An entirely different requirement is introduced however, that of finding a host. Perhaps we should not say entirely different, for in both cases food is of the essence.

But to feed upon the prey from the outside when the predator is larger and to feed upon the prey from the inside when the predator is smaller requires different techniques for finding the food. Toward this end interesting adaptations have been evolved to aid in the completion of the life cycle of a parasite.

Besides the two examples already given, of Polystoma and Fasciola, several additional cases will aid in rounding out this part of the trematode story

Haematoloechus (Pneumoneces)

If one performs even occasional dissections of freshly killed frogs it is difficult to avoid detecting the frog lung-fluke, Haematoloechus. For this parasite the life history is only incompletely known. A dragonfly, Sympetrum, which serves as food for the frog, brings in the metacercarial stage.

In the stomach of the frog the metacercariae hatch and the young flukes migrate through the esophagus to the glottis and then down to the lungs. Here they mature and reproduce. It is known that the nymph stage of the dragonfly "ingests" young cercariae by way of the rectum which, in this animal, serves the unusual function of respiration.

But in the direction from frog to insect there are gaps in the knowledge of the life history. How does the parasite leave the lung of the frog and then get to the dragonfly? Proof is required, not conjecture.

Opisthorchis (Clonorchis)

Man is by no means exempt as a host for trematode parasites. One of the most important in the Orient is Opisthorchis, more generally known as Clonorchis, which lives in the human bile duct. Embryonated egg capsules, containing miracidia, are discharged with the feces. These miracidia are atypical in that they are not free-swimming, but hatch only if they are first ingested by a snail, Bythinia.

In the snail host the usual redial and cercarial generations are formed; and the latter leave the snail. If Opisthorchis cercariae behaved in the same way as Fasciola, i.e. encysted on grass, the further continuation of the life history would be greatly jeopardized (but, for some humans, not entirely eliminated).

Fortunately for the survival of this genus, the tropisms of its cercariae lead not to encystment but to penetration of the flesh of a fish which is much used as human food; of the family Cyprinidae (carp), in fresh water. Add to this the fact that fish is often eaten raw in the Orient and it becomes apparent how the life cycle is completed. Perhaps we begin to see better now why predation from the inside of the prey involves special adaptations.

Schistosoma (Bilharzia)

For very special reasons we include the human blood fluke Schistosoma, or Bilharzia, which is the same but by another name. It was pointed out above that all Platyhelminthes are hermaphroditic. Schistosoma is an exception to the rule. Not only are the individuals of separate sex, but the sexes are dimorphic in structure and unusual in behaviour.

The female is longer and more slender than the male and, whether by preference or not, she is never found alone. The females, indeed, remain sexually immature unless in association with males. In a longitudinal fold of the body the male carries a female with him wherever he goes. The animals always occur in pairs in the rich blood of the hepatic portal system of man.

Not only is food no problem in this habitat but, through the pairing habit, mating is no problem either. The female leaves the male temporarily only to lay her eggs. Even while still encapsulated within the egg shell, the miracidia developing within are capable of a histolytic action upon the tissues of the human host.

This is of aid to them in their migration into the intestine and also into the bladder; and they emerge from the human host via the orifices of both these organs. The next phase is aquatic. The miracidia now hatch from the eggs and penetrate into a snail where they go through several generations and emerge as cercariae.

The cercariae enter the human host, but do not seem able to survive the environment of the stomach. If they enter by way of the mouth they go directly into the blood through the mouth membranes; or they may bore through the outer skin of the body. The latter opportunity is afforded to them by the human host while bathing, a habit which is otherwise not to be condemned.

It is interesting that all of the individuals derived from one egg, through the miracidial and cercarial generations, are of the same sex. Therefore cercariae of potentially opposite sex must enter the human in order to set up mating pairs.

Both Schistosoma and Opisthorchis are said to be able to live in man for as much as thirty years. Not only does this appear to be an extraordinarily long life span for this type of an animal, but the duration indicates that the relationship need not be particularly devastating to the host.

CESTODA

This, the final class of the phylum Platyhelminthes, carries the account of parasitism further along its way. While in trematodes free life is retained in the larval state, almost all of the cestodesthe tapeworms-are parasitic at all points of the life history. And, where trematodes have lost their epidermis, cestodes have lost both epidermis and gastrodermis.

We have here, therefore, a most unusual type of animal-made up largely of the derivatives of only one body layer, the mesoderm. (How about the nervous system?) Adult tapeworms are almost invariably found within the intestine of vertebrates. This location, with digested food all around them simply for the taking, must indeed be close to a worm "heaven."

There is no need for locomotion in quest of food; and there are no locomotory structures. Therefore even the musculature of the body-which would need to be developed for locomotion-is reduced. Ectoderm and endoderm are gone. Mesoderm is reduced. How much can there possibly remain?

Reproductive organs, and very little more, as we shall see. In structural degeneration the price of parasitism can be very high, and whereby parasitism imposes a peculiar type of life upon the individual the species is enabled to survive. Without implying that there is necessarily any evolutionary significance in this procedure, let us build up the body of a typical tapeworm, starting with the simpler forms.

At once we are confronted with an exception to the statement that all tapeworms live in the intestines of vertebrates. There is a little red annelid worm, Tubifex, which harbors within it an even smaller tapew-

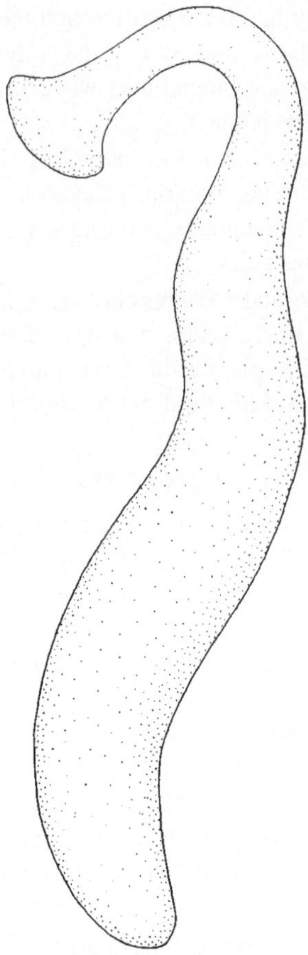

Figure 5.11: Caryophyllaeus.

orm, Archigetes. This is the only known cestode which matures within an invertebrate host. Archigetes is about a half-centimeter long, with a pair of shallow suckers at one end and a narrow tail region at the other.

The body is covered with a cuticle, and cilia, of course, are absent. The interior is made up almost entirely of reproductive organs. The egg hatches a sixhooked larva, the hexacanth stage, which is typically cestode.

Also cestode is the absence of an alimentary system. If not for the nature of the larva and the absence of intestine, Archigetes might be taken for a trematode. There are other cestodes too-such as Caryophyllaeus, Amphilina, and Gyrocotyle-which don't look like tapeworms, but nevertheless are tapeworms. This raises the question as to what causes a worm to look like a tapeworm, and when is the worm actually a tapeworm?

Briefly, a worm is a tapeworm when it is a platyhelminth without digestive system and without an ectodermally derived epidermis. To

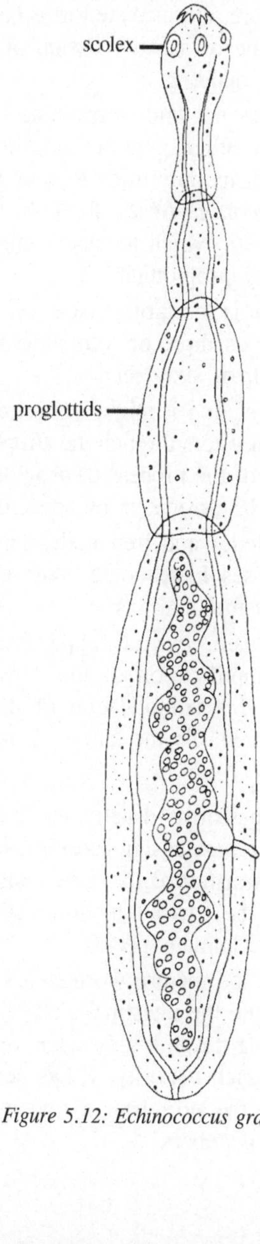

Figure 5.12: Echinococcus granulosus.

look like a tapeworm the animal must have an additional qualification. It must have a body composed of units called proglottids and an anchoring section, the scolex.

But there are a few tapeworms, as those named above, which possess a single-unit body, while others, yet to be mentioned, have a great many units, and there are intermediate forms between. The process of forming proglottids is one of asexual fission of the scolex (scolex means worm) by transverse budding.

When the "scolex" does not bud, forms like Caryophyllaeus and Gyrocotyle are found. In other genera budding is very limited. *Echinococcus granulosus* forms only three or four proglottids. Six are a feature of *Davainea proglottina* of the fowl. In the smallest human tapeworm, *Hymenolepis nana*, which attains a length of about a half-inch, there are up to twenty proglottids.

Diphyllobothrium latum is the largest tapeworm found in humans, and there may be as many as three or four thousand proglottids in a rather awesome total length of sixty feet.

On the basis of the foregoing it might be assumed that tapeworms arose from trematode-like ancestors through the atrophy of the alimentary system and the appearance of the process of proglottid formation. This view is, however, held to be erroneous by specialists in the group.

It is believed that cestodes and trematodes have had independent origins and that both classes have come, but separately, from the parasitismprone rhabdocoel turbellarians.

Where there is parasitism, two accompanying effects are to be expected. These are a simplification of the general body structure (reproductive excepted) and a complication of the life history. The former we have already noted. To the latter we now turn once more.

Life History

The life history of tapeworms usually involves an alternation of hosts, but not always so. Archigetes egg capsules, for example, may be picked up by one Tubifex worm directly from another. The life history of Hymenolepis can also be carried to completion within a single host, usually a child of the human species.

Embryos produced by the mature worms pass out with the feces, or they may bore instead into the intestinal wall of the same individual and from there, first passing through a cysticercus stage, return to the lumen of the intestine to reach maturity. It has been found with other genera of tapeworms that the presence of one parasite in hibits the development of additional members.

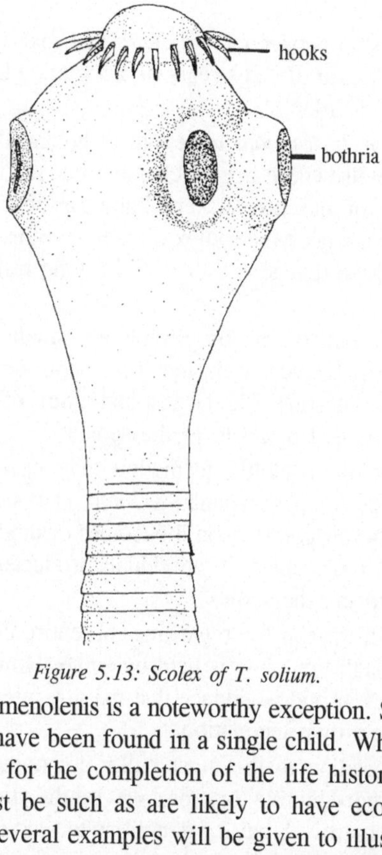

Figure 5.13: Scolex of T. solium.

Therefore, Hymenolenis is a noteworthy exception. Several thousand of these parasites have been found in a single child. When two or more hosts are required for the completion of the life history, it is obvious that the hosts must be such as are likely to have ecological contacts with each other. Several examples will be given to illustrate this point.

Of three tapeworms that live in man, *Taenia solium*, *T. saginata*, and *Diphyllobothrium latum*, the young stages of the first two are found in animals which are used as human food-those of *T. solium* in the pig, and those of *T. saginata* in beef.

It is easy to see how they get into the human. But the young stages of *D. latum* live in a small crustacean. Here a third host, a fish eaten by man, is found in the life history. For *Dipylidium caninum*, which attains maturity in the intestine of the dog, it is apparent that the flea serves admirably as an intermediate host.

And *Otobothrium crenacolle* (*Poronotus tricanthrium*) of the shark, is found encysted when young in the flesh of the butterfish. *Taenia saginata* and *D. latum* are treated below as examples of the common life histories. Since, as humans, we ourselves are their hosts, perhaps we owe them special mention.

Taenia Saginata

The relationship between *T. saginata* and man has been known to endure for life. A case of sixty years of association between a man and his worm is on record.

The scolex of *T. saginata* is devoid of hooks (that of *T. solium* is shown in Figure elsewhere in this chapter) but sufficient anchorage is secured by means of muscular suckers, known as bothria. In a constricted region known as the neck the scolex divides by transverse fission at the rate of eight or nine divisions a day, and a long train of proglottids is thereby formed.

When first produced the proglottids are small and thin, but they enlarge as they are moved back and have opportunity to share in the food found in the intestine. The largest and oldest of the proglottids are to be found at the end opposite to the scolex.

The process of proglottid formation may be compared with the strobilization of the Aurelia scyphula, which produces ephyra in somewhat the same way. By this comparison it becomes evident that the tapeworm may be thought of as a chain of individuals produced by the budding of the original member, the scolex.

There is little reason for regarding the entire complex as a single individual, although this view is held by some. However, the anatomy of the worm does provide evidence that may be interpreted either way, according to one's own inclination.

Before proceeding to the most bulky components of the worm's anatomy, the reproductive organs, we might first dispose of less conspicuous structures. A pair of ganglia is located in the scolex. From them longitudinal nerve cords run through the entire chain of proglottids. In line with parasitic habit, the nervous system is not highly developed in structure or in function.

Also running the length of all of the proglottids is a pair of excretory canals. At the posterior end of each proglottid there is a connecting duct between these canals. Flame bulbs are scattered through the mesenchyme. As the series of proglottids behind the scolex is scanned in sequence, the male reproductive system is encountered first, which shows it is the first to develop since female organs are not found until farther along.

The male organs consist of large numbers of testes scattered through the proglottid and from each testis there is a duct, the vas efferens, which leads to a common vas deferens. The vas deferens leads to a genital atrium, where it enlarges to form a muscular protrusible penis. In the female system there is a bilobed ovary, followed by oviduct and

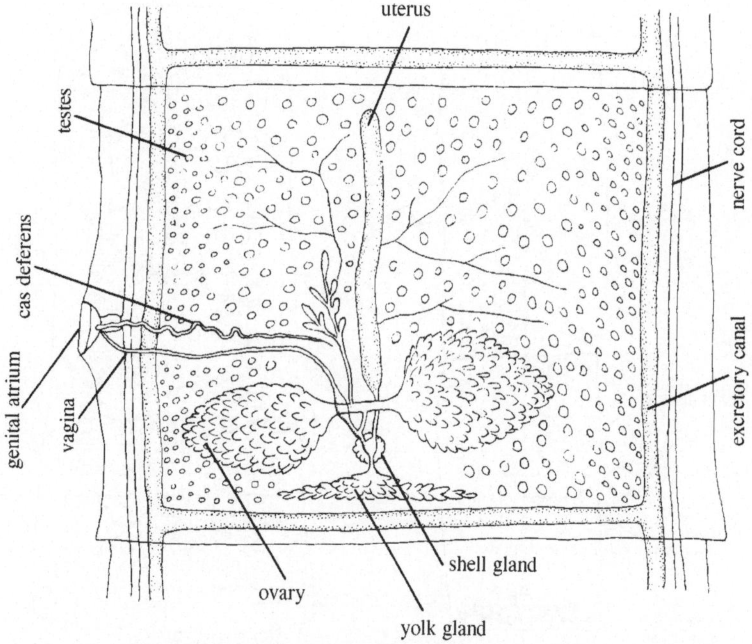

Figure 5.14: Mature proglottid (showing nerve cords).

vagina. The vagina opens into the genital atrium. Besides serving as an outlet for the ovary, the oviduct also receives a yolk duct, which carries nutrients provided by a large vitelline gland.

Where yolk duct and oviduct join there is found a shell gland for encapsulating the egg. A blind sac, at first small but capable of tremendous growth, also arises from the oviduct. This is the uterus, serving to store accumulating eggs.

Fertilization is accomplished by means of introducing the cirrus (penis) of the proglottid (which in reproductive behaviour acts fully as an individual organism) into the vagina of the genital atrium-i.e., self-fertilization.

Copulation may also occur between different proglottids of the same chain, or between two different chains if, as is unlikely, two happen to be present. It is conceivable that all three methods might take place. In time the proglottid reaches the end of its chain as a fully developed unit, and is then released and passed out with the feces. By now its gonads have become much reduced in size, or they may even have disappeared entirely.

The uterus is greatly enlarged, with many side branches, to

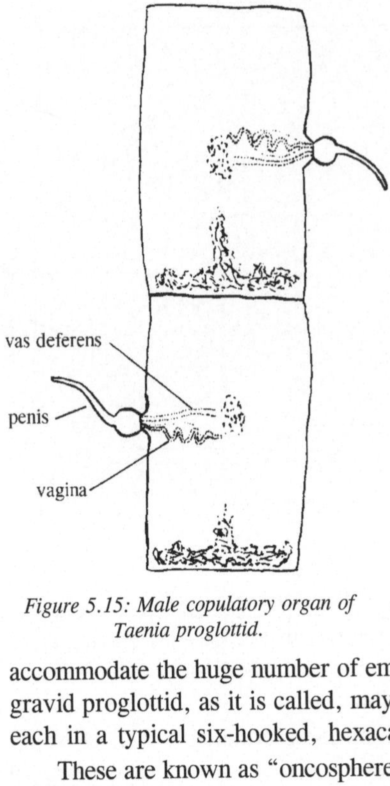

Figure 5.15: *Male copulatory organ of Taenia proglottid.*

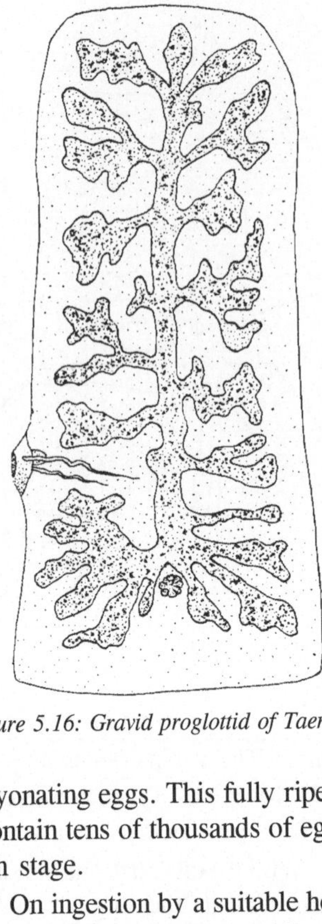

Figure 5.16: *Gravid proglottid of Taenia.*

accommodate the huge number of embryonating eggs. This fully ripe or gravid proglottid, as it is called, may contain tens of thousands of eggs, each in a typical six-hooked, hexacanth stage.

These are known as "oncospheres." On ingestion by a suitable host, in this case cattle, the hexacanths become active and claw their way into the musculature where they metamorphose into cysticerci. The cysticercus is a scolex in a dormant, inverted, condition. It is aroused to growth activity when ingested by the human host.

Taenia Echinococcus (E. Granulosus)

In the life cycle just described man harbors the mature tapeworm, and cattle carry the larval stage. But in the case of the dog tapeworm, *Echinococcus granulosus*, the reverse is true and man is the intermediate host. The dog-tapeworm is very small, only a few millimeters in length. The cysticercus may be several inches in diameter, however, and can reproduce by budding in this stage. If perchance lodged in a vital organ like the brain, the effect on the human can be very severe, even fatal.

Diphyllobothrium Latum

Of the intestinal inhabitants of man, *D. latum* is the largest and the

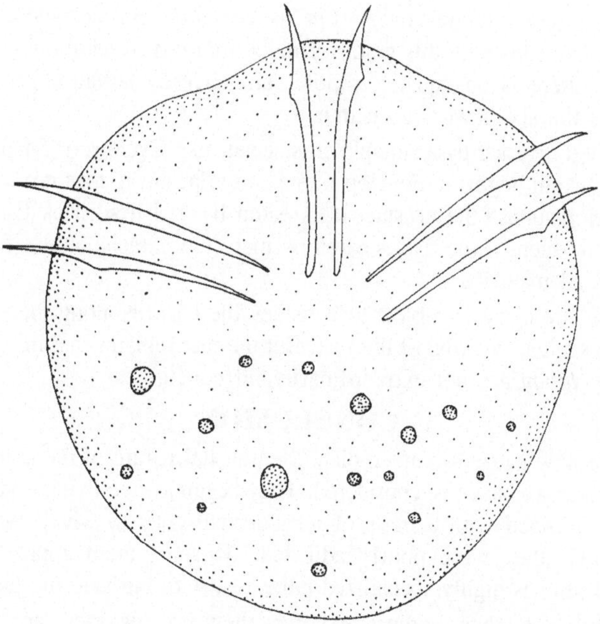

Figure 5.17: Hexacanth.

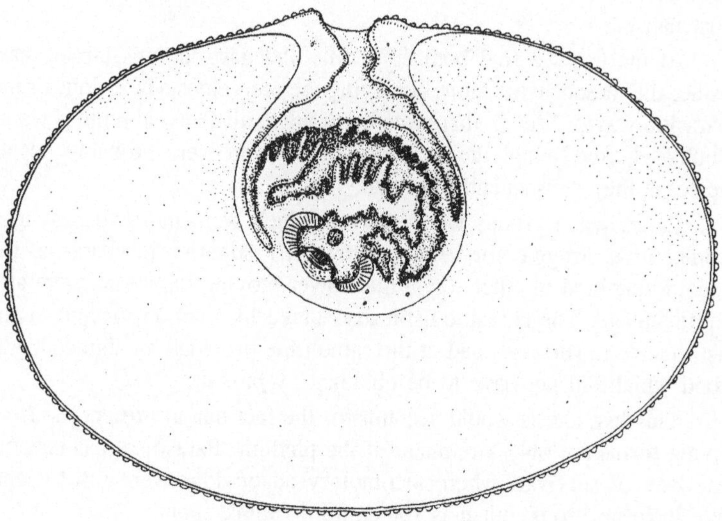

Figure 5.18: Cysticercus.

most injurious of tapeworms. Let us conclude our consideration of cestode parasites with this giant form. *D. latum* is of additional interest because there is an aquatic, motile, ciliacovered larval stage, which contains the six-clawed hexacanth.

When ingested by a suitable crustacean, like Cyclops or Diaptomus, the hexacanth begins to develop into a cercaria, but it does not continue to develop unless the crustacean is eaten by a fish such as Esox, the pike. And then, if the fish is eaten by man, the parasite attains full size and sexual maturity.

The life cycle is subject to considerable hazards along the way, of course; such as cooking of the fish. But the fact remains that infestations with *D. latum* are not extraordinarily infrequent.

CONCLUSION

We now pause to contemplate the unusual nature of the animals of the phylum we have just considered. They began as free-living organisms, newly provided with a mass of mesodermal cells to which, we have suggested, they were poorly adjusted. Most of them appear at the present time as highly specialized parasites, with intricate life histories.

Ultimately their bodies, and thus their life histories, are formed from the derivatives of the single cell layer-the mesoderm-which originally was a handicap to their free mode of life. At the beginning the epidermis protected the mesenchyme and the gastrodermis provided it with sustenance.

At the end we find both epidermis and gastrodermis largely cast aside; the mesenchyme alone achieving the marvelous adaptations of the parasitic way of life. In that remote era when all Platyhelminthes were, doubtless, free-living, the problems of survival were probably not as acute as they subsequently became.

Later, when groups were evolved which were more adapted to a competitive struggle for existence by their superior mechanisms for locomotion (and in other ways) the slower-moving flatworms were at a disadvantage. The parasitic habit discounted locomotion, or almost so, as a factor in survival, and at the same time provided an abundance of food which did not have to be obtained by pursuit.

This hypothesis would account for the fact that at present the free-living forms are only a remnant of the phylum. Parasitism has become the way of survival, where locomotory adaptations were insufficient. We have no proof, but it is something to think about.

6

PHYLUM ANNELIDA

As the size of animal bodies derived from the primitive evolutionary stems increased, there was at first nothing as effective for moving the bodies of the larger forms about from place to place as ciliary mechanism was for the small. Gradually the way was paved for the appearance of such adaptations. In pseudocoelomate animals for the first time, the body wall was separated from the intestinal tube by means of the interposition of a fluid-filled region between the two.

Later, in coelomate phyla, muscles were so divided by the body space that body wall and intestine were enabled to perform muscular contractions suited to their specific needs. In such animals surface ciliation was lost or the cilia became adapted for different functions, such as respiratory ventilation.

Sometimes the cilia indirectly served locomotory needs, as when they actuated the hydraulic devices of the echinoderm water-vascular system, or when they served to charge the proboscis and collar of the Enteropneusta. But animal life, so basically dependent for its nutrition upon the ability to move about from place to place in search of food, must have become increasingly handicapped by the lack of specific locomotory adaptation as effective for large bodies as cilia were for the small.

At one time this could not but have been a critical evolutionary problem. Something needed to be added, and these necessary adaptations appeared in the form of appendages on a segmented body. First, consider the nature of a true metamere. Unlike annulation of the cuticle, true metamerism appears to be more than a means of providing flexibility. It is a mechanism for producing controlled movements.

Toward the fulfilment of this function the essential ingredient of the metamere is an internal partition, the septum. The septum more or less confines the coelomic fluid in separate annular compartments. And it must be clearly understood that in the improved locomotory technique we are about to encounter in the phylum Annelida, coelomic fluid plays an important role.

So, too, do circular muscles, which have heretofore been absent or only slightly developed. Let us first assume a wormlike animal with circular and longitudinal muscles in the body wall, but no coelomic fluid within the body cavity. Contraction of the longitudinal muscles would shorten the length of the animal, and contraction of circular muscles would only decrease the diameter of the body.

But if coelomic fluid is present the effect of the action of the circular muscles would, in this event, be quite different. For, liquids being relatively incompressible, the coelomic fluid reacts to the effect of muscular pressure upon it by flowing out into regions of lower pressure along the length of the animal.

In this way the body is extended, and it should be apparent that no real extension could occur without the intermediate effect of the coelomic fluid. The mechanism is basically hydraulic. Now for the role of the septum. By virtue of the confining effect of septa, each segment of the body becomes a separate unit of motion.

If the coelomic fluid is compressed transversely the segment lengthens. If compressed longitudinally, the segment thickens. If the fluid is compressed on one side, the segment lengthens on the opposite side, and curvature ensues. Because of the presence of septa each segment is enabled to act in movement separately from the others and the body as a whole acquires a far greater versatility of motion than was heretofore possible.

There may be increase in length at one region, perhaps the anterior for exploratory purposes, and shortening elsewhere. Bendings, to bring about changes in the direction of movement, are easily effected. And the entire body, through use of the longitudinal muscle alone, has not lost its ability to undulate as in the roundworms.

The mechanism so far described accounts for movements of the annelid body itself, but does not go very far to explain the movement of the animal through the environment. In order best to translate body movements into locomotion, purchase must be obtained upon the surrounding medium.

In the case of a solid substrate, spicules might be sufficient to hold one end of the animal while the other end is pushed or pulled forward. But crawling (and certainly burrowing), is not usually a rapid method of locomotion. Greater speed can be attained if the animal swims.

Body undulations alone can account for swimming but, appendages adapted for the purpose are of great aid. True locomotory appendages, as they first appear in the annelid phylum, are paired paddle-like organs arranged in lateral series on the body. Except for a very few segments at the anterior and posterior ends of the body, which are too small or otherwise occupied, each segment possesses a pair.

While the appendage is a fleshy, i.e. muscular, organ in itself, it is swept through the medium chiefly by the movements of the muscles of the body wall to which it is attached. The annelid type of appendage is a momentous advance in the development of animal locomotion, but it is far from being the last word.

The effectiveness of the appendage in swimming depends upon undulations of the body and considerable waste of energy is therefore involved; since, in lateral motion, the body must move through a much greater distance than the distance between two points in a straight line. Furthermore, in crawling movement, the appendage as it now first appears is not designed to lift the body off the ground and the surface of contact between body and ground is, consequently, large.

For perfectly smooth bodies only the mass would be a factor in determining the force of friction which needs to be overcome, but the actual contours of a body being dragged must add greatly to the work that needs to be done. In spite of such limitations in application, we recognize the appendage as an organ for moving large bodies, as the cilium was for the small.

And modifications to overcome the difficulties outlined may soon be expected to appear. Many a person has held a sandworm or an earthworm in his hands without realizing that here is an animal that has attained one of the great evolutionary peaks. The annelid worm is more of a worm-a more intricately constructed worm-than any of the many other types of worms in existence.

The annelid may be regarded as the ultimate in worms, and it is the thin sheets of mesenteric tissue-the septa—which are more than anything else basically responsible for worm eminence. It is not intended to imply that locomotory utopia has been attained in annelids, nor that all are equally proficient in the art. Some still show a decided tendency to remain in one location, as *Polychaeta sedentaria*.

And in the most active of the polychaets (*Polychaeta errantia*) the speed of movement from place to place still falls far short of what is yet to appear among invertebrates.

But evidence of the superior value of the annelid plan over that of other worms is found in the fact that a free-living habit has been retained and generally prevails among them, whereas in the Aschelminthes there are a great many parasitic members.

THE POLYCHAETA

Of the several classes in the phylum Annelida it is now believed that the Polychaeta represent the original stem. Accordingly, we shall build our picture of the phylum around the sandworm or elamworm, a polychaet formally known as *Neanthes virens;* formerly, and still commonly, as *Nereis virens*.

Through its use as fish bait, many have a definite, though incomplete, concept of Neanthes. Let us free it from the bait bucket, the better to find out what manner of beast it really is, in its proper habitat.

NEANTHES VIRENS

Though capable of active swimming, Neanthes is found secluded in burrows in the sea bottom during daylight hours. This might be thought a matter of discretion as the better part of valor. Obviously Neanthes off the hook is even more alluring to fish than Neanthes on; so Neanthes digs in during the day.

Covered by sand in its burrow, Neanthes is protected against most of its predators, but not all-horseshoe crabs, for example, plow through the sand in search of food. In the sand there is physical safety but an inadequate oxygen supply. The worm could not exist there without some adaptation to overcome this difficulty.

First, it is necessary that the tube should not collapse and that its ends remain open to the sea. This is accomplished by the secretion of a mucus lining, which cements the sand grains together sufficiently for the purpose. Second, there is need for ventilation of the water within the tube.

Such is provided by appropriate undulating movements of the animal's body. In its tube Neanthes lies quietly, gently and rhythmically undulating its body in a dorso-ventral plane.

The Parapodium ("para-," alongside; "podos-," foot)

The locomotory appendages, or parapodia, of Neanthes are fleshy and flattened extensions of the body wall, laterally situated in pairs. Each segment is provided with a pair except the first segment, the peristomial, and the last, the caudal, which have none. The parapodium is a biramous structure. A dorsal portion, the notopodium, is structurally differentiated from a ventral portion, the neuropodium. Each of these rami is again partially divided into two.

The notopodiurn is larger than the neuropodium, and it is especially significant because of its extra surface and its rich supply of blood. Although the entire surface of the animal serves for the exchange of carbon dioxide and oxygen with the environmental water here, in the locomotory organs, additional opportunity is provided for respiration.

This is an advantageous location, for locomotory movements and respiration go well together. The parapodium is an organ with the specific characteristic of surface area. Such is required for swimming, and also for the gas exchange of respiration. Besides, the movements of the appendage which bring about locomotion also serve to ventilate its surface in relation to respiratory needs. Of course, while the worm lies in its tube there is no locomotion.

At this time undulations of the body draw a current of water through the tube and this current acts in the same way with regard to surface ventilation as does free movement of the worm through the environment.

It is interesting to consider the fact that respiration is sometimes associated with the alimentary tube, as we have observed in the holothurians and in the chordates; and sometimes it is associated with the body wall, of which the parapodia in this instance are a part. The physiological requirements are, in all cases, the same.

Surface is needed-surface that is well supplied by circulation with body fluids on one side, and exposed freely to the environmental medium for ventilation on the other side.

We are not quite yet finished with the appendage which is, indeed, an organ of many parts. Projecting from the dorsal surface of the notopodium and from the ventral surface of the neuropodium, one on each, are thin, tentacle-like structures, the cirri. These are especially touch-sensitive. If we now include sensation as a function of the appendage we find that it is a device used for swimming, crawling, breathing, and feeling.

Also, it digs. Even more: close to the neuropodial cirrus there is an excretory opening, the nephridiopore, and so the annelid appendage plays a part in excretion. Let us add reproduction, because the nephridiopore may serve for the discharge of gametes. When we eventually arrive at a consideration of the leg of the crustacean, we should recall these functions and see how they are allocated there.

Let us now assume that, by means of ambulatory action of the parapodia, the worm is about to move out of the tube. It becomes evident that the mechanism so far described is not yet complete, for soft fleshy lobes would not be satisfactory for this purpose.

There is obvious need for stiffening, so that the force of motion shall be effectively transmitted to the body. Stiffening of the parapodium is provided by two rods, the aciculi, running in the long axis. One aciculum braces the neuropodium and the other the notopodium. Muscles are attached to the base of the aciculum.

They help to move the appendage and also to extend it outward from the body in order to grip the sides of the burrow. At the outer edge, where there is actual contact, the parapodium is studded with

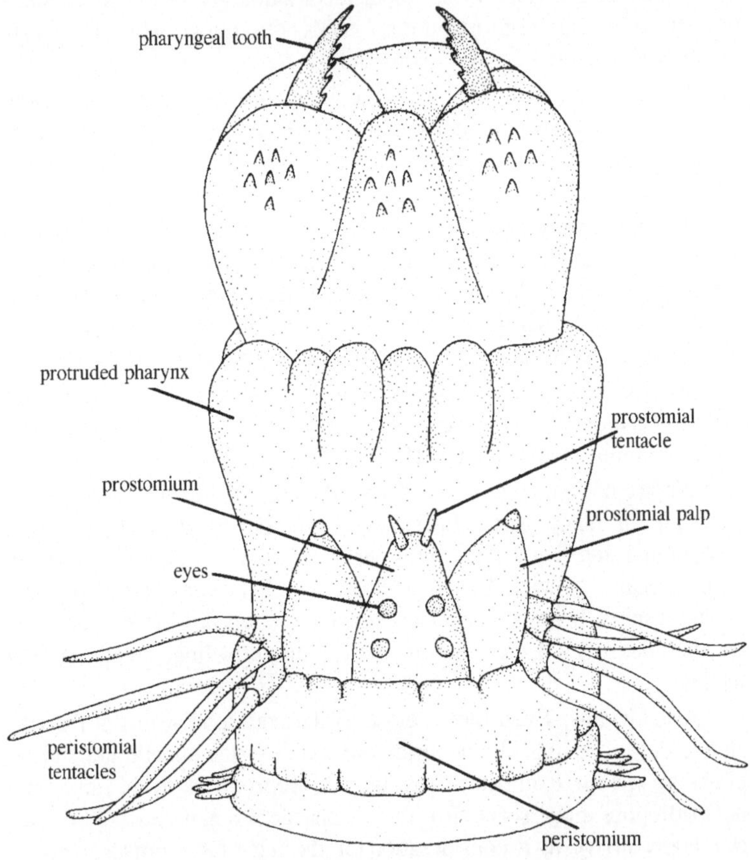

Figure 6.1: Anterior end of Neanthes, with pharynx everted.

numerous setae to provide traction. Each bristlelike seta is expanded distally into a narrow blade.

Head and Body Structure

As the worm moves out of the burrow, usually at night, the head appears first. The head is composed chiefly of the prostomium, which is a short, proboscis-like structure derived from the anterior-dorsal aspect of the peristomium. The peristomium is the first full segment of the body.

The mouth of the worm is formed by, and contained within, the peristomium. The prostomium bears a pair of small tactile tentacles anteriorly, a pair of plump probably taste-sensitive palps laterally, and two pairs of eyes dorsally. Also on its dorsal surface is a pair of ciliated pits, apparently for taste sensation, The prostomium is, therefore, the chief sensory center of the head; but contributing also are two pairs of comparatively long tentacles which originate on the peristomium.

Embryologically the peristomium is a fusion of two segments. Segments following the peristomium gradually enlarge until a maximum diameter for the body is attained, but otherwise all of them are very much alike, each bearing a prominent pair of lateral parapodia.

Posteriorly the worm tapers down again in diameter, and all the segments are alike except the very last, This, the caudal segment, lacks parapodia, but does have a pair of trailing sensory cirri. Formation of additional metameres, as the worm grows in length, occurs in front of the terminal caudal segment.

Food-Getting

When the worm is out of its tube the nature of the body undulations changes. While the worm is in the tube dorsal muscles act "antagonistically" against ventral muscles. Out of the tube the muscles change partners and those on one side of the body are opposed to those on the other side.

Instead of movements in a dorsoventral plane, the animal now weaves from side to side as it takes off to swim. If food is encountered a muscular portion of the alimentary tract, the pharynx, is everted through the mouth. Two formidable pharyngeal teeth appear and are extended widely as a consequence of the eversion of the pharynx.

When the pharynx is drawn inwardly, this action brings the teeth together like a pair of tongs which clamp the food, and aid in dragging it into the mouth. Surprisingly large objects can be engulfed in this way, either as a whole or piecemeal. The bite of a Neanthes is forceful and can easily be detected by the human hand, showing the power of the pharyngeal mechanism.

This method of tooth action is quite different from that in which teeth are set in solid jaws, and the jaws are worked by muscles. It is also different from mandibles that are independently supplied with muscles, as in the arthropod phylum.

Musculature of the body wall

The major muscle masses of the body wall of Neanthes are reminiscent of those of a roundworm. The largest muscles run longitudinally. There are four such. Two are situated dorsally and two ventrally. We have already observed that to produce the dorsoventral undulations that are of value in ventilating the worm's burrow, both dorsal muscles work as a team, and are opposed by the ventral muscles.

For locomotory undulations the muscles on one side of the body act as a team, and are opposed by those on the other side. For shortening the length of the animal all, of course, would contract together. The type of muscular activity and the harmonic waves found in undulatory movements are determined and controlled by the nervous system.

A continuous layer of circular muscle fibers lies outside the longitudinal muscles in the body wall. Circular muscles do not equal longitudinal ones in bulk but they are very significant in their effect. By means of contraction of circular muscles the coelomic fluid is put under pressure and the somites are forced to lengthen, either one by one or several at once.

Through the possession of this faculty controlled exploratory behaviour is greatly facilitated. For example, the head of the worm can be extended out of the burrow while the major part of the animal lies securely within. This type of reaction is not possible when only longitudinal muscles are present, as is the case with roundworms.

The functional development of circular muscles is therefore a great advance. To complete the structure of the body wall it is necessary to note the presence of strands of oblique muscle which connect the sides of the animal with the floor. And outside the circular muscles there is the single-cell-layered epithelium, as generally found among invertebrates, covered by a thin cuticle.

Also associated with the body wall are systems that indirectly support locomotory activity. These are respiratory devices, already described, and organs for excretion, nervous coordination, and circulation.

Excretory System

Lying close to the ventral body wall, in every segment that bears

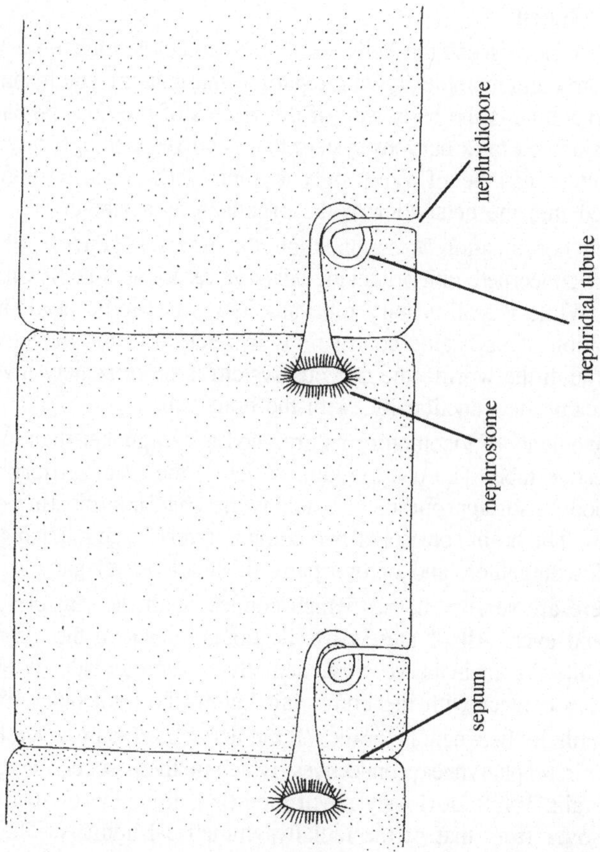

Figure 6.2: Nephridial structure, schematic.

parapodia, is a pair of nephridia. The structure of the nephridium extends into two segments. While the main nephridial tubule and the external opening, the nephridiopore, lie in one segment, the nephrostome-the ciliated funnel that draws material into the nephridium—is supported in the anterior septum and opens into the next anterior segment.

The much coiled tubule itself lies within a mass of syncytial protoplasm that is well supplied with blood vessels. We must assume that the nephridium is more than a simple conduit for the discharge of material gathered by the nephrostome. This is an inference based on the length of the tubule and its close association with the blood.

Perhaps micro-chemical tests will soon be performed to compare the composition of the coelomic fluid, which enters the nephrostome, with the excreta that emerge from the nephridiopore.

Nervous System

As we have seen, the body wall of Neanthes is built on a higher level of structural complexity with regard to musculature and locomotory adaptations than is the body wall of the worms of previous phyla. This indicates a need for a nervous system that is correspondingly advanced, for effectors can be of value only if their activity is harmoniously integrated into the behaviour of the organism as a whole.

Such coordination is supplied by the nervous system, which is primarily concerned with producing adaptive responses to environmental stimuli. While the alimentary tube has its own specific needs-for the coordination of peristaltic contractions in relation to the movement of food through the worm—the nervous system is more acutely involved, anatomically and functionally, with the body tube.

Movements of locomotory nature need to be quicker than those of the digestive tube. The prostomium, which is the chief sensory center of the body also, appropriately, contains the chief coordinating center, the brain. The brain consists of two comparatively large median ganglia lying close together, and of two pairs of small lateral ganglia.

There are sensory nerves which connect with the tentacles, cirri, palps, and eyes. All of these parts lie dorsally, above the alimentary tract, while the main nerve cord, actually two cords side by side, is ventral, in contact with the body wall below the alimentary tract.

Continuity between the brain and the nerve cord is provided by two pairs of circumpharyngeal connectives, which tie the first ventral ganglion to the brain. While obviously much modified, this plan of structure is a carry-over from that of the radiallysymmetrical animals. The nerve ring of the cnidarian becomes a nerve oval in the flatworms, and the nerve oval of the flatworm is represented by the double nerve cord of the annelid, with the encircling ring about the alimentary tract now very small.

Only in the chordates has this ring been dispensed with, and the nervous system there lies entirely on one side of the alimentary system. The first ventral ganglion of Neanthes, and the two that follow it, bear two pairs of lateral nerve branches. The anterior pair runs into the segment immediately anterior to the one in which the ganglion itself is situated.

The second pair serves the segment of origin. All of the remaining ganglia of the long ventral chain are similarly provided with nerves, but have an additional pair within the segment; three pairs in all.

The comparative complexity of the nervous system of Neanthes indicates that we have in the annelid worm a higher level of organization than in any of the worms of previous phyla; a conclusion which is borne out in the other body systems. It can therefore be said that the annelids represent the highest peak in the development of purely wormlike bodies, since in the phyla which follow a new trend appears.

The plan of development in length, which has been the theme in worms, there gives way to one of specialization of body regions and the body then becomes shorter and more compact. Apparently an unlimited segmental plan of body organization does not provide sufficient space for the development of organs in bulk.

But, perhaps most important, it seems to introduce difficulties in coordination. This is already indicated here, in the annelids, by the appearance-at least in some of the genera-of "giant nerve fibers" longitudinally oriented within the nerve cord. These transcend segmental boundaries and allow for more rapid communication between head and tail, which are so far removed from each other.

Another moment devoted to the nervous system will teach a lesson that is deep and important. The "brain" of an annelid-and this has been done with Neanthes and leeches-can be experimentally removed. The animal is then still able to move about. But the movements are non-adaptive.

They are not responsive to the nature of the stimulus, and movements cease only with the onset of fatigue. This indicates that the most basic function of the brain is one of inhibition; it is to know when to stop. In our emphasis upon the "creative powers" of the human brain it is well to remember that the animal brain appears to have been originally intended for inhibitory control, and timely inhibition remains the essential ingredient of all adaptive behaviour, even in humans.

Internal Plan of Structure

There is nothing distinctive about the basic tube-within-a-tube plan of structure of Neanthes. It is in the general nature of enterozoan organization to have two major body tubes, one for locomotion and one for nutrition. The two tubes in annelids are, however, tied together at regular intervals by the septa, which also divide the coelome into a chain of liquid-filled compartments.

In this respect the annelid worm is different from all other types of worms. Such septa are not found in previous phyla, and in no subsequent phylum are they so arranged. We may regard the septum then as the key distinction of annelid structure.

The inner worm-the digestive tract—is suspended within the outer worm-the body wall-by means of the septa. Movement is essential to each of these parts of the organism. And the need of moving selected portions of the environment, the food, through the inner worm follows the need of moving the outer worm through the environment in search of food.

These needs are mutually complementary. As food is moved through the alimentary tract, from portal to portal, it is mechanically and chemically processed in order to release and appropriate the contained nutrients. In truly coelomate animals, like Neanthes, there is a positive muscular mechanism all along the alimentary tract for the movement of its contents.

Like those of the body wall, the longitudinal muscles face the coelome. The circular muscles lie toward the lumen of the intestine where, by contraction, they exert pressure upon the contents. A peristaltic wave of contraction keeps the materials moving slowly toward the anus. Of course, less force is necessary for alimentary movements than for locomotion, and alimentary musculature is less in bulk than that of the body wall.

The pharynx of the animal is lined by an inward extension of ectodermally-derived cells which here, as on the epidermis, secrete a covering of cuticle. At the esophagus, endodermal lining begins and cuticular lining is absent. The esophagus is a short tube extending for about four or five segments, and is provided with a pair of esophageal glands.

The specific function of these glands has not been determined in Neanthes, but somewhat similar glands in crustaceans are known to produce proteolytic enzymes-perhaps here also. The passage between esophagus and intestine is guarded by a sphincter muscle. It may be inferred that closure of the sphincter prevents regurgitation of food from the intestine.

There is no structural stomach as such, but between the septa, in each segment, the intestine enlarges somewhat into a pouch, and functions of stomach and intestine are combined. The system is therefore known as a stomach-intestine. At the posterior the intestine passes into the rectum which, like the pharynx, is lined with cuticle. Terminally there is the anus, lying between two sensory caudal cirri.

The Blood-Circulatory System

In contrast with pseudocoelic worms-where there is none such present-the need for a special circulatory system is indicated in annelids for several reasons. Chiefly, they are as follows: The alimentary tube, which previously was a gastrodermis of unicellular thickness, now by the addition of muscle is composed of many layers of cells. It is probably the requirements of these cell layers—their need for oxygen and for the removal of metabolic wastes-which, more than anything else, can be correlated with the presence of a blood-circulatory system.

Of course, digested food components from the lumen of the alimentary system are distributed to other parts of the body through the circulatory system. But it is unlikely that nutritive factors are limiting. Food can be stored within cells and the need for immediate renewal is not urgent.

The body wall of the aschelminthes is at least as thick as the alimentary tract now being considered, and the former seems to be adequately supplied with nutrients from the pseudocoel, by diffusion. But the body wall of the annelid is now thicker than it was in the aschelminth, and the circulatory system speeds the passage of respiratory gases to and from the epidermis.

Considered along the longitudinal axis, septa would appear to be a factor affecting circulation. The liquids of the coelome are not fully free to circulate as they are in a pseudocoel, although the septa are perforated and do not constitute a complete block. Finally, excretion is now carried on in localized organs and the need for continuous and positive straining of the fluids of each metamere through the nephridia requires a circulatory system.

For these reasons direct transfer by diffusion from cell to cell and from body region to body region is, evidently, no longer adequate in the annelid body. Although some annelids surpass Neanthes in this respect, the circulatory system as found in Neanthes is fairly typical. There is a specialized fluid for circulation-the blood—which is bright red in colour because of haemoglobin present in solution.

There are no erythrocytes. It is interesting that the "bloodworm," or "fourjawed worm," Euglycera, does possess erythrocytes, so notable in chordates but a rare occurrence among invertebrates, although we have encountered them as early as in the Rhynchocoela. Moreover, Euglycera cannot be taken to represent the annelids, because it has no blood vessels.

In this animal the coelomic fluid, with the contained erythrocytes, is circulated by means of cilia on the coelomic epithelium. Such ciliation in Neanthes is limited to dorsal patches. The blood of Neanthes flows from ventral to dorsal in each metamere through segmental vessels. Along the length of the body it flows toward the anterior on the dorsal side, and toward the posterior ventrally.

Figure 6.3: Diagrammatic representation of Neanthes blood circulation.

The chief source of power to circulate the blood is found in the dorsal vessel, the walls of which are contractile, and which is also surrounded by separate circular muscle fibers. But peristaltic contractions are not limited to the dorsal vessel. They occur generally throughout the system, except for the long ventral vessel where none has been demonstrated.

The passage of blood from the ventral to the dorsal vessel is not direct. On leaving the ventral vessel each of the lateral, or segmental, blood vessels divides into two branches. One forms a capillary meshwork within the walls of the intestine, the other likewise in the body wall. Only then do the branches reunite to form the lateral vessel that arrives at the junction with the dorsal.

Obviously then, as contrasted with that which left the ventral vessel, the blood poured into the dorsal vessel is much modified in composition. Nutrients have been added from the intestine. In the body wall the carbon dioxide content has been lowered, and the oxygen level increased.

Of course, in passage through the nephridia, nitrogenous wastes have been reduced and other regulative changes, such as in water content, probably have been imposed. At the anterior end the dorsal vessel divides into two branches which lead to capillary meshworks in the walls of the esophagus.

These capillaries reunite and empty into the ventral vessel. In the esophageal region blood flows from dorsal to ventral, an exception to the general rule. At its posterior end the ventral vessel, in turn, divides into two and these pass around the rectum, to drain into the dorsal vessel.

Reproduction

The coelome of Neanthes is lined throughout with epithelium, and we are concerned with this epithelium now because it functions as a gonad.

From the ventral region of the coelome gametes are produced, and these are stored in the coelome. Gonads, uteri, seminal vesicles, and the like, are not differentiated. The coelome serves in all these ways. In the breeding season worms of both sexes swim freely together, in "schools," near the surface of the water.

This "mating behaviour" occurs at night in relation to the phase of the moon, as mating in the animal kingdom often does. Gametes are discharged into the sea either through the nephridia-which makes them, in effect, urogenital organs-or by rupture of the body wall. The proximity of the animals to each other tends to insure contact between eggs and sperm. Fertilization takes place in the sea.

The development of the Neanthes zygote has been intensively studied and is an excellent example of spiral cleavage and mosaic development. The first two cleavages lay down the four macromeres from which the endoderm of the larva is derived.

The micromeres then produced by cleavage from the macromeres arise as successive quartettes of which the first three (twelve cells) give rise to the ectoderm and all of its derivatives, such as epidermis, nervous system, and the lining of the alimentary tract at the anterior and posterior ends. Up to this point there have been five divisions. Mesoderm first arises from one of the cells of the sixth division-the fourth quartette.

The phylogenetically significant trochophore larva, possessed mutually by annelids and mollusks, is not seen in Neanthes since the eggs hatch in a post-trochophore three-segment stage.

OLIGOCHAETA

In the general nature of their body plan and structure the Oligochaeta have much in common with the Polychaeta, so much so that both are usually united in the class Chaetopoda. However, externally the oligochaet shows much atrophy of structure and internally considerable hypertrophy. This can be illustrated in the earthworm *Lumbricus terrestris* which, like Neanthes, is well known as an angling worm.

LUMBRICUS TERRESTRIS

All of the more or less prominent external features of Neanthes - parapodia, tentacles, palps, cirri, eyes-are absent in Lumbricus. The only vestige of the appendage is found in the form of four pairs of setae on each segment, but these cannot be seen with the unaided eye. They are detectable by touch.

There are many more setae in Neanthes than there are in Lumbricus-hence *"poly*chaeta" for the former, "oligochaeta" for the latter. The most conspicuous external feature of Lumbricus is the clitellum, a region of several segments swollen with glands and situated about one third the length of the body from the anterior.

Musculature

Instead of two pairs of longitudinal muscles as in Neanthes, there are in Lumbricus a dorsal pair, two ventral pairs and a median ventral muscle. Moreover, these have been expanded to form an almost continuous layer of longitudinal fibers underlying the circular. Consequently the bending movements are not limited to those of the undulating type, and exploratory capacity is more refined.

Alimentary Tract

The digestive tract of Lumbricus is more differentiated in several respects than that of Neanthes, in adaptation to the difference in feeding habits. Lumbricus is generally an unselective feeder. It may ingest bits of vegetation such as grass-leaves, but chiefly the worm swallows portions of the complete environment—the earth—in which it lives and through which it moves.

This is in a way a fortunate combination of locomotion and ingestion, for there is no loss of energy devoted to seeking out food. Everything the worm encounters as it burrows through the soil is taken into the mouth. Perhaps the organic content may be meager in some locations, but there is at least something to "keep body and soul together" or the worms would not be found there. Darwin, in his studies on the earthworm, estimated that there are as many as 50,000 of them in an acre of land (compare with soil nematodes), moving 18 tons of soil a year in their wanderings through the acre.

Most apparent among the structural differences in the alimentary tract is an enlargement of the posterior portion of the esophagus to form a food-storage organ, the crop, and this is followed by a muscular grinding sac, the gizzard. In the pharynx jaws are absent, in relation to food habits, and in the esophagus the esophageal glands have been reduced in size, in apparent correlation with a low protein diet.

In addition to the circular and longitudinal muscles of the Neanthes pharynx, that of Lumbricus possesses many radial fibers, attached internally between the pharynx and the inner surface of the body wall. On contraction these dilate the pharynx and open the mouth as the worm fills itself with earth. This method of ingestion is quite different from that employed by Neanthes, but then the media and the food are also different.

The stomach-intestine of Lumbricus, like that of Neanthes, expands outward in each segment between septa, increasing the volume of the digestive cavity. Besides, there is a long intestinal ridge, the typhlosole, suspended from the roof. The typhlosole increases intestinal surface by perhaps fifty per cent and thereby has the same effect as would coiling of an intestine one and onehalf times its original length.

However, the typhlosole occupies space in the lumen of the intestine and doubtless interferes with the free passage of intestinal contents. It therefore may not be as suitable an adaptation for increasing available digestive surface as is coiling.

The typhlosole indicates disharmony between body and alimentary tubes. The intestine is too short to meet the nutritive needs of the body. A more efficient animal would result if the body were shorter and the intestine longer. An opportunity is therefore presented for an evolutionary change in design. This will come in later phyla.

"Hearts"

While the circulatory system of Lumbricus is, on the whole, quite similar to that of Neanthes, there are some conspicuous differences. In Neanthes two of the segmental vessels at the anterior end carry blood from the dorsal to the ventral vessel, while here in Lumbricus there are five pairs for the purpose-ten in all-and these are direct without capillary slowdowns. In both, these connecting vessels are quite muscular and are often referred to as "hearts."

Reproduction

Unprotected gametes cannot survive in a dry environment and various animals meet this situation in various ways. With some exceptions terrestrial crustaceans, for example, go back to the water for mating. Internal fertilization is the ultimate adaptation. Lumbricus mating behaviour lies between these two.

The reproductive system of Lumbricus is designed to provide, on the land, a liquid environment for external fertilization. The reproductive organs of Lumbricus are concentrated in the anterior end of the body, in the region before the clitellum. They originate from the ventral portion of the coelomic epithelium, in segments nine to fourteen, and the largest ones-sperm storage organs, or seminal vesicles—are found wrapped around the esophagus.

This is a peculiar location for sex organs, but it does not in any way interfere with their function, and it serves the needs of the earthworm. Seminal receptacles are also conspicuous, but ovaries and testes are small and covered over by the other organs.

Lumbricus is monoecious and the difficulty of mating off in pairs is lessened. Any mature worm can act as a mate to any other. In Lumbricus finding a mate is simply finding another worm. Sperm ducts open through the floor of the fifteenth segment, and oviducts through the fourteenth. But these are not all of the sexual openings.

In the groove between segments nine and ten a pair of seminal receptacles open, and another pair in the next posterior groove. In all, Lumbricus has four pairs of pores for genital function. Three of the pairs have to do with sperm transfer.

Mating occurs by means of bringing together and overlapping the anterior portions of a pair of mature worms in such manner that the floors of the two bodies lie together, but oriented in opposite directions.

Where the animals are abundant and the burrows are close together, this can sometimes be accomplished without either animal leaving "home," a factor of obvious survival value. To leave the burrow completely is a dangerous procedure for a worm. The body is soft and defenseless, and enemies wait without.

As the animals meet and cling together in the mating reaction, there is a profuse secretion of mucus that temporarily binds them together. Each then discharges the sperms that have been accumulated previously in the seminal vesicles. External longitudinal grooves on the body help to guide the sperms to the openings of the seminal receptacles, where they are received.

The copulation phase is now complete, and the worms separate. It should be noted that fertilization has not occurred, only a mutual exchange of sperm from one worm to the other, in which each animal has acted as both male, a donor of sperm, and female, a receiver. After parting the seminal vesicles are empty of sperm, and the seminal receptacles are filled with sperm from the other worm.

After the mating partners have separated the secretion of the clitellum becomes particularly heavy and a short mucus band is formed around this part of the animal. By drying the band hardens somewhat on the exposed surface, while still quite moist within, and the worm slowly disengages itself by working its way out backward.

During the course of this procedure the genital openings are drawn in succession through the tube of mucus. First come the openings of the seminal vesicles, but these have already discharged their sperm and have nothing further to contribute at this time. Then the openings of the oviducts pass, and eggs are deposited within the tube.

Last, the tube passes over the seminal receptacles and sperm which previously entered here during copulation are released. It is at this time, outside of the body of the animal but in a liquid medium, that fertilization takes place. By this interesting procedure external fertilization takes place in a terrestrial animal.

The zygotes develop into miniature worms within the mucus tube, which has shrivelled into a cocoon. It is said that, for *Lumbricus terrestris*, only one worm eventually emerges from the cocoon, the survivor apparently being the most active and vigorous of the lot and having engulfed the rest as food. The struggle for existence thus begins very early for Lumbricus, and tests of fitness come even before emergence into the outer world.

COMPARATIVE FORMS AMONG THE POLYCHAETA

Neanthes, and to a lesser extent Lumbricus, have served as types to represent the bristle-bearing worms, the Chaetopoda, of the annelid phylum. Before proceeding further let us consider a few departures from type. First the Polychaeta, since oligochaets are probably themselves a departure derived from ancestral polychaets.

Order Errantia

Neanthes is a member of the order Errantia; not because it errs or deviates from the true type, but because it represents the polychaets that are of a wandering nature. In this order the protrusible pharynx

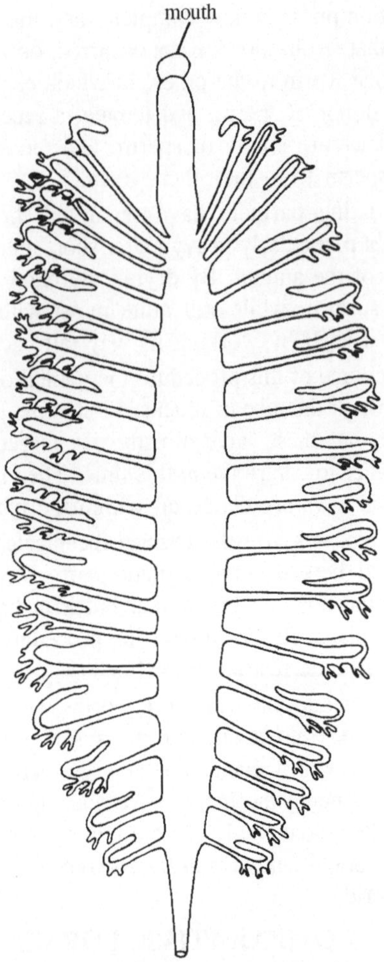

Figure 6.4: The digestive system of Aphrodite.

with attached jaws, which we emphasized above, is characteristic. In the order Sedentaria the pharynx is not protrusible, and there are no jaws; and the segments are specialized in different ways in regions along the length of the body.

The Sedentaria live in fixed tubes and feed microphagously. Among the Errantia, departures from type take place both in habit and in structure. When the roll is called of the Errantia some strange members appear.

First, let us consider *Neanthes* (Nereis) *limnicola*. There is nothing very unusual about the structure of *N. limnicola;* but it lives in fresh water. This requires drastic, though invisible, physiological modification. If a specimen of *N. virens* is placed in fresh water its life is shortened to a matter of minutes.

What evolutionary adaptations have occurred in the physiology of the skin and of the nephridia of *N. limnicola* which enable it to overcome the osmotic forces of a fresh water environment? The adjustment of salt balance is a universal problem for the inhabitants of fresh water, and it is met in different ways.

Among the Polychaeta, *N. limnicola* is a very unusual departure

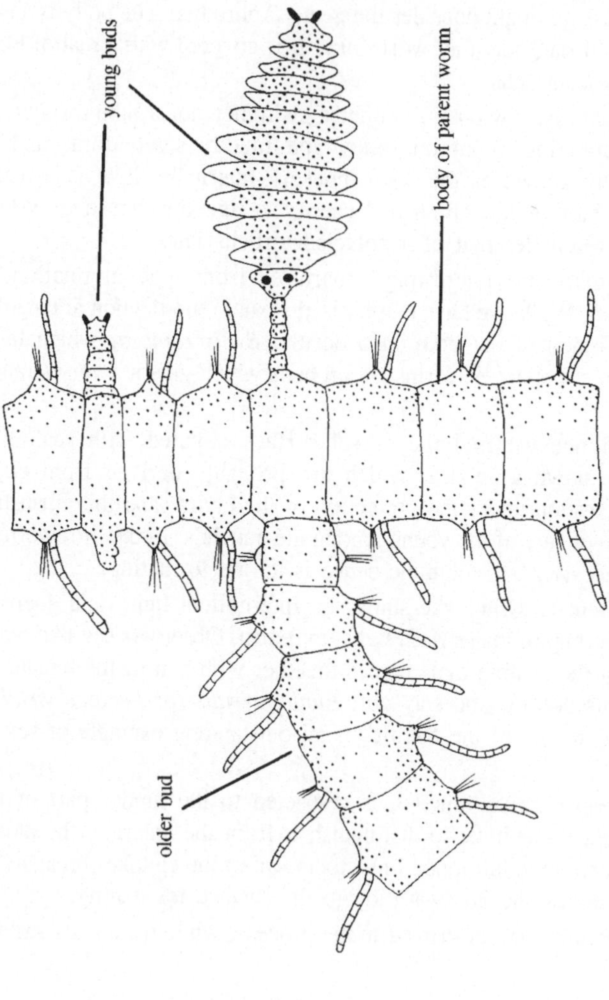

Figure 6.5: Lateral budding in Syllis.

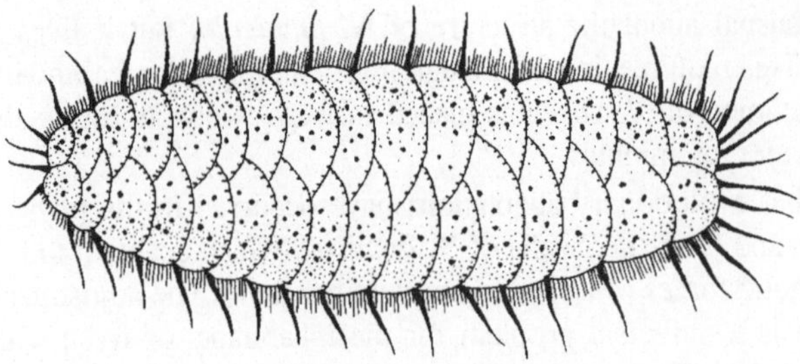

Figure 6.6: Polynoe.

from physiological type. As an example of departures from typical form and structure we might consider the genus Aphrodita. The body is short and wide and flat, not at all worm-like. It is covered with a mat of long dorsal iridescent setae.

Aphrodita is, obviously, neither a swimmer nor a tube-dweller. It is found crawling about on sandy and muddy sea-bottoms and is appropriately known as the "Sea mouse." Internally there is in each segment a pair of muchbranched caeca, so that the digestive system somewhat resembles that of a polyclad turbellarian.

Then there are interesting departures from type in relation to reproduction. While we have emphasized sexual reproduction among the annelids, fission of the body also occurs. *Syllis ramosa*, which lives within deep-sea sponges, forms lateral buds which give it a very strange appearance.

In Polynoe we find the dorsal surface covered with scale-like structures known as elytra, which are probably derived from cirri. Embryos develop under the protection of the elytra, and this furnishes an example of care of the young among the annelids. In the "fireworm," *Odontosyllis enopla*, bioluminescence is an aid to mating.

As a female swims she shows an intermittent light, and soon an encircling group of males flash lights in return. Observers say that when the light of the leading male comes together with that of the female all of the lights go out, and stay out! *Eunice viridis* (or *Leodice viridis*), the "palolo worn" of the Pacific, is an outstanding example of sexual periodicity.

The reproductive function is restricted to the hinder part of the body, called the epitoke to distinguish it from the anterior, the atoke. Once a year, in the full moon of October, all of the epitokes break away from the atokes and go swarming to the surface for mating.

The epitokes are destroyed in the process, while the atokes survive in their burrows to form new epitokes that will function again in the following year. The abundance of these worms during spawning is so great that they are awaited and collected by the natives of the Samoa and Fiji islands.

These, and other worms, would seem to have much to commend them as food, for those who might care for this type of food. There are no bones, feathers, or fur to contend with. While Polychaeta Errantia are capable of pursuing and subduing smaller animals, they themselves are highly attractive items of food for larger animals.

It must be because of this that some of them have been driven, evolutionarily speaking, to take shelter. Many, as Neanthes, resort to transient burrowing. Some even have permanent tubes. Diopatra constructs a long, roomy, permanent burrow in the mud and sand.

There is an internal smooth parchment-like lining of mucus which extends above the bottom like a chimney, to prevent silt from sifting in. Out of the chimney the worm extends its anterior, and snatches at any food organisms which chance to come its way.

Hyalinoecia also forms a permanent tube, but in this case of lightweight chitinous material, which it drags along as it moves from place to place.

Order Sedentaria

Among the Sedentaria, tube dwelling has become the prevailing mode of life. The nature of the tube and respiratory adaptations to life in a tube are points of interest.

Arenicola burrows constantly through the sea-bottom, as Lumbricus does on land, but this is accomplished with the aid of parapodia that have become reduced to rudiments composed only of setae. The pharynx, which is exceptional in that it is eversible like that of the Errantia, assists in burrowing. In the middle region of the body the segments bear segmentally arranged tufts of gills that are of parapodial origin.

Chaetopterus, in contrast to Arenicola, lives in a permanent tube. It is a looped, double-ended tube imbedded in muddy bottoms, with both ends projected upward into clear sea water. The tube is soft and of a consistency that gives the animal its common name "Parchment Worm."

In the middle region of the body there are a number of flabby parapodia that have become modified into fanlike sweeps to pump water through the tube. Like most of the Sedentaria, Chaetopterus is a microphagous feeder. The small particles of food drawn in with the water current are trapped in mucus for ingestion. The stream of water also ventilates the tube, facilitating the exchange of respiratory gases, and carries out the wastes of the digestive and excretory systems; and gametes, too.

Living in the tube with Chaetopterus, near the openings, are small crabs of the genera Pinnixa and Polyonyx. They are better equipped to deal with any larger organisms that might enter than is Chaetopterus, and at the same time acquire food and shelter for themselves. A very curious additional property of Chaetopterus is that, enclosed as it is in a tube, it is luminescent.

Upon the value of this we can only speculate. Certainly in this instance the light is not used as a mating signal, as in Odontosyllis. Perhaps the glow emanating from the tube attracts small organisms and these, venturing close to the openings, are caught up in the incurrent stream of water.

In Chaetopterus we see an example of adaptation to draw the environment to the animal, when locomotion has been given up in favour of protection within a permanent tube. Some of the Sedentaria build a hard tube, of lime, often in the form of a coil. Such are found in the common genera Hydroides, Serpula, and Spirorbis.

Gills are developed from the palps of these worms, where they can easily be extended out into the sea water and quickly retracted within the tube if necessary. An operculum is also formed from a palp, to close the tube against aggressors. Whereas polychaetes are generally dioecious, Spirorbis is unusual in that it is hermaphroditic. Also, the eggs of

Spirorbis develop within the operculum, which is modified to form a protective pouch for the young. Amphitrite builds its tube of sand and mud with the aid of long tentacles derived from the prostomium. These undoubtedly also serve as gills, but there are in addition three pairs of branching gills from the segments just behind the prostomium.

The gills are bright red in colour, and the tentacles reddish or orange, which indicates why these animals are known as "flower worms." For an example of a geometrically constructed tube, that of Cistenides would be difficult to surpass. It is made of sand grains carefully selected for size and shape, and firmly cemented together in the form of a cone. The worm is usually found partly buried, with its tube, in the sand; but the tube is strong and Cistenides can crawl around and change locations, dragging its tube along.

Parasitism Among the Polychaets

Annelids apparently originated, in their time, as actively moving, predatory worms. Despite their own desirability as food for larger forms, they have as a group maintained the predatory way of life, even though many have been able to survive only as burrowers and tube dwellers, for their own bodily protection. Among the polychaets, with rare exceptions, parasitism is unknown. (One possible exception is the Polynoe-like worm *Antinoe parasitica*, which is found under the elytra of *Lepidametria commensalis*, another of the Polynoe group.)

But regarded as related to the Polychaeta Errantia is a peculiar group known as the Myzostomaria. We shall omit the nature of the structural peculiarities of the Myzostomaria-although some students will investigate this for themselves-and point out only that they are parasites.

For some reason they have become involved only with echinoderms, and are found on the surfaces of crinoids and within starfish. Such narrow distribution as parasites seems to indicate a special relationship that in the absence of evidence falls within the realm of speculation. This anyone is qualified to do for himself.

COMPARATIVE FORMS AMONG THE OLIGOCHAETA

We note first that, while Polychaeta are almost all marine, Oligochaeta occur in fresh water and on land. Enchytraeus may be mentioned as an exception. Enchytraeus lives on the beaches between tide marks, but very few other oligochaetes are found anywhere near salt water.

Since Oligochaeta seem to have been evolved from Polychaeta, a change in osmotic relationships is one of their important adaptations. Terrestrial oligochaets, like Lumbricus, generally live in burrows in moist soil. A few find the organic contents of manure heaps more to their liking-e.g., Eisenia, which thus approach the nutritive habits of the saprozoic nematodes.

A terrestrial oligochaet of the tropics, Megascolides of Australia, holds the record for size. Megascolides may be as much as eleven feet long, and the sounds of its locomotion are said to be clearly audible. The possible use of Megascolides as an angle worm is a thought to excite the imagination.

Aquatic oligochaets are usually small in size. Some, like the well-known Tubifex which is used as food for aquarium fishes, form mucus tubes in the mud. Others find shelter by commensal habit. Aelosoma and Chaetogaster, as examples, are often found in association with fresh-water sponges. Branchiobdella lives on the gills of the crayfish (see Dioctophyme), to which it holds fast with the aid of a sucker at the posterior end of the body. In this respect Branchiobdella resembles the Hirudinea, which now follow.

Hirudinea

Unlike Polychaeta and Oligochaeta, Hirudinea lack bristles on the body and cannot, therefore, be included as Chaetopoda. Also, the coelomic space is much reduced. We might at once note an exception in the leech Acanthobdella, since it possesses both bristles and a well-developed coelome, and utilize Acanthobdella as a connecting form to draw the Oligochaeta and Hirudinea together in our minds.

The two classes do show considerable resemblance, and the latter may have evolved from the former in ancestral times. The anterior sucker of the leeches-although not present in all -when present contains the mouth and serves as a feeding organ.

The posterior sucker has no relation to the alimentary system. The anus lies dorsally to it, and the sucker acts only as a holdfast. Suckers are also used in ambulatory locomotion, one holding on while the other, not so employed, is moved forward or drawn up behind. In swimming, capably performed by undulations of a dorso-ventrally flattened body, suckers are not involved.

In feeding habit leeches are generally predators upon smaller animals. Haemopsis, for example, usually devours snails and smaller worms; although it is also a blood sucker. Leeches often feed upon blood, which is a substance of unique nutritive properties. This might best be regarded as a special form of predation, and not as parasitism.

Let us then not think of leeches as parasites, but as predators which often feed upon prey larger than themselves. Following attachment to the surface of the "host" by means of the posterior sucker, the animal punctures the skin by means of three sharp jaws and imbibes a deep draught of blood. Jaws are present in the order Gnathobdellida, but the Rhynchobdellida have a piercing proboscis instead.

Within the alimentary tract of the leech, blood is prevented from clotting by an enzyme, hirudin, a necessary adaptation for blood-feeding. Because of their predilection for blood, use was made of leeches, in days not long gone by, to reduce uncomplimentary symptoms such as bruise-blackened eyes. In times more remote, when disease was regarded as due to "bad blood," the leech occupied a regular place in medical practice.

In relation to its feeding habits the alimentary tract of the leech shows a greatly enlarged crop with many pouches. The medicinal leech *Hirudo medicinalis* is able to draw up about a year's supply of blood at one feeding, about three times its own body weight. To understand the prodigious nature of this act we might imagine a human attempt to consume three times the body weight in food at one meal.

Most of the coelomic space of the leech is filled with the alimentary tract, in the form of the enlarged crop, and the rest of the coelome is obliterated by a parenchyma of connective tissue; perhaps to hold the body together against the strain of the enclosed food.

Leeches have a fixed number of body segments-thirty-four. Externally, however, there are many more superficial annulations, as many as fourteen per segment. The true metamerism of the body is indicated by the ganglia of the nervous system.

It is of special interest that the greatest concentration of ganglia is found at the posterior end where, in relation to the orienting movements centered about the posterior sucker, seven ganglia are fused together. Appendages are absent in leeches, as they are in the oligochaetes, and so cannot be used as a sign of segmentation.

In Branchellion, however (which has the added distinction of ability to prey upon electric eels), paired gills are present. But this is an exceptional adaptation among leeches, since respiration is generally through the skin in the Hirudinea, as it is in the Oligochaeta. Excretory and circulatory structures, likewise, are similar.

It might be noted that in *Hirudo medicinalis-and* perhaps in some other leeches also-the nerve cord is contained within the ventral blood vessel. Such unusual morphology is encountered again only among the arachnids.

Hirudinea are hermaphroditic, like the Oligochaeta, and the gonads are situated in the anterior portion of the body. Also, the production of young includes the formation of a protective cocoon in which the embryos develop. A notable difference, in comparison with oligochaetes, is the presence of a penis and a vagina, so that insemination is possible, and takes place, within the body.

But this is not so in all of the leeches. In Glossiphonia, for example, sperm are simply deposited in a packet upon the skin of the female. They are apparently able to penetrate the body on their own, and reach the ovaries.

Since they are found in fresh water, in the sea, and upon the land, Hirudinea obviously have a wider ecological distribution than do either Oligochaeta or Polychaeta. Of the terrestrial forms Haemadipsa, a forest dweller, makes some tropical regions almost impenetrable to man.

Some Additional Types of Annelids

We do not wish to stress, nor call undue attention by omission, to the formerly much-emphasized class Archiannelida. These annelids were previously regarded as the most primitive members of the phylum, and ancestral to the other classes. This was their chief distinction. The Archiannelida are now thought to be advanced forms that are secondarily simplified; as represented in Polygordius.

There are other groups of worms which may be more or less closely related to the annelid phylum, or they may not. These are the Sipunculoidea (e.g., Phascolosoma) and the Echiuroidea (e.g., Urechis), which are sometimes brought together as Gephyrea, whether the name is given to a separate phylum or a class of the annelid phylum.

A group known as the Priapuloidea (e.g. Priapulus) has also in the past been considered as possibly related here. But there is much doubt about the taxonomic standing of all three, and little would be gained by an attempt on our part to go into the changing classification of these obscure groups.

It might be noted that in their embryology there is usually a trochophore larva and that in the adult nephridia are generally present. Metamerism is shown, but fleetingly, only in the Echiuroidea. The Gephyrea are very sluggish in movement. They are found burrowing in sand and mud along the seashore, feeding on detritus. They give evidence of being degenerate forms, evolutionarily most unsuccessful.

The common name “peanut worms” sometimes applied to the Sipunculoidea might well be extended to cover all of the Gephyrea, with regard to their general significance among present-day worms. We do not mention the Gephyrea entirely in vain, however. Among the Echiuroidea is to be found a biological extreme, and such are always interesting. Bonellia males and females are certainly not very much alike.

The female is a small ovoid animal, a few centimeters in length, which lives a concealed life in the burrows of other animals and similar protected habitats. For feeding a ciliated proboscis is extended out of the burrow. The proboscis-up to three feet-is many times the length of the animal. Small and timid as the female may be, the male is more so. He lives a microscopic life in the shelter of the female excretory duct, which also acts as an oviduct.

These are certainly the deepest depths to which male virility has descended in the entire animal kingdom. As eggs pass out of the body of the female, the male fertilizes them. Fertilized eggs are discharged

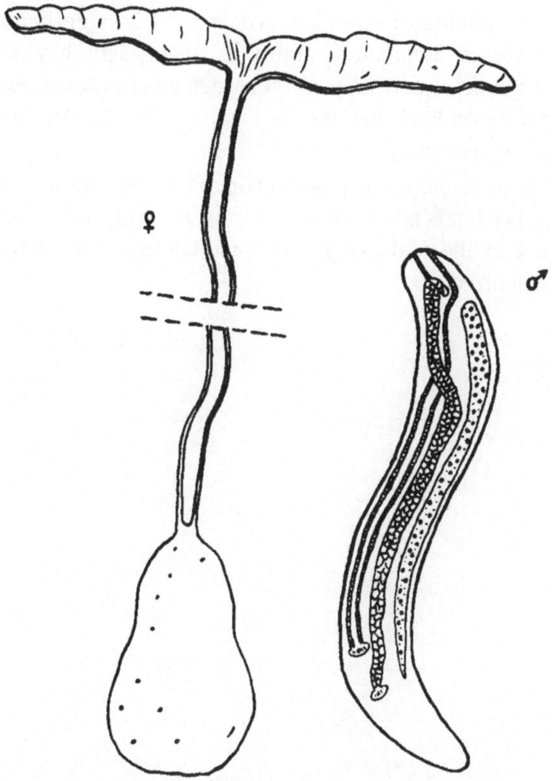

Figure 6.7: Bonellia-male much enlarged, proportionately.

into the sea, where they develop into ciliated larvae. Any such larvae which come into contact with an adult female are believed to enter the mouth and eventually they find their way to the nephridia.

Their development is suppressed, and they become males as described. If a larva escapes contact with a female, however, it develops into a female and then itself acts toward males accordingly.

And yet, although often referred to as such, this is not a case of parasitical relationship. True parasitism can exist only between animals of different kinds. Here it is all in the family, so to speak, and it is of benefit to the species.

CONCLUSION

As we take leave of the phylum Annelida, and of the minor phyla associated with or included with it, we should carry with us a mind-picture of a representative form like Neanthes; an active, alert, predacious animal, with its septa, its segments, and its parapodia.

These are adaptations which are especially significant for a reasonable level of locomotory ability in water, but they would be unsuitable to a general terrestrial realm despite an occasional exceptional annelid surviving on land, like the earthworm or leech. For locomotion on land legs are needed.

They will be found in the phylum which follows. But legs alone are not enough. Skeleton is also necessary. For increased speed of locomotion other systems of the body—e.g., sensory, coordinating, respiratory,- must be harmonized.

7

PHYLUM ONYCHOPHORA

In the annelid locomotory appendages extended out sideways from the body wall, and were used in part as sweeps in swimming. Here, in the *phylum Onychophora*, the appendages are directed downward. This simple change is of the greatest significance. Now, for the first time, we encounter an animal that walks.

This is a most profound achievement. The foundation has been laid for an entirely new way of locomotion. No longer need the body be dragged over the medium it is in contact with. It is now raised upon legs, and frictional *impediment* to movement becomes a minor factor.

This is especially important for animals that live on land, for the *buoyant* effect of water is absent and the full weight of the body must be dealt with. And yet, despite this new feature which they possess, the *Onychophora* are not an *outstanding* success. To develop the actual mechanical means for moving about on the land is an advance in only one body system.

A fuller, more successful, adaption to a terrestrial environment would involve a great many other systems. Particularly is it necessary for a new water balance to be attained between the animal and its environment, and here the onychophorans are especially weak in their adaptation. It would be too much to expect complete terrestrial adjustment to occur in one group. Progress is slow in nature.

Only the essential first steps were taken in onychoporan evolution, but there is evidence that they were sufficient to give the onychophorans

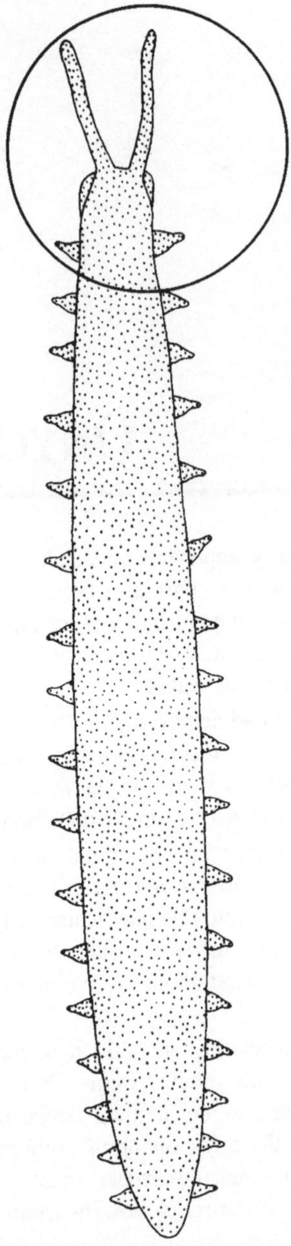

Fgure 7.1: Dorsal view of Peripatus.

widespread distribution upon the land in early evolutionary times. Then, as other more perfected groups appeared, the *Onychophora* were forced back.

They remain only in isolated pockets of survival, as we find them today. Although there were once additional genera—even one which lived in the sea, named Aysheaia-only the genus *Peripatus* still survives. The *Onychophora* possess the distinction of being a phylum with a *single* genus.'

THE PERIPAFUS HEAD

It is sometimes said that Peripatus has no head but it would be more correct to say that Peripatus has no neck, since there is no constriction between head and body. The neck is a valuable aid in the use of the head, but the absence of the former by no means rules out the presence of the latter.

In the absence of a neck, however, we must look to other criteria for identifying the head: eyes, and certain distinctive appendages. There are sensory antennae—a single pair—on the first segment, with a pair of small shining eyes behind them. The second appendages of the head are the jaws, but these are not easily visible since they are contained within the mouth.

Nevertheless the jaws are derived from appendages, and are independently movable. To facilitate the taking of food the mouth is

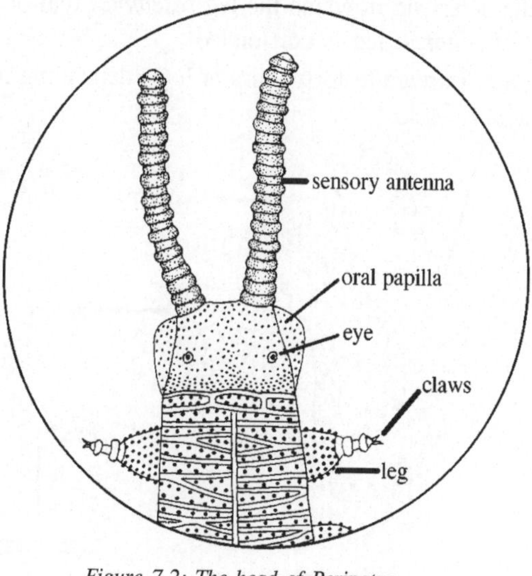

Figure 7.2: The head of Peripatus.

directed ventrally, toward the ground. This arrangement should be compared with that of Neanthes, where the mouth is directed anteriorly and the *jaws* are an integral part of the pharyngeal mechanism.

Also within the mouth, formed anteriorly from the roof, is a rasping tongue with chitinous teeth, somewhat like the radula of the *mollusks* which we shall encounter later. The third pair of *appendages* consists of stumplike projections known as "*oral papillae*," which contain the openings of a pair of large slime *glands*.

Through the oral papillae a stream of slime may be accurately thrown for a distance of several inches. This is a *precocious* reaction, if compared with humans, but now it is part of the essential behaviour of the animal serving both for defense and for the capture by entanglement of insects and other small *organisms* to be used as food.

Ascribing the latter function has been questioned, however. *Antennae*, jaws, and oral papillae are appendages of the head, and they show that the head is composed of at least these three segments, which are *otherwise* not distinct.

The Body

Peripatus is a short, wormlike animal, attaining a *maximum* length of about three inches. The *segmentation* of the body, like that of the head, is best related to the appendages. Each of the body appendages is in the form of a cone-shaped leg. *Terminally* each leg bears (two) claws, a characteristic in which the leg *resembles* that of an arthropod, but the *onychophoran* leg is not jointed.

There are fourteen to forty pairs of legs, depending on the species.

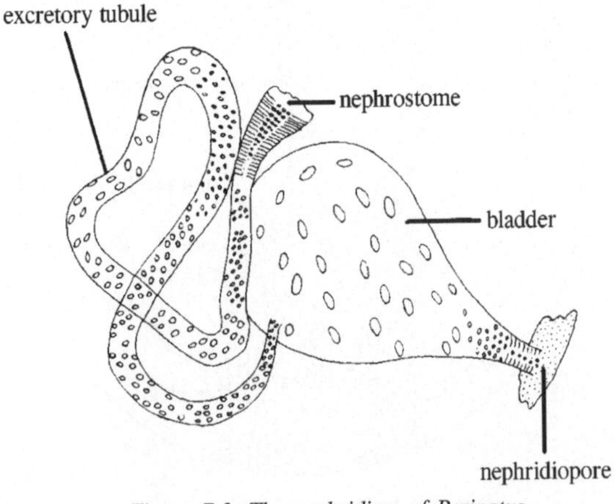

Figure 7.3: The nephridium of Peripatus.

A nephridial opening lies on the inner basal region of each leg, as on the annelid parapodium. These paired nephridial openings, arranged in series, give evidence of the internal segmental nature of the excretory system. The body shows numerous external circular annulations, but these are far greater in number than the pairs of appendages and therefore without metameric significance.

They are only wrinkles in the cuticle, comparable with those on the body of a leech, and bear no relation to basic segmentation as shown by appendages and nephridia. Posteriorly the body terminates in the anus while somewhat anterior and ventral to the anus, in both male and female, lies the genital opening.

Beneath the cuticle is an epidermis and a thin muscular body wall composed of circular, longitudinal, and transverse fibers. The appendages are themselves muscular, and move independently of the muscles of the body wall.

The Alimentary Tract

The alimentary tube is straight and simple. Following the mouth, with its jaws and spiny tongue, is a short, muscular pharynx, supplied with a pair of large salivary glands.

It is extremely interesting that the salivary glands of Peripatus are derived from nephridia, whose function has been here modified to secrete fluids for lubricating the passage of food into the digestive tube. (It was noted above that it is not saliva which Peripatus expectorates, but a slimy secretion especially provided for the purpose.)

The pharynx is succeeded by a short and narrow esophagus, which is followed in turn by a much wider and thin-walled stomach-intestine. The *stomach*-intestine makes up the longest part of the digestive system, and it then *narrows* down into a rectum that controls anal discharge.

CIRCULATORY SYSTEM

The blood-circulatory system of Peripatus is not at all like that of an annelid. The blood flows through the body spaces between the intestine and the body wall. There is only a single formed vessel. This lies dorsally, under the body wall, and runs through the full length of the animal. Blood enters from the *haemocoel* through paired ostia, provided with valves to prevent *backflow*.

The ostia lie opposite each pair of legs and are an indication of segmental nature in the circulatory system. No one seems to have determined in which direction blood flows through the dorsal vessel, or "*heart*." Presumably it is from posterior toward anterior, if similar to

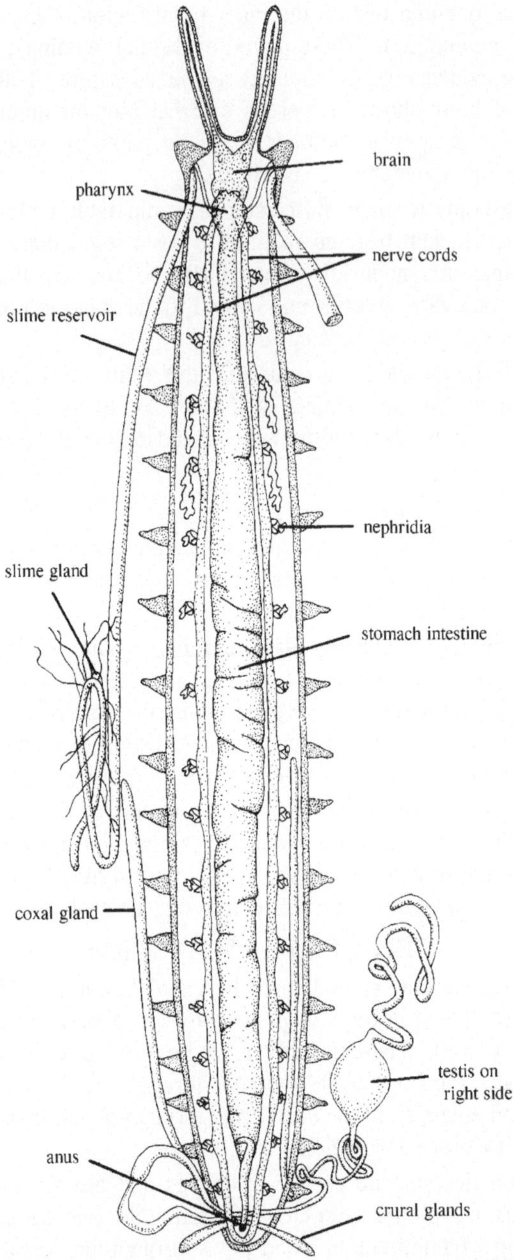

Figure 7.4: Alimentary and other internal organ systems of Peripatus.

the annelid. The elaborate system of vessels of the annelid is not present. This is an "open system," and the body cavity is a haemocoel, as in arthropods.

The low level of muscular activity of the body doubtless contributes, in part, to the ability to get along without a more positive circulatory mechanism. Perhaps most important is the fact that the blood has been *largely* relieved of the function of *transport* of *respiratory* gases.

RESPIRATION, AND WATER EQUILIBRIUM

It will be remembered that respiration requires a large area of moist surface for the exchange of oxygen and carbon dioxide to and from the tissues of the body. In aquatic animals the body surface itself, unless covered by an *impervious* layer, is effective in this function. Frequently the surface area is increased by the *proliferation* of gills, as we have observed in some of the *annelids*.

In a terrestrial animal the need for conservation of water, which is not readily available in the environment, combined with the drying effect of the atmosphere, rule out the general adaptation of the skin for respiratory use. *Nevertheless*, a large moist surface must be provided. Since this cannot be done externally, the *mechanism* is developed internally.

In Peripatus the respiratory system consists of long moist tubes that arise from external openings, the stigmata or spiracles. Unlike those of arthropods, these spiracles are irregularly scattered over the surface of the body, and therefore show no relation to metamerism.

This may or may not be an indication that the respiratory systems of *Onychophora* and *Arthropoda* (tracheate classes) have an independent origin. The air ducts, or tracheae, are simple and unbranched in the *Onychophoran phylum*. They penetrate deeply into the body, and carry *respiratory* gases directly to and from the organs.

Because the surface for gas exchange is internally located, there is much less loss of water than if a similar area were spread out exposed to the atmosphere. *Nevertheless* the loss of water is still considerable, and this is likely the most limiting factor in the terrestrial life of Peripatus.

More than any other factor, it probably restricts the genus to the moist tropical regions in which it is found. Unlike those of later, more perfected, systems the stigmata of Peripatus are not equipped with any closing device. Water loss is very many times greater (about forty

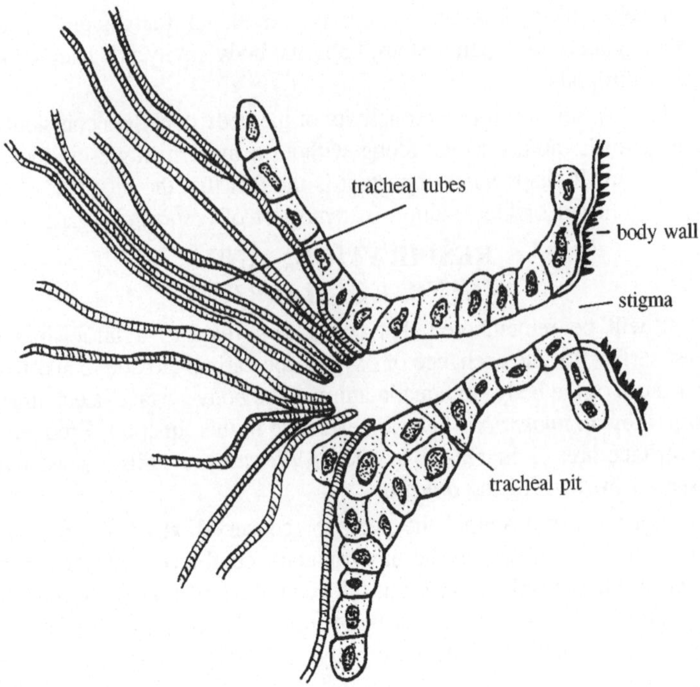

Figure 7.5: A respiratory organ of Peripatus.

times) than that of a caterpillar, with which Peripatus might be *compared* in bulk and level of activity.

Reproduction

As they are in *respiration* water considerations are also critical in other areas of the animal's activity. Gametes cannot be freely scattered through a terrestrial environment. At the least, *insemination* must be internal. The egg may then be *protected* by a shell for external *development*.

If not so protected development must also be internal. While in a few species of Peripatus the zygote is cast off within a shell, in most species fully-formed miniature individuals are developed within the body of the mother. It is curious then that there is no mechanism for insemination. Here is another point of imperfect terrestrial *adaptation*.

There is no copulatory organ for introducing sperm into the genital system of the female, and there are no secondary sexual characteristics whatsoever, except that the genital orifice of the male is somewhat smaller than that of the female (of course, the male is not required to give birth to young). Sperms are discharged in packets, or spermatophores, which are deposited upon the surface of the *female body*.

The sperms somehow find their own way into the oviducts. The female possesses a pair of ovaries and a pair of oviducts. The latter enlarge distally into uteri, and here the young develop. Uteri join in a common vagina which opens to the exterior between the last pair of *walking legs*.

It is through the *vaginal* opening that the young are born. Like those of the excretory system, from which they are derived, the genital ducts are ciliated. This point is significant since cilia are not present in the *arthropod phylum*, with which the onychophorans do share certain other *structural* features already brought out.

Nervous System

The Onychophora present many surprising structural arrangements, and the nervous system is not the least of them. For a phylum which is far enough along in some respects to be compared with Arthropoda, the nervous system is very primitive. In the dorsal region of the head there is a brain, in the form of a pair of cerebral ganglia.

A pair of long nerve cords, widely *separated*, run from the brain through the ventral length of the body to the posterior end. Here the nerve cords join together. Although the cords thicken slightly near each pair of legs, there are no ganglia. At intervals there are lateral nerve *connectives* between the two cords.

These are more frequent than the probable segments that make up the body, and therefore without metameric significance. On the whole the nervous system of the *phylum*—where legs and tracheae have been first attained—is on the level with that of the flatworms, the earliest *triploblastic* animals.

CONCLUSION

What is *Peripatus*?

Peripatus is a combination of features that are reminiscent of annelids, arthropods, and flatworms. In some special respects, *Peripatus* is simply itself. It has been assigned great prestige as a living connecting link, representing ancient *ancestral* stock.

Peripatus is a "*shy*," nocturnal, slow-moving animal, with evidence strongly indicating that it is in the process of bowing out of the living scene. We shall remember it as the first animal with a true leg; an *appendage* which raises the body off the ground.

It can walk upon the land and, *imperfectly* as it is adapted to the water requirements of a terrestrial existence, it has possibly walked upon the land for *greater* eras of time than any other truly *terrestrial* animal.

8

Phylum Arthropoda

In the *annelid* worms the metamerically—arranged locomotory appendages, as seen in *Neanthes*, were in the form of paddles projecting laterally from the sides of the body. Onychophoran appendages were turned ventrally and thereby became legs, capable of *holding* the body off the ground. Not very far off the ground, to be sure, but nevertheless off and, consequently, *Peripatus* could walk.

This is our first animal which is able to walk and, as biologists, we should take great pride in it, however *vicariously*. We now accept animals with legs too much as a matter of *course*. The first walking steps taken in the evolutionary scale were comparatively ineffectual.

This is so because *onychophoran* legs are short and, after orientation, length is a major factor in the functioning of a leg. Other things being equal, an animal with longer legs is able to walk, or run, or leap, better than one with short legs.

Onychophoran legs are muscular, but muscle alone is not enough to form a long leg. An essential ingredient-skeleton-is missing. But skeleton, as such, is stiff and would prevent movement. The evolutionary problem was one of supplying stiffening material without stiffening the leg. This is the great achievement found in the *arthropods*.

As with many great *achievements*, it was accomplished in a simple manner by introducing soft spots in the skeleton. These are the joints. Joints should not be taken for granted; they are a truly great advance. They have given the phylum Arthropoda its name and, perhaps more than any other *arthropod* feature, joints opened the way for the animals in this phylum to become the *dominant* group they now are.

In only two *phyla* do we find long legs. These are the Arthropoda and the *Chordata*. In both, the legs are stiffened with *skeleton*, and in both they are provided with joints. Of course, the method of *employing* the skeleton is different in the two *phyla*.

A true leg is designed to exert effective thrusts against the body, otherwise it would not fulfil its *locomotory* purpose. And the body must, accordingly, be built to receive the thrust. In arthropods the body is enclosed in a capsule of *skeleton*, more or less jointed to allow for *flexibility*.

The *skeleton* is secreted by the epidermis and encloses all of the soft parts within, thus affording them the important additional benefit of protection. But, being outside of all other parts, the *skeleton* occupies the largest dimension of the body and tends to be great in bulk and heavy in weight. As the animal gets larger a point of diminishing *returns* must soon be reached, where too much energy is required to move the weight of the skeleton itself.

This would place a limit on the size of arthropod animals. We find that they are comparatively small. Both phyla-Arthropoda and Chordata-in which the conflict between flexibility and skeletal support has been successfully resolved, have been eminently successful. It is as yet not certain which is destined to be more successful.

Certainly man, selfacclaimed as the most outstanding of the chordates, finds himself in uncomfortable competition with some of the jointed-leg invertebrates. It would be an oversimplification to state that the success of the arthropods is due entirely to the application of a little stiffening material to the leg.

However, the mechanical advantage of a leg with skeleton over one without skeleton is obviously so great that we may assume that the difference in destiny between the two invertebrate phyla which possess true legs-*Onychophora* and *Arthropoda*-began on the basis of this distinction. Success in nature has only one clearly *measurable* index, that of numbers.

The Onychophora are a phylum in deep decline. There is only a single genus barely surviving in scattered pockets here and there in the moist, warm regions of the world. By contrast the Arthropoda contain more genera, more species, and more individuals than perhaps all of the other metazoan phyla put together; and they cover the earth from pole to pole.

Such seems to be the significance of the leg; with skeleton for support and jointed for *flexibility*.

THE USE OF LEGS IN CLASSIFICATION

Besides its locomotory properties, the leg has many other aspects of significance in the arthropod phylum. It is not surprising that it is of value in classification, even as locomotory organelles were in protozoans.

As a first step, Arthropoda may be recognized as composed of two subphyla, the subphylum Mandibulata and the subphylum Chelicerata. What does this have to do with legs? We find that, while *originating* as adaptations for *locomotion*, arthropod legs become modified for many *additional* uses.

One of these is concerned with the processing of food. The mandible is a much shortened leg, heavily skeletonized and designed to serve the mouth in the chewing of food; it is a feature of the groups that compose the subphylum *Mandibulata*: *crustaceans*, *insects*, and some lesser ones. In the spiders and their relatives, of the *subphylum Chelicerata*, there are no mandibles.

Instead, the bases or shoulders of some of the walking legs are designed to nibble food. This is a very interesting combination of functions. The same appendage that served for the pursuit of food by locomotion may then act to masticate the food for ingestion.

Legs or modifications thereof are also *taxonomically* significant because of their position or numbers. In the location that *Mandibulata* have appendages (legs) modified to form antennae, *Chelicerata* have them as claws, or chelae. *Diplopoda*, or *millipedes*, are distinguished by the presence of two pairs of walking legs on each body segment of the adult animal, while *Chilopoda* (*centipedes*) have only a single pair to a segment.

The *Arachnoidea*-spiders and related forms-have four pairs of legs on the cephalothorax; insects, three pairs on the thorax. And so it goes. In case after case, the functionally significant leg is also of *taxonomic* importance.

There are several arthropod classes which are relatively minor, and we shall quickly dispose of these with very brief *treatment*. All of them are in the *mandibulate subphylum*.

Class Trilobita

Trilobites are no longer found as living forms. They were small animals of the sea, usually up to about ten centimeters in length, although some attained to almost a meter.

They have had their day in ancient seas and have, apparently, been forced from the scene by more capable successors. Most distinctive of the structure of a trilobite is the fact that the body was divided by longitudinal dorsal furrows into a central and two lateral regions. Along the length, head, thoracic, and abdominal regions were somewhat differentiated. The head bore a pair of compound eyes, a pair of uniramous *antennae*, and four pairs of biramous *appendages*. The numerous additional appendages of the body were all *biramous*. The Trilobita are a primitive group which live only in our *remembrance*. Their significance is *historical*.

Class Chilopoda

The centipedes are wormlike terrestrial arthropods with the body flattened dorsoventrally. The head is provided with eyes, a single pair of antennae, a pair of mandibles, and two pairs of maxillae. On the first segment behind the head there is a pair of maxillipeds ("*maxilliped*," "*jaw-foot*"), which contain *hypodermic* poison glands for *subduing* prey.

Each of the rest of the body segments, except two terminal ones, bears a single pair of walking legs. Breathing is by means of tracheal tubes and excretion through *Malpighian tubules*. The latter discharge through the hinder end of the *intestine*, which is straight rather than *coiled*. The genital system opens separately at the *posterior* end of the body.

Class Diplopoda

Millipedes are also wormlike tracheate *arthropods* and are enough like centipedes so that the two groups were at one time classified together as the *Myriapoda*. However, there are some points of sharp distinction. Not the least of these is that in the adult *millipede* each body segment is supported on two pairs of legs.

This is brought about by the embryological fusion of segments in groups of two. The head of a millipede, unlike that of a centipede, has only a single pair of *maxillae*, and the body is strongly arched in crosssection, not flattened as in centipedes. The absence of poison claws is reflected in the fact that millipedes are typically scavengers; while *centipedes* are *predacious*. Finally, for some strange reason, the gonads of a *millipede* open *anteriorly*, on the third segment of the body.

Because of the differences in structure it is better not to assume too close a relationship between *centipedes* and *millipedes*, but to regard them as separate classes.

9

CLASS CRUSTACEA

Crustaceans, insects and arachnids are the now dominant triumvirate of the arthropods, and these three chapters will consider them in this order. We have already noted that the arachnids occupy a separate group at the subphylum level because of distinctive modifications of their appendages.

Appendage characteristics may also be used as a rule of thumb to sort crustaceans, insects, and arachnids into their respective classes. Arachnids are separable from the others because their initial appendages are claws rather than antennae. Insects, in turn, have a pair of antennae first (followed by mouth parts); crustaceans have two pairs of antennae.

EUBRANCHPUS, A PRIMITIVE CRUSTACEAN

The body of a crustacean is sometimes much longer than it is wide, but in some crustaceans these axes have been considerably reversed, and the width is greater than the length. So much so that the animal even moves laterally, in a direction parallel to the longest body dimension.

These are the crabs. Appendages are basically biramous and leaflike, somewhat like the parapodium of a Neanthes, but jointed. More advanced types of appendages take various shapes and forms. In primitive crustacea we find the more or less wormlike bodies and the biramous leaflike appendages, as in the genus Eubranchipus, the "fairy shrimp", to which we shall first turn our attention.

It seems reasonable to assume that crustaceans originated in the sea but, curiously, Eubranchipus is not found in this habitat. Other seemingly primitive genera, like *Artemia salina*, show wide tolerance to salt concentration; from brine pools chemically saturated with salts to waters of very low salinity.

But Artemia will not reproduce in salt concentrations lower than that of the sea, which may be an indication of evolutionary origin. Eubranchipus is about one inch long, and swims with its eyes oriented toward lesser illumination. This means, generally, that it swims upside down.

The animal is composed of twenty-five segments (one of which, the first, disappears during development). This is additional evidence of extended length, i.e. wormlike nature, since more advanced crustaceans possess only twenty segments. There are five segments in the adult head (six embryologically), twelve in the thorax, and seven in the abdomen. As in other "entomostracans" ("entomo-," insect; hence, "insectlike"), the abdominal segments are distinctive in that they bear no appendages.

The first two pairs of head appendages are sensory antennae, but in the male the second pair is modified for clasping the female during copulation. After the antennae there is a pair of appendages that are shortened, thickened and turned inwardly to form chewing mandibles.

The fourth and fifth pairs of appendages are maxillae, which aid in holding food during mastication. On the base of the second maxillae are the openings of the excretory organs. We should note, then, that sensory, reproductive, feeding, and excretory functions are associated with the head appendages and thereby become functions of the head.

Dorsally the head carries a pair of compound eyes on stalks and, anterior to these, there is retained the single median eye that served the larva. Of the twelve thoracic segments the first eleven possess locomotory appendages of broadened, bladelike structure adapted for swimming. These appendages are also provided with bristles for straining food out of the water.

This, the microphagous method of filter-feeding, is found in many of the smaller crustaceans. Between their bases the appendages are hollowed out to form a groove along which food is wafted toward the mouth. Here food particles are consolidated into masses with the aid of a sticky secretion emanating from the labrum, or upper lip, and are chewed by the mandibles.

The last pair of thoracic appendages are copulatory organs in the male, and form an egg basket in the female for brooding the developing embryos. The openings of the gonoducts are also on the twelfth, or last, segment of the thorax.

Like the young of many groups, those of crustaceans are quite distinctive. There is a larval stage, the nauplius, which shows three pairs of appendages and a single central eye. In Eubranchipus, like other primitive crustaceans, the nauplius is a free-swimming stage.

In more advanced forms the nauplius is superseded by later stages while the organism is still developing within the egg. With the exception of the first antenna, which is uniramousand this is so in all crustaceans-the appendages of Eubranchipus are of the biramous type.

The biramous pattern is the original pattern, but in later members of the class it is often outgrown and supplanted by the uniramous. The change from biramous to uniramous occurs by the inhibition of the development of one of the rami while the animal, and its appendages, are still very small.

The biramous appendage consists of a basal stalk, the protopodite, which arises from the body. The protopodite is typically composed of two segments in series, although in some crustaceans one or both of these may be divided again to give a maximum of four, never more. After the protopodite the appendage forks into two branches.

The inner branch is known as the endopodite, and the outer one as the exopodite. All of the variations which the crustacean appendage may manifest-from mandible to walking leg (periopod), from maxilliped to swimmeret (pleopod), from antenna to uropod-can be traced back, although sometimes with difficulty, to the primitive biramous plan.

This is an exercise in serial homology. No matter how different the appendages may be in appearance and in function, the original plan of their structure is the same, part for part. Internally, we find that Eubranchipus is built on the usual tubewithin-a-tube plan of structure, but the alimentary tube is aligned within the body tube in a rather odd manner. The esophagus, the stomach, and the digestive glands all lie within the head region.

A blood vessel is situated dorsally to the intestine. Through a pair of ostia in each segment blood is drawn into the blood vessel from the body cavity. The blood is pumped forward and discharged again into the body cavity at the anterior end. The dorsal blood vessel may therefore be functionally recognized as a heart, and the body cavity as a haemocoel.

The circulatory system is simple, and comparable to that of Peripatus. The flow of haemocoelic fluids apparently suffices to ventilate the internal organs. There are, of course, no tracheal tubes as in Peripatus. In larger crustaceans we shall find specific provisions for aerating the blood, and for directing the flow of blood through respiratory channels.

This will be brought out later, in connection with the lobster. Anterior to the esophagus, which runs inward at an angle from mouth to stomach, there is a brain. There is a nerve ring from the brain around the esophagus and there are two ganglionated nerve cords, widely separated from each other in a manner not unexpected among primitive animals.

It will be remembered that the nerve cords of Peripatus are also separated. While widespread in spatial distribution, Eubranchipus is greatly restricted seasonally. Tolerance to temperature is very limited-from about four to fifteen degrees Centigrade-and, consequently, the animals appear soon after the spring thaw and disappear again with the onset of warm summer weather.

Behind them they leave resistant eggs that carry the species over to the next favourable period. Eubranchipus is defenseless against aggressors but, fortunately, in the temporary ponds which it inhabits predators large enough to attack it are not frequent. We shall remember this form for comparison with the lobster, but first a few words about crustacean taxonomy.

CLASSIFICATION OF THE CRUSTACEA

Until fairly recently the class Crustacea was divided into two subclasses. Small crustaceans without abdominal appendages were placed in the subclass Entomostraca; larger ones with abdominal appendages, in the subclass Malacostraca.

This distinction is now out of date. With regard to size, we should understand that animals of one taxonomic group may be small and those of another large, and do not belong to their respective groups because of their difference in size. Other more fundamental characteristics must be present. Size, itself, is purely secondary. The crab Pinnixia, which lives in their tubes with the annelid worms Clymenella and Chaetopterus, is two millimeters long and six wide.

It is a malacostracan. Eubranchipus, an entomostracan, is over two centimeters long. If size were a valid criterion then the taxonomic position of these two should be reversed. On the basis of what features, then, are the crustaceans classified? It is not surprising that locomotory adaptations-the appendages-and derivatives of them, are important.

It is, again, indicative of the basic significance of locomotion in animal life. The adaptations developed for moving about in the environment are linked with the position attained in the evolutionary scale.

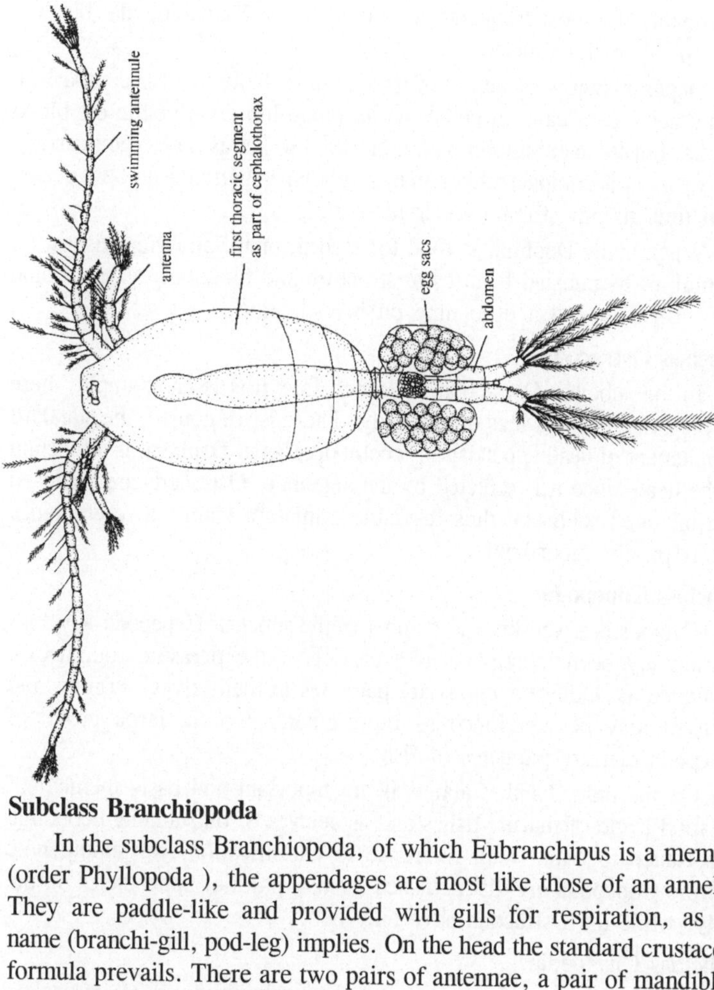

Figure 9.1: Cyclops, a common fresh water copepod.

Subclass Branchiopoda

In the subclass Branchiopoda, of which Eubranchipus is a member (order Phyllopoda), the appendages are most like those of an annelid. They are paddle-like and provided with gills for respiration, as the name (branchi-gill, pod-leg) implies. On the head the standard crustacean formula prevails. There are two pairs of antennae, a pair of mandibles, and two pairs of maxillae.

Since this is the same for all crustaceans, it cannot furnish a basis for further classification. Branchiopoda are different from other subclasses in that the rest of the appendages are uniformly branchiopods, as already described.

Order Cladocera

It is rather curious that, while crustaceans presumably originated in the sea, the members of this primitive subclass are so predominantly freshwater animals. The "water flea" Daphnia, of the order Cladocera, is probably the most frequently observed of the Branchiopoda, but it is not typical of the subclass.

Daphnia swims by action of its antennae. Note this for comparison with other crustaceans. It possesses haemoglobin dissolved in the blood plasma, but its haemoglobin is not believed to act as an oxygen carrier. The heart is a compact rather than a tubular organ and its beat ceases from time to time for no apparent reason.

When using Daphnia as food for Hydra, or for aquarium fishes, let us think of its unusual features of structure and function. Perhaps some will wish to spend a little time on investigation.

Subclass Ostracoda

In the subclass Ostracoda, of which Eucypris is an example, there are only two pairs of legs on the body. There is, of course, the standard complement of head appendages; locomotion, as in Daphnia, is a function of the head since it is effected by the antennae. Ostracods are enclosed in a bivalved shell and thus resemble miniature clams, a resemblance that is purely superficial.

Subclass Copepoda

Cyclops is a well-known member of the subclass Copepoda. Cyclops has already been mentioned as a carrier of the parasitic roundworm Dracunculus. Other copepods are parasites in themselves. Argulus and Lernaea may be mentioned as representatives of a. large group of copepods that are parasites of fish.

On the other hand, Calanus is an important and basic member of the food cycle of marine fishes and as such is of outstanding economic importance to man. With reference to classification, we should note that the Copepoda are distinguished by five pairs of appendages on the body, while the Ostracoda have only two.

Subclass Cirripedia

The omnipresent barnacles-rock barnacles and goose barnacles, ship barnacles and whale barnacles-were a taxonomic mystery to observers of older times. Some thought they were clams. Others thought that they were created by spontaneous generation from the feathers of sea birds. At present we recognize them as members of the crustacean subclass Cirripedia.

The most striking feature of a barnacle is its skeleton, which is hardened with lime and arranged in the form of protective plates about the body within. The typical barnacle lives along the shores of the sea, exposed to the turbulence of the surf, against which the skeleton serves

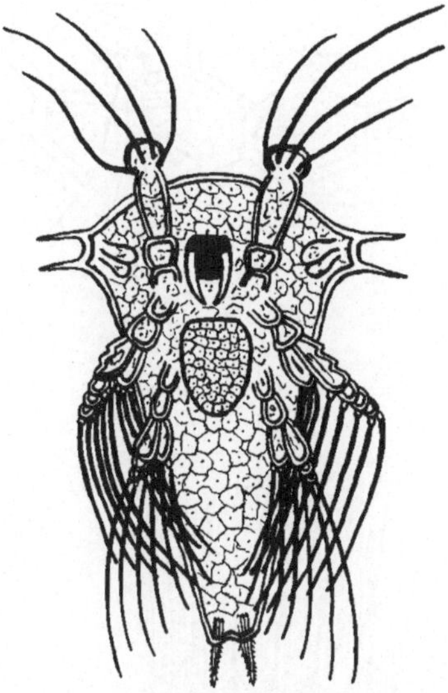

Figure 9.2: The nauplius larva of Sacculina, free living.

as a mechanical protection. To survive the periods when it is exposed by the receding tide to the heat and drying effect of the air it has physiological protections. Shore barnacles live a rugged life in these respects. But feeding is a different matter.

The adult barnacle is a sedentary animal, attached, lying on its back straining food particles out of the sea water and wafting them toward the mouth, with its appendages. From attachment to inanimate objects it is not a long step to attachment on a live host.

And so we find some barnacles on whales and other deep-sea animals. Of these, *Scalpellum regium* is interesting because of sex dimorphism. How is an attached female barnacle, constantly on the move due to the swimming of its host, to find a mate?

The chances are slight. In Scalpellum the females are comparatively large and the males very small. Once contact has been made, the female thereafter always carries the male with her (compare Schistosoma and Bonellia).

In Sacculina we have a barnacle that has gone beyond physical attachment to actual nutritive parasitism, and paid the usual price of such association in structural atrophy. Sacculina hatches from its egg as a typical crustacean larva, the nauplius. It grows and metamorphoses as a free-living form into the bivalved cypris stage, so called because it resembles Eucypris.

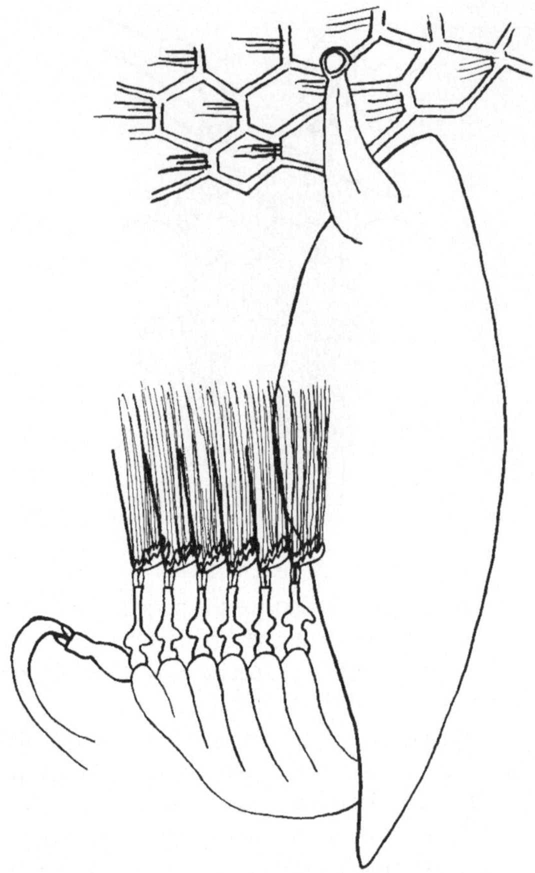

Figure 9.3: The cypris stage of Sacculina, on attachment to the host.

Then, by means of the antennae, Sacculina attaches to the thin ventral skeleton on the abdomen of a crab and its behaviour and appearance cease to resemble the usual barnacle. Sacculina leaves its own skeleton and passes within that of its host, never again in its lifetime to look or act like a barnacle.

Proliferating like a tumor, wandering rootlike growths pervade the tissues of the crab and absorb nutriment. Finally, on maturity, a sac containing the reproductive organs bulges out of the crab and recognizable nauplius larvae are produced, to reestablish the identity of the parasite. Morphologically, Cirripedia are noted for six pairs of legs on the body, besides the appendages of the head—but as we have seen they are without locomotory function.

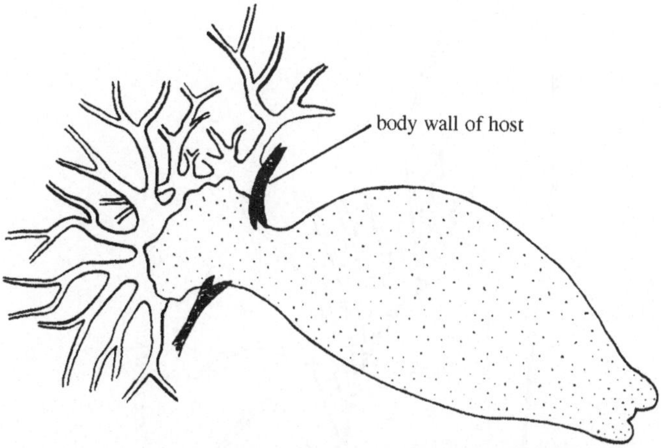

Figure 9.4: The atrophied form of Sacculkina as a parasite.

The antennae, which in previous subclasses often served as locomotory organs, here secrete a cement that fastens the larva to the substrate upon which the animal lives. It is significant that, in relation to their peculiar sedentary habit, four out of the five orders of the subclass Cirripedia have become partially or entirely parasitic.

Subclass Malacostraca

In the subclass Malacostraca, which includes the largest of the crustaceans, as well as many of very modest size, appendages are developed to the very end of the body. Typically there are five pairs of head appendages, eight pairs on the thorax, and six on the abdomen; nineteen pairs of appendages in all. Usually all three body regions of—a malacostracan are well developed.

There is a recognizable head, thorax, and abdomen; but there is no neck and there is no waist. These are extremely important omissions and, in view of the handicaps thereby placed on the flexibility of the body, they should not be ignored.

Insects have made much of such simple constrictions. Lobsters, shrimps, fresh and salt water crayfishes, and crabs compose the subclass Malacostraca, which also includes the dorso-ventrally flattened isopods, like the wood lice and pill bugs, and the laterally flattened amphipods like "beach fleas."

HOMARUS AMERICANUS

To round out the view of crustaceans gained from a consideration of one of the most primitive forms, Eubranchipus, we shall now turn to one of the most advanced, the American lobster, *Homarus americanus*.

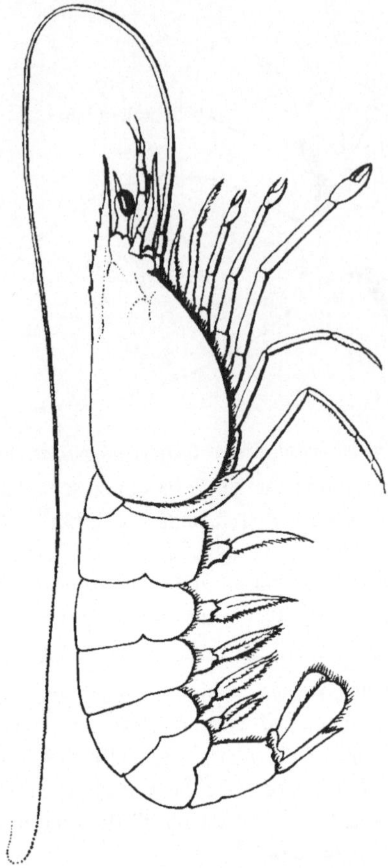

Figure 9.5: Peneus, adult.

Homarus is an animal in which biological importance as a type form is combined with widespread gastronomic appeal. The economic life of many a coastal village in New England and Canada is dominated by lobstering. Traps, constructed like slatted crates, may be seen piled high on the wharves when not in use.

These "lobster pots" are baited with codfish heads or other fishmeat and lowered to the sea bottom. Each is marked in position by a wooden "lobster buoy." The traps are periodically hauled to the surface and the occupants, if any, discreetly removed, for the lobster does not take kindly to such treatment.

The Lobster's Early Development

The lobster does not begin its free life in the nauplius stage. A nauplius larva is found as a swimming form in all previous subclasses

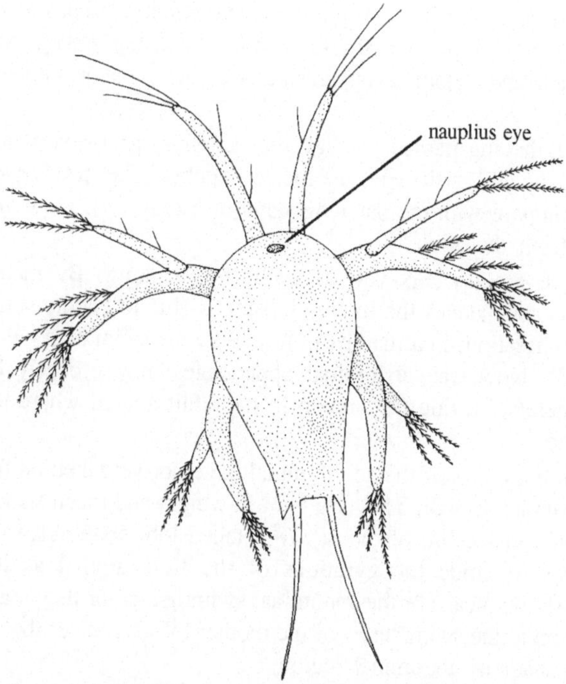

Figure 9.6: The nauplius larva of Peneus, showing presumptive anten nules, antennae, and mandibles now used for swimming.

of the Crustacea, but among malacostracans it is restricted to a very few such as the prawn Peneus.

We shall therefore utilize Peneus to illustrate what must be the inherent developmental pattern. The nauplius stage possesses three pairs of appendages, which will later be incorporated into the head region of the animal as antennules, antennae, and mandibles.

At first, however, these appendages of the prawn nauplius are used for swimming. It is interesting that in primitive crustacean genera, like Daphnia and Eucypris, swimming function is retained by the head appendages even in the adult condition.

But in more advanced forms, as the thoracic appendages make their appearance, the nauplian appendages lose their swimming function and convert to sensory and feeding activities.

This is so in Peneus, and in this stage the abdomen is as Yet unsegmented and without appendages. The larva is now known as a "protozoaea." In the zoaea stage that follows, segmentation of the abdomen begins, and when the abdominal appendages appear the animal is said to be in the mysis stage of development. Perhaps a better and more informative name is the schizopod ("split leg") stage, since both the thoracic and abdominal appendages are now in the primitive biramous condition.

After having passed through the nauplius, protozoaea, and zoaea stages while still in the egg, the lobster hatches as a mysis or schizopod larva (compare with the hatching stage of a crayfish). How different it still is from the adult.

There are no legs yet, as such, for walking. By means of its biramous appendages the minute lobster is able to paddle actively in a forward direction, in a manner quite unlike the swimming behaviour of the adult. Now, the abdominal appendages may properly be called "swimmerets," a title they retain in the adult animal where it has less relevance.

The big claws of the adult animal have not yet taken on their spurt of differential growth. They are light in weight and much flattened. For some time in the life of the newly hatched lobster the claws are used as planes to guide the gyrations of the little animal as it paddles vigorously by means of the abdominal swimmerets; or they may be used to hang on to the swimmerets of the mother lobster, tinder the protection of her capacious abdominal region.

The swimming phase in the early life of the newly hatched lobster is gradually supplanted by crawling habit as the thoracic appendages are modified from the biramous condition into uniramous walking legs. This involves the hypertrophy of the inner ramus, the endopodite, and the suppression of the development of the exopodite.

In the abdominal region biramous condition is retained by the appendages. Particularly noteworthy at this time is the fact that the last appendages become greatly enlarged to form the uropods of the adult, for swimming.

During embryological development, because of the invagination of the epidermal layer from which it is secreted, skeletal material is laid down in the form of a thin tube extending into the body at both mouth and anus. This is particularly so at the mouth end, where ectodermal penetration is deep and gives rise within the stomach to the teeth of the gastric mill.

Here and there the skeleton also works its way into the body in the form of stalks, or tendons, for the attachment of muscles-for example, the long mandibular tendons attached to the mandibles and connected with the mandibular muscles in the dorsal region of the head. In the

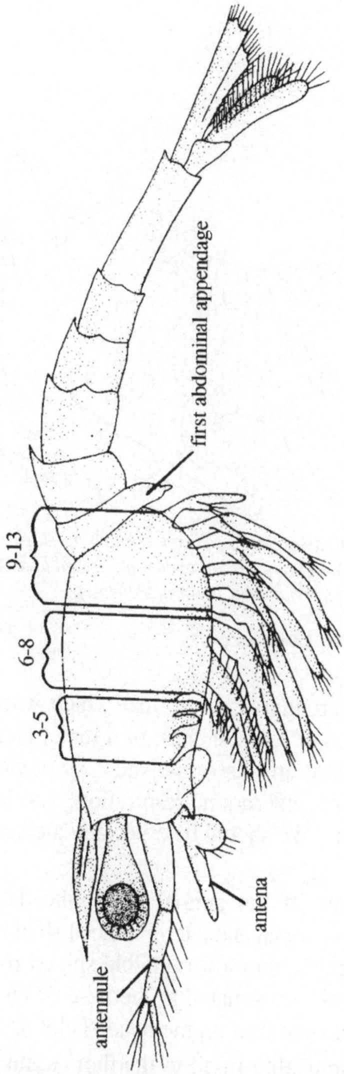

Figure 9.7: Mysis stage of Peneus. First two pairs of appendages now serve as antennae, 3-5 as mouth parts, 6-8 developing as maxillipeds. 9-13 the thoracic "walking legs," are now biramous swimming organs. The first abdominal appendage has appeared, while the terminal uropods are farther advanced.

floor of the thoracic region invaginated exoskeleton makes up a perforated horizontal plate, the endophragmal shelf, to which muscles of the proximal portion of the legs and also the powerful flexors of the abdomen are anchored.

Of course, the bulk of the exoskeleton remains on the outside, both as a protective wrap and as a brace for the various appendages so that they may perform their mechanical functions.

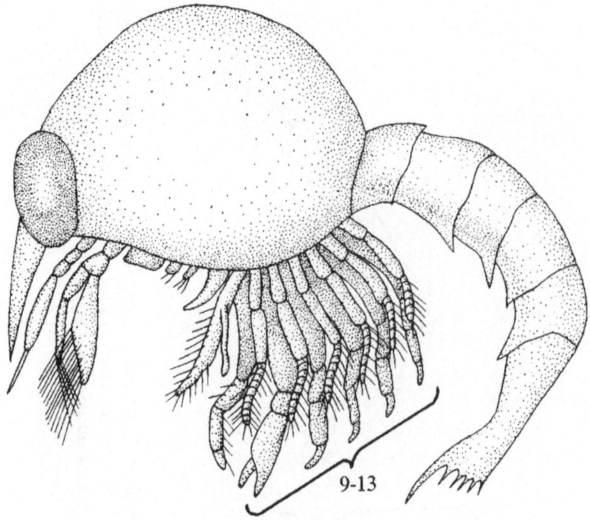

Figure 9.8: The lobster (H. vulgaris), in its schizopod hatching stage. Walking legs (9-13) are biramous on hatching, and there are no abdominal appendages as yet. (Eggs are larger and contain more food material than those of Peneus.)

Appendages of the Adult Lobster, and Related Structures

The adult lobster is an aggressive animal which wanders over the bottom of the sea in search of food, shelter, or a mate. Here appendages are directly involved. They are also involved less obviously in other functions such as sensation, excretion, respiration, and various phases of the reproductive process. We should be especially alert not to overlook secondary functions.

The first two regions of the animal's body-head and thoraxare contained within a common dorsal and lateral skeletal shield, the carapace, which is drawn out anteriorly into a formidable spined rostrum. A pair of eyes, on movable stalks, are situated at the base of the rostrum, and they may be laid back into grooves on the head skeleton for protection.

Since the head is immovably fused to the thorax and cannot, in the absence of a neck, be turned in direction, the presence of movable eye stalks is valuable compensation. Like those of other crustaceans the eyes of the lobster are of the compound type. This means that they are composed of many visual units, the ommatidia.

There are about ten thousand ommatidia in each eye. They are bundled together lengthwise to make up the compound eye. Each ommatidium is an independent visual unit, of cylindrical shape. It is

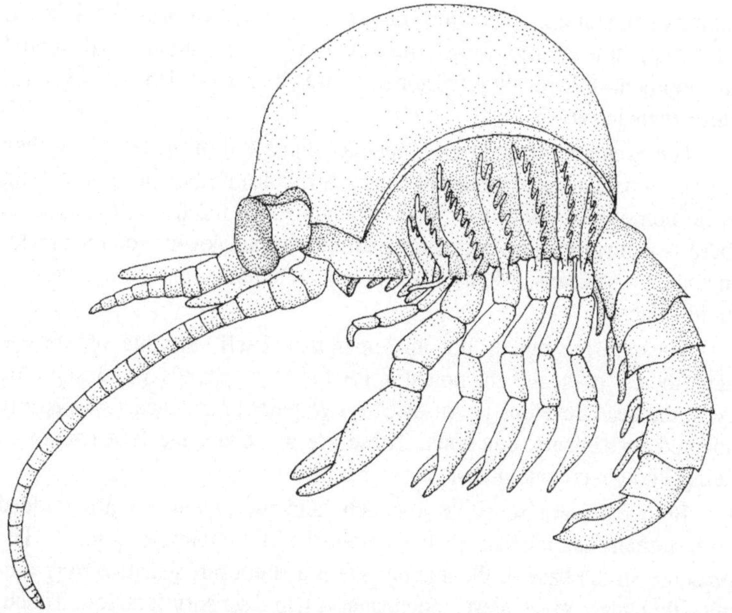

Figure 9.9: The hatching stage of a crayfish. Walking legs are uniramous as in the adult, and abdominal appendages have appeared. (Eggs are larger than those of the lobster.)

insulated on the long axis by a layer of pigment which prevents the passage of light rays, entering at the outer end, from one ommatidium to the other.

But, after the animal is in the dark for a time, the pigment is contracted toward the outer ends of the ommatidia, and the immediate effect of subsequent exposure to light is one of general stimulation. Later the stimulation is specific and each ommatidium receives at its inner nerve-sensitive end only those light rays which are parallel to the long axis.

It would appear, then, that after becoming light-adapted an eye of this type would be especially able to detect movement in the environment. At the same time the possibility that it can form images, though probably rather imperfect ones, is not excluded.

Curious as it may seem, sight is not the most important function of the eyes. They also serve other, rather unexpected purposes. Housed in the eye stalks is a pair of sinus glands that seem to be the chief endocrine organs of the body.

The secretions of the sinus glands control the phase of contraction of the hypodermal chromatophores, and thus determine the shade of colour of the animal. They also determine the rate of beat of the heart, the frequency of moulting, the level of blood sugar, and sexual development. Obviously a lobster that loses its eyes is deprived of much more than its vision.

The eyes are appendages ("append"-hang on) of the head, but they are not appendages in the usual sense. Structurally they are not thought to be homologous with the other appendages of the body. If this is so there is a curious morphogenetic finding that has never been explained: In some crustaceans, when an eye is lost an antenna may be regenerated in its place.

Thus, if the eye is not an appendage itself, the site of the eye nevertheless possesses the potential for forming appendages. Besides the eyes, the head develops in crustaceans two pairs of appendages especially adapted for sensory functions. These are antennae, the first pair often being known as antennules.

Both pairs are sensitive to touch, and the antennules are studded with numerous hairlike setae, responsive to chemical stimuli. The presence in the base of the antennules of a statocyst, sensitive to gravitational change, gives these appendages a triple sensory function. Touch, taste, and balance are all associated with the antennules.

The statocyst is a hollow, saclike organ that opens to the exterior through a pore. Inside it is lined with touch-sensitive hairs, but these are not exposed for contact with outside objects. They are in specific relationship with sand grains which have been introduced through the pores.

The lining of the statocysts, and the sand grains contained within, are shed at each moult and subsequently replaced. (This inspired an investigator-Kreidlto supply freshly moulted shrimps with iron filings to replace the sand grains normally available. When the animals were then placed in a moving magnetic field the function of the statocysts was most dramatically demonstrated.)

In the second pair of antennae two unrelated functions are combined. Besides being more highly touch-sensitive than perhaps any other part of the body, antennae-like antennules-contain pores at the base. These are excretory openings (compare location with Eubranchipus) leading from organs of urinary collection and discharge. It is easy to see, but a little difficult to accept, that the lobster urinates through its head.

Following the antennae there are nine pairs of appendages related to nutrition, either entirely or in part. Three of these pairs are on the head. First are the mandibles (composed almost entirely of protopod) which are situated one on each side of the mouth. The mandibles are the shortest and "stockiest" of the appendages, and on the basis of size it is interesting to find them immediately following the antennae, which are the longest.

The mandibles "nibble" bits of food from larger masses, for entry into the alimentary system. Two pairs of maxillae, behind the mandibles, assist in passing food to the mandibles. When not occupied in this way, the second pair of maxillae may be engaged in its most distinctive function, which is to participate in the respiratory process.

They act as water scoops, or gill bailers, which ventilate the gill chamber in the thorax by drawing water out of it. By this means it will be noted that the water current sweeps in an anterior direction past the head, and the urinary discharge is not swept back to the gills. The maxillae are the last appendages derived from the head.

The first three pairs of thoracic appendages also serve the mouth by picking up and passing food fragments to the maxillae, but they are successively longer than the maxillae and become increasingly leglike in appearance. They are appropriately called maxillipeds. Thoracic appendages then continue, and are completed, with five pairs of walking legs or periopods (composed largely of endoped).

The first pair is, however, not true to name. The first pair of "walking legs" consists of the powerful claws, the chelipeds. These are the bulkiest appendages of the body, and do not contribute to ambulation. They are adapted for aggression and for defense. They grasp and dismember food masses, or food organisms, and the smaller pieces are then passed on in chain sequence to maxillipeds, maxillae, and mandibles.

Of all nineteen pairs of appendages, it is only the last four thoracic pairs that are truly ambulatory. By means of them the lobster's long, unwieldy body is lifted off the ground and the animal is enabled to walk.' Even these four pairs are given additional functions.

The two pairs of walking legs behind the chelipeds possess miniature chelae that help to pick up small pieces of food which may have fallen to the ground. It happens, too, that some of the walking legs are involved in genital function.

In the female it is the sixth pair of thoracic appendages-two behind the chelipeds-which contain oviduct openings at their base. The last, or eighth, pair of thoracic appendages serves the male in a similar way, for the discharge of sperm.

We have not yet done with the versatile crustacean appendage; beginning with the second pair of maxillipeds, gills are derived from the base of the appendage itself and are therefore part of its structure and function. Such foot-gills, or podobranchiae, are found back to the fourth pair of walking legs.

At this point the gradient toward gill formation appears to have run out in the lobster, for neither the last walking leg nor any of the appendages posterior to it possesses gills.

The gills of the feet, like all gills, are tufted thin-surfaced structures of considerable total surface area. It is necessary to compensate for the fact that respiratory gas exchange is not possible through the general body surface, since this is now a hypodermis which secretes and underlies the impervious exoskeleton.

And, in spite of their great surface area, foot-gills alone are evidently not enough. The lobster is a bulky animal. There are differentiated organ systems and, particularly, large muscle masses within. All are dependent for their energy upon atmospheric gas exchange. And so we find that, besides the six pairs of foot-gills, there are fourteen additional pairs that arise from the body wall close to the legs.

Now we can visualize a situation which might have become the "Achilles' heel" of the lobster. Generally protected as the animal is by exoskeleton, it has need for exposing voluminous, delicate, and vulnerable structures to the sea for respiration. Here the protective function of the carapace, which extends down over the gills as a shield from above, becomes apparent. By action of the maxillae a stream of water is drawn through the gill chamber thus formed.

The water enters posteriorly and ventrally and is channelled over the full length of the gills in each segment by means of separating plates known as "brachts," which are also part of the leg structure. Since the gills cannot be safely exposed to the open sea, the sea is brought to the gills.

Sensation, feeding, excretion, defense and offense, ambulation, reproduction, and respiration, are all associated with the "legs" of the head and thoracic regions, and their structure is adapted accordingly. In the abdomen the situation is simpler. The first five pairs of abdominal appendages, although known as swimmerets (or pleopods), have little to do with locomotion.

In the adult male the first pair becomes stiffened rods, each hollowed out as a groove medially along the length on the inner side, for the transmission of sperm from the genital openings of the male into the sperm receptacle of the female. In the female the first pair of pleopods is considerably atrophied.

This is a secondary sex characteristic by means of which the two sexes may be most readily recognized. The next four pairs of pleopods, by paddling action, assist the lobster in walking. A major function of the pleopods is found in the female, where they serve for attachment of fertilized eggs. Here, by gentle undulations, the eggs are assured of freshly aerated sea water, which is essential to their development.

The last pair of abdominal appendages have the same structure and function in both sexes. Together with the telson they form a scoop, which is the swimming organ of the adult (compare with Daphnia and Callinectes).

The effective stroke is such as to draw the animal backward. Swimming is neither for recreation nor pursuit. It is an escape mechanism. In it the harmony of the lobster's design is apparent. As it hurriedly leaves the scene, back end first, of an indiscreet aggression-perhaps with a lobster larger than itself-the eyes are extended outwardly on their stalks so that, in the absence of a neck, it is still able to detect the way.

And the heavy spines of the rostrum at the anterior end, together with the highly formidable chelae, always confront the pursuer. This is an interestingly effective system of adaptations for, in changing from aggressive to escape behaviour, there is no need to turn around. No time is lost and there is no exposure of the relatively defenseless posterior.

The swimming muscles are the largest in the animal's body, particularly the powerful flexors of the abdomen. These originate on the dorsal surface of the endophragmal shelf and have intricate insertions from segment to segment of the abdomen to provide for flexion. The extensors, being required to exert less force, are much smaller in total mass than the flexors.

The extensors are dorsal in position and also run longitudinally from the thorax into the abdomen. In spite of the difference in bulk it is possible to discern in this arrangement of muscles-a pair of longitudinal dorsal muscles and a pair of modified longitudinal ventral muscles-the basic plan of the roundworm and of the annelid.

But, whereas roundworm and annelid muscles on one side of the body generally work as antagonists to those on the other side to produce body undulations, the ventral muscles of the lobster work as a team and the dorsal muscles work as a team, to produce flexions and extensions.

The body of the lobster no longer consists of a chain of substantially identical metameres but rather of more or less similar metameres in three groups-the head, the thorax, and the abdomen-each with segregated, though overlapping, functions. Sensation, ingestion, and excretion are performed by the head; ambulation and respiration by the thorax; swimming and egestion by the abdomen.

Gametes are discharged in the thorax but are thereafter controlled-both sperm and eggs-by appendages of the abdomen. The appendages of the animal while basically, with the possible exception of the antennules, biramous in plan of structure, have become specialized in adaptation to the functions performed.

From the long second antenna to the short, squat mandible, from the slender copulatory pleopod of the male to the wide, paddle-like uropod-they can all be traced to a similar embryological pattern. This fashioning of similar parts to different use demonstrates the adaptability of nature. It is an exercise in serial homology.

The Digestive System

Within the body tube is the food tube. As in Peripatus the mouth is not terminal, but ventrally situated on the head. The esophagus runs in a ventral-dorsal orientation and soon opens into a capacious stomach. The stomach is a dual one and its linings are embryologically and functionally different.

There is a large cardiac portion for temporary storage, and a small pyloric stomach where digestion begins. Up to the pyloric stomach the alimentary system is lined with invaginated epidermis and the property of secreting skeletal material is present. This entire section is covered internally with a cuticle which, at the junction of cardiac and pyloric stomachs, is thickened and elaborated into a system of plates and bars.

Here a calcified gastric mill, composed of two lateral and one dorsal tooth, is situated and here food receives its final mastication. Only small particles, about ten microns in size, can enter the pyloric stomach, for the transit is guarded by a system of fine filters composed of setae.

Any materials taken in by the lobster which cannot be reduced to this size are expelled again through the mouth. Even after the cardiac stomach relatively little digestive process takes place in the general run of the digestive tract, but rather in a pair of diverticuli thereof. These are connected with the pyloric stomach and form a large bilobed liver, the hepatopancreas.

This is the largest component of the digestive system, and here the bulk of digestive and absorptive action occurs. Food particles are taken into the hepatopancreas. It is composed of numerous tubules with a great amount of combined surface, but the physiology of the organ is not fully known. Besides digestion the hepatopancreas, like a liver, probably acts to regulate the composition of the blood.

The alimentary tube which runs from the pyloric stomach to the rectum is a true intestine, for (unlike that of the crayfish) it is endodermally lined. However the short length and small diameter of the intestine preclude any significant digestive contribution. After the intestine, the rectum-in the last abdominal segmentand the anus are again ectodermally lined, as was the foregut.

Because of the stomach and the hepatopancreas, the alimentary system is most expanded in the cephalothoracic region, and here body musculature is scanty. In the abdominal region, on the other hand, body musculature is greatly enlarged due to the huge flexor muscles, and the alimentary system is slight in bulk.

The small amount of space which remains between the muscular and digestive systems, chiefly in the cephalothorax, is filled with parts of the nervous, excretory, circulatory and reproductive systems.

The Nervous System

Within the head and between the bases of the eye stalks, which contain the sinus glands of endocrine function, lies the cerebral ganglion or brain. Thus the centers of nervous and endocrine coordination are close together, even as in vertebrates.

The cerebral ganglion is in nerve contact with the antennules, the antennae, and the eyes, and also with other parts of the head. It would appear, therefore, to be the chief sensory center of the nervous system. Around the alimentary tract the double nature of the nerve cord becomes clearly evident, where it encircles the esophagus as a pair of circumesophageal nerve connectives between the cerebral and subesophageal ganglia.

The subesophageal ganglion is a complex made up of the individual ganglia of the segments bearing mandibles, maxillae, and the first two pairs of maxillipeds-five in all. The cerebral ganglion is protected by virtue of its position at the base of the rostrum, while the subesophageal ganglion and the ganglia of the thorax lie in a region protected by the endophragmal shelf above and the exoskeleton below.

This is of interest in analogy with the neural canal of vertebrates. From the circumesophageal ring a stomogastric nerve supply runs to the esophagus and the stomach. Nerves which control the rate of beat of the heart originate in the first subesophageal ganglion, but the stimulus to initiate the beat comes from nine nerve cells which are located in the heart tissue itself.

Between the ganglia of the third and fourth walking legs the nerve cord again clearly reveals its double nature as the components separate and allow the sternal artery to pass between them. In the abdomen the nerve cord is at its simplest as it runs just above the artery, with ganglia and lateral branches in each segment.

While the nervous system is built on a segmental basis as a chain of ganglia, within the cord there are four giant longitudinal fibers which again, as we have seen in annelids, transcend segmental boundaries. The long fibers must be especially useful in the swimming escape reaction, which is an over-all response involving the entire animal.

Excretion

Tucked into the head, anterior and ventral to the esophagus and stomach, are a pair of excretory organs known as green glands because of their tinge of green colour. Each is composed of a ventral secretory portion and a dorsal bladder for the storage of urine. An excretory duct runs to the base of the antenna, where there is a pore provided with a valve for closure.

The antennal and ventral thoracic arteries carry a rich supply of blood to the green glands, particularly to the glandular portion where the terminal portions of these blood vessels end in small blood sacs so that, in effect, the excretory glands lie in a pool of blood. In their function of excretion of urine, and in the related functions of regulation of salt and water content of the body fluids, the green glands are aided by the hepatopancreas and the gills.

Circulation

There are no veins in the lobster to carry blood back to the heart. The blood, under pressure, finds its way back through the spaces between the various organs. These spaces, serving instead of veins, constitute a haemocoel. The blood plasma transports all of the soluble components needed by, or produced by, the specialized cells of the organism.

By the presence in solution of a proteinaceous copper compound, haemocyanin, the oxygen-carrying capacity of the plasma is enhanced. The functioning of the blood is dependent upon its fluid nature, but the life of the animal depends on the capacity of the blood to solidify on injury. For this purpose there are at least two distinctive cell types.

There are explosive corpuscles which disintegrate quickly and promote clotting, and there are thigmocytes that contribute fibrils to strengthen the clot. Related to blood and clotting is a special reaction adapted to a life in which limbs are often damaged. A predetermined breaking point is provided on the limbs.

Here, by constriction of special muscles, the injured member is cast off in a reflex action known as autotomy. At the breaking point a diaphragm of tissue is located to slow the loss of blood, so that a clot may more easily be formed.

Unlike the venous, the arterial flow of blood is conducted through a system of arteries which insures each organ of an individual supply of incoming blood and, moreover, that the blood will be aerated. High pressure, to bring about flow, is transmitted to the blood by contraction of the muscles of the heart.

The heart is centrally located, and suspended in the dorsal posterior portion of the thorax by means of three pairs of elastic fibers which also serve to expand it and bring in blood. The heart lies within a pericardial blood sinus, from which blood is drawn through three pairs of valve-guarded ostia. The arteries which lead from the heart also have valves at their bases to prevent backflow of blood.

When the heart expands there is no place for the blood to come from except the pericardial sinus, and when it contracts there is no place for the blood to go except out through the arteries. By its contractions the heart moves blood from the pericardial sinus to the arterial system, reducing pressure in the former and building it up in the latter.

Blood is directed to the antennules, the eyes, and the brain through an ophthalmic artery which arises from the midline of the anteriodorsal margin of the heart. A pair of antennary arteries, which originate on either side of the ophthalmic, carry blood to the rostrum, the antennae, the green glands, the mandibular muscles, the hepatopancreas, the stomach, the gonads, and to muscles of the thorax and abdomen; besides supplementing the blood supply of the ophthalmic artery.

An additional supply of blood is also brought to the hepatopancreas through a pair of hepatic arteries, which arise from the heart below the antennary. While five arteries originate in the anterior wall of the heart, only one arises posteriorly. This is the dorsal abdominal. It runs above the intestine and sends a pair of branches ventrally in each segment.

Through the dorsal abdominal and its branches, blood is supplied to the abdominal portions of the hepatopancreas, the sex organs, and the abdominal muscles and appendages, as well as the intestine. From the base of the dorsal abdominal, quite close to its origin from the heart, an unpaired sternal artery is directed ventrally.

The sternal follows a course to one side of the intestine and between the two tracts of the nerve cord, which are here separated to accommodate it. Then the sternal artery divides into a posterior branch known as the ventral abdominal artery and an anterior branch, the ventral thoracic.

The ventral abdominal artery carries blood to the nerve cord and to the last two pairs of walking legs. The anterior thoracic appendages, including the massive chelipeds, and the mouth appendages, are supplied by the ventral thoracic artery.

Blood, specifically distributed by arteries in the manner described, now flows into the ventral thoracic sinus, because of the lower pressure there. When the heart pumps blood out of its own pericardial sinus, the pressure in the latter is reduced below that of the ventral sinus and causes blood to move from the ventral sinus toward the heart.

It is in this transit that the blood is aerated; between ventral (or sternal) sinus and heart, the system of gill sinuses is interposed. It is significant to note that the blood circulation of the lobster is especially adapted in relation to respiratory needs. The blood system of an insect will stand out sharply in contrast.

Reproduction

A pair of tubular gonads lies close to the stomach, one on each side, and extends into the abdomen alongside the intestine. In the female, and usually also but not always in the male, the gonads are connected transversely with each other just anterior to the heart.

From approximately the middle region of each gonad a gonoduct proceeds to the sexual opening on the leg. As it matures the ovary goes through various shades of colour, from light gray to yellow, orange and eventually dark green. Light gray indicates that the eggs have recently been released, dark green that they are ready for discharge.

Copulation occurs in the dark green colour phase of the ovaries, but the eggs are not immediately discharged. Impregnation takes place while the skeleton of the female is in a softened condition. This means that moulting is also correlated with the green colour phase of the ovaries. Because of the generally aggressive nature of the animals, it may be fortunate for the male that the female is in a relatively helpless condition while sperms are being introduced into the seminal receptacle.

But what is it that then stays the male from destroying and feeding upon the female? Somehow chivalry, however ephemeral, possesses the male lobster at this time. Sperms are known to be able to remain in functional condition within the seminal receptacle of the female for at least two years, though normally the eggs are discharged from the ovaries within a month or two after copulation, at which time they are fertilized.

The time lag between insemination and fertilization may be associated in part with the need for thoroughly rehardening the skeleton of the female, for it is about to endure its greatest strains. "Birth" is a solitary process. The female lies in protective seclusion with the ventral side uppermost, and an egg basket is formed of the flexed abdomen. The eggs are discharged and directed to the egg basket, where they become attached to the swimmerets.

There may be as many as 5000 eggs in an eight-inch lobster, or up to 100,000 in a sixteen-inch animal. These the lobster will carry about with her for a period of eleven months, aerating them by gentle undulations of the swimmerets and protecting them with her body while they develop to the swimming schizopod stage.

During this time, of course, there is no moulting. Such parental care of the young is a newly emphasized form of behaviour, which will reach even greater heights in other classes of the arthropod phylum. Do not allow the contribution of such behaviour patterns to the survival of the species to be overshadowed by advances in structural design.

ADAPTATIONS OF OTHER MALACOSTRACA, AND TAXONOMY

In the higher crustaceans integration is the keynote. Not only are the segments integrated into well-developed body regions, but the regions are integrated into a body which acts as a unit; and the animal itself is integrated into a specific environment. These relationships will be illustrated with a few examples from various orders.

Order Isopoda

Among isopod crustaceans are found such genera as Idothea of the sea, and Oniscus the "wood louse" and Porcellio the "sow bug" of the land; the latter are neither lice nor bugs, of course, but crustaceans. In isopods the body is flattened dorsoventrally, and only the first thoracic segment is fused with the head.

There is no carapace. As compared with the rest of the body the abdomen is short and its appendages serve for respiration. There are gills in the aquatic forms, and the gills are adapted to serve in moist environments among those Isopoda which are terrestrial. In Porcellio the respiratory structures, in the form of plates, are provided with air tubes so that gas exchange occurs within them and there is less water loss.

Eggs develop within a brood pouch formed by the thoracic appendages and they hatch out in miniature adult form. There is no need for an external watery environment even for the young.

Order Amphipoda

Unlike the Isopoda, which are dorsoventrally compressed, amphipods are flattened laterally. Orchestia, the "beach flea," is an amphipod commonly found in beach debris. As in the Isopoda there is no carapace, and only the first thoracic segment is fused with the head.

However, the abdomen of the amphipod is more developed than that of the isopod, and the last three pairs of abdominal appendages are adapted for the leaping reaction characteristic of this group. The first three pairs of abdominal appendages are used in swimming, and respiration is carried on by means of gills on the thoracic appendages.

Order Stomatopoda

Squilla (Chloridella), "the mantis shrimp," is another creature that technically must renounce its namesakes, being neither insect (praying mantis) nor decapod crustacean (shrimp), despite superficial resemblances to both. Squilla has five thoracic segments grouped with the head, which is covered by a shallow carapace that does not cover the thorax.

The rostrum, which includes the first two head segments, is movable. This is of value because Squilla lives in the sand with only the head fully exposed. Instead of chelipeds, as in the lobster, there is a small pair of maxillipeds on the fourth thoracic segment.

The function of food capture is assigned to the second pair of maxillipeds, which are long and extensible like analogous appendages of the praying mantis. Respiration is a function of the pleopods, on the abdomen, which are provided with gills.

Squilla is a large animal, approaching the size of a lobster, and its abdominal region is correspondingly large and well developed; but the telson and uropods are not paddle-like. They are heavier and spiny, adapted for digging rather than swimming. Why is Squilla not placed in the same order-Decapoda-with the lobster? Two outstanding reasons are the short carapace and the fact that the gills are on the abdomen rather than on the thorax.

Order Decapoda

With the lobster in this order are crustaceans such as shrimps and prawns in which all three body regions are well developed, but there are also others, like the hermit crabs, in which the abdomen is more or less atrophied. And, finally, in the true crabs, there is practically no abdomen at all; except in the females, where it is modified to form a brood chamber for the developing eggs.

The crab type of body presents a very interesting development in relation to locomotion. With the abdominal region practically absent, the weight of the body is centered over the legs where, on the basis of mechanics, it properly belongs.

The crab is much more agile and quick on its legs than the lobster with its heavy trailing abdomen. But the body of the crab is now often much shorter than it is wide and, with this organization, crabs have taken to moving in a lateral direction with one side of the body leading rather than the head. Further evolutionary modifications, in other systems than the locomotory, seem inevitable. What will they be? This we shall never know.

Of the common crabs Callinectes is one of the best known because, like the lobster, it is commercially captured for the market. The body is made up almost entirely of cephalothorax, and the abdomen, what there is of it, is tucked like a tail between the legs. Of the five pairs of so-called walking legs, the first pair is composed of chelipeds and the last are swimming paddles analogous in function, but not in method, to the uropods of the lobster.

This leaves three pairs devoted to ambulation; and for walking, it now appears, fewer legs are better than many. There are crabs, however, in which there is no adaptation for swimming and in them four pairs of legs are ambulatory, still a relatively small number. This is so, for example, in the spider crabs.

In spider crabs, like Libinia, the legs are very long for the small compact body and among them we find one of the giants of the invertebrate world, the oriental genus Macrochira having a leg span up to twelve feet.

There are a great many forms of special interest among the Decapoda, and we can mention only a few. Further reading, in other books, would be well rewarded. There is Emerita (Hippa) the sand mole, to which the author owes some fond recollections of angling-of days in which he sat on the white sand beaches of the Gulf of Mexico with Emerita on the hook and, motionless, observed the shadows that moved under water.

After a time a scarcely perceptible shadow would flicker near the crab on which his gaze was fixed, a shadow indefinably different from others which had occasionally passed that way. But then the quiet erupted into violent action until, with luck, there lay upon the sands a

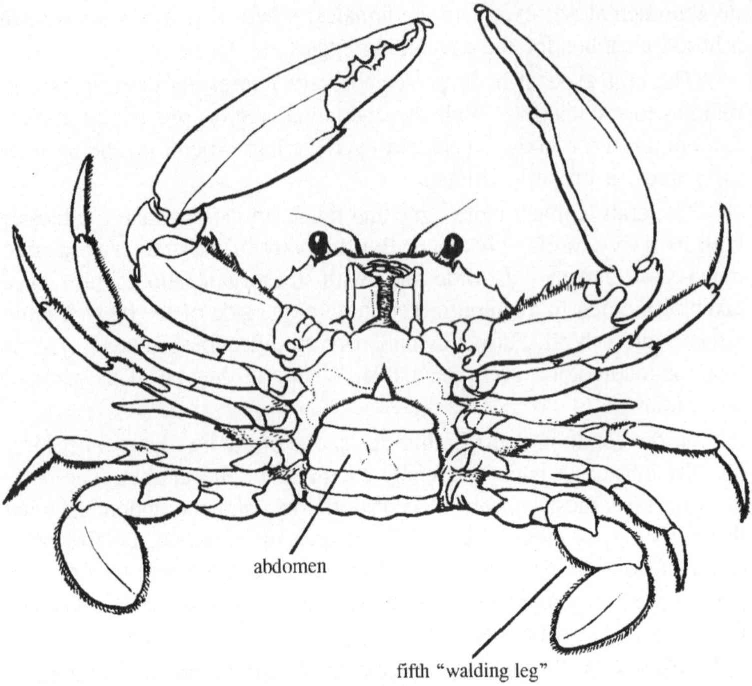

Figure 9.10: Callinectes female, ventral view.

beautiful silvery pompano, flapping violently to get back into his native realm. Emerita had lured him to his fate.

Emerita, though known commonly as the "sand crab" or "sand mole" is not a true crab. The abdomen is held under the thorax, but it is fairly well developed. A sturdy spade-like telson is especially notable which, together with the thoracic appendages, serves for rapid digging-in if exposed by wave action on the sand.

The entire animal is rather egg-shaped and highly streamlined, for it lives in a very turbulent environment on the sea beach in the surf zone. On each receding wave the head is thrust out and a pair of long feathery antennae become visible; they are used for straining small organisms from the rushing water. Then the animal draws quickly into the sand again, leaving no sign of its presence until the next wave.

Higher up on sand beaches lives another crab, Ocypode the "ghost-crab," which is a true crab. Because of its blending colour Ocypode is difficult to detect, but if observed it is capable of a surprising turn of speed, usually vanishing into its burrow before a pursuer can come close. Ocypode is highly adapted to terrestrial life, for the gills have

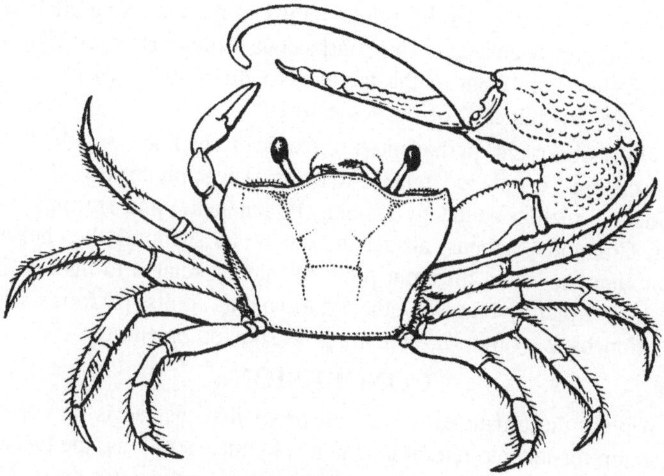

Figure 9.11: Uca, a fiddler crab.

disappeared as such and have been replaced by tufts of vasculated tissue suitable for aerial respiration.

Many crabs achieve protection through association with other objects. Dromia for example, already referred to in connection with sponges, carries a sponge on its back, and the sponge may grow around it leaving only moving parts exposed; or Dromia may hold over itself the shell of a clam as it moves from place to place.

In hermit crabs the abdomen is soft and atrophied, but it is not as small as in a typical crab like Callinectes. We find such hermit crabs as Eupagurus wearing an empty snail shell around the abdominal region, and the abdomen is coiled to fit the spiral of the shell. With growth of the crab the old shell needs to be cast off and a new one acquired, and this is a fascinating process to watch as the crab tries on several to obtain the best fit.

One of the large hermit crabs, Birgus the "cocoanut crab" or "robber crab," does not wear a shell, its abdominal region being protected by heavy exoskeleton. Birgus has the unusual habit of climbing cocoanut trees to obtain their fruit. In this genus we find some of the most interesting adaptations among crustaceans to life on land.

The chelipeds are used for scooping water out of available pools. The water is passed to the mouth by the maxillipeds, for drinking, and from the maxillipeds to the last pair of walking legs for moistening the gills.

Some special adaptations of crabs and other crustaceans appear to be related to mating. In the fiddler crabs, e.g., Uca, one cheliped of the male is greatly enlarged. This conspicuous member is waved vigorously through the air in front of the female and this is believed to convince her of the "manliness" of its possessor.

Other observers, perhaps less romantically inclined, say the waving of the cheliped is only a defensive reaction. The spiny lobster, Palinurus, produces a mating sound by rubbing its antennae, and shrimps of the genus Crangon (Alpheus) attract the female by snapping the chelae. In Gecarcinus there is a different point of interest related to mating. This is a genus which, while well adapted to land as adults, performs a mass migration back to the sea at mating season for breeding.

CONCLUSION

Among the crustaceans we find proof that the leg is an adequate adaptation for locomotion on land since, by means of legs, the body can be lifted off the ground and moved quickly from place to place. There is evidence also that a shorter, more compact, body has advantage over a longer, more unwieldy one, and that fewer legs are better than many.

The chief factor still tending to limit crustaceans to the aquatic realm is respiratory. When this is overcome in isolated instances we find crustaceans moving out onto the land and even up into the trees. We shall now proceed to investigate the specific adaptations the insect class has made in the basic arthropod plan to enable it to achieve its surpassing success.

10

CLASS INSECTA

We are inclined to think of insects as intruders into our homes, as aggressors on our bodies and on the bodies of our domesticated animals, and as destroyers of our crops and woodlands. But insects were already long established on this earth at the time when certain peculiar animals ventured down from the trees and began to fashion crude implements and otherwise alter natural surroundings to their own ends, becoming human.

When there were no humans there were no insect residents in human habitations, no insect feeders on human crops, and no insect vectors of human diseases. As humans we hold these things against the insect class. More objectively, we must give them credit for marvellous adaptations to a changing world.

It is because insects, like man, are such successful occupants of the terrestrial realm that we find ourselves so keenly aware of their presence. We shall examine them eagerly to determine the causes of their success on the land, which is above that of all other invertebrates.

With a knowledge of succeeding evolutions it is easy to look back upon the worms and see that they were literally overextended. Hindsight is far less taxing than foresight. In the worms metamere after metamere contained duplicated structures, and each element of structure more or less individually served the segment in which it was located.

Built on this plan, a long and unwieldy body was the result. In crustaceans there was considerable change. Although beginning still with the wormlike form of a Eubranchipus, the compactness and agility of the crab type were eventually achieved. This was accomplished by de-emphasis of the crustacean body region that was most wormlike-the abdomen. Now reduced in size, the abdomen was tucked under the thorax. The thorax became the locomotory center of a compact, well-balanced body. But, with a vestigial abdomen, other organ systems which might have been developed there had to be accommodated in the thorax.

Crowding of the thorax evidently produced unusual stress on the organism as a whole, for the normal ratio of body width to body length began to reverse itself. From the viewpoint of symmetry and locomotory mechanics this is a serious matter. A bilaterally symmetrical animal is designed to move forward, not sidewise.

So, even though some crustaceans became adapted for aerial respiration, their locomotory technique was "frustrating." In insects the thorax is specialized for locomotion-almost exclusively so. A well-developed abdominal region is present for other functions. The thorax is reduced to three segments, each with a pair of leg appendages.

Three pairs of thoracic leg appendages is the most outstanding characteristic of the class Insecta as a whole, and it has therefore also been known as the class Hexapoda. There is an abdominal region of between seven and eleven segments.

Eleven are found in the embryo and in more primitive orders. Seven comes with specialization, not as a matter of chance. Between the head and the thorax of an insect there is an important constriction, the neck. This allows the head to be turned independently of the body, and is therefore of great significance in behaviour. Likewise, a constriction is often present between thorax and abdomen-the waist.

Neck and waist allow for an agility heretofore impossible in a specialized organism stiffened with exoskeleton. It is these two natural incisions in the body, the neck and the waist, which underly the name Insecta: "By insects I mean such creatures as have nicks or notches on their bodies, either on their bellies or on both backs and bellies" (Aristotle).

Their functional significance is, however, more important than the name. Wings are an outstanding characteristic of insects, but they are not always present and, when present, some forms are used only on special occasions. The fact that the most primitive orders of insects do not have wings shows that wings are an innovation in the class, and are not handed down from some other group.

Also, in some of the advanced orders and in some genera of certain orders, wings have been lost, but this is the exception and not the rule in insect evolution.

The body of the usual insect is not dragged on the ground like that of a worm but, as in the more evolved crustaceans, is carried high on the legs. Besides, with the aid of wings when such are present, the insect can disassociate itself entirely from the ground, and flight-the highest achievement in locomotory skill of all invertebrates-becomes a common method of moving from place to place.

With the greater speed of movement made possible by legs and wings, a heavily armored exoskeleton is more of a handicap than a benefit, particularly so since the buoyant effect of water is not present to offset the weight. An exoskeleton is present in insects, but it is chitinous and light in weight, and a minimal impediment to movement. Where extra strength is needed it is provided by means of hollow tubular braces.

Now mobility itself becomes a form of dynamic protection against enemies, replacing the static benefit of exoskeleton in bulk. To allow for contractions and expansions of the body in relation to air breathing, the skeleton is not only divided segmentally but also dorsoventrally on each side of the body.

In the abdominal segments dorsal plates, the terga, slide over ventral plates, the sterna, and each segment can be contracted or expanded in diameter. The same design provides also for the movement of wings, which are lateral extensions of the terga. It is probably for reasons related primarily to locomotion that insects constitute the most successful form of invertebrate animal life on land, although other contributing reasons will be considered later. But first we shall establish a base of general information by a study of the roach, *Periplaneta americana*.

PERIPLANETA AMERICANA

There are hundreds of kinds of roaches, but most of them avoid human habitations. The commonest to be found as co-residents with humans are *Blatta orientalis* and *Blatella germanica*, neither of them native to the United States.

They arrived as immigrants, in successive waves, the first quite possibly having come over on the Mayflower.' Both Blatta and Blatella are much smaller than Periplaneta, the latter, as roaches go, being a rugged, clean-cut specimen about an inch and a half in length. Periplaneta is a native American.

In Southern areas it may be found in the field, but in the colder regions of the north Periplaneta seeks shelter in human residences. It is, however, less common there than Blatta or Blatella.

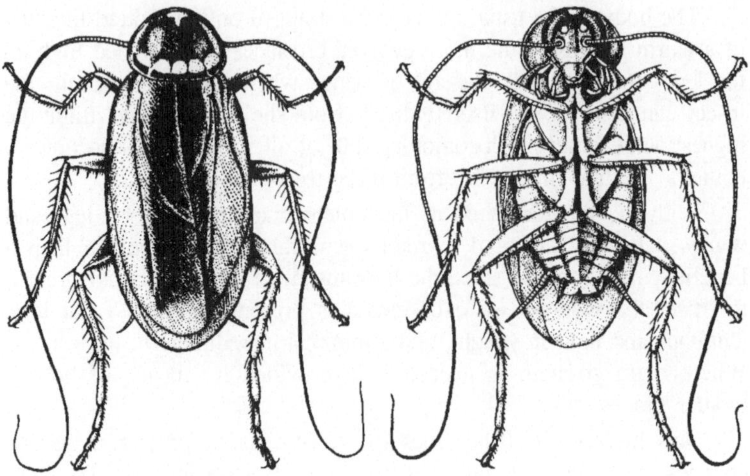

Figure 10.1: Periplaneta, dorsal and ventral views.

External Anatomy

The body being much flattened dorsoventrally, Periplaneta is enabled to run into shallow crevices for protection. The legs are especially adapted for running and a surprising turn of speed is shown. Periplaneta is also proficient in flying but does not often resort to locomotion through the air.

Because of the neck, the head can easily be turned, and since the eyes are not on stalks as in crustaceans, the use of the neck is helpful in surveying a broad horizon. Also, the movable head facilitates feeding. The mouth can be applied directly to the food, without the need for accessory food-handling appendages such as the maxillipeds of the lobster.

The head is composed of six segments thoroughly fused together. The thorax is made of three segments somewhat more distinct than those of the head. Eleven segments are assigned for abdominal use, but the posterior ones are telescoped together and not individually visible in the adult. Between thorax and abdomen there is, in the roach, no waist to speak of and flexibility is here, accordingly, limited.

As compared with a crustacean there is a reduction in the number of pairs of appendages on each of the body regions. Of antennae there is only a single pair. These are situated dorsally on the head immediately in front of a pair of compound eyes which -appropriately in a head that is itself movable-are not on stalks.

There is a pair of mandibles and one pair of maxillae as such. Second maxillae are present but they are fused together to form a lower

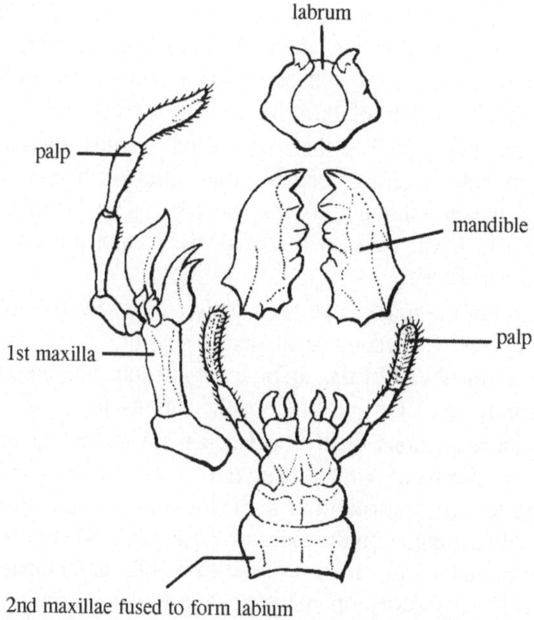

Figure 10.2: The mouth parts of a roach.

lip to the mouth, the labium. The upper lip, the labrum, is not derived from appendages. A soft, median tongue extends into the mouth cavity from the labium. There are, then, four pairs of appendages, or their derivatives, on the head, as contrasted with five pairs on the lobster head.

On the thorax each segment bears a pair of running legs, and wings arise as extensions of the terga of the mesothoracic and metathoracic segments. No species of insect has wings on the prothoracic segment, and it is rather curious that this segment has shown no potential for wing formation. In the roach, only the metathoracic wings are fully adapted for flight.

They are light in weight, membranous, and expandable into large flying surfaces. When at rest they are folded lengthwise around the point of attachment as a radius. The mesothoracic wings are heavier and act as non-folding shields for the flying wings when the latter are not in use.

In flight the mesothoracic wings are extended laterally and probably help to keep the insect in the air by acting as planes, while the metathoracic wings vibrate and propel. On the thorax only the legs are comparable to crustacean appendages. Wings are new, and without precedent. Vestiges of appendages are found on the abdomen of the embryonic roach, but in the adult abdominal appendages are absent except at the posterior end where they are represented in the genital parts and also in a pair of terminal sensory cerci.

These are the "ears" of the roach, found in this unusual location. Other insects have auditory centers on the sides of the abdomen, as in the case of the grasshopper, or on the legs as in katydids, but few insects seem to have them on the head except mosquitoes, where the antennae are auditory.

The cerci of the roach have been shown to be sensitive to vibrations up to 800 cycles per second, a moderate soprano range. Between the ears at the terminal end of the abdomen is the anus and below them the genital opening, in a curious positional relationship.

Quite inconspicuous on the surface of the insect are pores called spiracles, or stigmata, which lead into a system of tracheal tubes penetrating to all internal parts of the body. The spiracles are symmetrically arranged on the sides of the animal. There are two pairs on the thorax and a pair on each of the first eight abdominal segments. Of the twenty respiratory openings none is found on the head.

Alimentation

The alimentary tube starts from the mouth as a short slender pharynx and continues as a narrow esophagus to the posterior end of the thorax. A pair of salivary glands-really double on each side-drains into the mouth, but there is no room for further expansion of the alimentary system within the head, and the thorax is rather fully occupied by the muscles of wings and legs.

Starting at the posterior end of the thorax and extending into the abdomen is a capacious crop, where food coming in from the mouth is accumulated. The crop is followed by a muscular gizzard with a gastric mill composed of six teeth, for further mastication of food. At this point the foregut-with lining embryologically derived from ectoderm-ends.

Before food can enter the midgut the particles must be small enough to pass through a sieve of bristles. Having entered there is provision to prevent return, for the foregut is fitted into the midgut in a valvular arrangement which prevents backing up.

The midgut is short and in the form of a loop. The hindgut, after a straight muscular run of ileum, turns into a larger looped colon and terminates in the anus by way of a muscular rectum.

The feature to be especially noticed in the insect is that, while the body is short, the alimentary tube is longer. The one-to-one ratio of intestinal tube to body tube that prevailed in most previous groups has been altered. The body has become shortened and more compact, but the alimentary system has not conformed.

There are important physiological considerations involved. Food needs space and time for digestion and related processes. As the food moves along, following the contours of the alimentary tract, looping provides more space than if the tract were straight. And, perhaps more important, the greater length of the intestine means that the food is retained within the body for a longer period of time in transit from mouth to anus.

An additional device to provide both space and time is the presence of eight blind intestinal sacs, the gastric caeca, which arise in a circular arrangement immediately posterior to the gizzard. By secretion from the salivary glands water is added to the food in the mouth, and water is reclaimed by resorption in the hindgut. It might be said that the water is put out on loan to serve the various phases of digestion. With the saliva in the mouth a potent starch-digesting enzyme, amylase, is added.

Lipase and proteinase find their way into the crop from the pyloric caeca, and the crop becomes the major organ for the digestion of all three food components. It is true of all insects that, unlike crustaceans, there is no liver present. The fact that salivary glands are always found appears to be related to the need for water in digestive function and to the fact that, in terrestrial animals, extraneous water does not enter with the food.

After digested nutrients are absorbed through the lining of the gut, chiefly in the midgut, the hindgut reclaims water. This last phase of the digestive process is of great importance in terrestrial adaptation, since water is in short supply. Finally, we might note that a well-fed roach is a fat roach, since excess nutrients are stored in the form of a fatty layer inside the body wall.

Excretion

A functional association is found in Periplaneta, as in other insects, between alimentation and excretion. Although "ears" may be situated near the anus, at least excretory organs are no longer in the head (as they were in crustaceans), but are located within the abdomen where they appear more properly to belong.

The system consists of a mass of fine tubules suspended in the abdominal haemocoel and gathered together into six clusters that drain into the most anterior portion of the hindgut. This is not merely a relationship of position for, by means of such association, the fluid discharge of the Malpighian tubules is subjected to the dehydrating action of the hindgut.

In excretion as well as in digestion there is, consequently, provision for the reclamation of water. In addition, the interior surface of the rectum is thrown into a number of longitudinal folds, providing increased surface for this important function. Like the foregut the hindgut is also lined with ectodermally—derived epithelium and this extends into the Malpighian tubules, which may therefore be considered structures of the skin that "sweat out" nitrogenous wastes in soluble form.

The wastes are then converted to uric acid crystals which, being relatively insoluble, require little water for their transport and are passed out with the feces.

Besides a major tube for alimentation and many small tubules for excretion there are also tubes for respiration, circulation, and reproduction. The internal anatomy of Periplaneta is a study in tubes.

Respiration

The innermost recesses of the body are in direct air contact with the atmosphere through a system of tracheal tubes with valve-guarded spiracles on the surface of the body. By repeated branching a very extensive capillary system is formed (compare Peripatus). The air tubes are lined with cuticle near the surface, but the finer terminal branches are moist and permeable. Here gas exchange with the body fluids takes place in very much the same manner as it would between a blood capillary and the surrounding plasma.

Respiratory gases are inhaled and exhaled by means of pressure changes produced by contractions of the musculature of the body wall and transmitted through the body fluid to the tracheae. It is believed that increased respiratory surface is made available on need by partial resorptive draining of the contained fluid of the capillaries.

Circulation

In the usual animal the most critical function of the blood system is to deliver oxygen to the tissues and remove carbon dioxide. Here in the insect the blood has been relieved of this function, and the change is reflected in the structure of the bloodcirculatory system. There is only a single major vessel, the heart.

It is a relatively simple dorsal tube somewhat expanded in the abdominal region to form a series of gentle segmental pouches. Blood, enriched and purified by contact with alimentary, Malpighian, and tracheal tubes, is drawn into the heart through valvular ostia and forced forward into the head.

After sifting through the tissue spaces of the head and thorax and serving these regions in their various needs the blood is reconditioned by the organs of the abdomen and then, once more, taken up by the heart. No specific respiratory channels in the circulatory system are required, as they were in the lobster, and blood flow can be more tranquil and less limiting on the life of the organism.

Reproduction

In the insect the genital system, which sometimes in other animals is associated with the excretory or even with the alimentary, stands alone. It is a system of great intricacy, highly adapted for the purpose of bringing sperm and eggs together in a terrestrial environment, where the gametes cannot be scattered at random.

In addition, the system in one way or another provides for the protection and early development of the zygotes. In the male Periplaneta the essential reproductive organs are a pair of testes located dorsolaterally in the fourth and fifth abdominal segments.

Sperm tubules, the vasa deferentia, carry sperms to the seminal vesicles where they accumulate. With the aid of the secretion of a phallic gland the sperms are packaged before copulation into capsules called spermatophores. Also, at copulation, the secretion of the phallic gland is utilized to cement the spermatophores to the opening of the sperm-receiving organ of the female, the spermatheca.

As part of the copulatory apparatus there is a system of hooks and spines. These include a "titillator" for prying open the female genital

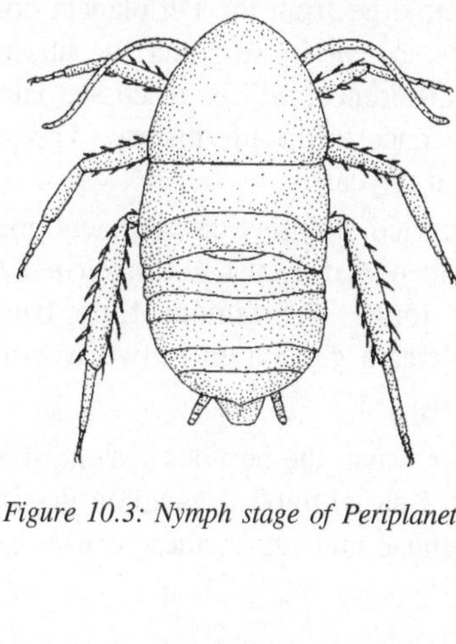

Figure 10.3: Nymph stage of Periplaneta.

chamber and, besides the titillator, two additional phallomeres to bring the genital openings of the mating individuals into proper alignment.

There is also a pseudopenis to lock the animals together for the period of copulation, which lasts for over an hour in the roach. Now, after the preliminaries, the spermatophore is passed down the ejaculatory duct of the male into the spermatheca of the female.

The male Periplaneta is genitally precocious. The sperms are formed in the nymph stage of the life history, and then held in readiness for use by the adult. In the female there are a pair of ovaries which extend through the fourth, fifth, and sixth abdominal segments.

Via a common oviduct the eggs are carried into a genital chamber known as the gynatrium, where they meet with the sperm from the spermatheca. A pair of colleterial glands now pour their secretion into the gynatrium and an ootheca, or egg case, is formed about the zygotes. While hardening, and before laying, the egg case is shaped by three pairs of forceps—like gonophyses within the gynatrium. Each ootheca contains sixteen eggs.

In spite of added complexities and terminology, we should realize that the basic features of the reproductive process itself are no different in Periplaneta than they were in the first terrestrial animal, Lumbricus. A very complete analogy can be drawn.

In passing we note that the seventh abdominal segment, contains a large compound ganglion of the nerve cord. This, no doubt, is needed to coordinate the complex nature of sexual events. It will be remembered that in the leech, in relation to the special function of the posterior sucker, there was also a concentration of ganglia at the hinder end of the body.

The young that emerge from the Periplaneta ootheca resemble the parents fairly closely except in size and the absence of wings; this latter, an important difference, will be discussed later at greater length because of its significance to the life history. The young roach attains full maturity in about a year.

This is a 'long period as insect development goes, but it is not the longest. The "seventeen-year locust," *Magicicada septendecim*, takes seventeen times as long. The famous little fruit fly, *Drosophila melanogaster*, completes a generation in two weeks.

Coordination

As in many other ways, the nervous system of an insect resembles that of a crustacean. A large bilobed ganglion lies in the head between the bases of the antennae and serves these organs as well as the eyes.

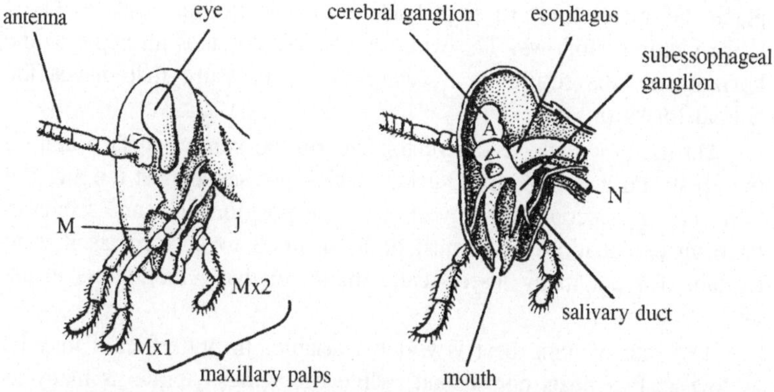

Figure 10.4: Head of Periplaneta, showing position of cerebral ganglia.

The nervous system then separates into two constituent trunks around the pharynx. From these trunks branches go to glands of endocrine function located at the sides of the esophagus, and these branches continue dorsally as a visceral nervous system.

As the trunks around the pharynx rejoin they form the first ventral ganglion below the esophagus, which supplies the ventral portion of the head including the mandibles. Now leaving the head, there are three ganglia in the thorax, primarily concerned with locomotory movement.

In the abdomen a chain of six ganglia is found, the last and largest being a fusion of several in correlation with the high level of activity at the posterior end of the abdomen. Large tracheal tubes that parallel the nerve cord indicate the high respiratory requirements of an active nervous system.

WINGS AND INSECT CLASSIFICATION

Among invertebrates, wings are the unique achievement of insects. Since it is in the nature of animal life to go from place to place, and there is no more effective way than to go by air, the dominant position of the insect class can be understood.

Spiders, too, show a trend toward the air, as we shall presently see, but in spiders it is of a rather passive nature, and there are no wings. The typical insect flight-wing is a lightweight vibratile organ of broad expanse that can react effectively with the low-density aerial medium.

It is a dorsolateral outgrowth of the integument of the body braced by tracheae and found in pairs on the mesothoracic and metathoracic segments only. As the wing is moved up and down in a dorso-ventral plane the stiffer forward edge leads while the trailing surface, being more yielding, follows. The width of the wing makes an angle to the horizontal. This results in a vector of air pressure that drives the animal forward.

On the down stroke the vector acts on the ventral surface and on the up stroke it is the dorsal surface which presses against the air. But how may we account for hovering in one position? No one seems to have an explanation. This must be as difficult to perform as it is to explain, for not many insects can remain relatively motionless in the air.

The rate of wing beat is widely variable. In butterflies it may be as low as five beats per second, while bee wings vibrate as many as 200 times per second and the housefly moves its wings 300 times per second. An extremely rapid vibration rate of about 1000 beats per second is credited to some of the tiny midges.

Not all types of insect wings are equally adapted for flying, nor do all insects possess wings. And, among those which do, some fly only on considerable provocation. On the other hand many insects are capable of rapid and sustained flight; among these the migratory locust (*Melanoplus spretus*) and the monarch butterfly (*Anosia plexippus*) are notable.

The monarch butterfly covers a migratory route of about 1000 miles. Among those which fly fast, common dragonflies can attain a speed of fifty miles an hour. If we attempt to attribute this to the two pairs of equally developed flying wings of the dragonflies then we find that the hot flies with only a single pair of wings equal the dragonflies in speed; but, perhaps not in agility, for the target of the bot flysheep, cattle, horses—is large, while the target of the dragonfly is small.

Dragonflies utilize mosquitoes as food, to a large extent. It is interesting that this predator-prey relationship is followed through the life history, for the young of both dragonflies and mosquitoes are aquatic and the adults of both are terrestrial.

Apterygota

The most primitive insects are wingless and they are grouped together in the subclass Apterygota. Here are included several comparatively obscure categories of which perhaps the best known representative is the silverfish, Lepisma, of the order Thysanura. Lepisma may, not infrequently, be observed making rapid transit through a bathroom or a library.

These would be commendable locations if they were in pursuit of cleanliness or erudition, but to the silverfish they mean only moisture on the one hand, or food, in the form of the organic material in book bindings, on the other.

Another of the Apterygota, *Anurida maritima* of the order Collembola, is somewhat seagoing, being found along ocean beaches. Insects do not seem to be able to adapt themselves to marine habitats, and it is a point of special interest when they are found there.

Although not belonging with the Apterygota, we might mention at this time the amphibious marine beetle, Aepys, and the bug Halobates, which may be found afloat far out at sea, but these are exceptions to the rule.

Pterygota

Winged insects, even though they may by secondary adaptation have lost their wings, belong in the subclass Pterygota. The Pterygota are again divided on the basis of the nature of wing development into the divisions Exopterygota and Endopterygota. A little more will be said about this classification in relation to metamorphosis, but we can see again the role played in taxonomy by locomotory structures.

Wings are the most important single characteristic for placing insects into related orders. The proof of this statement will serve also to introduce the major orders of the Pterygota. Basically there are two pairs of flight wings. It is in the variation of these two pairs that distinction between orders is to be found.

Orthoptera

In the order Orthoptera our type form, Periplaneta, is situated. Here (along with other roaches) grasshoppers, crickets, katydids, praying mantids, and the wingless walking sticks are also found. In the Orthoptera the metathoracic wings are thin and membranous and, when at rest, are folded along their length in the manner of the old-fashioned lady's fan.

The mesothoracic wings are thicker, of a somewhat leathery texture, and act as protective covers for the underlying flying wings. In flight the metathoracic wings are spread out to their full expanse and are vibratory, while the cover wings are held out laterally and help, to support the weight of the body by acting as planes in the air.

Hemiptera

The sub-order Heteroptera, of the order Hemiptera, is composed of the true bugs. No other type of insect is really a bug. Bugs possess a forewing that is leathery only at the base. The distal portion is thin and membranous, like the metathoracic wing.

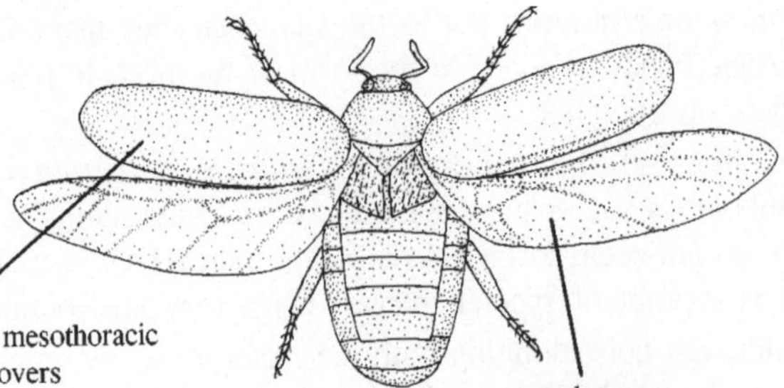

Figure 10.5: The wings of a beetle.

Among Heteroptera are stink bugs, chinch bugs, squash bugs, assassin bugs, various kinds of water bugs (pond skaters, water boatmen, back swimmers), and bedbugs. The bedbug has no wings and perhaps we should know its name, *Cimex lectularius*, because it is an insect that is sometimes very close to man.

In aphids, scale insects, cicadas, and the like the forewings are uniform in texture and are held like a peaked roof over the abdomen when at rest. This is in the suborder Homoptera.

Thysanoptera, Plecoptera, Ephemerida, Odonota

The orientation of the articulating joint of the wing is a point of distinction in other orders besides Hemiptera. Among the Thysanoptera, or thrips, and Plecoptera, the stone flies, the wings are in a horizontal position when at rest, while in the Ephemerida, the May flies, they are held vertically.

In the dragonflies, order Odonota, wings are held at right angles to the body, while in the damsel flies of the same order they are in parallel position.

Coleoptera

Mesothoracic wings are most highly developed as protective wing covers in the order Coleoptera (beetles) where these wings meet together in the midline of the body when at rest and form a hard, turtle-like case under which the membranous flying wings are folded and concealed. Beetle wings seem to be the most noisy when in action.

The Hercules Beetle of Africa is said to drone along with the sound of an airplane and our own May beetles or June beetles (Lachnosterna, or Phyllophaga), when flying at a screen during the evening, are far from inaudible.

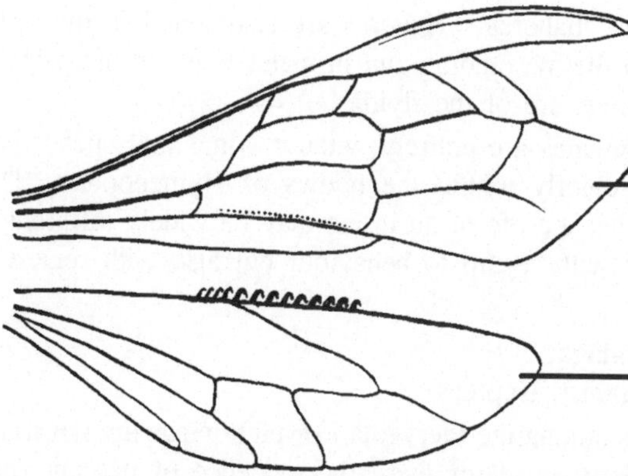

Figure 10.6: The wings of a honey-bee.

Hymenoptera, Mecoptera, Lepidoptera

Among ants, bees, and wasps, in the order Hymenoptera, two pairs of membranous flying wings are stowed parallel to the body, one pair above the other, when the insect is not flying. In flight, by means of a row of hooks on the leading edge, the metathoracic wings are locked to the mesothoracic pair to form a single pair of functional units of large, effective area.

Similar devices are found among scorpion flies, order Mecoptera, and in butterflies, order Lepidoptera. However, the best known wing characteristic of the Lepidoptera is colouration rather than flight. Lepidopteran wings are usually covered with a shingle-like layer of scales of various hues.

Some of the most brilliant colourations of butterfly wings are due, not to reflection of pigments, however, but to prismatic refraction of light rays by the scales. One of the most beautiful examples is found in the South American *Morpho cypris*.

Diptera, Strepsiptera

The advantage of two pairs of wings locked together in flight over a single pair of equal total area appears to lie in the more compact stowage possible when the wings are at rest. Certainly the members of the order Diptera, in which only the mesothoracic wings are developed into flying surfaces, are not poor flyers.

The metathoracic segment is, nevertheless, not without flight significance. This segment bears a pair of knob-like stumps on short stalks, regarded as modified wings, which undergo a rapid whirling motion and act in the nature of gyroscopic stabilizers. Such modified wings are known as "halteres." Halteres are also found in the order Strepsiptera, but on the mesothorax and in males only. In Strepsiptera the metathoracic wings are of the flying

type, but the females are entirely without wings and spend their lives as parasites, chiefly within the bodies of Hymenoptera. This illustrates the fact that the life of an insect may be widely different in the sexes, not only with regard to behaviour but also with regard to habitat.

Psocoptera, Mallophaga, Anoplura, Aphaniptera, Isoptera

There are cases among the Pterygota in which wings are not found even in whole orders. In all of these the evidence of descent from winged ancestors is clear, and there need be no confusion with the true Apterygota. Examples of wingless Pterygota are the Psocoptera, or book lice, so called because they are often found browsing among old books for nutrients; also the Mallophaga or biting lice, the Anoplura or sucking lice, and the fleas.

Fleas, order Aphaniptera (Siphonaptera), are known for the power of their muscles. These little insects, perhaps an eighth of an inch long, can leap for as much as a foot. This would be equivalent to a human leap of over 500 feet. The strength of flea muscles is dramatically illustrated in flea circuses.

The devastating spread of the great plagues of the Middle Ages is also due to the ability of the fleas (carriers of the disease) to leap from host to host. Finally, with regard to wingless Pterygota, the absence of wings in some members of insect societies like those of the ant (Hymenoptera) and the white ant (Isoptera) is so well known that it hardly need be mentioned.

There are more kinds of wing variations among insects than we can mention, and there are more orders of insects than we have so far mentioned in connection with wing variations. Some of these will yet appear in other connections.

LEGS

Although wings are the distinctive locomotory adaptation of insects we must not forget that insects, like crustaceans, also have legs. But since this is not a new development we shall give legs only briefer mention. Running is a primary method of locomotion, and it is well developed in many insects. The roach, the silverfish, the ant, the tiger beetle, are a few insects which can make rapid progress on their feet.

Figure 10.7: Gryllotalpa, the "mole-cricket," showing leg adaptation for burrowing.

A good many insects are capable of using their legs for the initial acceleration required to leap into the air and then fly, as, for example, the leaf hoppers and the grasshoppers. And some simply leap without subsequent flying, as the flea.

We cannot include the click beetles as leaping insects, although they propel themselves relatively high into the air, because they perform this from a recumbent position by a snap of the waist. When the appearance of neck and waist was pointed out it could not have been foreseen that one of these articulations might actually become a means of moving the body from place to place.

Let it be clear, though, that the click beetle utilizes the waist to throw itself upward and away only when it finds itself overturned. The legs of some insects are adapted for supporting the weight of the body on a surface film of water, and such e.g., the pond skaters, may be found walking or skating on quiet stretches.

Others, the water boatmen and back swimmers, have metathoracic legs modified into oarlike sweeps; but the water boatmen swim "face down" while the back swimmers row themselves about upside down like little boats. Some of the water bugs are very large -up to four inches- and prey upon fish. Although all now mentioned are Hemiptera, other orders also, like Coleoptera, show leg adaptations for aquatic use.

Insect legs are not only adapted for moving on the ground as well as on and in the water, but some are fitted especially for underground use. Outstanding is the modification of the prothoracic legs of the mole cricket (Orthoptera) for digging.

Of course legs themselves are only tools of the muscles that operate them. Weight for weight, insect muscles are far more powerful than those of vertebrates. A honey bee, for example, can exert a pull of twenty times its own weight.

MOUTH ADAPTATIONS AND INSECT ECONOMICS

Aside from escape, the capability of an insect to get about from place to place would be of little service to it if it were not equipped to take advantage of the foods to be found on arrival. We might put it somewhat differently and say that the insect moves about until it encounters .the type of food for which its mouth parts are adapted.

The basic mouth adaptation of an insect is for chewing, as in the roach. There is a flattened, grinding type of mandible. The mandible is followed by another appendage modified to serve the mouth. This is the first maxilla-toothed, spooned, and palped to aid the mandible.

Mandibles and maxillae are enclosed by the upper lip, or labrum, in front and by the fused second maxillae acting as a lower lip, behind. The economic importance of the chewing type of mouth parts depends on what the insect chews.

Mouth parts of the chewing type are put to destructive use by such insects as the locusts and grasshoppers that destroy crops and vegetation. The Japanese beetle, *Popillia japonica*, chews orchard fruits by preference but in need will take almost any form of vegetation. The termite is a notorious chewer of wood, both natural and when processed as lumber.

In this habit it might be joined, more rarely, by Camponotus the carpenter ant, by Lyctus the powder-post beetle and by Anobium the deathwatch beetle; but Camponotus, Lyctus and Anobium chew for shelter rather than nutrition.

Anobium can be detected by sound, for it beats its head against the wood walls of its self-made galleries. This is a mating signal, but was commonly supposed to presage death for humans, thus bestowing upon a humble insect an undeserved but memorable name. Tribolium, the flour beetle, and Tenebrio, the meal worm, chew flour and cereal grains.

Dermestes, the larder beetle, feeds on skin, feathers, hair, and other more common proteinaceous foods like meats and cheeses. Anthrenus, the museum pest (a beetle), enjoys the dried carcases of other insects and is, accordingly, a form which the entomologist detects with dread in his collections. *Anthonomus grandis*, the cotton boll weevil, likes cotton.

Leptinotarsa decimlineata is the Colourado potato beetle, now also found in Eastern states. Lasioderma is a tobacco-chewing beetle. Sitodrepa has been called the goat of the insect world because this beetle eats anything-including dried pepper, ergot, and belladonna. A more attractive name, which Sitodrepa has„ also earned, is "drug store beetle"; its "meat" is all others' poison.

In these forms it is chiefly the young that do most of the damage because of the demands of growth, but the adults feed in a similar manner. In many insects the adults lack functional mandibles, and *only* the young are destructive. This is so in the order Lepidoptera, from which the following examples are drawn.

We can start close to home with the clothes moth (Tineola) or go out into our orchards with the codling worm (Carpocapsa) and the tent caterpillar (Malacosoma). In the garden we find the corn borer (Pyrausta) and the corn earworm (Heliothis). In the cotton fields there is the pink bollworm (Pectinophora) which, unlike the boll weevil, is a lepidopteran.

Particularly destructive in forests are the tussock moth (Hemerocampa), the brown-tail moth (Euproctis), and the gypsy moth (Porthetria). Bombyx, the silkworm, is in the same category with the above in the fact that chewing mandibles are found only in the larva.

But it is, of course, on the positive side of the economic ledger since there is a return in silk for the "fodder" consumed. Generic names are given in each case to make it easier for the student to investigate further on his own.

Figure 10.8: Lepidopteran mouth parts, showing characteristic maxillary sucking tube of the adult stage

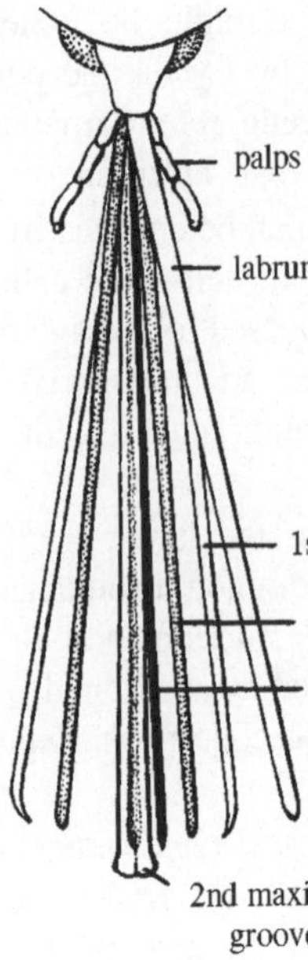

Figure 10.9: The mouth parts of a mosquito.

While mandibles are vestigial or absent in adult lepidopterans it is the maxillae that are drawn out to form, between them, a long sucking tube that is usually coiled, but can be uncoiled to reach into the depths of a flower for the nectar stored there.

It is this tube which is emphasized as a taxonomic characteristic of the order Lepidoptera, but the larval mouth parts are far more important from the economic viewpoint. Only the larvae can chew and they supply nutrition for the life history. The adults, fitted with harmless sipping tubes, are otherwise devoted almost entirely to sexual functions.

Adults of the order Diptera also have a sucking tube as part of their mouth equipment, but it is in this case formed from the stiffened lower lip, the second maxillae; and the sucking tube encloses a spiny tongue, stylet-type mandibles, and sometimes also maxillae.

While adult butterflies can only suck, adult flies can bite and suck. However, it is only female dipterans that are so adapted. Male mosquitoes, gnats and biting flies are accordingly innocent of the annoyance attributable to the species. The male sex is also innocent of after effects such as malaria, yellow fever, sleeping sickness, and other dipteran-

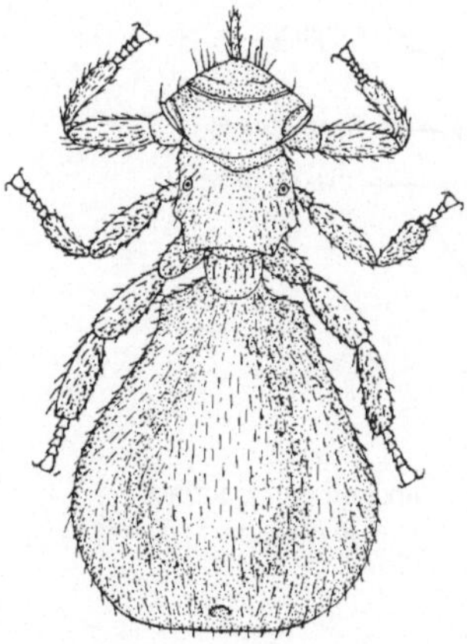

Figure 10.10: Melophagus, a dipteran, which acts as a "sheep tick."

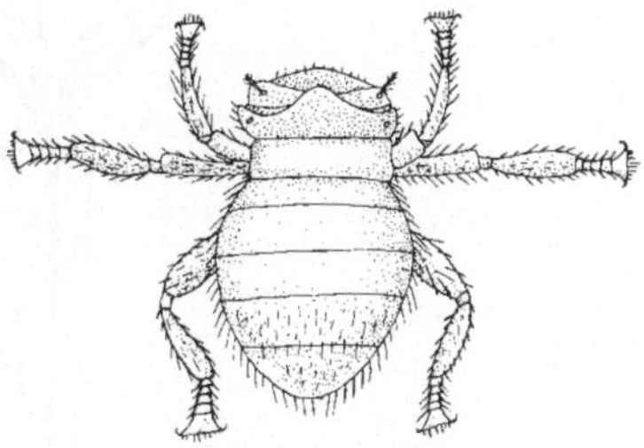

Figure 10.11: Braula, a dipteran, which acts as a ''bee-louse."

carried diseases. Among economically important dipterans there is a tiny immigrant gnat that may have come in with the Hessian troops during the Revolutionary War.

The effect of the Hessian fly (Mayetiola) continues to be more troublesome than the troops ever were, for it is a very important destroyer of wheat plants in the field, and wheat is our most basic food crop.

On the other hand, larval stages of tachinid flies (family Tachinidae) are internal parasites of many noxious insects and help to control their numbers. Demonstrating similar carnivorous food habits are the larvae of Sarcophagidae, which feed on flesh. Some prefer their food well ageddecayed-and, like Lucilia, have shown a measure of usefulness in clearing the fine recesses of festering wounds.

Among dipteran copyists there is a "sheep tick," *Melophagus ovinus*, so-called because it resembles a tick, and there is a "bee louse" (*Braula caeca*), which resembles a louse. But, as is the case with mimics, neither is what it seems to be.

Both insects are dipterans and, moreover, they are to be regarded as instances of convergent evolution rather than mimicry. We do not have far to seek, however, to find examples of actual mimicry in the Diptera. Syrphidae, the "flower flies," which feed on honey and nectar, are harmless, but they resemble bees and wasps in appearance.

The mouth parts of hemipterous insects are modified from the basic type shown in Orthoptera in a way rather similar to the modifications in dipterans. There is a tubular labium enclosing elongated mandibles

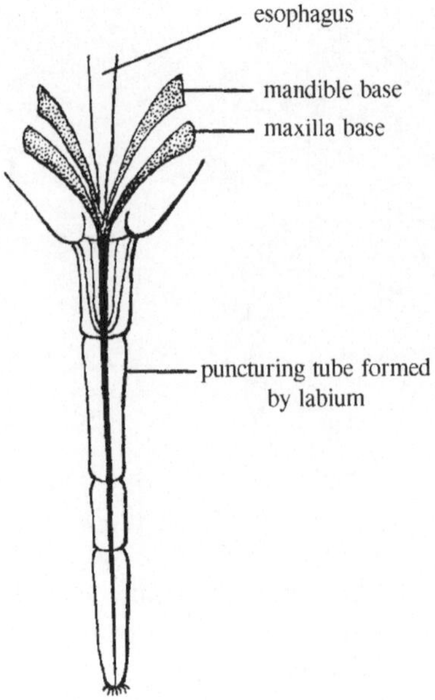

Figure 10.12: Mouth parts of a hemipferan.

and maxillae; but in both sexes. The proboscis—the tubular labium-is a hard tube and is capable, with the aid of the other mouth parts, of puncturing the surface of both plants and animals. These insects subsist upon various types of liquid diet. We find among them the economically important scales and aphids, which feed on plants.

There are others which show a preference for animal juices; such are the bedbugs and the assassin bugs. The assassin bug *Reduvius$_s$ personatus*, if it enters houses, feeds on bedbugs, but it is known to sample the human host too.

Another assassin bug, *Triatoma sanguisuga*, feeds on large insects in the field, but when opportunity offers, seems to prefer humans and gives a vicious, painful bite. Carnivorous insects such as the dragonfly, the dobson fly, and many of the beetles have a mandible of the chewing type, but the mandible is pointed and toothed for flesh-eating.

We shall close the account of insect mouth parts with emphasis on beneficial aspects. Outstanding is the beetle Calosoma, the "fiery hunter," which performs a valuable service in destroying noxious forms. And there are the "ladybird beetles"—Adalia, Coccinella, Rodolia -which feed on aphids and scale insects. Rodolia is the famous little ladybird that was brought from Australia to save the orange groves from scale insects.

METAMORPHOSIS

During their lifetime practically all animals go through changes of form, but in insects the changes fall into regular patterns that are characteristic of the various orders.

The life of an insect is often divided into periods of distinctive function. Often only the larva is concerned with nutrition and the adult, taking little or no nourishment, is devoted entirely to reproduction. Sometimes the allocation of function is not so sharp.

Feeding may occur in both young and mature, and sexual phenomena may begin before the adult stage is attained, as in the roach. In some cases locomotory, nutritive, and reproductive habits and adaptations are so widely different at different stages that the corresponding life phases cannot be recognized as belonging to the same species. A phase of sharp transition, the pupa, must first ensue.

Changes in structure and in adaptation, of whatever kind, from youth to maturity, are expressed in insect metamorphosis. In the most primitive orders of insects, the Apterygota, there is no metamorphosis. This means that a small insect, quite like the adult, hatches out of the egg. Among Pterygota, as in bloodsucking and biting lice, we may also find that there is no metamorphosis; but this condition is rare.among the Pterygota and related to special adaptations.

Generally, Pterygota may be divided into two groups, the Exopterygota and the Endopterygota. In the former, metamorphosis is often said to be "incomplete," but this is not a very meaningful term. "Gradual" metamorphosis would be better and, technically, "hemimetabolous" is used.

Insects with hemimetabolous metamorphosis are hatched out of the egg in a condition somewhat resembling the adult, but the head is oversized and there are no wings. As the insect feedsfeeding is a continuing function throughout the life of the hemimetabolous form-it moults periodically to accommodate the increasing body size.

Wings appear as external buds and gradually develop in successive moults; the body proportions of the adult are attained because of a higher growth gradient in the posterior regions. Mouth parts and feeding habits are the same for all stages except when the young-known in hemimetabolous insects as nymphs—live in a different type of environment from the adult.

These are the orders of the hemimetabolous insects: Orthoptera, Dermaptera (earwigs), Isoptera (termites, or "white ants"), Plecoptera (stone flies), Embioptera or Embiodea (a rare order of few species),

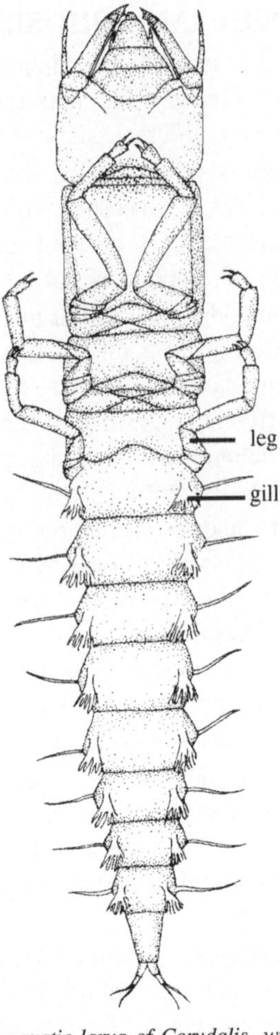

Figure 10.13: The aquatic larva of Corydalis, with gills on abdomen.

Psocoptera or Corrodentia (book lice), Ephemerida (May flies), Odonota (dragonflies and damsel flies), Hemiptera, Mallophaga (biting lice), Anoplura (sucking lice), and Thysanoptera (thrips).

Stone flies, May flies, dragonflies and damsel flies have nymph stages that live in water. In such cases the distribution of air within the animal is, nevertheless, in insect fashion, i.e., through tracheal tubes, but exchange between the tracheal system and the environment is by means of gills. This is a very interesting readaptation of a terrestrial respiratory mechanism for aquatic use.

Mayflies (Ephemerida, from "ephemeros," daily or lasting but a

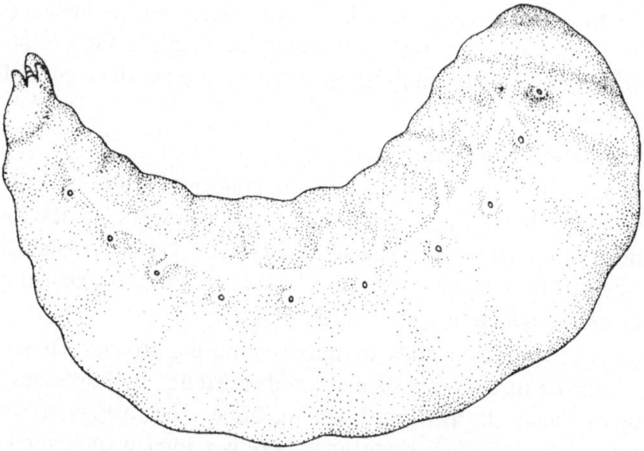

Figure 10.14: The worm-like larva of a honey-bee.

day) are especially noted for the brief duration of the winged, adult, phase. Several years may be spent in underwater growth, but the adult mates, lays its eggs and dies all within a few hours.

Among holometabolous (completely metamorphosed) insects aquatic young are also prominently encountered. For example in Corydalis, the Dobson fly, of the order Neuroptera, there is an aquatic larva, the "Hellgramite", and it is provided with gills. The Corydalis larva crawls out on land and goes through a pupal stage, during which it is transformed from a wormlike animal into a large insect with two pairs of prominent wings.

All of the Trichopteran larvae are aquatic (they carry little shelters made of twigs or pebbles), and so are the pupae; like the larvae and pupae of some of the Diptera, e.g., mosquitoes. The life history of the holometabolous orders-Neuroptera, Meuoptera (scorpion flies), Trichoptera (caddice flies), Lepidoptera, Coleoptera, Strepsiptera, Hymenoptera, Diptera, and Aphaniptera (fleas)—is characterized by an abrupt change from the larval to the adult condition.

This occurs within a single moulting period, known as the pupa. The pupa is often referred to as a resting stage, because there is no locomotory or feeding activity, but the term is otherwise most inapplicable. Internally an extremely intensive structural reorganization is carried out during the "resting stage."

The features of the larva are resorbed and-from predetermined aggregates of cells laid down in advance during the larval period, and known as imaginal discs—the structures of the adult are developed.

A wormlike animal enters the "resting stage" and an insect emerges. There is no more remarkable metamorphic magic anywhere and, like the more familiar metamorphosis in higher groups, it is controlled by hormones.

The Pupation Hormone

Imaginal discs may, in a way, be compared with egg cells. Both are dormant biological systems with fixed pathways of development, awaiting stimulation. The egg is usually activated by a stimulus from the sperm; the imaginal disc by a hormonic stimulus emanating from prothoracic endocrine glands in the insect.

The prothoracic glands are quiescent during growth. They become active during metamorphosis and are then excited by hormones from a group of gland cells associated with the brain. The analogy between egg cells and imaginal discs shows that there is a fundamental similarity in biological chemistry no matter on what level it is studied.

It is noteworthy that at one time hormones were thought to exist

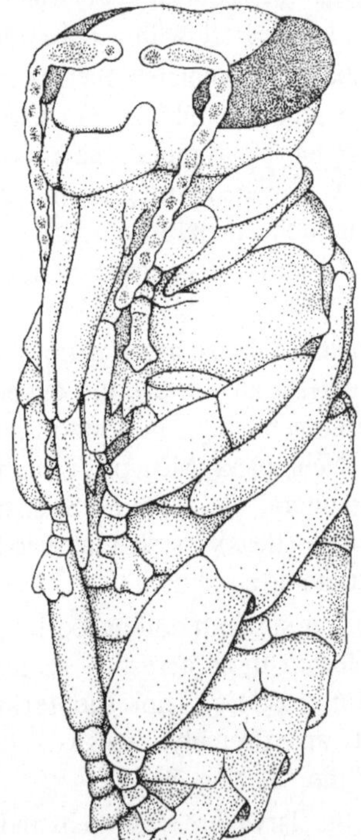

Figure 10.15: The pupal "resting stage" of the bee.

only in vertebrated animals. They were regarded as a chemical feature of distinction between these two types of animal, somewhat in the same manner as Aristotle had taken the presence or absence of blood as a distinction.

Jumping to conclusions is a favourite pastime, even in science, but it is not difficult to understand an error after it has been corrected. The misconception with regard to the limited occurrence of hormones was evidently due to the fact that the first such substance, secretin, was found in 1901 among vertebrates, and when the first invertebrate hormone was discovered in 1917, vertebrate endocrinology was already a well-established field of investigation.

Now for a bit of hindsight. Secretion is a general function of all living cells. Hormone production must be an aspect of that function. It is logical to assume that different types of cells within an organism evolve specific adaptive responses to the chemical environment set up about them by the emitted products of other cells; just as living organisms as a whole adapt themselves to other species in intricate ecological relationships.

Probably all morphologically distinctive cell-types produce chemically distinctive metabolites to which other types of cells respond. It remains only to find them. Such substances are hormones, just as carbon dioxide to which the medulla of the vertebrate brain reacts in coordinated response is a hormone.

There is nothing extraordinary about the discovery of a pupation hormone produced by the insect brain in 1917, except that it was the first invertebrate endocrine substance to be demonstrated. Sex hormones are now recognized in flatworms, annelids, and insects, molting hormones in crustaceans and insects, and others have also been isolated in mollusks and arachnids.

COMMUNAL LIFE

In a survey of this kind we must consider, with the insects more than with any other group, how we may adequately bring our study to a halt; completeness is out of the question. Because of their economic significance insects as a whole, and in all their minutiae, have occupied human attention more than any other group.

There are so many special phases of entomology-genetics, embryology, behaviour, colouration, mimicry, protective resemblance, luminescence, hibernation, migration, control, distribution in space and time, speciation-that it is only possible to mention some of them by name.

One aspect that should not be ignored is the emergence among insects of a special way of life in which not the individual, nor even a mating pair of individuals, is the unit of survival. In communal life only the social group as a whole can survive.

Insects show all gradations of communal life. Mosquitoes simply drop their eggs into the water and, in this single act, discharge their obligations to the survival of the species. The female grasshopper digs a burrow in the soil which provides physical protection for the developing young, but nothing more.

The solitary wasp goes somewhat further, in provisioning the burrow for its young, which it will never see, with a supply of fresh and available food in the form of a grub or caterpillar rendered motionless by inoculation with the sting. (This is a simple and effective method of food preservation, a method worthy of admiration.)

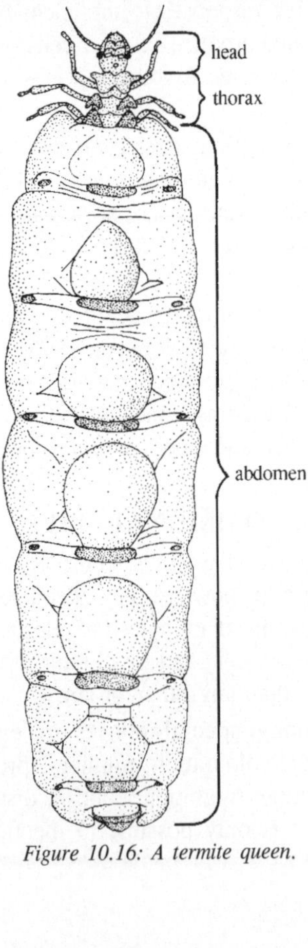

Figure 10.16: A termite queen.

These are instances at the bottom of the scale of social life for, aside from contact between the sexes, their exponents live strictly solitary lives in relation to others of their kind. In the obscure earwig we can see the first step of something more, for the female broods her young under her own body for their protection.

Highly developed social insects live together in a society to which each contributes some essential service, and outside of which none can survive. The life of the termite and the life of the bee are both excellent examples.

The Termite and the Bee

The central member of the colony is a fertile female, the queen. The functional duty of the queen is to deliver the eggs of succeeding generations, only that and nothing more. The queen of the tropical termite Macrotermes has a head and thorax of normal size-about the same size as those of a true ant-while the abdomen is about four inches long and an inch and a quarter in diameter.

Functional and structural specialization is so great that this queen is physically unable to do anything but lay eggs. There is little resemblance to the slim and graceful young queen who winged her way on the nuptial flight. Then her function was to meet her mate, and for that she was then adapted.

Now it is her function to produce the young and in this she is now proficient beyond imagination. It is said that she can lay as many as 36,000 eggs a day in sustained performance. With this capacity she may well leave as many as 900 million immediate descendants, in a fertile life that lasts for about thirty years.

The Apis (honey bee) queen is a busy "mother" too, but she can produce only about 1000 eggs per day. In the course of her lifetime, about five years, perhaps about a million young might be produced. Although impressive by other standards, in relation to those of the queen termite the maternal efforts of the bee are merely puny.

After the nuptial flight the king and queen termites cast off their wings and both settle down together in the colony. The successful suitor of the queen bee, however, having served his purpose, is destroyed in the process of mating. The queen returns alone, but with a supply of sperm sufficient to last for her productive life. (It is interesting that a queen bee will not mate in the hive although it has been found in the practice of beekeeping that artificial insemination can be successfully performed.)

The queen bee lays either fertilized or unfertilized eggs, apparently

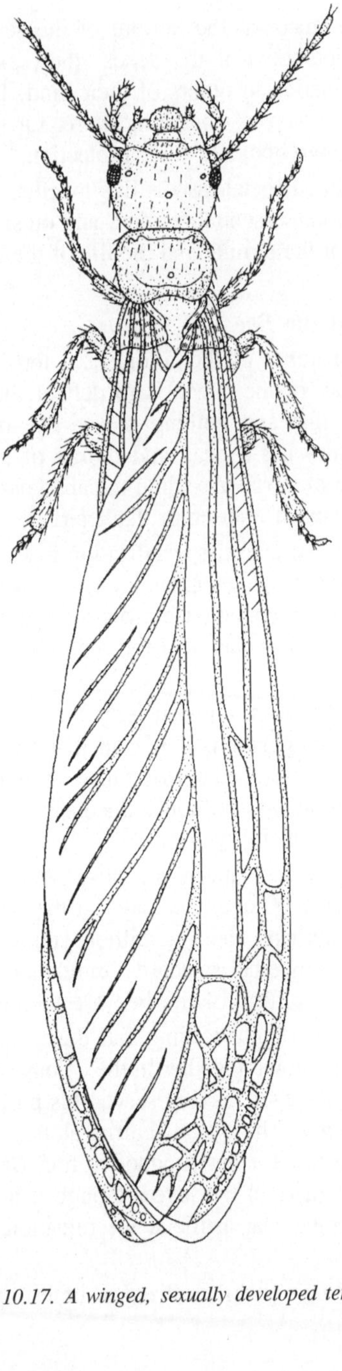

Figure 10.17. A winged, sexually developed termite.

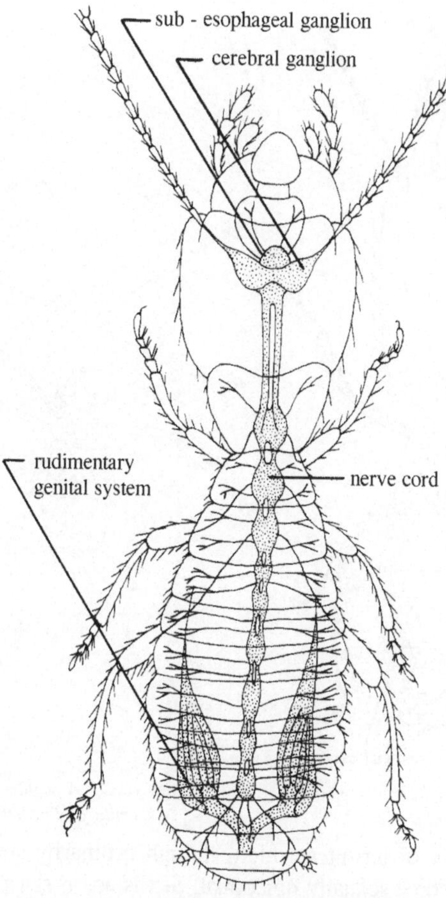

Figure 10.18: A termite worker.

at her own "discretion" depending upon the composition of the colony. Fertilized eggs develop into females. Unfertilized eggs develop only into males, and the queen lays no more of these than is necessary since the contribution of males to the life of the colony is limited to the nuptial flight.

Supernumerary males would simply mean more mouths to feed. In the termite nest, besides sexual males, there are also sterile males which take part in the work of the colony. In the beehive this is strictly "women's work," carried on by sterile females. The queen bee is able to control the sex of her offspring, while the termite queen is not.

Mating termites are darkly pigmented, winged insects, while their offspring are wingless, colourless (white), and sterile. But individuals

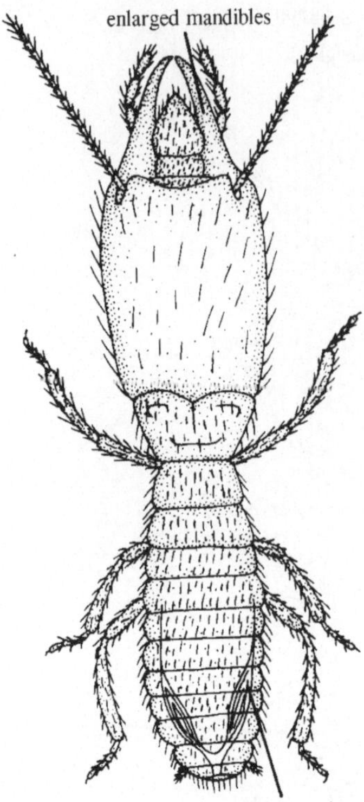

Figure 10.19. A female termite modified as a soldier.

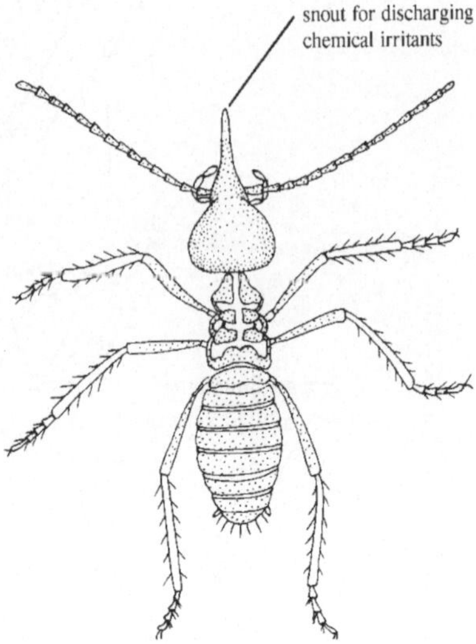

Figure 10.20: A nasute soldier termite of Borneo.

exist in the colony of termites which, though ordinarily sterile, retain the capacity to become sexually functional. Sex is not as sharply reserved in termites as it is among bees.

Workers, male and female, build the nest. It is built subterraneously in colder regions but in the case of Macrotermes it is aboveground, in the form of a "castle" cemented together of earth and saliva, and it may be as much as thirty feet high.

The workers also raise the young and feed all individuals that cannot feed themselves. This includes the queen and also the soldiers who defend the colony. The mandibles of soldiers are so greatly enlarged in the function of defense that they are useless for feeding. Among termites, soldiers are such without regard to sex, either male or female, but sterile in either case.

The bee colony is defended only by its females. The sting so employed is a modified part of the female genital system, the genital system having defense as its only function in the usual, sterile, female bee. Defense among insects is assigned to various parts. Presently pertinent is the fact that there is a genus of termite, Nasutitermes, in which the head is modified into a nozzle for spraying obnoxious fluids.

Termites, with the aid of Hypermastigidae, engage in a mode of nutrition based on wood. Bees-the female workers-forage afield and collect nectar. Mixing this with saliva, they carry it back to the hive in their crops. They also bring a load of pollen in a basket formed by special modification of the legs.

In the hive these materials are turned over to workers that tamp down the mixture about each freshly-laid egg in its cell. The cells are kept open for a time, but not all are treated in the same way. Some are filled with nectar and pollen as it comes from the field. In a very limited number of cells only food that has been worked over by the digestive glands of hive bees is deposited.

This is "royal jelly." When the cells are filled they are sealed by the hive bees-young workers that have not yet gone out into the fieldusing wax collected and brought in from tree buds. If submerged in royal jelly a fertilized egg completes its development in sixteen days and hatches as a queen. If nourished on common fare the egg becomes a sterile female in 21 days. A male is derived from an unfertilized egg, in 24 days. The majority of the offspring are sterile females, determined by the queen mother when the eggs are laid.

A few, also determined by the queen, are males or drones. But the queen cannot decide her own succession. New queens will emerge depending upon how the workers treat the fertilized eggs. There may be a system of checks and balances in this behaviour pattern (see below), During the cold months of the year the temperature of the beehive is maintained at about 60 degrees or higher through the metabolic heat generated by wing movement. Bees in a hive are never in a state of hibernation.

During the winter when no food is available, they feed on stored honey. As the hive is nonproductive during the winter season this serves only to deplete food previously collected. Perhaps the advantage lies in the fact that the colony is in readiness to make the earliest use of spring blossoms. Among social insects the entire group is the unit of survival. No single individual can long exist alone. There is little or no freedom of choice among the members, but there is a system of checks and balances.

The queen bee by laying fertilized or unfertilized eggs determines the ratio of males to females. The worker bees, by feeding processed or unprocessed food, control the formation of new queens. The males are a luxury in the usual life of the hive. They work not and want not, but a small number are maintained for their potential services to new queens.

In a highly integrated unit of life of this kind, where the constituents are not the cells of an organism but the individuals of the colony, how is coordination between the parts effected? It has been shown that bees have a sign language of their own. On return to the hive, a bee goes through a ritual of bodily movements that are related to its experiences in the field.

They show both the distance and direction from which the bee has come. The load carried back gives evidence of what might be expected at the point of origin. Perhaps the number of movements from side to side in the dance of the bee is a repetition of the number of times it swerved from side to side on the homeward flight.

If the flight pattern of the bee is characterized by deviations of constant periodicity from a straight line-as is the movement of many animals-then the dance would be an indication of distance. At any rate, while the dance behaviour of the bee may be perplexing to the human observer, bees of the hive seem to have little difficulty in interpreting it.

And, having started out, how does the bee maintain its direction? Like tent caterpillars on the march, bees seem to respond to the rays of polarized light in the atmosphere, the "sun compass."

Ants

Would any account of insects, no matter how brief, be complete without a special word on ants? Probably not. The author has never forgotten a story told to him years ago by a then former worker on the Panama Canal. For amusement in their leisure time, he said, the men would capture an anteater and toss it into the midst of a herd of army ants on the move.

And the anteater would begin to eat out of satisfaction at the plentiful supply of food, and he would eat to satiation and then, as the ants came inexorably on, he would continue to eat out of desperation. The scene ends with the army of ants marching on, leaving behind it the bones of the anteater.

There is the story of army ants crossing a stream. The vanguard marches right in. Others behind walk on the backs of those in front until the stream is bridged. Most of those underneath may be killed. But it is the army which is the unit of life, not the individual. And it may be taken for granted that the queen ant (ants have a colonial organization resembling that of bees) was safely carried across.

These are good stories. But it appears that Eciton, the American legionary army ant, does not travel in groups large enough to substantiate them. Dorylus, the African driver ant, might overcome a mammal, or the soldiers of Atta (below) might bite one to death; but Eciton is probably innocent of the deed.

Nevertheless there is some point in Maeterlinck's suggestion that "the insect does not belong to our world. One would say that it comes from another planet, more monstrous, more energetic, more insensate, more atrocious and more infernal than ours." Although the soldiers of Atta are well able to protect the group, the working Atta is a farmer ant that collects bits of leaves and carries them back to the nest.

Here it sows the leaf mulch with fungus spores and tends and eventually harvests the developing fungi for food. As in bees, control of the diet determines the development of the workers of various kinds, of soldiers, and of winged males and females for the nuptial flight. Some ants are not as industrious as the group as a whole is reputed to be, for they make slaves of others and have the latter do their work for them.

Leptothorax, for example, is a slave, and Harpegoxenus is the slaver. Likewise, respectively, *Formica fusca* and *F. sanguinea*. Aneuretus is a primitive ant which possesses a sting to subdue other insects as food and is therefore regarded as related to the wasps. Also the ant Paraponera, of the tropics, with a more powerful sting than a hornet.

CONCLUSION

There are about a million known kinds of animals. Five per cent are chordate as against about 70 per cent insects. The remaining twenty-five per cent include all other known animals. Such lopsided dispensation of species demands an attempt at explanation.

First we note the small size of insects. Since beetles comprise about forty per cent of all insects, let us consider the factor of size in the order Coleoptera. The smallest beetles are less than $^1/_4$ mm. in length. The largest include such as *Goliathus giganteus* of Africa, four inches long, and *Macrodontia cervicornis* of South

America, the beetle champion at six inches. In linear dimension there are some insects which are even larger. There is, for example, the moth *Erebus agrippina* with an eleven-inch wing spread, and there are tropical walking sticks over a foot in length.

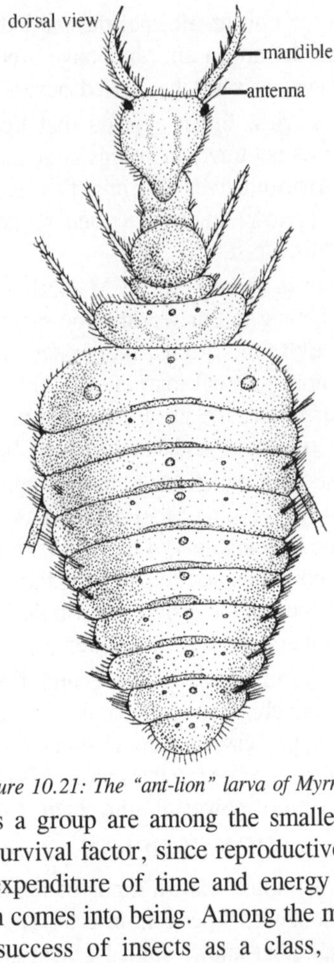

Figure 10.21: The "ant-lion" larva of Myrmelion.

But insects as a group are among the smallest of animals. Small size is a positive survival factor, since reproductive maturity is attained with a minimal expenditure of time and energy for nutrition before another generation comes into being. Among the many factors that may account for the success of insects as a class, not the least is the tremendous fecundity made possible by the quick turnover of generations.

A single pair of houseflies, for example, possesses the potential—if all descendants survived and also reproduced-of producing 191×10^{15} individuals in a season of five months. This is approximately 100×10^{9} times as many people as there are on the earth, and the flies would outweigh the people by about 20,000 times. (We estimate the weight of flies at about 50,000 to the pound and the weight of humans at an average of 100 pounds, including young and old.)

All living things are, however, fecund beyond any hope of realization. Biological success is not due to fecundity alone. There are innumerable special adaptations which, in individual cases, must be taken into account

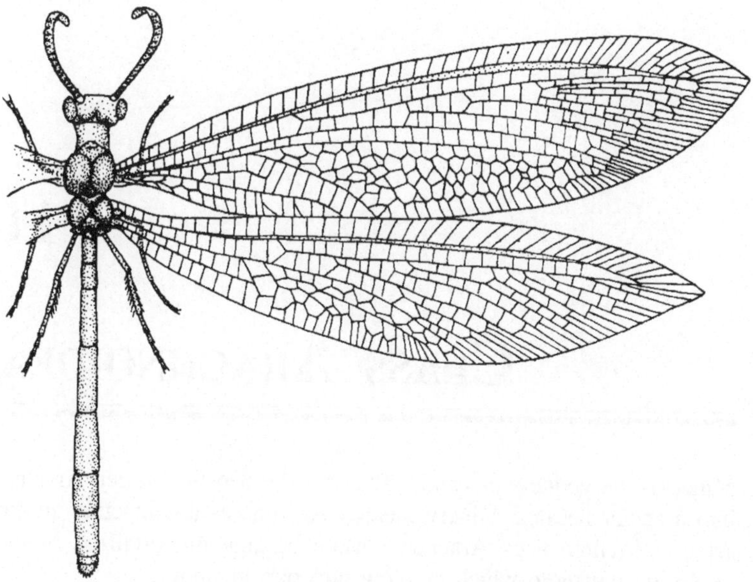

Figure 10.22: Myrmelion adult, (of the order Neuroptera).

as survival factors: protective resemblance, like that of the deadleaf butterfly Kallima which, when it alights, disappears into a cluster of leaves as if into a magician's hat; repulsive taste or odor like that of the aphis lion Chrysopa-which is, incidentally, very useful in controlling aphids-or of the stinkbug Euschistus; stinging power, equally effective whether administered by the hairs of the saddleback caterpillar Sibine, the beautiful wingless wasp Mutilla, or an angry bee; food-capturing habits including the swift flight of the dragonfly in pursuit of the mosquito, or the sand trap of the ant lion Myrmeleon for the capture of its prey.

Great fecundity, small size, and special adaptations can, however, be found among animals other than insects. In the last analysis the ability of insects, in the words of a famous Civil War general, to "get there the fustest with the mostest" is their outstanding distinction. The locomotory adaptations of insects surpass those of all other terrestrial invertebrates.

11

CLASS ARACHNOIDEA

Minerva, the goddess of handicrafts, transformed the maiden Arachne into a spider because Minerva feared Arachne as a competitor in the art of weaving. Thus Arachne's name became immortalized in the group of animals to which we now turn our attention.

Besides the weavers, or spiders, the class Arachnoidea includes such forms as the ticks, mites, scorpions, king crabs, and perhaps even the curious little bear-animalcules, or tardigrades, all of which do not weave. In name, Arachne has mothered them all, and some of her "descendants" have come close to inheriting the earth, for it is estimated that there may be as many as two million little spiders practicing their art on an acre of land.

Yet, while the spinning ability of spiders is perhaps unsur-passed, it is not unique. The silkworm is an insect, not a spider. We shall even discover that there are clams that can spin out an admirable thread. To find the key of relationship among the rather diversified creatures included in the class we must seek elsewhere than in spinning proficiency.

Again, as in so many cases which have come before, we find it in relation to locomotory adaptations, How many of the appendages of the body are reserved and specialized for the function of locomotion? One pair per segment, as in the centipedes? Two pairs per segment, as in the millipedes? Five pairs on the cephalothorax, as in the decapods? Three pairs on the thorax, as in insects?

None of these arrangements fits the arachnids, but four pairs of essentially ambulatory appendages on the "cephalothorax" fits them all. The little bear animalcule, Macrobiotus, clumsily crawling about in its freshwater habitat on four pairs of stumpy (but unsegmented!) legs, is

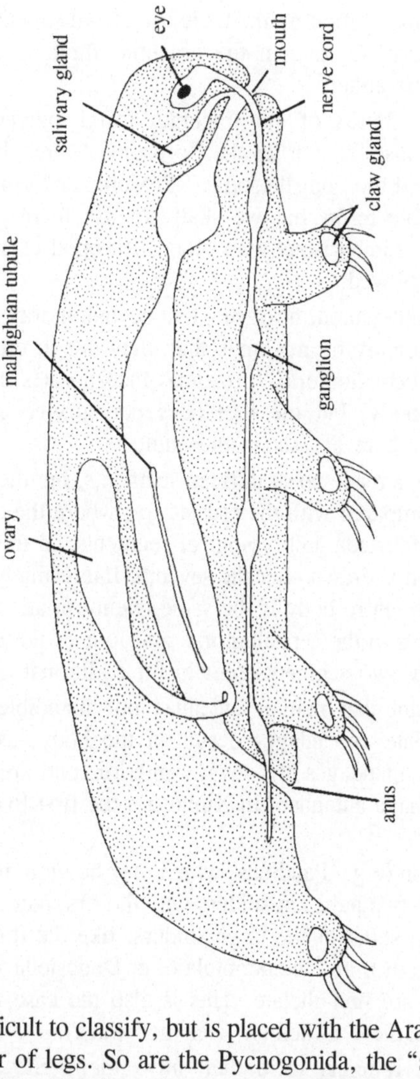

Figure 11.1: Macrobiotus, the "bear animalcule."

otherwise difficult to classify, but is placed with the Arachnoidea because of the number of legs. So are the Pycnogonida, the "seaspiders," with body so minute and legs so long that extensions of the viscera are accommodated within the legs. And the nature and distribution of the legs of the king (or horseshoe) crab, Limulus (Xiphosura), points to the fact that the animal is not a crab at all, but an arachnid.

Body Regions and the Distribution of Appendages

Number of appendages is not alone distinctive of Arachnoidea.

Their nature and distribution on the body are also distinctive. Although there are three body regions in the arachnid there is no neck and sometimes no waist either.

The head and thorax of the arachnid, fused together to form a cephalothorax, is also known as the "prosoma," and the abdominal region is then called the "opisthosoma." Prosoma and opisthosoma are valid and acceptable terms but we shall not use them, as it will be easier to visualize comparisons with other arthropod classes if similar terminology is employed.

It should be understood, however, that cephalothorax and abdomen are made up differently in arachnids than they are in other arthropod classes. Now the cephalothorax (prosoma) incorporates the first seven segments of the body, but the first does not survive embryological processes, and so there are six in the adult.

The abdomen is made up of thirteen segments, but the first of these is also lost. As compared with the crustacean, where the cephalothorax includes the first fourteen embryological segments, in the arachnid the line of demarcation is drawn after the seventh. Interestingly, the number of segments in the entire body is the same-twenty in all. With only six developed segments in the cephalothorax and four of these occupied by walking legs, only two segments remain for additional appendages.

It is significant that neither antennae nor mandibles are among them. When chelate appendages occur on the body, as they almost always do, such appendages are always anterior, and are found where other arthropods have antennae. In Xiphosura the first five pairs are all chelate.

In the scorpion (e.g., Pandinus, which may be more than six inches long) it is the first two pairs. In spiders only the first pair of appendages is chelate. And in some of the large spiders, like the trap-door spider (e.g., Bothriocyrtum), and the tarantula (e.g. Dugesiella), even the so-called chelicerae are non-chelate. This is also the case in many ticks and mites (where there is neither neck nor waist).

But the rule remains valid that only among the arachnids are pincer-like appendages, like the claw of the lobster, found as the anterior appendage of the body.

Gnathobases and Related Adaptations

The lack of mandibles among the appendages of the arachnid would appear to be an embarrassing omission. The animal must eat! Let us recall that the mandible of the crustacean and of the insect is a "leg" adapted for chewing.

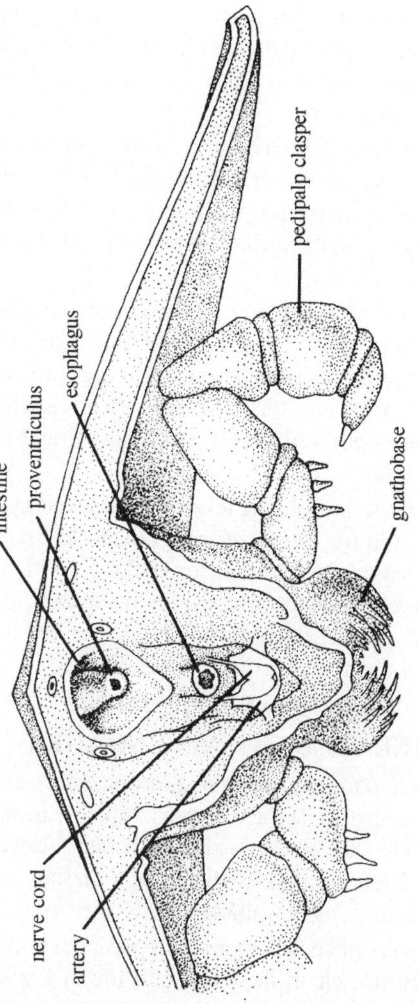

Figure 11.2: Xiphosura, cross-section.

This "leg" is extremely short and cannot possibly be used for locomotion. Among arachnids there are legs which, while serving locomotory functions, are also partially adapted for food mastication. The basal segment of the leg is especially fitted with spines on the side toward the mouth, this structure being known as a gnathobase.

In Xiphosura the second, third, fourth, and fifth pairs of appendages-four pairs in all-are provided with gnathobases. By a process which might be likened to the shrugging of shoulders, four pairs of them, Xiphosura chews its food. Evidently the king crab may look like a crab, and enjoy a crablike habitat, but its structural features, internal as well as external, show arachnid relationship. In the scorpion only the second, third, and fourth appendages are provided with gnathobases, and in spiders only the second pair.

There is evidence that the combination of locomotory and masticatory functions in one appendage is not a fully satisfactory one. Often there are poison glands for subduing prey, presumably so that the gnathobases may more easily be applied. In the scorpion the poison sting is in the tail.

Spiders generally have a poison gland in the cephalothorax which opens by way of a fang in the first pair of appendages, the chelicerae. Arachnid poison may be, drop for drop, far more virulent than that of reptiles; as in the notorious black widow spider Lacrodectus (even though it rarely bites and is still more rarely fatal), and in some of the tropical scorpions.

The strongest evidence pointing toward the inadequacy of gnathobase mastication is found in the trend toward a liquid diet among arachnids. In scorpions the pharynx is modified for sucking up the juices of food masses first crushed by the gnathobases, and in spiders food is digested externally through the action of enzymes discharged with the bite. Liquid nutriment is then sucked into the stomach.

OTHER ADAPTATIONS RELATED TO APPENDAGES

While the first pair of arachnid appendages is chelicerate, the second pair-the "pedipalps"-serve a sensory function in spiders. The tip of the pedipalp of the male spider is also employed for delivering sperm to the female. In Xiphosura the pedipalp is a clasper for holding the female and is also used as a walking leg.

The last four pairs of cephalothoracic appendages provide a crawling type of ambulation; notable in the usual web life of a spider. But those of the wolf spider Lycosa, which builds no web, are adapted for running down its prey, and the spider Salticus is proficient in leaping.

Misumena, a "crab spider," moves sideways like the true crabs of the crustacean class. In the Australian flying spider, *Attus* (*Saitis*) *volans*, extensible flaps of the abdomen assist the legs in making unusually long transits through the air. The last pair of walking legs of Xiphosura terminate in clusters of spade—like processes which provide the traction required for forcing the carapace forward in the manner of a bulldozer, as the animal plows through the sand and sifts it in search of food.

Additional Features of the Cephalothorax

Besides appendages, the cephalothorax hears a number of simple eyes on the dorsal surface, except in Xiphosura where one pair of the eyes is compound. The compound eyes of Xiphosura are, however, not regarded as homologous with those of other arthropods. A mouth is located ventrally, and coxal glands, comparable to the green glands of the crustaceans, open by ducts between the legs.

The Abdominal Region

The abdomen of Xiphosura is conspicuously different from that of other arachnids because of the presence of six pairs of platelike structures on the ventral surface, each pair fused together at the midline. These may represent appendages which-except for a single, much smaller, pair on the scorpionare absent in other arachnids.

For its aquatic life the king crab has gills, arranged like the pages of a book, on the posterior surface of the abdominal appendages. In other, terrestrial, arachnids these book-gills or lung-books, as they would here be more properly called, are sunk into pits that form pulmonary sacs. The adaptation to retard desiccation is obvious.

The scorpion has four pairs of such pits. Spiders have only two pairs, or a single pair, but there is also a tracheal system and a muscular mechanism for compressing and expanding the abdomen in respiratory movements. Mites and ticks have only tracheae.

Malpighian tubules are also found in the abdomen of the arachnids, except in Xiphosura, but they seem to be derived differently from those of insects since they are associated with the midgut and not with the hindgut. On the anterioventral surface of the abdomen there are genital openings, while the anus is terminal.

Only in Xiphosura is any active locomotory function associated with the abdomen. The abdominal plates serve for slow swimming movements, usually while the animal is in an upside-down position.

Blood and Nervous Systems

The blood system of arachnids is of the open type as in other arthropods, but the system of arteries is more extensive; most notable in Xiphosura is the fact that arteries enclose the cerebral ganglia, the circumesophageal ring, the ventral nerve cord and its major branches. Functionally, the advantages of bathing nervous tissue directly in blood cannot be doubted, but structurally one can only regard this arrangement as another indication of the strange evolutionary pathways taken by this group of nonsocial arthropods.

THE SILK-CENTERED LIFE OF A SPIDER

Spiders are spinners, and the uniqueness of their way of life is based on silk. While Xiphosura possesses special abdominal swimming plates, and the scorpion a telsonesque sting, the spider has two or three pairs of abdominal spinnerets that connect with silk-producing glands. These are useful in all stages of the spiders' life.

Male spiders often spin little webs to receive sperms that, after discharge, they scoop up with the pedipalp and transfer to the genital system of the female. The male appears to approach the female with caution. The female is usually much larger, equal sometimes to a thousand males in weight, and she tends to regard the male as food.

Therefore, in some species, the male first ties the female down with silk before proceeding with the affair of mating. In other species he may offer the female a silk-wrapped bundle of food to engage her attention while he deposits his sperm. In the typical species measures such as the above are not necessary and the female is induced to cooperate by a courtship dance performed by the male, although he does not always survive the dance.

Also, in some species, males and females live together in tranquility. While the young of scorpions are born alive, the eggs of spiders are laid in little silken cocoons, often carried around for protection and therefore fastened to the body of the mother by silken threads. Trap-door spiders such as Cteniza dig burrows in the ground which they line with silk and protect with a silk reinforced lid.

In this burrow they lay their eggs and in it, under protection, the young develop. It is common for young spiders after hatching to pay out a silken thread long enough to lift them into the air. They have been found afloat as high as 10,000 feet, and this is of value in the dispersal of the species.

The use of silk often extends to the food capturing habits of later life, but not always. The house spider Scytodes-several species of spider are "domestic"-ejects some sticky material to pin down her prey. In Australia there is a so-called "Bolas spider" that secretes a short thread of silk at the end of which there is a sticky globule. This is whirled around and around by one of the legs and used to capture the spider's food. Most spiders are, however, more passive.

The usual method of food capture is by means of a silken web, intricately constructed of sticky and non-sticky threads. The common food of spiders consists of insects. It has been estimated that the total weight of insects destroyed by spiders each year approximates that of the human population; and surprisingly large insects may be caught, for the strength of silk is many times that of steel.

While spiders are entirely terrestrial in basic adaptations, some live under water. In this respect, too, they utilize silk. The waterspider Argyroneta builds a dome of silk, anchored with threads to aquatic vegetation, and fills it by carrying down bubbles of air. For mating, males and females are found living in adjoining domes, with silken passageways connecting the two.

CONCLUSION

Although spiders can move about with agility and even with considerable speed, their locomotory devices are no match for the wings of insects. Yet insects are their natural prey. This is possible because of the ability of the spider to build a trapping web of silk to which the prey arrives through its own superior locomotory capacities.

The insect's achievement having been turned against itself, the spider takes its toll. Lacking also the chewing mandibles of insects, arachnids subdue prey by means of poison glands, macerate it with gnathobases, liquefy it externally, and draw it into the alimentary system by a gut especially adapted for sucking.

Ticks and mites, lacking even silk glands, adhere to other animals and to plants in an ectoparasitic relationship, and engorge themselves with the juices of the host.

Only the marine Xiphosura still retains the chewing habit, without the adaptations to perform it very effectively, and plows laboriously through the sand in search of prey too slow to elude it. But we cannot say that Xiphosura form a very successful group.

12

Phylum Mollusca

The mollusk, like the molluscoid, is a triploblastic, coelomate animal that spends its early life as a swimming trochophore larva. Like the molluscoids, it shows no metamerism. We have seen metamerism in relation to the annelid type of bodily movement, and we have seen the great role played by the arthropod appendages, developed in relation to metameric body structure.

In the absence of metamerism it should therefore not be surprising that primitive mollusks are slow-moving, creeping forms. But the most advanced members of the phylum have evolved adaptations whereby they are among the swiftest marine forms. This is something we want to look into, and understand.

Early mollusks were apparently wormlike, but unlike other "worms" they were endowed with two significant bodily features. The entire ventral side formed a locomotory foot, and the dorsal side was composed of a mantle of glandular tissue.

With these distinctive adaptations, variously modified as we shall see, mollusks have been able to survive in the water and on the land, and eventually they attained a structural level unsurpassed in the invertebrate world. Thus, while we have held the mollusks to the last in our consideration of invertebrates, they do not fall into the category of "least."

Amphineura

In the class Amphineura we find the simplest of the mollusks, and presumably the most primitive. Like worms, they are built on a plan of a straight alimentary tube within an uncomplicated body tube. On the

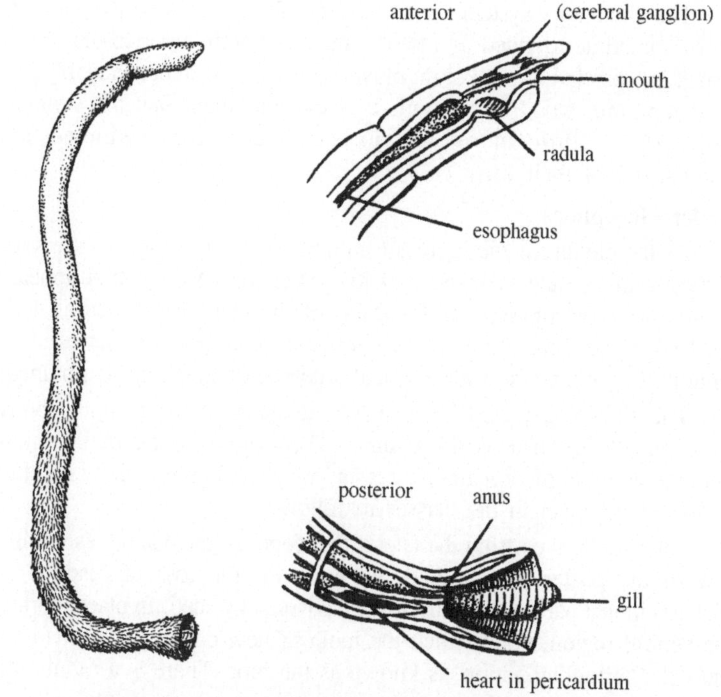

Figure 12.1: An aplacophoran mollusk. Chaetoderma nitidulum.

ventral surface there is a ciliated groove that is the locomotory organ. A cuticle covers the body and, perhaps portentously, there are calcareous spicules secreted within the body wall. As yet there is no shell. Such mollusks are placed in the order Aplacophora (or Solenogastres) of the class Amphineura.

As might be deduced from their organization, the Aplacophora are slow-moving animals. They browse on bottom flora and fauna with the aid of a peculiar new adaptation, known as the radula. This is a rasping, ribbon-shaped organ studded with minute chitinous teeth. In use the radula, supported by a cartilaginous rod-the odontophore-is slid back and forth, scraping off small particles of food.

The radula is to become an outstanding characteristic of the mollusk phylum. It is present in all classes except one in which it has evidently been lost. The Aplacophoran nervous system-a good index of evolutionary level—is composed of a circumesophageal nerve ring with a cerebral ganglion, and two ventral nerve cords widely separated as in primitive worms. There is a supplementary pair of nerve cords more lateral in position.

The circulatory system is also very simple. There is only a pumping heart, sometimes divided into two chambers, within a pericardial blood space. In correlation with slow movement there is, understandably, no need for rapid blood circulation. It is evident, then, that the simplest mollusks are little more than unsegmented worms with certain peculiarities of their own.

Order Placophora

As the phylum name implies ("molluscus," soft) mollusks are soft-bodied animals, and there is need for protection. A shell first appears in the order Placophora (or Loricata) of the class Amphineura. This shell takes the form of eight calcareous plates arranged in series as in Chiton. The animal is protected, and a degree of flexibility is retained.

The shell is secreted by a dorsal, glandular portion of the body wall, already defined as the mantle. The mantle is one of the most outstanding of all molluscan features and we should be especially mindful of its development in the classes to follow.

Gills are derived from the lateral free edges of the mantle, especially toward the posterior end, and make up for the loss of respiratory function in that part of the body surface covered by shell. In placophorans the ventral region, upon which the mollusk now creeps by means of a muscular wriggling action, is known as the foot. There is a radula for

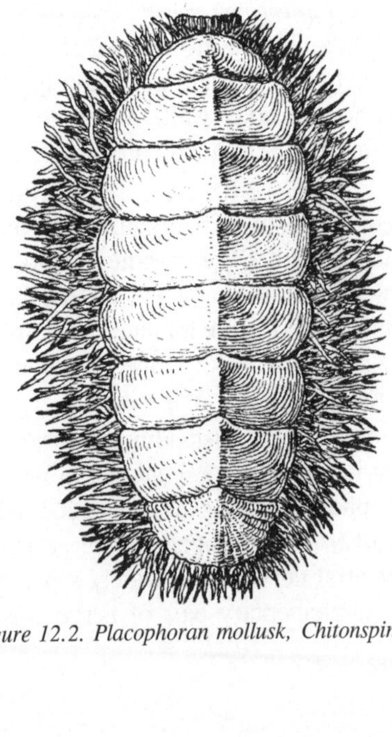

Figure 12.2. Placophoran mollusk, Chitonspinosus.

feeding, as in Aplacophora, and the nutritive needs of the bulkier body are provided through added digestive surface in a coiled intestine.

The heart lies in a large pericardial sinus, and it is composed of two auricles and a single ventricle. By means of ciliated funnels, blood is drawn directly out of the pericardial sinus into a pair of kidneys. The blood is processed and returned to the body, while extracted metabolic wastes are discharged through pores near the posterior end of the animal.

The Placophora, unlike Aplacophora, live in shallow coastal waters. We therefore usually think of the Amphineura as chitons, but it should be remembered that the earliest amphineuran mollusks were very wormlike and had no shell.

Pelecypoda

With the class Pelecypoda, or Lamellibranchiata, we enter more familiar ground (at least in a gastronomic sense). The common edible members of the mollusk phylum are pelecypods.

In the class Pelecypoda the mantle is divided into two lobes emanating from the mid-dorsal region of the body. The animal is enveloped in these two soft sheets of tissue, one on each side. Because the mantle is primarily a glandular organ for shell secretion, the shell is also in two parts; and this becomes the outstanding recognition characteristic of the class.

In whatever other respects bivalve mollusks—common clams, oysters, mussels, scallops, and "shipworms"—differ from each other, they are alike in the possession of two shells, or valves. The shells are hinged together dorsally and protect the soft body between them.

Although the shells are, as a rule, heavily calcified and can be held firmly together by muscular action, the starfish is able to open bivalves, the drumfish can crunch through even the unusually heavy shells of the southern oyster, the gull utilizes the weight of the shell of the clam against itself by dropping it to crack it open and get at the meat inside, and several types of predatory snails can bore directly through bivalve shells.

The ventral portion of the body of a bivalve is typically composed of a pointed, hatchet—shaped foot (Pelecypoda means hatchet-footed) for burrowing into the sand or mud, as in the clam Venus, which we shall consider below. But Arca, the blood clam—so called because of the presence of haemoglobin as a blood respiratory pigment-possesses a flattened foot upon which it creeps, and in Cardium the foot is bent and capable of leaping action.

Understandably, the shell is an impediment to locomotion, and under its encumbering weight bivalves show a low level of locomotory ability. Many, after initial motile larval life, are permanently fixed. The oyster, for example, cements itself to some solid base by its right valve, while the left valve acts as a flat protective lid.

Other sedentary bivalves, like the edible mussel (Mytilus), may hang attached by means of byssus threads secreted by a silk gland in the foot. In the clam Pinna, of the Mediterranean, a golden thread is formed, of so fine a texture that it has been woven since ancient times into a fabric known as "Tarentine Cloth."

In Biblical times byssus linen was manufactured in the textile town of Beth Asbea in South Judea. With regard to silk production it is odd to find Pinna the clam and Bombyx the moth in the same company as spiders; but we have pointed out before that spiders are not the only spinners. The best-and it is a most peculiar best-that bivalves can do in the way of locomotion is shown in the clumsy swimming technique developed by scallops such as Pecten.

Ordinarily Pecten lies quietly on its right side, straining food out of the water. When it moves it does so suddenly, by snapping its valves together. Water is forced out between the valves at their hinge and a jerky swimming action, ventral side first, results. If Pecten exerts itself unusually vigorously water is forced through the gape of the valves and the swimming direction is reversed.

Any observer of the swimming behaviour of Pecten will be impressed at once with the imperfection of the adaptation. Bivalves are obviously not designed to swim. But since Pecten does swim, a correlated development appears. Pecten, unlike other pelecypods, has eyes. But where? Like its biological companions in the class Pelecypoda, Pecten has no head.

The eyes are found, like two rows of bright little beads, along the edges of the bilobed mantle. Swimming is evidently a secondary adaptation in Pecten. Nor do all scallops swim, and even the young of Pecten are attached-by byssus threads as in Mytilus, above.

VENUS MERCENARIA

As a general representative of the bivalved mollusks we shall take the common hard-shell edible clam or "quahog," *Venus mercenaria*. Venus is found on sandy-muddy sea-bottoms and, as clams go, is fair-sized, attaining a maximum of about four inches.

Others, like *Turtonia minuta*, are less than an eighth of an inch in length when full grown. The toheroa clam of New Zealand, *Amphidesma ventricosum*, which is like a quahog, is much larger than Venus. Like Venus, Amphidesma is also used as human food, and the number which may be taken is set by law. The largest known bivalve is the "bear's-paw," *Tridacna gigas*, of the Philippines.

A good-sized specimen, about four feet, weighs up to 600 pounds including the shell, but the edible body within only amounts to twenty pounds, wringing wet. The edges of the Tridacna mantle are beautifully coloured in violet and yellow hues, like a border of blossoms-to be admired but not molested, for to be clamped by the valves would be no laughing matter.

Venus lies in its environment with the anterior end down and the anal end up. Siphons, which are posterior extensions of the mantle, reach into the clear water above. Venus does not burrow very deeply, and its siphons are short. (The soft-shell clam, *Mya arenaria*, goes deeper and its siphons are correspondingly longer.)

The animal is enclosed within its two shells, which meet in a hinge formed of interlocking processes, the "teeth," on the dorsal side. Inserted into the hinge is a tough, elastic ligament, which tends to keep the valves open. Against the resistance of the hinge ligament the force of a pair of adductor muscles, attached -between the shells, is constantly required to keep the edges of the mantle lobes in contact.

Only in this position is the water system of the clam properly operative. The animal lies in its own protected little pool of water with the mantle lobes in contact with each other at the edges, and is guarded by the two hard shells. If the shells are widely agape the clam is dead or dying.

It is of comparative interest that in the edible mussel Mytilus only the posterior adductor muscle is well developed. In the oyster only the posterior muscle is present, the anterior one being completely undeveloped.

Gills and Their Uses

Between the mantle and the body proper, Venus has two gill plates on each side, attached dorsally and with ventral edges free. The gill plates are composed of individual filaments locked together by long intermeshing cilia. In more primitive clams, e.g. Amusium and Nucula, the gill filaments are separate.

Short cilia on the gill surfaces maintain a water current which enters through the ventral siphon and is expelled through the dorsal siphon, after making a circuit of the mantle cavity and being directed to the dorsal siphon by an excurrent, suprabranchial chamber. Like a sponge, the clam is dependent on this stream of water for all its needs. A clam does not pursue its food, nor does it move to seek a mate. All things come and go by way of the water current, as the animal lies "head" down in the sand, with its ciliary pumping mechanism in action.

Into the exhalent current carbon dioxide, nitrogenous wastes, feces, and genital products are discharged. Thus the gills-because they are the source of the water current-play a part, directly or indirectly, in nutrition, respiration, excretion, egestion, and reproduction. They serve as an adaptation which, in large part, compensates for the absence of locomotion and makes survival possible in this sedentary mode of life.

Alimentation

The clam is a filter-feeder. As the water current passes over and through the many small openings between the gill filaments food particles are trapped in mucus secretion and the mucus directed in strings toward the mouth. Here the food strings come under the control of a ciliary current derived from two pairs of labial palps at the sides of the mouth, and the food is thus directed for ingestion.

There is no radula or odontophore in pelecypod mollusks-another evidence of atrophy of the head region—and nutrition is necessarily microphagous. The alimentary system consists internally of an esophagus, a stomach with liver attached, a coiled intestine, a rectum, and an anus. Feces are discharged at the base of the dorsal or exhalent (excurrent) siphon, where they are caught up in the outgoing water stream and expelled.

Supported in a fold of the intestine and extending into the stomach is a rod-shaped structure known as the "crystalline style." This rod is continuously rotated by the cilia of the intestine, and simultaneously forced against a cuticular thickening within the stomach. Thus abraded the crystalline style releases an amylolytic enzyme for the digestion of carbohydrate. At its posterior end the style is reformed.

This highly peculiar mechanism for forming amylase, found also in some of the gastropods, is known only among mollusks. Food particles from the stomach enter a large digestive diverticulum, the liver, where they are taken up intracellularly for fat and protein phases of digestion. Digestive process also occurs within the intestine.

We have encountered some unusual locations for certain organs before—the excretory glands in the head of the lobster, the ovaries near the eyes of Euplanaria, and the hearing devices alongside the anus of the roach-and here in the clam we find another, for the rectum is set within the ventricle of the heart.

That this is so in the majority of the pelecypods-due to the fact that, in embryogeny, the ventricle grows around the rectum-makes it no less strange. It has been shown that cardioregulating nerves are present in the heart of Venus, as they are in the hearts of other animals, and that these nerves secrete neurohormones of antagonistic nature; either to speed or to slow the beat as might be required.

Acetylcholine is the inhibitor and 5-hydroxytryptamine excites. It seems that, in the clam, the proximity of these and other chemical substances to the rectum does not interfere with the functioning of the latter; perhaps they stimulate.

But some of the chemicals extracted from mollusk heart tissue, in very small amounts, bring on symptoms of schizophrenia when injected into humans. (Probably a structural association between heart and rectum, such as found in the clam, if it occurred in the human, would also bring on schizophrenia).

Circulatory and Excretory Systems

By the contraction of the ventricle blood pressure is raised within the heart and the blood is thereby forced out-via anterior and posterior aortas-to the intestine, the foot, the mantle, and also into the blood sinuses of the other organs.

The absence of capillary meshworks is an indication of an "open" blood system, but veins return the blood to a pericardial chamber which is a remnant of coelome, as are the cavities of the gonad and the kidneys. Because it has, in this transit, passed through the gills and especially through the mantle (which contains important respiratory surface), the blood arrives in the pericardial chamber suitably reconditioned for respiratory purposes.

Communicating with the pericardial chamber are a pair of nephridia, or kidneys. There is a glandular portion followed by an internally ciliated bladder. The bladder discharges into the mantle chamber, where nitrogenous wastes are swept out in the exhalent stream of water. The blood taken up by the pair of auricles out of the pericardial chamber for transmission to the ventricle has thus been served by both respiratory and excretory organs.

The Nervous System

For the coordination of its activities Venus possesses a nervous system which consists, in common with those of other mollusks, of three basic pairs of ganglia. Cerebral ganglia lie at the sides of the esophagus and are connected with each other by a nerve tract that passes anterior to the esophagus. Inasmuch as there is no radula and there are no eyes or tentacles, the cerebral ganglia are one of the very few indications of an otherwise atrophied head. (It can be more correctly said of bivalve mollusks that they have no head than it can of animals like Peripatus, in which the head is present and only the neck is missing.)

From the cerebral ganglia nerve connectives run to a pair of pedal ganglia in the foot, and to a pair of visceral ganglia near the posterior adductor muscle. The simple and decentralized condition of the nervous system in sluggishly moving mollusks like Venus should be kept in mind for comparison with the most advanced members of the phylum, like Loligo, in which locomotion is a very highly developed function.

Reproduction

The gametes of Venus are produced by a pair of gonads that develop around and between the loops of the intestine. Like other products destined for the outside environment, the gametes are discharged into the posterior portion of the mantle cavity where they are caught up by the exhalent water current and expelled through the dorsal siphon into the sea.

Fertilization and development are external. Embryology includes a swimming trochophore larva which, since the adults cannot move very far from the site where they settle, is a valuable aid to dispersal of the species.

Venus individuals are either male or female, although the sex of other common bivalves may alternate between male and female. In the oyster a brood of young may have been derived from a parent which served them as a mother, while in a subsequent year the same individual will act as a father to another brood. (Similar examples can be found among univalve mollusks.

In Crepidula, for example, an individual begins life as a male and later converts to female. Compare also with roundworms, as *'Rhabditis nigrovensa*.) Thus, in some mollusks, an occurrence which is regarded as phenomenal when encountered in the highest groups of the animal kingdom can still be normal behaviour.

In further relation to reproduction of bivalves it is of interest to note an adaptive stage in the development of fresh-water clams (mussels). The eggs are not freely discharged into the water, as in Venus, but are trapped in mucus on the gills, like particles of food. Here they are fertilized by sperm carried in by the inhalent water stream, and they develop into minute larval bivalves known as glochidia.

In this stage they are swept out of the mantle and, on encountering a fish, clamp to the gills or to the surface of the body, depending upon the species of mussel. The glochidia live as parasites for a few weeks, feeding on the body fluids of the host, and then drop off to settle down to adult life as free-living forms on the bottom. A twofold advantage evidently accrues from this way of life.

The danger of being swept down into the sea, which would be a disaster to these fresh-water forms, is eliminated by "riding" the fish during early life when the clam is light in weight and would be easily upset by water turbulence.

At the same time the young clams are widely dispersed by an animal whose locomotory powers are equal to the task. Since "one good turn deserves another," it is interesting to note a reversal of the relationship. The eggs of a fresh-water fish Rhodima, the bitterling, are attached to the gills of a mussel for a time.

Scaphopoda

This is a small group of mollusks that live somewhat like common bivalves, with head downward in the sand. There are no eyes, but the head is more complete than that of the bivalves, since the typical radula of the mollusks is present in the mouth.

The scaphopod body is elongated like that of a worm, but the intestine is curved back on itself so that the anus comes to lie near the same end of the elongated body where the mouth is found. There is a muscular burrowing foot, triangular and pointed something like the "hatchet-foot" of the bivalves; but the shell is quite different. It is long and tubular, and open at both ends.

There is a current of water through the upper open end for ventilating the inner surface of the mantle which, again as in bivalves, serves as a respiratory organ. There are no gills. Food is taken in at the lower, wider, end of the tube with the aid of a cluster of tentacle-like organs that surrounds the mouth.

Food consists of foraminiferans and other organisms of like size, found abundantly in the sea. Scaphopods are all marine. The best known exemplar of the scaphopod mollusks is the genus Dentalium.

Gastropoda

In the gastropods the foot is designed for getting about from place to place, but at a "snail's pace." In correlation with change of habit there is modification in bodily adaptations.

In contrast with the Pelecypoda and like the Scaphopoda, Gastropoda possess an undivided mantle and, consequently, an undivided shell. The body is elongated in the dorsoventral axis, like that of the scaphopods,

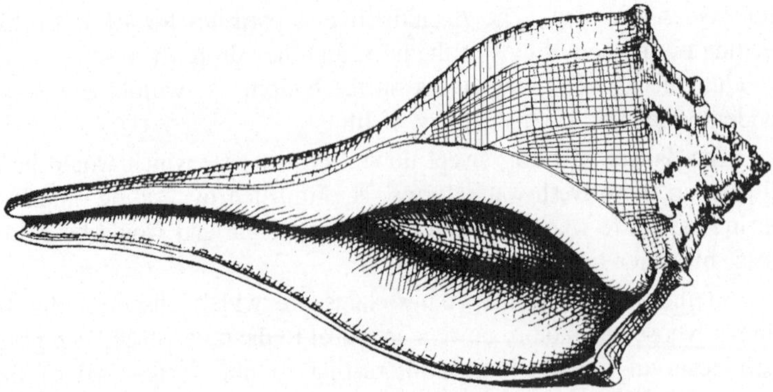

Figure 12.3: The shell of Busycon.

but coiling causes it to appear much more compact, and the mantle and shell are both coiled. The head, now with well-developed eyes, projects out of the anterior end of the opening of the shell. The ventral region of the body forms a crawling foot (Gastropoda means "bellyfooted").

The coiled visceral hump remains within the shell, into which the entire animal can retire for additional protection. Often the shell opening can be closed by an operculum, which is otherwise carried on the dorsal side of the foot while the animal is moving about.

Only rarely are gastropods inactive in locomotion, slow though it may be. Only rarely, as in the genus Vermetus (also known as Vermicularia) are they permanently attached. (Vermetus is noted for living in large masses of attached tubes, which form "worm rock"). While in the genus Caecum there is gliding by ciliary means, (as in the aplachophoran amphineurans), the prevailing mode of gastropod locomotion is creeping by minute muscular undulations of the foot.

Progress is not rapid, but it is faster than ciliary locomotion. Haliotis, the abalone, has been clocked at a rate of about eighteen feet per minute. (A clam, by comparison, plows along at the rate of only a few feet per hour.) It is interesting that some snails have evolved the ability to swim.

For example, Aplysia the sea hare or sea slug is a crawling form with a reduced shell, but by means of fin-like extensions of the foot it can also swim. Certain gastropods have become entirely pelagic. Clione is a little snail about an inch long that is found swimming in large schools near the surface of the sea. It is representative of a group of gastropods known as the Pteropoda, or sea butterflies.

A coiled shell is found only in the embryonic stages of Clione.

disappears and the foot is modified into a pair of here is still another group of pelagic sea snails, the which Carinaria is an example. But the typical gastropod ıming for its traditional undulatory ambulation.

Th... of Gastropods

Not quite all of the gastropods have a radula. There is a little snail, *Odostomiatrifida* (which occupies a curious habitat on the siphon ends of the soft shell clam, *Mya arenaria*), that falls into this category. But almost all gastropod mouths are equipped with a radula, and also with a pair of chitinous jaws, and there is a change in this class away from the filter method of feeding shown by the bivalves.

Many of the gastropods are herbivorous. Haliotis, which on the West Coast is collected and prepared as abalone steak, feeds on algae, and for some reason shows a preference for red algae. Young Aplysia also prefer red algae but later changes its diet to the green and brown. Limax, the land slug, and Helix, the edible land snail, feed upon terrestrial vegetation.

Especially notable in relation to herbivorous food habits is the huge land snail *Achatina fulica*, which is up to nine inches long. Achatina is edible, like Helix; spread by man over large areas, it has then become highly destructive to agriculture. The capacity of the radula extends beyond vegetarian uses. In many snails the radula becomes an organ of active aggression, and its application becomes a matter of economic importance to humans when the radula of gastropods like Thais and Urosalpinx is used in feeding on pelecypods like clams and oysters.

Busycon, a whelk (large marine snail) to which we shall soon give additional attention, uses both foot and radula in its feeding. The powerful foot plows through the sand and seeks out the bivalve, and the radula bores through to get at the meat inside.

The feeding habits of Aeolis, a sea-slug, are worthy of special mention because this gastropod shows preference for marine hydroids and the cnidoblasts, which are ingested, migrate to the surface of the mollusk where they provide nematocyst protection as if they were still part of the animal in which they originated.

Twisting of the Visceral Mass

In gastropods the alimentary tract is much longer than the anterior-posterior axis of the body and in this relation we find one of the unique features of the class. While in other types of animals with coiled intestines the body remains straight, here in gastropods both coil together.

The coiling process begins in the "veliger stage" of embryogeny (following the trochophore), at the time when the foot and the shell are first formed.

While the head and the foot retain the usual positional relationship, the mantle and underlying visceral mass begin to rotate. The first twist displaces the mantle cavity, which is originally at the posterior end of the mantle, toward the right side of the animal. Torsion continues until the mantle cavity is at the anterior end of the body. In this relocation procedure the anus is carried along and comes to lie in a rather bizarre position near and above the head.

The ventral portion of the visceral mass and of the mantle now remain in this orientation, rotated about 180 degrees or a little more, while the dorsal part of the animal continues to spiral for several revolutions. Twisting of the dorsal hump affects the organs of the body in such manner that those of the left side tend to disappear.

After torsion these would have been found on the right side; and this accounts for the fact that in adult gastropods the right kidney, the right gill, the right auricle of the heart, and other corresponding parts of the initially bisymmetrical organ systems are often absent.

BUSYCON (FULGUR)

Busycon is a carnivorous marine snail about nine inches Tonga whelk. It feeds upon the bivalve members of its own phylum, and is in competition with man for clams and oysters. The animal moves along by means of muscular contractions proceeding along the length of the foot, which is well lubricated with mucus provided by a pedal gland at the anterior end.

A head with a pair of eye-bearing tentacles projects anteriorly above the foot, while between and below the tentacles there is a mouth and protrusible proboscis. In a middle position dorsal to the foot is the visceral mass under its enveloping mantle. The latter is tucked into the shell, which is coiled about an axis known as the columella.

The right side of the body is provided with a columellar muscle by means of which the body can be drawn into the shell and, at the posterior end, the dorsal portion of the foot carries the operculum, a skeletal plate that fits into the opening of the shell and secures the contracted animal within.

While adapted for aggression against non-aggressive prey, Busycon is itself unprovided with active means of defense against predators. When disturbed it contracts, visceral hump followed by head and foot into the shell, with the operculum acting as a seal.

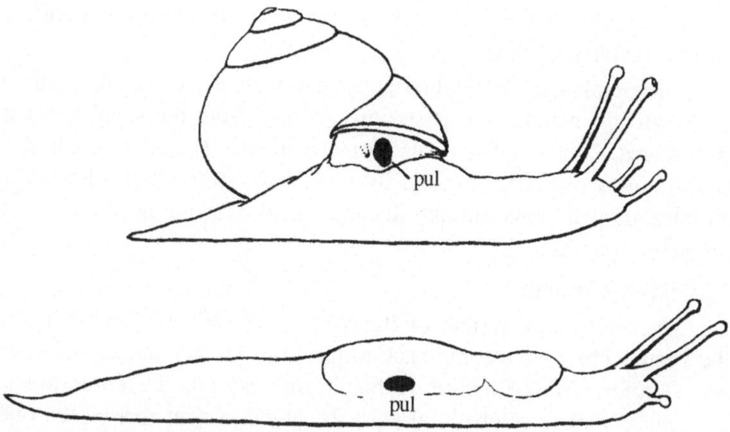

Figure 12.4: Helix above and Limax below.

Gills and Lungs of Gastropods

Within the mantle cavity of Busycon there is a single gill, that on the left side. Strategically situated near the gill and bathed by the same current is a water-tasting organ known as an osphridium. In the mantle, in contact with the gill, is the hypobranchial gland which protects the gill by a constant secretion of mucus.

It is of interest that in terrestrial gastropods there are no gills at all. Instead the mantle cavity is richly supplied with blood and acts as a lung, much in the same way as the gill chamber of terrestrial crustaceans like the ghost crab. Examples of such respiratory adaptation in terrestrial gastropods are found in Limax and Helix.

Even more interesting is the fact that many fresh-water snails, like Planorbis, Physa and Viviparus (a live bearer) also possess mantle lungs instead of gills. In these pulmonate snails the edge of the mantle is drawn out into a siphon, well illustrated in Viviparus, which is thrust into the air from time to time for respiratory exchange.

Finally, the mantle cavity of some "pulmonate" snails has become readapted for gas exchange in water, acting again as a gill, and trips to the surface are infrequent or nonexistent. These facts are often cited as evidence that the pathway of gastropod evolution from the sea to fresh water has been via the land.

Alimentation

When feeding, the proboscis of Busycon is extended, and the radula, supported by the underlying cartilaginous odontophore, is applied to the shell of the prey. A hole is drilled and the soft parts within are extracted and ingested. Food passes through the proboscis and enters a narrow esophageal tube.

The esophagus is supplied anteriorly with the ducts of a pair of large salivary glands, and posteriorly, a duct from the small pancreas is received. The esophagus leads into a tubular stomach which is in connection with a large bilobed liver. And the stomach is followed by an intestine that vents through the anus, held over the head on a short projecting papilla.

Circulatory System

The circulatory system of Busycon is typically molluscan in that the venous channels leading back to the heart lack epithelial walls and are therefore in the nature of blood sinuses; but the latter are so constricted that functionally at least the blood system is a closed one. The heart, within a pericardial sinus, is typically gastropod because, besides the large muscular ventricle, there is only a single auricle.

The second auricle, like the second gill, has been lost in the embryological contortions which have produced the twisted body.[3] An enlargement of the aorta serves as a "secondary heart" to build up pressure, and this, together with the ventricle, provides considerable force and therefore rather brisk circulation.

Nervous System

Understandably, because of the higher level of activity, the nervous system of Busycon is more intricate than that of Venus, but the major ganglia of the Venus system are discernible in Busycon. A pair of cerebral ganglia lies above the esophagus.

The location of the pedal ganglia close under the esophagus, and connected to the cerebral ganglia by a nerve ring, is evidence of a trend toward concentration of the central nervous system. However, the visceral ganglia still lie far removed, in the vicinity of the kidney.

Also there are several pairs of accessory ganglia not found in Venus. Perhaps the most noteworthy of these are the buccal ganglia, connected by nerves with the cerebral, and related to the mouth apparatus occurring in snails but not in clams.

Reproduction

The gonad is found in the dorsal portion of the visceral mass, between the lobes of the liver. In the female an oviduct leads from the ovary into a nidamental gland (function given below), and the system has its outlet near the anus. In the male the sperm duct terminates in a permanently extended penis. The penis projects from the visceral mass above the head, and below the anus. This location must be taken as another curious effect of embryological torsion.

Fertilization is internal. Embryos develop within egg cases composed of the secretion of the nidamental gland and moulded into distinctive shape by the foot. As many as 1500 eggs may be produced at a single laying, and these hatch from the egg cases after development into miniature snails.

There is no free larval stage. The distinctive trochophore is known among the Gastropoda, but only in more primitive forms, e.g., the limpets. While the number of eggs does not begin to equal, by far, that produced by Venus, compensation results from the fact that fertilization, being internal, is more certain. Also, development within egg cases is under protected conditions not present when the eggs are freely exposed to the sea.

It is of comparative interest that some snails, like the terrestrial species Helix and Achatina, and the fresh-water Viviparus, are hermaphroditic. Copulation and exchange of sperm are then mutual between mating partners and two separate broods of young result from a single mating, thus adding to the fecundity of these forms.

CEPHALOPODA

To the slow-moving or sedentary mollusk the shell is obviously an invaluable though not always an invulnerable protection

against its enemies. Of enemies there are many, both from outside the mollusk phylum and also within. But the weight of the shell is a decided handicap to locomotion, and thereby limits the scope of feeding methods. It is significant in this respect that members of previous classes were either filter-feeders or herbivorous, neither of these types of feeding being dependent on rapid locomotion.

At most, capacity for predation was limited to prey that was even slower in movement than the predators themselves (including here as prey such unusual forms as cnidarians and sponges).

The mollusks of the cephalopod class are cast in a new mould. By distinctive modification of the same basic features previously present, the foot and the mantle, rapid locomotion becomes possible, and active predation appears within the mollusks as a common way of life. Thus, from Amphineura to Cephalopoda, the relationship between locomotory adaptations and animal behaviour can be illustrated in a single phylum.

In other evolutionary lines the highest levels of locomotory technique are attained in relation to metamerism. Since mollusks are unsegmented, a different scheme of high-speed locomotory mechanics might be expected. This is indeed the case.

Locomotion

The mantle, which is the source of the protective but encumbering shell in other classes, becomes the major organ of locomotion in cephalopods. Concomitant with the return to speed of movement among cephalopods, a level of bodily organization has appeared that is unsurpassed among all other invertebrates and which, in some respects, is comparable with that attained by the vertebrates.

It is interesting that the shell is not entirely absent among cephalopods. In the pearly nautilus, as we shall see, it is chiefly the effect of its weight which has been circumvented. But in the squid there remains only a mere vestige of the shell, and this has been taken within the body wall to serve other purposes than protection.

The shell of the pearly nautilus (*Nautilus pompilius*) resembles that of a large snail, but the resemblance does not extend beyond superficial appearance. The shell is spirally coiled in a single plane. As the animal grows it moves outward, secreting an enlarging bore, and from time to time closing off the inner regions by means of transverse walls.

Only the largest, outermost, chamber is occupied, but a membranous tube, the siphuncle, remains behind, connecting to the innermost chambers and keeping them filled with gas. The resulting buoyancy enables the animal to crawl and even to float. Crawling is accomplished by means of numerous, suckerless tentacles-close to one hundred-situated about the mouth.

Based on the presence of four gills, the pearly nautilus is placed in the subclass Tetrabranchiata which in the past contained numerous living members but which now is composed of only a single genus. Evidently, the slower moving Tetrabranchiata, shell-protected but shell-encumbered, have not achieved a successful adaptation for survival.

The majority of the Cephalopoda are found in the subclass Dibranchiata. While the two gills here found are a recognition characteristic of taxonomic value, of far greater significance is the fact that in this group there is emphasis on locomotion.

The Dibranchiate cephalopods are agile and quick moving, and the shell has all but disappeared in most cases. It would be difficult to escape the conclusion that the success of the Dibranchiata, in contrast with the Tetrabranchiata, is correlated with locomotory power.

There are two orders of Dibranchiata, based upon the number of arms. The Octopoda have eight arms, and the Decapoda have ten. In both the shell is conspicuous only by its relative absence. True, in the argonaut, or paper nautilus (*Argonauta argo*), there is a complete shell, but of most peculiar nature. First, it is found only in the female and, being secreted by a pair of the arms, it is unconnected with the mantle. The animal may leave it at will.

Secondly, the shell is of a parchment-like consistency and light in weight. The shell of the argonaut is utilized as a brood-chamber, for the protection of the developing young. The prominent members of the order Octopoda are, quite naturally, the octopuses. The arms are used for crawling, and membranes between the arms enable an octopus to swim with these as well as by means of a water jet emitted through a siphon.

But the octopus is not very fast and in the capture of food it relies largely on stealth, usually lying concealed in rock crevices or in self-constructed shelters of loose stone. For real speed among cephalopods we must go to the order Decapoda, which includes the cuttlefishes but which will be represented in our consideration by the squid.

LOLIGO, THE SQUID

It is a far cry from the ciliary method of creeping locomotion shown by primitive Aplacophorans to the advanced technique of jet-propulsion to be described in the squid. It seems almost incredible that such a range could have been developed from the same basic molluscan equipment, the foot and the mantle. But let us look at the evidence.

The Symmetry of the Squid

The body of a squid is long in the dorsoventral axis -the lesser axis in most animals-and short from anterior to posterior. As it lives and moves, the squid is oriented with the posterior portion of the body downward and the anterior portion upward. The functional axis has been rotated 90 degrees clockwise from the morphological.

The Mantle and the Foot

The mantle, which encloses the visceral mass, is conical and very muscular. It is composed of high-speed muscle, faster than most. The muscle of the squid mantle takes 60 thousandths of a second for a contraction, while that of a lobster claw requires 200 thousandths. It is interesting, and understandable, that the muscles of the dragon-fly wing are faster than either of the above, needing only 40 thousandths of a second for contraction.

These speed factors for locomotory muscles become more meaningful when viewed in contrast to visceral contractions which show a time range of from several tenths to several full seconds.

Embedded within the morphologically anterior ("dorsal") region of the mantle is a penlike, chitinous skeletal support. (In the cuttlefish, e.g., Sepia, the skeleton is calcareous and finds various commercial uses as "cuttlebone.")

Externally the mantle is drawn out into lateral finlike extensions and internally at the sides there is a pair of gills. Because the anterio-posterior axis of the body is comparatively very short, the head and the foot have been brought closely together; and the anterior (morphologically) portion of the foot is modified into a cluster of ten arms, situated about the mouth. Posteriorly the foot takes the form of a funnelshaped siphon, the expanded portion of which lies within the free edge of the mantle.

Locomotion

On expansion the mantle draws water through the gap between its edge and the edge of the siphon. In this phase the orifice of the siphon is closed by a valve, which makes it inoperative as a locomotory device and also prevents the products of various visceral systems, whose openings reach into the siphon, from being swept back into the mantle cavity. When the mantle contracts the siphonal gap is closed and the siphon orifice is open.

Water, under high pressure, is then forced out of the orifice. This is the jet which propels the animal, with the mantle leading and the headfoot trailing. Reversal of direction is accomplished by the simple expedient of bending the tip of the siphon backward. When swimming in pursuit, with the head forward, the arms are held closely together to reduce water resistance, but it seems likely nevertheless that greater speed is possible when the streamlined mantle end of the animal is leading.

This would be an escape reaction and it consequently appears that, in locomotory adaptation of the squid, escape takes a higher priority than aggression. The "flying squid," *Ommnastrephes illecebrosa, is* capable of such great speeds that schools of them have been observed to fling themselves out of the water to a height of many feet, apparently in an attempt to elude large predacious fish.

The fins alone, by undulatory movements along their length, can produce a gentle, exploratory swimming behaviour, but in rapid swimming they assist in initial acceleration and then appear to act only as stabilizers, while the arms held together act collectively as a rudder.

The Arms and the Jaws

The ten arms of a squid are not all alike. The fourth pair is longer and, unlike the others, provided with retractor muscles, and especially adapted for the capture of food. The fourth pair of arms is sometimes known as the tentacles, but whether "arms" or "tentacles" it should be remembered that all are derived from the mollusk foot.

On contact the tentacles are first made fast, by means of suckers with which all of the arms are provided, either along the entire length or only terminally. Attachment is of a dual nature. After the mouth of the sucker is applied the body of the sucker is expanded, and this brings about a reduction of pressure within.

The greater force of the water outside holds the sucker firmly against the surface of the object. In addition, the inner rim of the sucker is set with a circle of chitinous teeth which sink into the flesh of a victim, holding the sucker doubly fast. In the Octopus there are no teeth in the sucker but, instead, a "caruncle" in its center which, working like a receding piston, builds up a force of attachment which may be greater than the mechanical strength of the tissues themselves.

As predator and prey are drawn together by the retraction of the tentacles, the remaining arms are applied and the two animals are held firmly against each other, with the mouth of the squid in contact with its prey-generally fish or crustacean.

This provides opportunity for the utilization of the squid beak. The beak is composed of a sharp jutting lower jaw, V-shaped, and a smaller upper jaw which slides past and within the lower on contraction of powerful muscles, thus moving the cutting surfaces effectively by each other. This is the most formidable weapon of the squid, by means of which it can inflict considerable injury.

A little farther within the mouth is an odontophore and radula, the usual mouth parts of a mollusk. Salivary glands, which discharge into the mouth cavity, do not secrete digestive enzyme, but form a poison that quiets the prey.

The Alimentary Tract

Following the mouth cavity a narrow esophagus leads into a thick-walled muscular stomach. There is a capacious caecum attached to the stomach, and the caecum receives a combined duct from the pancreas and the liver.

Up to this point the alimentary tract is oriented away from the mouth, into the visceral cone. But now from the stomach, at a point near esophageal entry, the intestine turns back in the direction of the mouth. Then, via rectum and anus, feces are discharged into the base of the siphonal funnel, and ejected with the water stream.

Escape

Larger squid eat smaller fish, and larger fish eat smaller squid. The occasion may arise when the squid, in pursuit of prey, finds it expedient to reverse its siphon and take off. If there is desperate need for escape the squid may simultaneously discharge a few bursts of sepia from an ink gland which lies in contact with the rectum, and whose orifice is directed into the outgoing water jet of the siphon.

The puffs of ink in part conceal the squid but probably act chiefly to divert the predator while the prey makes its escape. At the same time, the excitement causes the animal to darken in hue by dilation of the numerous chromatophores contained in the skin.

These defensive measures seem quite in harmony with the advanced method of jet locomotion, and they may be easily observed in a squid held in captivity; but experience will show that, for aesthetic reasons, it is best to keep out of range of the ink gland.

Gills and Kidneys

Besides the mechanism for defense, many other systems are aided in their function by the circulation of water set up within the mantle. The gills lie in the mantle cavity and their ventilation is thereby tuned to respiratory needs, for the more violent the locomotory exertion the more rapidly will the water within the mantle be changed. This also benefits the function of excretion, for a pair of kidneys, extracting wastes from the pericardial coelome, discharge into the mantle cavity.

Blood Circulation

The higher level of activity of the cephalopods generally, as contrasted with other classes of mollusks, is reflected in the mechanics for circulating the body fluids. There would be little gain in effective gill ventilation, for example, if respiratory gases then taken up were not quickly moved to the motor organs.

Nor would the positive flushing out of excretory wastes have purpose if the pericardial blood were not subject to rapid circulation. The blood-circulatory system is to chemical coordination between the various organ systems what the nervous system is to motor co-ordination.

There is a three-chambered heart in Loligo, consisting of a well-formed ventricle and two auricles. The latter, for reasons that will soon be clear, need not be, and are not, strongly developed.

Through an anterior (morphologically ventral) and a posterior aorta, the ventricle forces blood into capillary meshworks in all of the organs of the body. Practically, the blood system is a closed one. Blood from the head region is returned through an anterior (ventral) vena cava. The anterior vena cava divides into two vessels that are joined by a pair of postcaval veins just before the blood of these combined vessels arrives at the gills.

Now the blood is received within a special pair of branchial hearts, which build up the pressure for effective passage through the gill capillaries. From the gills the blood enters the heart auricles and is transmitted to the ventricle. The outgoing blood circulation from the ventricle, which enters the arterial system for distribution to the bodily organs, thus consists entirely of aerated blood.

Physiologically, this is a single-pump system, like that of a fish. Unlike vertebrate hearts with two auricles, there is no qualitative difference in the blood within the two auricles of the squid. But the squid has two gills (Dibranchiata) and an auricle to receive blood from each of them separately.

Evidence that the heart of the cephalopods is adapted in this manner to the respiratory system is found also in the Tetrabranchiata. In the latter there are four gills. For each gill there is a heart auricle to receive blood, but then all four auricles transmit their blood to a single ventricle.

Structurally the heart of the squid is a three-chambered heart, and the heart of the nautilus is a five-chambered heart, but functionally and qualitatively the cephalopod heart works like the heart of a fish, certainly not like the three-chambered heart of an amphibian, nor the four-chambered heart of the higher vertebrates; except that in the fish the blood is aerated immediately after leaving the heart, while in the cephalopod it is aerated just before arrival in the heart.

The presence of individual branchial hearts to improve the circulation through the gills of an animal like Loligo is of particular interest in relation to the high activity level of this form. Oxygen is probably the most limiting factor in its metabolism, and oxygen cannot be stored like nutrients. Yet oxygen must be immediately available in amounts sufficient for the needs of the moment. In a predacious animal like the squid such needs can become quite urgent.

Reproduction

It is because the mantle has become adapted into a powerful water-pumping mechanism that the outstanding aquatic locomotory achievements of the squid are possible, but the mantle is closely wrapped around the visceral organ systems, and this introduces special problems of communication between them and the outside environment.

In the functioning of the reproductive system the solution to the problem has taken a strange turn. Squids are either male or female. There is no hermaphroditism and there is no sex reversal, although both have been encountered in some of the members of previous classes of mollusks.

The gametes are not broadcast into the water and there is clearcut need for sexual contact between mating individuals. Yet a male squid approaches a female with each tightly wrapped in a thick muscular mantle; and, in spite of this handicap, the male succeeds in impregnating the female.

In the male a ciliated funnel of the vas deferens gathers the sperms released from the testis. The vas deferens carries the sperms to a spermatophoric organ, where they are packaged into clusters called spermatophores. The spermatophores are discharged by a muscular penis, but the penis lies within the mantle cavity, near the rectum, and cannot reach the female.

Gametes pass from the ovary of the female into the oviduct through a ciliated funnel, as in the male. Farther down, the oviducts are thickened to form a glandular portion-the oviducal glands-from which a secretion is derived which encapsulates the individual eggs. Like the sperms, the eggs when shed are contained in groups.

They are embedded in a gelatinous matrix supplied by a pair of large nidamental glands. But how are the eggs fertilized? The first zoologist who discovered a wormlike object wriggling within the mantle cavity of cephalopods regarded it as a parasitic worm, and gave it the genus name of "Hectocotylus."

Either it was not observed, or the significance was overlooked, that "Hectocotylus" occurred only in female "hosts." It was subsequently found that sperm packets are taken up by an arm-of the fourth pair in the squid-and deposited by the arm within the mantle cavity of the female. In the squid the tip of this arm is cast off with the spermatophore, while the male argonaut loses an entire arm in mating.

It is this arm, or part of an arm, which was the "Hectocotylus" of earlier zoological times, and the arm so modified is now known as a hectocotylized arm. The female squid temporarily stores spermatophores in a sperm receptacle located below the mouth, within a fold of a membrane that runs between the bases of the arms. The egg clusters the female takes into her own arms—at which time, or previously, they are fertilized-and, while sticky with nidamental secretion, they are attached to some solid object in the environment.

A trochophore stage occurs while the eggs are still encased, and the young emerge as miniature squids. From the time of hatching they swim by pumping action of the mantle. `It is evident that the squid is endowed with a rather unusual arrangement for bringing sperm and eggs together, and that this adaptation is related to the modification of the mantle into a swimming organ.

Coordination

We have shown that we have in the squid an animal of active and intricate behaviour. It is predictable that the nervous system will reflect this status, for it is in the nervous system and the associated sensory organs that the relative development of an animal can most easily be assayed. Of all of the environmental stimuli to which an animal is

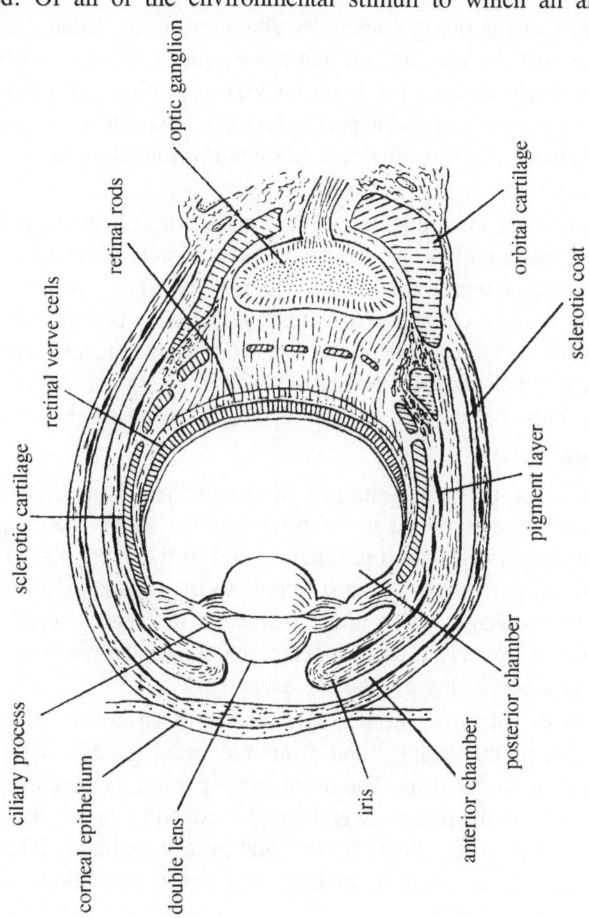

Figure 12.5: The eye of a squid.

receptive, light, predominantly, has the characteristic of speed. Auditory stimulation is slower, and olfactory is slower still. The eye, therefore, is an excellent index of evolutionary level, because a high order of response presupposes a high order of stimulus perception. In this measure of evolutionary level the squid eye does not fail. There is no comparable eye in any other group of invertebrates.

Arthropod eyes are of a completely different type, and there is no doubt that the cephalopod eye is able to see perfect images. The evolution of the cephalopod eye has converged on that of the vertebrates, and has surpassed the latter in some respects. Because the nerve fibrils leave the sensory elements at the rear of the retina, there is no blind spot in the cephalopod eye.

Also, focus is brought about by alteration of the distance between lens and retina, as in a camera, and not by change in shape of the lens as in the vertebrate eye. The latter method, operating as it must within very close tolerances, would appear to be more subject to error, especially in a framework that lacks the precise support afforded by the vertebrate skull.

A better eye is of course useless unless functionally supported by the rest of the organism. An incidental illustration is the bathyal squids, e.g., Thaumatolampus, that produce their own light by means of well-developed organs. Of greater universal importance is the development of a nervous system capable of receiving, discriminating and distributing the stimuli which the eye can detect; just as the motor mechanism of the body must be, and is, on a similarly advanced level.

The Brain

Within the nervous system of the squid there is a cerebral brain center that consists of a pair of fused ganglia above the esophagus. From the cerebral ganglia optic nerves run to the eyes, buccal nerves to the mouth parts, and statocyst nerves to the organs of equilibrium. Below the esophagus there are a pair each of pleurovisceral and of pedal ganglia, somewhat fused together and connected with the cerebral ganglia in a nerve ring around the esophagus.

From the pleurovisceral ganglia a pair of so-called "giant nerve fibers" run to the mantle, and from the pedal ganglia ten brachial nerves extend to the arms. The pedal ganglia also innervate the siphon, and nerves from the pleurovisceral ganglia extend to the various internal viscera. The cerebral, pleurovisceral and pedal ganglia are all recessed within cartilaginous elements making up a cephalopod "skull" that also encloses the statocysts.

The Peripheral Nervous System

The nerves emanating from the central nervous system, or from the brain, generally do not terminate directly in the organs that they supply. The optic nerves, for example, expand into an extraordinarily large pair of optic ganglia which lie in contact with the eyes. Similarly, the nerve fibers running to the mantle terminate there in a pair of large stellate ganglia, from which smaller nerves radiate out into the mantle.

Associated with the brachial nerves, there are brachial ganglia in the bases of the arms; and there are buccal ganglia associated with the buccal mass. Also under nervous control are the chromatophores in the skin. The chromatophores are pigment-containing cells with elastic walls. When not stimulated, the pigment is concentrated in small areas and the animal is pale in colour.

By means of tiny muscles each chromatophore can be stretched and the pigment spread over a larger surface area, thus darkening the whole animal. This effect is under the control of the stellate ganglia. When a squid receives an optical stimulus of alarm, one of the first responses is a blush of colour change that darkens the skin. This shows that the stimulus has traversed the optic nerves and passed through the cerebral ganglia to the pleural-visceral.

From the latter the giant nerve fibers have conducted the stimuli, with a minimum of delay, to the stellate ganglia in the mantle, whence they are spread out over the mantle and cause contractions of the chromatophore muscles. More intensive stimulation causes the muscles of the mantle itself to respond, and the animal darts away.

It is apparently only on rather extreme provocation that stimuli also travel from the pleurovisceral ganglia through visceral nerves to the muscles of the ink sac, and the concealing and diverting cloud of ink is discharged. (There is some evidence that, besides optical effect, cephalopod ink also anesthetizes chemoreceptors of possible predators.)

The squid is a highly responsive animal, as indeed it must be to survive. It is a favourite food of larger creatures than itself, like fish, but is well equipped with measures of defense. And smaller fish are outsped and captured by larger squid. This contest between the mollusk and chordate phylum continues even into the mammalian class, for the giant squid is a favourite food of the great sperm whale, and the squid is not readily submissive.

Titanic struggles in the sea between the squid, *Architeuthis princeps*, and the whale have been described as resembling volcanic upheavals. It must be quite a sight, a fifty-foot squid-with eyes about a foot in diameter-facing up to a whale even larger. Invertebrate eye against vertebrate eye, arms and beak against teeth, flippers against mantle, cartilaginous "skull" against bony skull, invertebrate brain against vertebrate brain, they are pretty evenly matched, invertebrate and vertebrate. Both are supreme examples of the enterozoic way of life-alert, predaceous, fast-moving.

INDEX

C

F

G

H

N

O

Q

R

S

T